Also by Karla Clark

Between Courses: A Culinary Love Story

Knotted Pearls and Other Stories

Annie's Heaven

a novel

Karla Clark

Jess —
Be intent on
things above ...
K. Clark
2010

authorHOUSE®

AuthorHouse™
1663 Liberty Drive, Suite 200
Bloomington, IN 47403
www.authorhouse.com
Phone: 1-800-839-8640

First published by AuthorHouse 10/16/2008

ISBN: 978-1-4389-0567-9 (sc)
ISBN: 978-1-4389-0566-2 (hc)

Library of Congress Control Number: 2008906879

Printed in the United States of America
Bloomington, Indiana

This book is printed on acid-free paper.

For Scott, Jordan, and Jonathan
In consideration of Love & Affection

And

In memory of Ryan Roy Cleary
Our tie-dyed superman

Acknowledgments

This book sprang from my own grief. My mother died in 1992 from metastatic breast cancer, three months before my second son was born. My nephew, the first grandson in our family, died in 2004 in a tragic suicide during his sophomore year of college.

One death was slow and expected. The other came out of nowhere.

I wrote this book in part to comfort myself. In imaging Heaven I was able to stay connected to my loved ones. I feel their presence every day. Love doesn't disappear; it just changes shape.

Thanks to all the lovers in my life: my husband Scott—twenty-five years in 2008! To my son Jordan who has a beautiful brain and a beautiful spirit. To my son Jonathan who spreads joy every day. To my dad, Frank Manarchy, who thinks all women are crazy except for his daughters! To my mom, Marge Manarchy, whom I miss everyday. To my sisters, Linda, Dana, Paula, and my brother Frank. To all my sisters- and brothers-in-law: John, Pam, Bob, Sue, Steve, Cheryl, and Jim. To my late mother-in-law and late father-in-law, Chris and Scotty Clark.

Thanks to all my "second" mothers: Rose Ciaccio, Mary Halbin, Rose Parlapiano, Maxine Lizer, and Nancy Stephenson.

I couldn't have written this book without having had interesting children in my life. I have lifted character traits from my own two sons, as well as from my nephews, Ryan, Sean, Steven, Jason, Justin, Nicholas, and Thomas in developing the boys in the story. Other boys

I thought about while fashioning the characters were friends Steven and Scott Broski, Phillip and Patrick Sudderberg, and Alex Greco. For the character of Tess, my nieces Margaret and Sarah Marie Sentovich provided ample inspiration.

Thanks to my many doctor friends and others in the medical community. Through my job as a pharmaceutical sales rep, I have come to know and respect you. You work so hard!

A hardy shout out to my book club (now called "The Bad Girls Book Club" because so few of us actually read the book!): Jane Sudderberg, Lisa Greco, Nonie Broski, Dawn Pratt, Maureen Morrisey, Lisa Lillie, Karin Kellogg, Julie Anderson, Jane Weiss Proudfoot, and Lana Ewing (who keeps me in jewels!).

Thanks to readers and proofreaders: Frank Manarchy, Sean Cleary, Paula Sentovich, Karen LaFasto, Dr. Richard Nora, Nick Sentovich, Kris Rummel, Dana Manarchy, Lisa Lillie, Kay Sentovich, and Carol Hanson. And a special thanks to my niece, Margaret Sentovich, for reading chapters aloud to me so that I could "hear" the written word.

Thanks to my friend, Giacomina Francik, for her special contribution; to Amanda Spohr, for introducing me to horses; and to Mare, our angel in a bathing suit.

Thanks to my agent and publicist, Mary McNamara Bernsten, whose zest for life and love of art is contagious.

Thanks to my editor, Linda Cleary, who has whipped all three of my books into shape. When I thought they were finished, it was Linda who bravely told me, no, there was still work to do.

And thanks be to God!

Author's Note

Socrates, Plato, and Aristotle all believed that philosophy begins with wonder. And so I wonder about Heaven.

Please, dear reader, know that throughout this story I allude to Heaven, and although I have attempted a rather thorough research of the subject—biblical, academic, anecdotal, and philosophical—in the end, my "Heaven" is based only upon my own robust imagination. Please do not take my descriptions literally as I have had no experience—in life or in near death—of Heaven, save for the slices of heaven I have found in love, faith, laughter, music, art, good books, dreams, delicious food, work, family and friends; in other words, the heaven on earth that we all can experience if we put ourselves in the right mindset. What is Heaven? I haven't the foggiest. I only know I want to end up there.

My father, a man who thinks deeply, reads widely, and loves greatly, recently replied this way when I asked him what he thought about our life's purpose, he said, "Honey, it's this: we are here to prove the existence of God—to ourselves by our thoughts and dreams, and to others by our words and actions." Bravo, Dad!

Two men please God—
one who serves him with all his heart
because he knows him;
one who seeks him with all his heart
because he knows him not.

--Nikita Ivanovich Panin

We cease grieving
not because something changes only within us
but because something changes
between ourselves and our beloved dead.

Sheldon Vanauken in "A Severe Mercy"

All things by immortal power,
Near and Far
Hiddenly
To each other linked are,
That thou canst not stir a flower
Without troubling of a star.

Francis Thompson

Chapter One

Annie Looking Down

O *NLY TWO PEOPLE in the whole wide world know the truth about how I died. And they're not talking.*

They blame each other but it really wasn't either one's fault. These things happen. Life. Death. Life.

Heaven isn't what you think. But not to worry, it's better. There are fewer languages: just one. There are more colors, but no way to describe them…they are as unearthly as angels or aliens. I can't tell you that the color "glessa'" is like yellow, although it is sort of like yellow. Then again, no, it's not. You may be saddened to know that we don't fly—per se—but we do move around a lot. There is much work to do here; we don't sit on clouds playing harps. And there are plenty of rules in Heaven, one of which is that I am forbidden to share with you anything that would alter your personal journey. I have permission to say this, while on earth, practice deep breathing, don't tattoo your body (God really doesn't like that), crack open a window in your bedroom at night—yes, even in the winter—and eat a lot of bananas. Trust me on that one.

You keep your name. I am Anne Louise (for my maternal grandmother) Hopewell Langdon. I go by Annie. My father bred horses; my mother was

1

a teacher. I have two siblings. I married well: an older man, nineteen years my senior, whom I love with every inch of my body and soul. He is a pediatrician in Rockford, Illinois, and we have three great kids. Really interesting kids. Not your typical run-of-the-mill average American kids, but some truly sparkling children. Oh, I know, every mother feels this way.

My husband was faithful, thoughtful, romantic, and most important for a good marriage—not around much. (This is his joke, not mine.) He gave me a lovely home on the river and while we tried not to spoil the children, they certainly enjoyed some "my-dad's-a-doctor" kind of perks. We kept it simple: I got to stay home with the kids and do the things I loved to do—mother, cook, garden, and give riding lessons out at my parents' farm. We limited our attendance to the countless balls and fundraising events we were invited to. We took camping vacations.

I was pretty, but not too pretty—good cheekbones, blonde, thin, but muscular. I was a runner. I adored the outdoors. I wasn't book smart—I earned average grades in school—but I think I possessed an extra dose of common sense that seemed to be lacking in some of my intellectual friends. My only hospital stays were for the births (ridiculously easy) of my children. I suffered no chronic ailments, I never sprained or broke any part of my body, and I never in my life vomited. Not once. But it's not just about staying healthy. Truly, one just never knows what's around the bend.

I had a perfectly beautiful life. I had a perfectly beautiful death.

It's just that... Well, mothers will understand this...remember the feeling you had at the birth of your child? Remember the euphoria? Remember how happy you were holding this new little life? And then remember being struck with a bolt of sadness because you missed having that little life inside you? How crazy was that? Here was your beautiful baby, your miracle, and yet you ached to feel the movement of life inside you. I guess you just miss it. That's how it is here: euphoria tinged with homesickness. You just miss it.

If Heaven is a mansion, then I am still in the foyer. At the end of the hall there is a door. The most beautiful thing you have ever seen, massive in size, intricate in carving, cut I am told from the precious wood of the montadu tree. The door is the color of sky and imbedded with precious gemstones that glimmer and gleam far more brightly than anything found on earth. The door will open when my life comes full circle. When things below are set right.

Chapter Two

Mitchell Langdon, M.D. (m.d. for "magnificent dad")

THE SKY IS water. Blue. Blue. Saturated blue. Mitchell Langdon lay in his boat—anchored to the pier in his back yard—bobbing blissfully, peeking at the vault of azure sky through his sun-visor fingers. He'd fallen asleep. Now he wondered what time it was and if he was sunburned. He closed his eyes again and listened to the late spring Sunday afternoon sounds: the whir of a lawn mower, a boat passing by, some light traffic on the bridge. He rubbed his eyes and wondered if his children had killed each other or burned the house down while he'd been hiding in his boat. He wondered if Tess had kept her promise and was making dinner. He wondered if a nine-year-old even knew *how* to make dinner. And he wondered if anyone knew that he was breaking his own rule by being on the boat alone.

Mitch had always been nomadically inclined. People exhausted him with their politics and their eggshell temperaments. The ways of the human race were always a mystery to him. He understood

4

their bodies—he was, after all, a physician—but everything else was baffling. Except for Annie. Annie was easy. Annie was quite possibly the most uncomplicated person Mitch had ever known. Easy to please. Low maintenance. She had her peculiarities but then so did Mitch. Some they shared, like their fastidiousness, rigid bedtime routines, and overprotection of each other and their three children. Some were completely original, like Mitch's excessive hand washing or his junk food addiction: three a.m. Doritos and Pepsi snacks—consumed on the sly, since he was, after all, a physician.

Annie's oddities ran along the phobia continuum, the most pronounced being her fear of water. As a little girl she was involved in a traumatic bath time mishap when a teenage babysitter kept Annie in the tub for hours in tepid water while she talked on the phone to her boyfriend. Afterward, Annie refused baths, screamed through showers, hated rainstorms, and never put a toe into a swimming pool. How ironic, then, to marry Mitchell Langdon, the proverbial water boy, champion high school diver, and lover of all aquatic sports.

Love overlooks such things, doesn't it? Love goes beyond limitations: likes and dislikes, character flaws, political biases. Even age. What did it matter that when Mitchell Langdon met Annie Hopewell, he was a forty-one-year-old bachelor and she was a twenty-two-year-old landscape architect? And what did it matter that Mitch lived in a house on the river and Annie detested even driving across bridges?

Mitch had been practicing medicine for a decade when he resigned himself to the fact that he was destined to live alone the rest of his life, so he sold his condo and bought a big old house on the Rock River and settled in. He'd grown up in the northwest side of Rockford and had always dreamed of returning to the old neighborhood where people knew each other's names, held block parties, and purchased Girl Scout cookies and Boy Scout wreaths from each others' children.

Mitch bought the old Victorian "painted lady," located in the National Avenue Historic District on the Rock River, and renovated it inside and out. It was a terrible waste of space for just one person, he knew, but he loved the quiet coolness of the capacious rooms and the constant view of the water. He was content to live alone, losing himself in a demanding carpentry or refinishing project. He loved to hole himself up in a place where nobody needed him—not patients, not staff, not pharmacies, the hospital, the nursing homes, the sales reps, and especially not the insurance companies.

For Mitch, the river was the main attraction. Geologically speaking, the Rock River was older than Lake Michigan, and as a boy, he and his family had spent every chance they could boating, skiing, and fishing on it. Now, living on the riverfront meant fishing off the pier or lying in his boat on a sunny day with a good medical murder mystery.

As for the house, he remained true to the period, style, and architecture, and at the end of four years had himself a grand old home. He loved that fact that his property was once the site of a civil war training center. His mother and sisters helped him with the decorating—his mother, commenting on several occasions that the only thing missing in the house was a wife and a couple of kids. But Mitch honestly didn't see a family in his future, and it had nothing to do with his appearance, emotional health, or sexual preference; it had to do with the fact that he was shy in social situations, a bit nerdy and bookish, and so devoted to his patients that he never could carve out much time for dating. He often wondered how other physicians with wives and children balanced it all. His partner had four children, all athletes and musicians that required chaperones, audiences, and constant taxi service. No, Mitch Langdon was content with a few dates a year—with friends of friends—and with his full but solitary life.

He sat up in the boat and rubbed his eyes. In a perfect world, in a *fair* world, Annie would be sitting across from him in the boat right now. He smiled, thinking about his Annie. When she was assigned to design the landscaping for his property she had no way of knowing that in one short year she would be his wife and living in his beautiful home on the river. Annie the landlubber, whose favorite thing was terra firma. She was in her element digging, transplanting, fertilizing. She stayed away from bodies of water, was careful even with her garden hose, as she disliked even a subtle spray of water on her legs.

On the day his life changed forever, Mitch had been putting the finishing touches on some oak bookcases he was building in his den. He hadn't heard the doorbell at first over the din of his circular saw, but when he opened the door, there was Annie, a young, vibrant woman with blonde hair and remarkable gray eyes. At first he thought she was his neighbor's daughter, an unemployed college graduate who was forever ringing his doorbell and asking to borrow odd items like a sprig of rosemary or a can of hearts of palm (all things he never had), but it was Annie, and goodness, the sight of her tugged at his left anterior descending artery. She was wearing a white form-fitting tee shirt with some kind of company logo above her right breast, tan khaki shorts, and white socks with brown work boots. Her face, arms, and legs were already tanned to a warm cinnamon and her long blonde hair was pulled back in a loose ponytail. She looked so alive and healthy it made Mitch stand up straighter. *Holy Moses*, his heart said. Suddenly, he wished he were wearing a clean shirt.

She asked if he was Mitchell Langdon and when he nodded she said she was Anne Hopewell from *River View Cottage Garden Design*. "Judy asked me to come out and get a look at the property. Take some pictures and get some measurements."

Mitch was thinking *Judy Who?* and *River View What?* All at once he was perspiring. "Oh, right, right. Judy Castree. Sorry, it slipped my mind. Come on in."

"Actually," Annie said, standing in the sunlight with her hands on her hips, "I was wondering if you might come out."

"Oh, yes, of course," Mitch said. "Let me just wash my hands." In the bathroom off the kitchen he washed his hands. Twice. His face, too. He scrutinized his reflection in the mirror and silently decried his age. He hadn't shaved that morning, had decided just this morning to grow a beard; now he realized a beard was all wrong and wondered if he had time for a quick shave. No, probably not. Would she notice if he changed into a fresh tee shirt? Yes, women noticed these things. If she noticed, what would she make of it? That he simply had good manners? That he was interested? Good lord, she was half his age and twice as good looking. Who was he kidding? What had gotten into him? Maybe he'd inhaled too much sawdust or an excessive amount of wood glue. He lifted up his arms to check his blue tee shirt for pit stains. Satisfied that his antiperspirant had done its job he headed outside to meet Annie Hopewell, future wife and mother of his three children. The woman who saved him from growing old alone, although here he was now, all alone in his brand new boat, missing Annie and wondering when his children would notice that he was AWOL.

Chapter Three

Come and See

I'M LOOKING DOWN to earth, through all the layers of atmosphere—from the Exosphere, Ionosphere, Thermosphere, Mesosphere, Stratosphere, and down to the Troposphere where all the weather takes place. You think a clear, sunny day on earth is gorgeous, well, you should see it from up here. Breathtaking.

I can see my family. I can see them hurting. They're stalled is what they are. Just zombies doing the bare minimum. I was the center of their earth. A mother usually is. And although a father is just as important in a family his absence isn't felt as deeply as a mother's. God intended the bond between mother and child to be so powerful, as a matter of fact, some of the cells from a baby are left behind in the mother after the baby is born. Yes, this is true, and when I crossed over, brain scientists were just discovering the "fetomaternal microchimerism" phenomenon. What happens is this: fetal cells enter the mother's blood circulation and remain there for years, developing into different kinds of tissue. But even more cool is that the fetal stem cells actually cross the mother's blood-brain barrier and move into her brain and can even help repair the brain! What a beautiful gift from God!—that a portion of your child resides forever in your brain. This is

God's way of rewarding women for the pain of childbirth. Pretty darn cool, huh? So, no matter how stinky your kids are to you, they do something nice for you on the inside by leaving an army of good little cell soldiers inside of you to keep you healthy.

Okay, okay, I know you have a lot of questions. You want to ask me if there is sex in Heaven, and food in Heaven, and animals in Heaven. You want to know who gets to Heaven. Which faith is the true faith. You want to know how big Heaven is and where Heaven is. You wonder how old you are in Heaven. Are we still married in Heaven? Does Hell really exist, and if it does, can people in Heaven see people in Hell? You want to ask me about reincarnation, evolution, creationism, the Big Bang. You want to know if Jesus was married. You want to ask me if there is music in Heaven and if Heaven is serious or funny. You want to know what our Heavenly body looks like. And you want to know what the heck we do in Heaven—with all that perfection and happiness, aren't we bored? Well, I can't tell you much; that would be cheating. Besides, I don't know all the answers yet myself. You see, you get to Heaven in stages, and I have only just passed "Go."

There are three stages in Heaven. In the first stage you discover your true self, in the second stage you commune with all the saints, and in the third stage you come to know God. I am in the first stage where you review your life. It's a quiet time, time for reflection, understanding, and purification. It's not unlike being rehabilitated. Heavenly Rehab.

You've been taught that there is no pain and suffering in Heaven, and while this is true—of course it's true!—it takes a while to get to that level of Heaven. In the meantime, while you transition, your heart can ache a bit as you review your life. My guide, a sweet little girl named Cecilia, tells me that vestiges of earthly heartache can follow us here and adhere securely to our souls. That's why it takes longer for some of us to completely let go. Especially for those of us who go quickly, such as in an accident. Those who die after long illnesses and have more time to prepare are more ready to say goodbye. For those of us who go tragically, God keeps us in the lower vault of Heaven a little longer to allow time to help put things in order.

God is so good and has allowed my guide Cecilia to take on the form of a nine-year-old girl, who resembles my Tess, in order to ease my missing of her. But Cecilia is no child; she's an old soul, with wisdom and knowledge that surpasses anything known on earth, packaged in the untarnished sweetness of a child.

It's been almost a year now (in earth time) since I crossed over—that's what it's called up here, not "died." There's a problem. My family…they're still faltering. They're stuck in the mud of grief. But the real issue is this: Luke and Danny are living a lie, Mitch is living with a lie, and Tess, well, my little Tess is just lying! Please pay attention here—the truth really does set you free. I want my family to be free; only then can they continue on their earthly journey, and only then can I continue on my Heavenly journey. For grieving is a process not just for the survivors, it is a process between survivors and their beloved dead. They need to heal before I can move on. And I need to heal before they can move on. Everything, yes, everything, is connected.

They haven't made much progress, my family. And although we are not allowed to intervene in earthly business, we are allowed to influence. We can nudge our loved ones when they need it and plant synchronicities (what many people mistakenly call coincidences) into their lives. We can pass on an intuition, an inkling, a hunch, a gut feeling, a suspicion, a sense, or a presentiment. We can coordinate with our loved ones' guardian angels and spiritual guides, and lastly we can pray for them. Did you think prayer stopped once we were in Heaven? Oh, sweet people, prayer is the language of Heaven.

So, you send out a brief message about the nature of the problem on earth, then another saint—yes, we are all truly saints up here—responds with a problem that might match up. Yes, often when you add two problems together the outcome is a solution. This is something that we don't understand well on earth. Or maybe we do intuitively. Sometimes the packages that bring about healing and love come in some pretty unusual wrapping. Here's how my guide Cecilia helped me word it: "Nice family— doctor and three kids—stuck in grief after death of wife/mother almost a year ago. Need something to shake them up and move them on." Here's *the reply we got back, and although it seems an unlikely solution, Cecilia assures me that I must trust in God: "Unconventional, quirky, free-spirit artist, her mother, and her daughter start over after a family tragedy. Need something to ground them."*

I won't kid you, it's a little hard to watch things unfold from up here, but there are only good endings. Notice how I didn't say 'happy' endings. That's only for Hollywood. This is Heaven.

Chapter Four

Princess Scout

TESS WAS NINE going on nineteen. A tiny thing, but wiry and strong, with dark blonde hair like her mother's, which she mostly wore in a ponytail that never stayed put. A little girl who lost her mother too soon, Tess only remembered the edges of Annie. The shape and scent of her. If she closed her eyes, she could see her mother's face, but the features were hazy, and if she tried to imagine her mother's voice in her ear at night, it sounded far away like the last faint reverberation of an echo. This frightened Tess as her mother had only been gone for about a year. What would she remember in five years? Ten? Fifty?

Tess looked like her mother (and for this she was grateful), especially her attention-grabbing gray eyes. She tried to love the same things that Annie loved—cooking, gardening, and horses—but she didn't really know how to cook, she didn't like dirt, and horses had always frightened her. The things Tess missed most about her mother were the lipstick imprints in that particular shade of raspberry left on Annie's cream-colored coffee cup, the way she always smelled like Lilies of the Valley, the exercises they did together in the morning, and the way she would braid Tess's hair while singing made-up, nonsensical songs: *There was a girl, her name was Tess, her smile was sweet, her room was a mess, she was so smart she could add in her head, and when she was tired, she went straight to bed.*

Now Tess stood on a kitchen chair at the stove with her ponytail falling apart and her mother's floral apron wrapped around her, wooden spoon in hand. The dog, Piper, a black lab, sat at her feet, keeping her company. Dinner was soup from a can. Two kinds mixed together. She had planned on a nice green salad but the refrigerator held only a half head of rusty iceberg lettuce and a somewhat mushy tomato, so she did her best with tearing the brown parts off the lettuce and cutting the tomato into small pieces to disguise its undesirable texture. Nobody really cared about eating anyway. But one of the things Tess remembered about her mother was that Sunday dinner was not optional.

Tess couldn't wait for school to be out. One more week and she would be free. Secretly, she hoped she could spend most of the summer with her Aunt Maggy, her mother's younger sister, Uncle Jack, and her cousins, Nat and Tim. Aunt Maggy was pretty, not as pretty as Annie, but pretty and sweet and fun. Tess loved how she doted on her, not having any daughters of her own. She called Tess *princess* and treated her to girly things like shopping sprees and girls' lunches. Since her mother died—a year ago this June—Tess had prayed feverishly to be adopted by Aunt Maggy and Uncle Jack.

But someone had to take care of things around here.

In one year there had been three housekeepers. And it wasn't that the Langdon kids were difficult, it was just that Mrs. Johnson's husband died and she moved to Florida to be near her daughter, Mrs. Bassey broke her hip and never fully recovered, and Karina decided to go back to college. A month ago, Tess's dad had found their current housekeeper: Mrs. Cally, a heavyset black lady with whom Tess had fallen in love immediately. She had just finished reading *To Kill a Mockingbird* and so began her fantasy that Mrs. Cally was Calpurnia, the spunky cook from the book. (Tess also fantasized that she herself was Scout.) Mrs. Cally was kind and efficient, but she wore a perpetual grimace

(Tess's dad said maybe it was because she suffered from arthritis) and so Tess kept a safe distance. Mrs. Cally only worked Monday through Thursday so on weekends the Langdons had to fend for themselves. On Mondays, when she returned, Tess would see her cluck her tongue at the mess that had materialized over the weekend. Tess wished she would complain about it—Calpurnia-style—lecturing about good manners, good hygiene, and how neatness counted, but she minded her own business while cleaning and cooking for the Langdons.

Every so often she would allow Tess to trail her and she would teach her a few things: how to load the washing machine, the correct way to fold a fitted sheet, how to polish silver until it shined. But when Tess asked her questions about her life, Mrs. Cally shooed her away.

The soup concoction was the result of an almost bare pantry. After morning Mass, her father had sent her brothers, Luke and Danny, to the grocery store. They'd come back with only pop and junk food. Somehow, they'd lost the list their father had written so now breakfast for the week would be a choice of Cherry Pop Tarts or Brown Sugar Cinnamon. Lunch—well they all bought their lunch, either at school or at the clinic. Dinner would consist of frozen pizza, Tater Tots, and Hot Pockets. Mitchell (Tess had taken to following Scout's lead in *To Kill A Mockingbird* and was addressing her father by his given name) had been furious but also had been too exhausted to go shopping himself and just let it go. So that's how tonight's entrée became cream of broccoli/bean with bacon soup.

Tess yelled to the direction of the river room (what the Langdons called their family room addition that ran the entire width of the house, providing a commanding view of the Rock River and downtown Rockford): "Someone come and set the table." Piper's ears perked up, as if to say, "*You talkin' to me?*" Tess read the expression and said, "I'm talking to the boys, Piper. Go get them, will you?" Piper, being beautiful but dumb, didn't budge. Tess shook her head. "You guys!" she hollered. When no one appeared, she called again. Nothing. She jumped down from her chair, lowered the gas on the burner, and headed for the river room, with Piper trailing. "I said: Someone come and set this table. Now!"

Chapter Five

Sir Luke, the Eldest

*L*UKE AND HIS brother were lying on the couch in the river room, one on each end, kicking each other every few minutes, urging the other to move to the love seat. Luke was older by barely a year, but seniority meant nothing in this house. Danny was eighteen, four inches taller than Luke, and his main purpose in life was to antagonize his older brother. A day did not go by without some form of agitation, aggravation, provocation, or pestering. Their mother always told Luke it was because Danny idolized him and that he had realized early on that he couldn't compete with Luke's athletic good looks and Einsteinesque brains. Mom said that Danny purposely went the opposite direction, choosing a grunge look, achieving average grades, and identifying with the music/art/theater students at school. Luke tried to keep these things in mind, but sometimes Danny simply asked for it. Here was a kid who ate potato chips with a spoon. He made inside-out sandwiches—one slice of bread in the middle of two pieces of ham. He'd open the fridge and grab a "squirt of mustard" snack straight from squeeze bottle to mouth. The guy was colorblind and had absolutely no sense of style, and he didn't know the difference between cosmetology and cosmology. Seriously.

On TV a scruffy looking kid was competing in a skateboarding championship, executing death-defying flips and jumps. Luke, impressed, tried to insert himself into the picture, but his cropped blond hair and football-player physique didn't quite cut it. Skateboarding would be a sport for Danny—if Danny had been in any way athletic. Still, Luke watched in awe, thinking that it must be the closest thing to flying.

"I could do that," Danny announced.

Luke didn't acknowledge his younger brother's braggadocio because he knew he was just talking to talk. Which is what Danny did best. Talked. Non-stop. At ear-piercing decibels. Luke shook his head. Danny sang a line from a Van Halen song: "*Jump! Ah, might as well jump!*" Luke kicked him.

"I was talking to the skateboarder," Danny told him, rubbing his shin. Sure he was. Between them, that word had become the worst four-letter word in the English language. *Jump!*

They used to get along. All their lives they were Luke and Dan-Dan, Lukey and Dandy. Then they were thrown together into that cesspool of hormones and peer pressure and competition called high school. For three years, Luke had to put up with his kid brother, and in the red-hot spotlight of high school, their differences magnified. They had always known their strengths—Luke was the brains and brawn of the operation; Danny was the idea man. For example, a favorite adolescent pastime had been riding bikes in the cemetery on North Main Street. If Danny got it into his head that it would be a kick to tip over a gravestone, his job would be done—there was the idea. Then Luke would deliberate, come up with a plan, and eventually, the execution. (Or in that case—fortunately—merely the attempt.) Yes, Danny was the incubator and he expected Luke to be the hatcher.

For years, Luke had endured Danny throwing out his idea bombs—always something provocative, something bold, something Luke never would have dreamed up on his own. He was always disappointed with himself for his eventual involvement. It was a wonder they had never been arrested for their antics. They could have been—should have been—many times.

Still there was brotherly love there. Luke himself, in his vanity, knew it would be hard to be his brother.

"That is so stinking cool!" Danny said. "I could do that," he said again. "That's a one-eighty Ollie."

Yeah, right, Luke thought. Danny didn't even own a skateboard. Luke shook his head and groaned.

And groaned again when he heard Tess screaming for someone to set the table. When Tess entered the room with Piper close behind, Luke quickly closed his eyes, pretending to be asleep. He heard Piper's toenails clicking on the hardwood floor and then Tess's exaggerated sigh.

"You guys are *not* sleeping," she said. Luke almost smiled knowing that Danny had had the same idea. He scrunched his eyes shut even tighter. He could just picture his little sister standing above him with her hands on her hips, shaking her head. But Tess would only be going through the motions. The whole world knew how she worshipped Luke. And usually Luke was sweet to her. Their mother's death had been hardest on Tess. She had just turned eight and had undergone a complete meltdown. She ended up needing a tutor because she had missed so much of the second grade.

"I guess Piper will just have to lick you awake," Tess threatened, as if this were the most terrible fate one could imagine. "Piper, lick 'em, girl, lick 'em!"

Luke had always loved his baby sister—the whole family treated her like a beloved pet. She was Daddy's little girl and Momma's big girl, and the kind of adorable little sister that Luke and Danny's friends— especially the girls—found irresistible. But lately, she'd become bossy and incorrigible. She wasn't so bad during the week when their housekeeper, Mrs. Cally, was here to help, but on the weekends, Tess decided she was the woman of the house and made sure everyone else knew it as well.

"Lick 'em, Piper. Come on!"

Luke braced himself for a big, wet dog kiss. Sure enough, he felt a warm, wet tongue tickle his left cheek. He grimaced—never a fan of dog saliva—and opened his eyes. Expecting Piper, he was surprised to see Tess standing above him, with her failed ponytail, remarkable gray eyes, and pink tongue poised for another lick.

"Sick!" Luke screamed and pushed Tess a little harder than he meant to. She tumbled and fell hard on her rear end. She looked dazed but didn't cry. Sometimes she was stronger than all of the men in the house put together.

"Luke!" was all she said, as she rubbed her buttocks.

"Cripes, Luke," Danny said, springing up from the couch.

"Act like a dog, get treated like one," Luke teased, wiping his cheek. He offered Tess a hand up and she took it. But Piper, seeing this, and mistaking Luke's hand offering as a second act of violence against his most favorite person in the family, nipped at Luke.

"Shit!" Luke yelled, drawing back his hand and checking it for teeth marks. There were none; the dog's teeth had just grazed the skin.

"Serves you right, Luke," Tess said, sticking out her tongue. "Now for your punishment, go set the table."

"Yes, Ma'am!" Luke said, saluting.

"Ha Ha," Danny said.

"You," Tess said, pointing to Danny, "have dishwashing duty." She turned dramatically and, nose in the air, started to leave the room.

"Who died and made you queen?" Danny yelled after her.

Tess stopped in mid-step. She turned around, her face contorted in horror, hot tears springing from her eyes. "How could you say such a thing?" she wailed. "How?"

Luke tackled Danny, hurling him to the couch. "You asshole!"

"I didn't mean it!" growled Danny, under Luke's weight. "I wasn't thinking."

Luke held Danny down for a few seconds more. "Yeah, well, that's no excuse. You're never thinking."

Chapter Six

Dan, the Man, that Can

*D*ANNY HELD BACK a gag. The soup was a disaster but no one dared say anything. Tess had been so upset by his "who died and made you queen" comment that she'd fled to her room. He'd had to pry her off her bed, piggyback her down to the kitchen, and promise to take her to Dairy Fair for ice cream after dinner and rent the movie *To Kill a Mockingbird*. The movie part was a lie because Tess knew darn well that she was not allowed to see the movie until she was older. But he had to say something. He felt like crap and contrary to popular belief, he wasn't heartless. The expression had just popped out of his mouth. It was something they had always said: *Who died and made you king? Who died and made you the referee? Who died and made you the babysitter?* He never would have said it if he had thought about it. He missed her too you know. Just because he was a guy and couldn't whine about it everyday didn't mean he didn't miss her everyday. Sometimes every minute.

"I like Calpurnia's soup better," Tess announced, obviously fishing for compliments.

"Tess!" Mitch said, in the middle of a spoonful. "Honey, you can't call Mrs. Cally that. It's not appropriate."

"But I mean it in a nice way, Mitchell. I love Calpurnia."

Mitch said, "I know, honey, but you better stick to calling her 'Mrs. Cally' and me 'Dad.' And what's all over your face, honey? Your face is all dirty."

Tess wiped her face with her bare hand and shrugged. Without Annie, Danny realized, Tess was turning into a tomboy; she always seemed to be dirty around the edges, and the corners of her mouth often showed evidence of her last meal. It was kind of disgusting. Danny wondered if his sister would turn into one of those girls that wasn't necessarily bad looking but could never seem to get it together appearance-wise. Annie used to brush Tess's long blonde hair several times a day, and make sure she brushed her teeth and cleaned her ears. Now Tess's hair was a mess of tangles and her fingernails revealed that no, she had not washed her hands before dinner, or before preparing dinner, for that matter.

Danny set down his spoon. He was glad that he promised to take Tess to Dairy Fair for an ice cream cone after dinner because then he could get himself a chilidog and a butterscotch shake. This soup was like chunky puke. Danny tried to guess which two or three soups Tess had mixed together to come up with this creamy surprise: Chicken Noodle, Cream of Broccoli and Black Bean? Chicken with Rice, Vegetarian Vegetable and Cream of Asparagus? After the first spoonful reached his lips, he'd almost blurted out, "I didn't know Campbell's had a new soup—Cream of Crap." Thank God, he'd caught himself.

He picked at the salad and wondered if he was missing brain cells or neurons or something that other people had that kept them from blurting out stupid things. Danny felt like he was the king of saying stupid things. Sometimes they were funny, but most of the times, they were funny *and* hurtful. And he didn't mean the hurtful part. Luke said he had a warped sense of humor. His dad often told him he was just a smartass. His mother though, well, his mother told him he had the mind and the delivery of a great comedian. That someday he'd probably be famous, but for now to tone it down and to try not to hurt people's feelings.

Danny knew he was different and that different wasn't always bad. But he also wondered if he was normal and *ab*normal was usually bad. Under his mattress at that very moment was a book called *Are You Normal? Do You Behave Like Everyone Else?* by Bernice Kanner. And, the funny thing was, according to the book, he was as normal as the average American man in the twenty-first century. He, like most people, rarely made his bed; reached behind the first gallon of milk in the dairy case to grab a fresher gallon; didn't use the slit in his briefs when urinating, but simply went over the top of his underwear; set his watch five minutes ahead (still, he was always late); buttoned his shirt from the top down; rolled his clean socks into balls; believed in an afterlife; had a bout of athlete's foot; believed in ghosts; and called in sick sometimes to work or school when he wasn't. So, on paper, at least, he was normal as the next guy.

His most unique trait was his love of words, his command of the English language. He studied *mondegreens* (a mishearing of a phrase or song lyric—"*Hold me closer, Tony Danza*" instead of "*Hold me closer, tiny dancer*"), *eggcorns* ("sparrowgrass" for "asparagus"), *malapropisms* ("we have just ended our 'physical year'" instead of 'fiscal year'), and *spoonerisms* ("fight a liar" instead of "light a fire").

Danny downed his iced tea in one gulp, belched loudly, and waited for his dad to comment. But there was nothing. Not even a look. Mitch was actually spooning the so-called soup into his mouth from a special blue bowl. He'd read that the color blue served as an appetite suppressant and may help you eat less. Mitch had put on at least ten pounds since Annie died. He seemed to be running on autopilot, his head hung over his bowl. Danny had noticed that his dad was especially out-of-it lately. More than a week had gone by without a threat to cut off Danny's long brown locks while he was sleeping, a warning about a summer job, or a question about registering for community college.

High school for Danny had been a bumpy ride. The only time he coasted was at the end of his junior year. Ashley Pallow had a little—

no a lot—to do with it. *Out-of-my-league*, he'd thought when he first saw her at his best friend Mathis's end-of-the-year swimming party. He knew she was the kind of girl that came with some risk of dependency, but he didn't care. She went to Keith, a pricey private school in town where many doctors sent their kids. Ashley Pallow in a powder blue bikini, already tan from spending spring break in Florida with her family. He would never forget the sight of her. The first girl he knew with a pierced nose.

By the end of the summer she broke his heart. But for three stinking cool months, she was his. Like Danny, she also had an attention problem so she understood his inner workings. They shared how it felt to be labeled and medicated and, worst of all, impulsive. "I don't mean to hurt people," she once told Danny in the back seat of his beater. (It's not what you think—Danny and Ashley never had sex…she was a good girl who was saving herself for marriage and Danny really respected that. It surprised him and frustrated the hell out of him, but he respected it all the same.) They were in the back seat because Mathis and his date were in the front seat. Danny had kept his contacts in too long and his eyes were so irritated he thought it might be better if Mathis drove. They'd gone to a movie—a stupid high school movie—and then sat in the car in the parking lot of Dairy Queen.

"I know," Danny had told her. "I don't mean to hurt anyone either." (He pronounced the word *either* with a long 'i' rather than a long 'e' because suddenly, in front of this particular girl, he wanted to sound intelligent.) "Just call me Captain Backfire," he told her, stealing the line from a John Mayer song.

Ashley found this comment to be endearing and she kissed him for it. He remembered the wet ice cream kiss. Even more clearly he remembered seeing her kiss someone else later that summer and breaking his heart.

"Come on, Scout," Danny said to Tess, breaking out of the painful daydream. "You ready to get that ice cream?"

Tess set her spoon down, ceremoniously, next to her completely full bowl of soup. "Yes, thank you," she said, smiling sweetly at her father. "I'm not hungry for soup after all."

Chapter Seven

May-December

OF COURSE EVERYONE *thought we were crazy. "Annie," they said, "he's so old!" But when they met Mitch—my friends and family—they changed their tune. They saw what I saw: a beautiful, kind, brilliant, mature man. Big deal that he was nineteen years my senior. I fell for him the first day I met him when I went to his house to take measurements for the landscaping he'd contracted with the company I'd joined right after college. He'd been doing some woodworking and the sawdust had coated his hair, making it look gray, and adding years to his real age. I took him for at least fifty. Even then, I was attracted to him. He could have been a hundred and I still would have loved him.*

I worked at his house for weeks. It was a beautiful piece of riverfront property in one of the oldest and nicest parts of town. The project included planting various trees to replace some old oaks that a severe storm had taken down the previous summer. We also put in over thirty shrubs and conifers and hundreds of bulbs and perennials. We lined the brick paved walk that led down to the pier with dozens of hostas. It really was a beautiful yard. I had no idea that in a year it would be mine.

Mitch wasn't home much of the time we were on the job. Most of the correspondence the crew and I had with him was by phone. But one Saturday morning I went by to check on some hydrangea bushes we had put in that were a bit "iffy" and he pulled into his driveway right before I did. It was about nine in the morning and the June sun was sweet in the sky, the breeze a pleasure to feel against my bare shoulders and arms. I had run that morning, after taking a short hiatus for a pulled hamstring, and I was feeling energized and happy in the simple, honest way you feel when your body cooperates with you. I had excused myself from a breakfast date with a guy I had been half-heartedly dating for the past couple of weeks, hoping to bump into Mitchell Langdon. But when I got out of my car and approached him, I was surprised to see that he wasn't gray after all, in fact, his hair was as brown as my younger brother's, and suddenly, I was shy and wished I hadn't come.

Mitch parked his car in the garage and then came out to greet me, or at least to see what the hell I was doing there on a Saturday morning. I was worried about the hydrangea bushes, I told him. Which ones were they, he wanted to know. He followed me over to the north side of the house where I pointed them out. He pretended to be interested in the genus and type and if they flowered or not. He said he couldn't picture them until I asked him if he remembered the scene from the movie "It's a Wonderful Life" when Jimmy Stewart and—oh, gosh, what's her name—were walking home after falling into the swimming pool at their high school reunion and she lost her robe and hid in the hydrangea bushes. "Oh, yes, yes, now I know," he said. "When Jimmy Stewart says, 'Now this is a very inner-esting situation.'" His impersonation was terrible but we both smiled. He fetched the garden hose for me so I could give the plants a drink, and then we talked more about the movie and our all-time favorite movies, and before I knew it I was in his kitchen and he was calling his sister, the movie buff (since this was pre-Google era), so we could relieve our aching brains and find out the name of…Donna Reed, of course, Donna Reed. And then he was scrambling up some eggs and telling me about his morning rounds at the hospital and how he loved babies and never got tired of witnessing the

25

miracle of newborns. He gave me a tour of the house, pointing out with pride all the improvements he had made to the 1898 carriageway.

And then he asked me if I would like a ride on his boat. For most of my life I'd been terrified of water, but Mitchell Langdon was enchanting and sweet and well, grown-up. I was twenty-two and the guys I had dated up till then had been babies. Here was a man. So I braced myself, put on a life vest, gritted my teeth, and suffered through it. We sped around the Rock River on a gorgeous late spring day and I tried to enjoy it. Afterward, when we docked at his pier, he suggested we sit on the boat and soak in the sun, but I faked the need to use the restroom, and so we ended up on his screened porch and talked more. He wanted to know all about me, how old I was, first of all. School. Family. Where I grew up. What I wanted to do in life.

We seemed to be opposites: he was quiet and brilliant; he loved water and didn't mind being alone. I was boisterous and of average intelligence; I hated water and loved a good party. But there was something there. Definitely something there.

I showed up the next Saturday, and then the next, and I think after one more Saturday, we were inseparable. Secret, but inseparable. I didn't want to tell my family about him, or my boss. It seemed to me neither one would be pleased that their daughter/new employee had fallen in love with an older man/customer. But I had; and so had he.

Once we revealed our secret to the world, things moved pretty quickly. We set an autumn wedding date. "Why so soon?" my mother asked, when Mitch and I announced our wedding plans. "He's not getting any younger, Mom," I teased, and squeezed Mitch's hand. I had always dreamed as a kid of getting married in a meadow, barefoot and on horseback, but my mother wouldn't hear of it (Mitch would have gotten married in a meadow, on horseback and naked if I'd asked) so I settled for a simple church wedding at our Catholic church in Belvidere. I wore white. I wore shoes. The horses stayed home.

We honeymooned in Montpelier, Vermont, during peak foliage season. It was romantic and restful and wonderful—except for the one waiter who thought Mitch was my father. Oh, well, we laughed and decided that our *age difference would likely raise eyebrows for the rest of our lives. And it was true. As we aged and Mitch grew grayer, I stayed blonde with the help of my hairdresser, which only seemed to make the age gap wider. Did we care? No.*

Once I read an article in a women's magazine that said May-December couples faced discrimination as intense as that encountered by same-sex couples or interracial couples. The article said that women in these relationships were more likely to bear the brunt of society's disapproval because younger women were often seen as gold diggers and older women were accused of trying to hold on to youth. There was a double standard though—it didn't matter if a man was with an older woman or a younger woman, he always got a wink and a pat on the back.

Mitch and I had seen the disapproving stares, had endured the "and for your daughter?" questions by stupid waiters. I caught men winking at my husband when he pointed me out from across a room. The thing was, we didn't care. For us it was a non-issue.

We settled into a comfortable life. The first two years I kept my landscaping job and we continued to fix up the house. We wanted to start a family right away, but it took a little while for me to get pregnant. Just when we were getting worried that there might be a problem, Luke was conceived. I had the easiest pregnancy and delivery, and Luke was a sweet and good-natured baby. This is so easy, we thought, let's have another one! Then Danny came along: colicky and sleepless. Okay, so this one wasn't quite so easy. But we didn't care. We had these two adorable little boys. Though they started out with totally opposite temperaments, they grew to be inseparable; where one was the other wasn't far behind.

When Luke was ten and Danny was nine, I began longing for another baby. The days were gone that my two little guys were in love with their mother; now it was their dad whom they idolized. They lived for his attention, his praise, his approval. I had to resign myself to the fact that my home had been overtaken by boys. I was outnumbered. So I approached Mitch one soft summer night and said I thought I still had a little girl in me and he said, "Well, there's only one way to find out."

Tess completed our family. She was our little princess and I'm embarrassed to say that when she was four and heard her friend Julianna's father call Julianna a princess, she was confused. "Is Julianna a princess, too, Mommy?" she asked. When I said yes, she scrunched her face and said, "I thought I was the only princess."

When the kids were young it was a laugh a minute. Honestly, you didn't even need to turn on the TV in our house, the kids were entertainment enough. Danny got interested in filmmaking and blossomed into a junior Steven Spielberg, producing hilarious melodramas, talk shows, reality shows, and the like. Luke was our walking encyclopedia, nicknamed "Mr. Probably-Knows-Everything" by his brother. Tess fluttered around just being cute—belting out songs day and night. Life was good. Life was so good.

***

So, I guess Mitch and I proved to everyone that we weren't crazy. Only death did us part. And now I'm here reflecting on my incarnation.

Nobody on earth wants to talk about Heaven. We seem to do a better job imagining Hell. Someone once said that people spend more time researching their vacation destinations than they do their final destination. It's scary to talk about the other side of death. It's scary to talk about anything that we don't understand. And really, Heaven would hardly be Heaven if we could define it with earthly words.

Cecilia is helping me to see things with my soul. Earth connects to Heaven. How is not important, but just remember that everything is sacred energy—every person, object, movement, and thought is energy—and exists in the universe forever. Of course energy takes on different forms, but energy leaves its fingerprint on the universe.

If Earth connects to Heaven then you connect to Heaven. Many of us have just forgotten how. Quiet time and introspection used to be a way of life, but nowadays these things have been replaced by technology and busyness. But getting in touch with your unconscious self is not a lost art. It's all a matter of perception. You have eyes and areas of the *brain that interpret visual patterns and energy, you have ears and areas of the brain that process sound waves, and you have a God-designed part of your brain—the right temporal lobe—that connects you to the Almighty, the Supreme Being, to Heaven, the universe, and to mystical experiences. Just as the fetus is connected to his mother by an umbilical cord, so we are connected to our Creator through an invisible silver thread of energy that bonds us to God. Have no fear! You are not like a dog on a leash; you are like a child holding hands with a loving parent.*

People used to be more connected to Heaven. In ancient times everyday rituals and customs were heaven-reaching. The celestial heavens were part of the everyday life of religion, politics, and art. Early cultures used the heavens to regulate agricultural cycles and certain rituals, and they believed the heavens to be the link that connected them to the universe. Christians will understand this concept through the Star of Bethlehem, which guided the Magi to the nativity. (And I can assure you, this is not just an ancient cosmogonic myth.) Think of all the ancient pyramids that were constructed like mountains, usually with seven or nine steps, which corresponded with the layers of heaven that ancients believed lay superimposed over each other.

Young souls are still close to Heaven; they still remember. Sometimes when Tess is lonely she goes to her room, lies on the bed, closes her eyes and waits for her music box—the one with the red ruby slippers on it that plays "Somewhere Over the Rainbow"—to play a couple of notes on its own. She senses that it's me visiting.

Chapter Eight

The Doctor is Out of it

{Oh, look! There's my husband! Cecilia lets me peek at Mitch at work. "He looks the same, but different," I tell her, which is what I always say when she allows me a glimpse of Mitch. His face is pale, his waist is thicker, and although his step is confident and his touch competent, there's a sluggishness about him that wasn't there before. I love watching him "doctor" since it is something I never could do while I was alive. And it makes me wonder about all the spouses who never really understand their mate's profession. I watch as Mitch peers into the ears of a small boy who is squirming in his mother's arms. "His ears are fine now," Mitch tells the mother. Her face is washed with relief and I realize that Mitch attends to more than just the little ones, but to the parents as well. No wonder so many of his patients' mothers fall in love with him!}

YOU COULD SAY that Mitchell Langdon was a traditionalist. His conservatism touched every aspect of his life from medicine to politics, from parenting to finance. He was a careful man. He folded his underwear neatly in drawers, inserted shoe shapers into his wingtips, and retained receipts and financial papers for the recommended seven years. He rarely borrowed money, used credit, or gambled with speculative investments. He paid off his mortgage in ten years, drove the same gun bolt blue Volvo for fifteen years, and was reluctant to dole out money to his children unless they earned it. He never diagnosed his pediatric patients over the phone, was old school in his treatment philosophy, meaning he was low on the intervention scale, never rushing to use prescription medications when good old acetaminophen and bed rest would do the trick, and he believed in listening to children, spending as much time with them and their parents as was necessary. He was gentle and good-humored with his patients and needless to say, they loved him.

But after practicing medicine for almost thirty years, Mitch was beginning to show signs of wear. Even before he lost his wife. He must have looked into the ears and throats of his patients hundreds of thousands of times. He wasn't tired of the children—he never tired of the children—but the parents could be difficult. As could the health system, the insurance companies, and his new young, greedy partner.

He noticed that he yawned more than he used to. One of his patients—a three-year-old favorite—even mentioned it, asking if he had "slept through the night." He got a good laugh about that one, but the way the child's mother looked at him—with compassion, not pity—he knew that she knew the truth: he hadn't had a good night's sleep since Annie died.

At least his days zoomed by when he was at work. The pace was brisk. He had an A-1 staff, skillful and courteous. One of his nurses, Liz, had been with him for over twenty years and could anticipate his moods and needs almost as well as Annie. And his receptionist, Margie, was a sweet grandma, round and charming, who had a knack for calming down anxious and panicky mothers as they described the specific color of their baby's poop.

The work was still interesting and challenging because there were always new treatment methods, clinical guidelines, protocols, and algorithms. Every day he skimmed the major pediatric medical journals because one only had to blink and there was a new treatment for asthma,

ADHD, or diabetes. Just the other day he came across an article in the Journal Pediatrics about a new treatment for acute infectious diarrhea in children to consider when the BRAT diet (bananas, rice, applesauce, and toast) didn't work. The study found modest success in treating children with *Lactobacillus*, which is found in the live and active cultures in yogurt. And he'd just read that French researchers found that the smell of vanilla can reduce apnea in premature infants who do not respond to drug treatment. His partner shared an abstract the other day that assigned some of the blame for childhood asthma to breathing in chlorine fumes from indoor pools. Blink and you could miss the answer to the SIDS mystery—it's likely caused by a brain stem disorder. There was new information cropping up every day on potty-training, breast-feeding, weaning, immunizations, developmental delays, tics, bed-wetting, sibling rivalry, sleep and feeding schedules, circumcision, autism, the pros and cons of the Hepatitis B and the Human Papillomavirus vaccines, and on and on. He had to keep up. His patients' good health depended on it.

By the end of the day he was drained. At four forty-five p.m. there were still three patients to see. He yawned his way through his examination of a small girl with a hoarse cough and high fever, and had to apologize to the mother, explaining that he'd been on call the previous night. Though the child's lungs were clear of pneumonia, he prescribed a two-day course of cortisone to reduce the inflammation around her vocal cords. This treatment was considered somewhat controversial and was uncharacteristically bold for Mitch, but since this child had had croup twice before he believed it was worth preventing complications. He wanted to keep her out of the emergency room. Mitch patiently explained his treatment plan to the concerned mother, then playfully bopped the three-year-old's head with the end of his purple tie and presented her with a stick of chewing gum and a sticker.

Finally he finished with his last patient. Looking at his watch, he thanked God he still had time to take Tess to her gymnastics lesson. Luke and Danny had ended up taking her the last three or four Thursdays, and he promised her last night when he tucked her in that he would take her. He'd pick her up at a quarter to six and then take her out for pizza at *Altamore's Ristorante* after her lesson. They hadn't spent much time together lately and a little time with just the two of them would be nice.

Mitch was in his office, hanging up his lab coat, when his receptionist peeked her head in and asked if he wanted to take one more case. "What is it, Margie?" he asked. Margie described the child's symptoms and Mitch said, "I better see her." He pulled his coat off the hanger and shoved his arms through the sleeves. Reluctantly, he dialed up Luke's cell phone. "Luke, sorry about this, but can you get Tess to gymnastics? I've got a surprise patient. Sick as a dog."

❧

The house was dark when Mitch got home. Piper greeted him ambivalently. Being a female herself, Piper had always favored the ladies of the house. She simply tolerated Mitch, Luke, and Danny. No one was home. He hit redial on his cell phone and Luke answered after the first ring. They were on their way home. Danny was with them and they had stopped for pizza.

"Is Tess mad at me?" Mitch asked.

"What do you think, Dad?" Luke answered.

So now he'd get the silent treatment. Tess was so like Annie that way. He and Annie seldom fought, but when they did, it was textbook: Mitch would break a promise (usually on account of a patient) and Annie would say she understood, but would grow silent and sulky. With Annie, it sometimes took flowers or Godiva chocolates, but with Tess, well, he didn't know what it took.

Mitch braced himself for Tess's rage when he saw Luke's car pull up the driveway. He decided nonchalance would be the best way to go. After all, he was her father and he was a doctor and doctors take an oath to help sick people and what if it had been her, that last sick patient, that little girl with a hundred and four temperature who couldn't keep

33

anything down and was possibly dehydrated? What if it had been her, and her doctor had sent her off to the urgent care or the emergency room where she would wait forever in a waiting room and possibly infect a lot of other people in the process?

As it was, Tess by-passed her father completely and so all the buildup was for naught. Danny stopped in and high-fived his dad and plopped into the chair next to him. Luke hovered in the doorway, shaking his head, holding a Styrofoam box. "Let her be, Dad," he said. "Let her pout for a while. You want some leftover pizza?"

"Can I sleep at Mathis's?" Danny asked.

"No and yes. Whatever you want."

{"Cecilia, I want to shake my husband! He needs to wake up! How long will Luke have to do the parenting around there? It's not fair!" Cecilia pats my hand. "Look at him, just sitting in the dark. I wish he'd turn a light on."}

The boys left him. He trudged to the kitchen to pour himself a glass of wine and then went back to his chair to sit in the dark. He'd never been partial to German white wines but they were Annie's favorite and so they had a couple of cases of *Piesporter Riesling Kabinett* on shelves in the basement. Somebody had to drink them. The moonlight found its way into the room and dusted the furniture with a powdery light. It made Mitch sad: the quiet rooms, the tasteless meals, Annie's garden full of weeds. And not enough time in the day to do anyone or anything justice. With Annie gone, everything suffered.

They were a cast of wounded characters, this family of his, yes, a walking cast of wounded. From all appearances it looked as if they were coping. They were "hanging in there," "keeping busy," "doing as well as could be expected." Oh, there were plenty of pat responses to the genuinely heartfelt questions posed by well-meaning people. But sometimes Mitch wished he could be honest. Imagine if when Mrs. Abbey from across the street caught him in the driveway one morning and in response to her "How's the good doctor faring?" he replied, "Like shit, actually." Imagine!

Mitch can put one foot in front of the other; that he can do. But the cloud never lifted. Something pushed intently on his chest, waking him in the morning, and keeping him awake at night. He should probably go in for a stress test, but—but nothing—he should just go in.

Don't get him wrong—there was plenty to live for. Goodness, he would never be so dramatic as to say without Annie there was nothing to live for. The kids he loved. But he couldn't keep up. They seemed so distant, as if they were running away from him in slow motion. Annie would know what to do. That was the irony—Annie would know perfectly well how to handle her own death. Mitch felt so out of the loop. Annie had run this household with ease and finesse—panache even. And she loved it. Mitch could barely remember which grades the kids were in. Well, Luke was easy. Luke was going to be a freshman in college. He should have been a sophomore but they had lost Annie last June, and come August, Luke just couldn't bring himself to leave, so he took the year off, worked at Barnes and Noble, took a computer class at the community college, and helped out with Tess. He still wanted to be a doctor—not a pediatrician like his Dad—but a neurologist or maybe a neuro-psychologist. Luke was fascinated with the brain. Mitch smiled, sitting there in his chair, remembering the day Luke, maybe four or five, had asked him, "Daddy, where do memories live?"

Danny had just graduated from Boylan High School, which seemed impossible since he seemed so young. It wasn't that he was immature... well, yes, it was that he was immature. He had crashed his car so many times it was a wonder it still ran. Danny loved all things grungy: clothes, hair, his room, his books and notebooks. He prided himself on being an eclectic-enigmatic-artist-musician. And as frustrating as this was, Mitch had to admit that it was Danny who made them all laugh. Danny had inherited Annie's creativity and exuberance. Luke had inherited Mitch's quiet conservatism. Tess was just Tess—a little blonde blob of estrogen circulating in a sea of testosterone, endlessly asking questions to which Mitch had no answers: "Where does the white go when the snow melts?" "Why are yawns contagious?" "Can you get a brain tumor from using your cell phone?" "Why do some people have 'innie' belly buttons and some people have 'outie' ones?"

It was Danny Mitch worried about most. Danny, with his James Dean squint, rebel killer eyes, and rock star hair. For all Mitch's preaching to parents about raising children with healthy self-esteems, he wondered where he went wrong with Danny. Sometimes the kid's self-esteem cup runneth over and other times he was completely bankrupt in that department. It was all or nothing with Danny.

Oh, Mitch knew most of his second son's problems stemmed from being the brother of a near-perfect child (it was so cliché!). The other part was pure genetics. Danny was a risk taker and seemed to be genetically drawn to intense stimulation. Behavior scientists called people like Danny "high sensation seekers"—mountain climbers, firefighters, parachutists, racecar drivers, even addicts and criminals. Mitch worried about his son's high sensation-seeking tendencies. Danny's own motto was: *Dan the man that can!* And most of the times he could, but what about the time he couldn't? That's what worried Mitch.

Sometimes, when Mitch was sitting in the dark, he allowed himself a moment or two of self-pity. If the tables were turned, he wondered, and he had died first, would anyone even miss him? There were times in the marriage when he had felt like the breadwinner and nothing more. But then Annie would do something special to make him feel wanted, loved, needed. He prayed to her for help. Sometimes at night he listened for her. Just maybe she was trying to send him a message. The other night he'd watched one of those psychics on *Larry King Live* and he had to admit he was impressed. Maybe there was something to it. But wasn't all that hocus pocus against the Catholic Church?

Well, the kids were getting help. Tess was seeing Miranda Burns weekly and Luke seemed to be doing okay with Dr. Bonovia. Even Danny (it had taken three professionals before getting it right) wasn't complaining about going to see his psychologist anymore, so at least that was something.

Well, you carry on. You plug away. You keep so busy there's no time for grief. You fill every minute of every day with something to think about, something to act upon. At work, there were endless patients and charts and dictation and politics. At home, there were bills and renewals and college applications and school functions and gymnastics and piano lessons and vet visits. And suddenly the house was falling apart: he needed new gutters, a new dishwasher, someone to change the toilet paper rolls since it was obvious he was the only one who ever did it. The driveway needed to be resealed, and he swore he saw a mouse scurry through the hallway the other night when he got up to use the bathroom.

He was just so tired. Maybe he should retire early. He was only sixty-three—Dr. Jurts worked until he was seventy-two, saying he was addicted to kids. Dr. Penter retired at sixty-five and then couldn't stand it and came back a couple days a week. Mitch considered other possibilities: pediatric hospitalist, something in administration, teaching at the school of medicine, but all involved change and change required energy and he was bust in that department. His own daughter looked at him as if he was going to croak any minute. She was always flinging the back of her hand to his forehead and asking him how he felt, how he had slept. She monitored what went into his mouth more strictly than even Annie had. Poor Tess. He knew she wished she had a young, vibrant father, like Julianna's father, Zeke Spellman, their neighbor to the left. Once Mitch had overheard Tess refer to her best friend's father as a "fun" father, implying that hers was a fuddy-dud. That was another worry. Tess didn't know yet that the Spellmans were moving away in a few weeks. Mitch was happy for Zeke Spellman; he would be a rabbi in the old Chicago neighborhood where he had grown up. But the move was going to be hard on the girls and it meant the Langdons would be getting new neighbors. The houses on their particular block of National Avenue stayed in families. People seemed to stay put. Suddenly, Mitch felt vulnerable. Very vulnerable indeed.

Yep, he would just hit the hay. The alternative wasn't very appealing: late night TV talk shows. Depressing. Tomorrow was Friday. For some people—normal people—that meant the weekend. That meant R & R. For Mitch, it meant he was one day closer to a massage. Ever since Annie died, he'd been getting weekly massages on Saturday mornings from a lady named Trina who had a nice set-up in her home. The fifty-minute Swedish massage that relaxed every muscle in his body had become the highlight of his week. He would never admit it, but he had become addicted to his massages. Just thinking about missing his eight a.m. appointment made him anxious. What was it? The routine? The quiet time? The stress relief? The aromatherapy? The tinkling music? Mitch knew exactly what it was: it was the only time he was touched by a woman anymore. It wasn't as if his life was devoid of any meaningful physical contact but it seemed to be so one-sided—Mitch touching patients with a physician's inquisitive palpitations, Mitch hugging Tess, squeezing Luke's shoulder, mussing up Danny's curls. But who touched Mitch? Trina did. And it was perfectly respectable and legitimate. Still, it often made Mitch uncomfortable—paying for services of pleasure. Yes, he was addicted to his massages.

Mitch's legs were leaden, and when he finally stood up to head up to bed, he had to stop to shake the sleep from his left foot. In the kitchen he put his wine glass in the sink but then before he knew it he was refilling it and flicking on the small TV on the counter. He was stalling. He knew sleep wouldn't come easy. How he wished the body could function without it.

On TV, David Letterman was schmoozing—oh, hell, what's her name—that actress with the big smile that everyone goes ga-ga over. See, that was another thing he lost when he lost Annie—half of his memory. Oh well, the actress's name didn't matter. She was teasing Dave about coming to fatherhood so late in life. "How old will you be when your son starts college?" she asked. Dave smarted back, "Somewhere between eighty and dead."

"Get used to it," Mitch told TV Dave. The jokes would last Dave's lifetime. There'd been studies that looked at the optimum age of parents, but over the years, Mitch had put less and less faith in the results of those kinds of studies. What did he really know about kids anyway? He'd devoted his entire life to their care and development but he knew next to nothing of the inner workings of their brains. Any hint of childhood mental disorder and Mitch quickly referred his patients to a pediatric psychiatrist.

He sipped the wine and looked around at the assortment of dirty dishes in the sink and on the counter. Before Annie died, he wouldn't even have *seen* the dishes, but now, he not only saw them but also collected them, rinsed them, and added them to the dishwasher. Yes, kids were total mysteries. Just the other day he'd had a teenage girl whose mother brought her in because she was worried she had mononucleosis. Turned out the fifteen-year-old was pregnant. The girl swore up and down to Mitch that she had never even had sex. "Never in my whole life!" And then there was Jacob Waller—athlete and math whiz—who stole his grandmother's car and drove it into a brick office building, killing himself and the custodian. What went on in these kids' heads? Or in his own kids' heads for that matter. How well did he really know his own kids? People were such a blend of genes, protein, enzymes, hormones, education, upbringing, culture, gender and health. It was a wonder we knew as much as we did about the human race.

An old quotation jumped into Mitch's head: "Life is a mystery to be lived; not a problem to be solved." But while you lived the mystery, you couldn't help but want to solve the problems. The biggest problem of all being the mystery surrounding Annie's death. He still didn't know exactly how it happened. Would he ever know?

Suddenly he felt tipsy. What was wrong with him?—he couldn't even hold his liquor anymore. Two small glasses of wine and… He closed the dishwasher door, pushed the "on" button, and flicked off the kitchen light. He trudged to bed, his stocking feet slogging on the wood floors. "Pick up your feet!" his inner voice reminded. Nothing came easy anymore, not even walking.

Upstairs, he peeked into Tess's room. She looked like a rag doll when she slept, arms this way and that, one leg hanging off the side of the bed. He tiptoed in and covered her lightly with the sheet. There were so many stuffed animals in her bed there was barely room for her. Of course Annie knew all their names. Poor kid.

Mitch wasn't snooping, but when he stepped into Danny's room (he'd already forgotten that Danny was sleeping at his friend's house) he noticed a journal on the nightstand. Annie had encouraged all the kids to keep journals. It was just like Danny not to think to hide his; he'd always been too trusting. When Mitch opened it, he chuckled at Danny's lefty scrawl. The first page read: "I beseech thee, do not enter. Please, these are the private ruminations of my bleeding heart. These are the secrets of my sacred soul. Pieces of my fragmented flesh. I ask for your respect and consideration in this matter. If you fail to respect my wishes, then F-you!"

Mitch couldn't help but smile…and peek. Mostly, there were scribbles about girls and stick drawings. Ashley Pallow figured into Danny's "ruminations" as did ideas for his documentaries. The most surprising and intriguing entries though were his questions about the afterlife:

"What is the soul? Is it electricity?"

"Pinch me. Am I really alive? What is this thing we call life? Existence. Resistance is futile."

"I read a quote by Woody Allen. Something about getting thrown out of college for cheating on a metaphysics exam. He looked into the soul of another boy."

"What's nearer to me—God or my own spirit?"

"Sometimes I feel like my soul expands and contracts in the universe. Is consciousness an optical delusion as Albert Einstein said?"

Albert Einstein? If the journal entries weren't written in Danny's unique handwriting, Mitch might have thought he'd picked up Luke's journal. It shamed him that he didn't know this side of Danny—this sensitive and curious side. Sometimes the kid seemed to just skim the surface. He'd misjudged Danny. What else had he misjudged? What else was right under his nose?

He didn't dare check in on Luke. He knew Luke was tired of being a pseudo mom and that he needed some space. Mitch tried to remember what it was like to be nineteen. At Luke's age he was already at Loyola studying his brains off. He'd set a personal goal for himself to ace every class he took and when he got a 'B' once in organic chemistry he fell into a deep funk. It took a long weekend in Palm Springs—a worried gift from his doting grandmother—to bring him out of it. Goodness, he'd been a serious kid. He hoped Luke would find a way to have some fun in college. Not too much fun, but some. He shook his head. What was he thinking? He didn't need to worry about Luke.

Mitch used the bathroom, brushed his stupid teeth, washed his hound dog face, and stripped off his clothes. In his bedroom, he stared at the king-size bed he and Annie had shared for almost twenty years. It looked as if it could eat him. He walked over to the dresser and started opening and closing drawers. Since Annie had died he constantly rummaged through drawers and closets, through plastic storage containers in the basement, through corrugated boxes in the attic, always searching for pieces of Annie. Secretly, he hoped to find a love letter. Just something small. When his sister Katie lost her husband, she found a letter he had hidden under the lining of his desk drawer. It was a poem, a love poem, addressed to her, a secret statement of love, words he could put to paper that he could not bring to his lips. He loved her simply, purely, and only.

{"What is he looking for?" I ask Cecilia, as we watch Mitch rummage through drawers in the bedroom. Cecilia just shrugs. My poor Mitch. This stress is not good for his heart. It's taken such a beating. Figuratively and literally. About a year before I died, Mitch's heart stopped beating. He was driving to the hospital on a cold January morning when something in his chest went ka-boom and he went into cardiac arrest. He veered into an oncoming car—thank God that driver and her little girl weren't seriously hurt—and passed out. My heroes, Dean Armour, Sr. and Dean Armour, Jr., father and son joggers, happened to be running in the neighborhood, witnessed the accident, attended to both drivers, called 911, and performed CPR on Mitch until the paramedics arrived.

What a terrifying experience! Mitch came out of it okay. He was resuscitated and rehabilitated. And after a pacemaker-defibrillator implant he was proclaimed good as new. But he was never really the same. There was a melancholy look about him that wasn't there before. It was a rude awakening for Mitch—the man who spent his days fixing others wasn't going to be able to fix himself.}

Mitch slammed the final drawer shut and dropped himself onto his bed. He didn't bother getting under the covers even though the air-conditioning was cranked. Mrs. Cally tucked his sheets and blankets in so tightly the bed felt gift-wrapped. He often woke up feeling claustrophobic. In just a couple of weeks, he would face the first anniversary of Annie's death. It was hard to believe that it had been a year of emotions and holidays and seasons and milestones, all without Annie. After June twentieth, there would be no more grieving hurdles. No more first Christmas without Annie, first anniversary without Annie, first Valentine's Day without Annie, first birthday, Fourth of July... Was there such a thing as a grieving graduation? If so, he would not be receiving a diploma this year. He was in no way ready.

Chapter Nine

Don't Cry over Steamed Milk

{*"What's Luke up to, Cecilia? May I see Luke, please?" Cecilia nods. I follow her finger and see Luke preparing an espresso at the café at Barnes and Noble. Luke! My oldest! The easiest kid in the world to raise! Just weeks before I died Luke had graduated from Boylan Catholic High School, where he'd had a fantastic year—he was valedictorian, state diving champ, and had had a couple of nice (but not too serious) girlfriends. In spite of his father trying to guide him away from medicine and into a less-frustrating career, Luke insisted he wanted to be a doctor and had been accepted at the prestigious University of Chicago. His path was set.*

Look how handsome he is! Smile! I want to tell him, for in spite of his good looks, he's rather shy. Oh, from the outside he appears to be easy-going, the kind that doesn't ruffle easily, but he's a great actor. Inside, my Luke is full of activity: his nervous stomach gurgles, his ethical conscience clamors, his analytical brain flickers and sparks. But Luke will do big things. We knew he was special and mature beyond his age right from the start. He walked and talked at nine months, could sing his ABCs at a year. He was doing puzzles at eighteen months. He fell in love with LEGOS and riddles and mind games. He was a science whiz, a history buff, and an adorable magician. Then he just grew into a scholar, winning at school contests, fairs, and competitions.

Mitch once told me that Luke was the perfect child. I knew what he meant but I told Mitch it was a dreadful thing to say! Perfection is a burden. Someone once said that perfection is the highest form of self-abuse and I think it's true because perfectionists are usually their own worst enemies. Luke always puts a lot of pressure on himself. Some of it is first-child syndrome, some of it is his father, but most of it is just how he's wired.}

LUKE MAKES COFFEE. This is what it's come to. Another Saturday night and here he was standing behind the counter at Barnes and Noble preparing a *venti 2% light-whip triple two-pump mocha* for a petite redhead who had more piercings on her body than a person ought to. Not so long ago he was on the other side of this counter. When the redhead reached for her drink Luke noticed a tattoo on her wrist that looked like a cell phone. He didn't understand tattoos or body piercing, and not just because he despised pain of any kind. He once read that tattoos were the expressions of the inarticulate, and although the statement was put forth by some highbrow old fogy, he tended to agree with it. At any rate it seemed to be a vestige of primitive behavior of which he himself wanted no part. Tattoos? I think not.

Seriously, the idea behind taking this job at the bookstore was that it would keep him in the circle of wisdom. He thought at the very least surrounding himself with books would help mitigate the blow of missing out on his first year of college. The truth was Barnes and Noble was overrun with caffeine-crazed kids who needed a place to hang out and spend their parents' money. Okay, that wasn't entirely true, but he couldn't believe the kind of money these kids shelled out for a lousy cup of coffee and a brownie the size of a sandwich. He was all for free enterprise, but where did it end? On the other hand, people could do worse on a lonely, dateless Saturday night than spend it with a cup of joe and a magazine. He'd done worse himself for nearly the last year, spending most of his free time carting around his little sister, reading books about the brain, doing the grocery shopping, paying the bills, and balancing his dad's checkbook. His friends had all gone off to college without him; a few he'd lost even before he'd graduated. Friends turned out to be so—temporary. This came as a surprise. He'd always thought his grade school friends would be his friends for life. But things happen along the way, unexpected things. Things you regret but can't change.

He often had to remind himself that he had done the right thing—staying behind for a year after his mom died. It was understood that he had made the supreme sacrifice for his family by staying back, but the truth was, had he gone to school, he likely would have flunked out. He was damn lucky that the University of Chicago granted him deferred admission. He really expected that he'd have to reapply and possibly end up at another school all together, but his heart was set on U of C and now, thankfully, he would be attending in the fall. Actually, it was more like mid-August. Just get through June and July and he would be home free. His life could begin. The plan was unfolding; his four years of studious discipline at Boylan had earned him the valedictorian title, which in turn awarded him acceptance into one of the best schools in the country. He was ready. He was ready right now.

But Tess did tug at his heart. She'd been sleeping in his room on a cot for several months now. Well, she could easily move it into Danny's room. Danny would be around for another year at least. (Since he had no idea what he wanted to do in life, he'd promised his dad he'd take classes at the community college before committing his time and his father's money to a four-year institution.) But it wasn't just Tess's sleeping arrangements that concerned Luke, this obsession with Harper Lee and *To Kill a Mockingbird* was disconcerting. Even more unsettling was the fact that Tess's lying was getting worse. It was subtle—Mitch missed it most of the time—but Luke picked up on things. He called her psychologist about it a few months ago and she said she was aware of it and that it wasn't an uncommon defense mechanism for children who had lost a parent. She was working on it. She couldn't say much, though, due to patient privacy.

Then there was Danny. Danny Luke could leave. Of course he loved him, but the kid was this side of weird. And although he possessed talents Luke himself longed for—the gift of gab, natural charisma, and a zest for life that comes from being truly fearless—he drove him crazy. Here was a grown man (at least physically) who would ride grocery store horses! Here was a guy who hopped on one foot down the halls in school his senior year for a solid week. (On a dare and he'd made a hundred bucks for doing it.) Here was a guy who talked—literally—in his own language, this stupid made up "tongue" that Danny used with his friend Mathis.

Danny had always embarrassed Luke. Even as a baby Danny would glom all the attention by charming the pants off people by smiling, winking, and waving at strangers. He would talk to anyone. Looking into people's grocery carts he would ask if they were throwing a party, or ask how they could possibly like sardines. Once when he was about five, Danny had asked an ambiguously-gendered convenience store attendant if he was a boy or a girl. Luke was mortified! Another time, he asked a kid with a Mohawk if he was a horse. And he just had to be obstinate. He had to say "Treat or Trick" every Halloween at the neighbors' doorsteps. Every Christmas he insisted on saying "Happy Christmas!" and every New Year, it was "Merry New Year!" He was always breaking an arm or wrist or spraining something and garnering sympathy from all corners of the earth.

Annie and Mitch had to remind Luke repeatedly that he was not Danny's guardian and that he did not need to monitor his little brother's every move. Still, Luke always felt Danny needed reining in. This bothered him about himself, that he had jealous bones in his body, but there they were. Now, he and his brother merely tolerated each other. Danny thought Luke was a snobby, intellectual jock, and Luke thought Danny was an ignorant, irresponsible hippie. Just the other day Luke had overheard Danny telling his friend Mathis that Luke was a self-made man who worshipped his creator—himself. It made

Luke wonder if he deserved the criticism. Did other people see him this way? He didn't mean to appear arrogant. He used to be smart *and* fun. Maybe he had become serious and humorless. Well, tragedy will do that to a person. Luke sometimes wondered, how, considering all that had happened, Danny could still act like a clown. And an idiot. He was forever leaping out of corners and shouting, "Jump!" in Luke's ear and then laughing when he did jump. Oh yes, between the two of them the word *jump* had become the dirtiest word in the book.

So, he made coffee and he chauffeured his baby sister around town. (Someday, when he was conducting Nobel-Prize-caliber research on the brain, he would look back at this time in his life and—what?— laugh, sigh, grimace?) He'd been forced to cut his hours at Barnes and Noble to accommodate Tess's busy summer schedule, carting her to birthday parties, piano lessons, and gymnastics. His father had begged him to quit his job altogether—that he'd pay him an exorbitant nanny salary—but Luke talked him into letting him keep a limited schedule, just enough to keep his sanity and a little pocket money. Not that he spent much money. He hadn't been on a true date in months. While Danny had countered his grief with mania, Luke had gone deep inside himself. It had taken a year to climb out and he wasn't home free yet. Dr. Bonovia was helping. That was another thing that worried Luke about leaving. Would he be ready to give up his weekly sessions? Surely he wouldn't be up for starting the process all over again with someone new once he got to school.

At first Luke disliked Dr. Bonovia. He was round and bald, wore an unruly beard, and laughed at his own jokes. But after a while, Luke got used to him. And, more importantly, Luke started to trust him. He never told Luke how to feel—or even how others in his situation had felt. Luke came to appreciate the doctor's odd brilliance as it emerged, for he understood the brain and offered scientific evidence of cognitive function and how the brain was wired for emotions. He suggested books for Luke to read. Working at Barnes and Noble made that an easy undertaking—he didn't even have to buy anything, but simply read on his breaks or before or after his shift. It was Dr. Bonovia who suggested considering a specialty in neurology or neuro-psychology. The brain, Luke found, was spectacularly fascinating. Especially his own.

As much as he liked Dr. Bonovia, he could never tell him the whole truth and nothing but the truth. The truth was something that Luke swore he would take to his grave for he knew with certainty that bringing the truth out into the light of day would be the death of him.

Luke waited on a ditzy-looking teenaged girl, skinny as a sheet of loose-leaf, who ordered a complicated coffee hybrid: *venti latte with two Sweet'N Lows, nonfat milk and a triple shot of espresso with legs.*

(LUKE'S FASCINATING BRAIN FACT: Women may be more at risk of eating disorders than men because of the way their brains process information.)

"Can I ask you a serious question?" the girl asked Luke, as she dug in her purse for money. When Luke nodded, she said, "When I make a cup of coffee at home for my father—he pays me for this, you see—and I add cream, it never gets the color he likes it, you know, kind of like a beautiful cocoa color. I keep pouring in more cream and it never changes color? What's the secret?"

Luke paused to make certain this young lady was serious. The look on her face told him she was. *Be nice*, his inner voice warned. "I think you just need to *stir* it," he said with a smile.

"With a spoon?"

(LUKE'S FASCINATING BRAIN FACT: Male brains are about nine percent larger than female brains, even after correcting for body size, but since both brains contain the same number of brain cells, we can't say that women have less mental capacity than men. Standing in front of him, however, was a female who could be an exception.)

No, with your finger, his inner voice said. "Yes, with a spoon."

"Hmmph," she said. "I really thought there was a special kind of cream or something. You must think I'm a space."

"No, not at all." *More like a ding-a-ling.*

Twenty minutes before closing, two girls with whom Luke had graduated came in and stood in line. While he finished up with the customer before them, they giggled and talked about what a drag it was to be home for the summer and living under their parents' roofs after having enjoyed so many months of freedom. Then Luke overheard the one that had been in his homeroom say, "Yeah, that's him," and nod in his direction. When it was their turn in line, they smiled at him and ordered iced Chai tea but they didn't let on that they recognized him. Just as well, Luke thought. He wasn't in any mood to reminisce.

When his shift was over and the stragglers were shooed away, Luke said goodnight to his manager and headed out to the parking lot. Look at what he drove! A van! How humiliating! His mother's blue Toyota Sienna van. A nice enough vehicle, yes, but it made Luke feel like a soccer mom.

He worried about losing his edge. There was no doubt about his looks—he knew he was good-looking. He'd been told since he was knee-high that he was going to "break all the girls' hearts." He liked when people told him that he looked like Matt Damon, although he wouldn't quite go that far. But he did take care of himself. Like his mom, he liked to run and ride horses, which helped keep him in shape. He wore his dark blond hair neatly cropped, spiked at the front a bit, and with the help of a good dermatologist and a good orthodontist, his skin and teeth were movie-star perfect. In spite of it all, Luke was shy and self-effacing. He was most articulate on paper. Conversation seemed to be an art lost on him. He always got tripped up with his own thoughts.

The person with whom Luke could share the most was gone. Yes, he could talk about just about anything with his mother—except for sex, and well, a few other things. Annie was a good listener and gave him room to make his own decisions while giving him good advice. He liked how she helped him uncover choices when a decision needed to be made and to weigh out those choices, even sometimes on paper, before making decisions. And it was his mother who taught Luke the difference between the "best" decision and the "right" decision. He missed her so much it hurt to even think about her.

He got into the van and started it up, idling while grabbing his CD case to see what he could find to match his dismal mood. A black Jeep pulled up next to him and the girl from his homeroom rolled down her window and motioned for Luke to do the same. Luke was confused. What could *she* want? The other girl wasn't in the car with her.

"Hi," she said. "Don't think I'm stupid. We had homeroom together. You're Luke Langdon, right?"

"Yeah."

"You don't remember me, do you?"

Luke wanted to lie and say no, he didn't remember her, that he suffered from *Prosopagnosia*, which was an inability to differentiate faces except for the most familiar ones such as members of one's family, but, the truth was she had an unforgettable face; he could pull her out of a crowd of hundreds. Her name was Karley, but he didn't want her to know he remembered. "Don't tell me," he said. "Kitra or Katrina or Kayla. Something with a 'K' anyway."

"Karley. Karley Lappos. I sat behind you. For four years I stared at the back of your head for fifteen minutes every morning. You have a mole in back of your right ear."

This freaked Luke out and he felt his right eyebrow raise—his idiosyncratic and telltale display of surprise. "Oh, right," he said, using a flat, emotionless voice, even though inside his heart was racing, his pits were dampening, and cortisol hormones were flooding his brain. He'd thought of asking her out once, but she was dating some older guy from another school.

"I wasn't very nice in high school," she said.

Luke found himself nodding. In high school, she was probably trapped in a stereotype that she herself had promulgated and then realized too late that it was shallow and lonely and unauthentic. "Well, I'm glad to hear that one year of college has redeemed you."

"I'm just nicer, that's all. Not so judgmental."

Luke never knew her well enough to know about her prejudices, but he did recall her aloofness. He'd always thought she'd seemed urbane and chic, more collegiate, while her peers seemed juvenile and inelegant. She was beautiful. That much Luke couldn't deny. And put together well. He guessed that this was a girl who devoted a lot of morning time to grooming. She had straight brown, layered hair, and well-applied make-up. (Luke hated when girls had clown faces— spider leg eyelashes, round blotches of pink on their cheeks, and worst of all, lipstick that went beyond the lips and onto the skin to give the illusion of fuller lips. Yuck!) Her skin was smooth, her fingernails were nice (he'd been obsessed with women with manicures because his mother, being a gardener, an artist, and a horsewomen, never had manicured nails) and she adorned herself with silver jewelry. If nothing else, Karley Lappos provided a nice view.

"I was sorry to hear about your mom," Karley said, her thin arm leaning out of the open window. "We all were. Did you know I came to the funeral?"

Luke was caught off guard. "You did?"

"A lot of us did. It was so sad."

"Yeah, well. Where's your friend?"

"She got bored."

"What about you?"

"I wanted to tell you something."

"Oh, and what might that be?"

"You still live on the river? On National?"

"Yeah."

"This is embarrassing, but, my aunt just bought the house next door to you. She and my cousin are moving in soon and if I were you I'd be moving out ASAP."

Luke didn't know why, but suddenly he found this conversation with this girl, who, for four years hadn't given him the time of day, very amusing. "And why is that? Are they axe-murderers or something?"

"Worse than that. They're bohemians."

"Is that all," Luke said, snickering. "Well, thank you for the heads up, Miss Lappos. I'll be sure to canvass the neighborhood."

"I am not kidding. You will not know what hit you until they have infiltrated your world and then it will be too late."

"How are you related again?"

"The mom is my mother's brother's wife, but my mother won't claim her. She's like this crazy woman. And the daughter, my cousin, well she's just strange—she studies saints and likes to give money to charity."

"That's terrible!" Luke said, feigning shock.

"They're moving here from Lake Forest. My uncle died. I heard the grandma might move in with them too since the house is huge. I think the grandma is crazy too. She's filthy rich but crazy. You got three crackpots there."

"I don't understand why you're telling me all this."

"Just as a friend."

"Oh, we're friends now?"

"Whatever. I told you I'm nicer now. I didn't have to sit out here in my car and wait for you to get off work. I could be at a party right now."

"So why aren't you?"

She shrugged. "Do you want to go?"

Luke laughed. Ninety percent of him wanted to go—just to feel normal again. But the ten percent that was still in high school said forget about it. "Naw, I gotta go."

"Suit yourself. Anyway, her name is Lee."

"Who?"

"My cousin, the nutcase."

"Thanks for the warning."

{*"Well," I say to Cecilia, "I don't know what's gotten into my son." That young lady was practically throwing herself at Luke! He needs to get out and have a little fun! Oh, I wish I could give him a kick in the pants. He's lost an entire year of his life just moping around. This is what a nineteen-year-old boy should be doing—going out to parties, not sitting home in front of his computer doing brain research. "What is going on with my family?" I ask Cecilia. She only smiles that knowing smile of hers.*}

The van didn't want to go home. Sometimes it had a mind of its own. Luke would be on his way home from work and then all of a sudden he would find himself parked in the cemetery or in front of the Holy Family chapel or at the bike path where a tree for his mother had been planted by her siblings. Tonight, the van idled in front of Rockford Memorial Hospital. Don't think about it, he told himself. And headed home.

Man, how his life had changed! And man, he missed his friends! Hardy was at UW Madison and had e-mailed that he was staying up there for the summer. He'd found a job in the library and would rather stay in the dorm than with his mom and new stepfather. Logan was home for the summer, but he was with his girlfriend Katie every spare moment. Then there were Drake and O'Connor. They were both home for the summer, he knew. If this was last summer, they'd be hanging out in Drake's pool, or they'd be belly-up to O'Connor's pool table, or else they'd be on his dad's boat. These two had been his best friends since grade school, but now they weren't even talking to him. "*You're dead to me,*" O'Connor had said in a mobster voice. And he wasn't kidding. O'Connor hadn't even come to Annie's funeral. Drake was there, but only because his parents made him go. Well, all the more reason to get away to school. Make some new friends. Make a fresh start.

He couldn't wait to get out of town. In his opinion, Rockford was a boring Midwest town, with barely a personality. Oh, his mom and dad loved the town; even Danny said he'd probably settle here after college, but not Luke. It wasn't that it was a hellhole or anything, but for a town of its size—over a hundred and fifty thousand people—it didn't have what Luke was looking for.

{"*I really don't know why he feels that way about Rockford," I tell Cecilia. I loved living in Rockford. It was big enough that there were always things to do, yet small enough that it still had a hometown feel. It was cliché to say, but we always said it anyway: Rockford was a nice place to raise a family. We're called "The Forest City" because of all the trees, and being a landscaper, trees were my passion. In 1915, when Rockford was given that nickname by a New York journalist, the city actually counted up all the trees inside the city limits to see if they really deserved the title. According to the survey there were 142,044 trees in Rockford, or 122 trees per city block. In the nineteen fifties we lost over 50,000 beautiful elms to an epidemic Dutch Elm Disease. I was a young girl and remember coming into Rockford from Belvidere (a thirty minute drive) and seeing huge tree trunks lying in streets. It looked like something out of a war zone. Rockford falls into a 4b planting zone and as long as I could garden six months out of every year, I really didn't care where in the world I lived.}*

Luke thought about Karley. What was that all about? (LUKE'S FASCINATING BRAIN FACT: the female brain contains more grey matter and has more specialized connections between neurons, which might explain why women are much better than men at interpreting both language and tonal variations in speech. In other words, Luke's exchange with Karley Lappos from high school homeroom had left him baffled, but, as he rewound their conversation in his head he couldn't help but think that Karley knew exactly what had just transpired.)

He came home to a dark house. Since his mom was gone the house seemed to sag, as if someone had pulled a plug and it had simply deflated. He found his dad sitting in the river room, no lights on, TV on but muted, with a glass of white wine in hand.

"Where is everybody?" Luke asked. Even Piper wasn't around.

"Tess had a minor meltdown. I just broke the news to her about the Spellmans moving to Chicago. She wants me to adopt Julianna immediately. I tried to explain that we can't adopt a child who already has parents. And she said, 'Well, maybe they can adopt me then since I only have one parent.' Anyway, I had her take a bath and go to bed early. She wants to try to sleep the entire night in her own room, in her own bed."

"Poor kid," Luke said, plopping down on the couch. "Julianna is like a sister. You know she doesn't mean anything by it. It's just a big blow."

"A second big blow."

"We better watch her lying now. The kid's a regular Pinocchio. Where's the annoying one?" Luke asked.

"If it's your brother to whom you so disdainfully refer, he is spending the night at Mathis's. Again."

"So there is a little good news."

"Luke! What's with you two? You used to be inseparable, and now when you need each other most, you can't seem to get along."

"He speaks *Lig* Latin."

"I know, I know. But don't let him get to you. He's just staying young a little longer than you did, that's all." His dad smiled. "Want some popcorn? How about I make us some popcorn and we put in a guy movie, something with 'Aww-nold.'"

Man. The last thing Luke wanted to do was sit with his dad in the dark, eat popcorn, and watch a stupid Arnold Schwarzenegger movie, pretending everything was okay. Pretending that Tess was sleeping peacefully, that his normal little brother was spending the night at a friend's, and that his mom was still out in her garden even though it was pitch black outside. (Annie'd put in a "moon garden" some years ago where all the plants were white or glow-in-the-dark silver and she would garden by moonlight and by the light of a 2000-watt spotlight.)

"I'm not hungry, Dad."

"Forget the popcorn, we'll just throw in *The Terminator*."

"I'm just not in the mood," Luke said, rubbing his eyes, feigning fatigue from a long day of schlepping cappuccinos. He didn't look at Mitch. He knew he'd see hurt in his eyes. They used to be buddies. "Hey," he said to change the subject, "did you know the Spellmans sold the house already?"

"That was quick," Mitch said. "How do you know?"

"This girl I used to go to school with came into the store. She told me. It was weird though, she said the new owners were her relatives and that they were bohemians and that we should run for our lives."

"Bohemiams, huh?" Mitch said. "We've never had bohemians in the neighborhood before. I think it sounds interesting."

"It scares the hell out of me."

"Oh, where's your sense of adventure?"

"It died," Luke said without thinking.

Mitch flinched and downed the rest of his wine.

***

(LUKE'S FASCINATING BRAIN FACT: You should do all short-term learning in the morning and long-term learning in the evening. That's why the last thing Luke did before he went to bed was to look at a picture of his mother. To etch her face into his long-term memory.)

Luke couldn't sleep. Tomorrow was Sunday but there would be no sleeping in because they all went to nine o'clock Mass at St. Peter's. Mass attendance was not optional in their household and whenever Danny or Luke put up a fuss about it, their dad would act as if they were damning their mother to Hell if they didn't go to church. This was one way in which Luke and Danny were alike: they hated to disappoint their father. So they set their alarms for eight-thirty, threw on clothes and sat in the pew smack dab in the middle of the right side of the cathedral, while Tess belted out the hymns and criticized the altar servers, dreaming of the day she would be in fifth grade and could "go on stage" (as she put it).

Luke lay on his back and tried to pray. He used to pray a lot. Never rote prayers (it was Tess who had a penchant for rhyming prayers: "Now I lay me down to sleep…") but casual dialogue with God. But now prayer was harder. Dr. Bonovia said Luke was angry with God, but that wasn't it. He just wasn't sure anymore if He really listened. Maybe God wasn't a listening kind of God. He wasn't sure. He used to be sure. Things were so much easier when you were sure.

Einstein, always a physicist, seemed to believe that God was the sum total of all the powerful forces in the universe. But then he also said when confronted with quantum mechanics that "God doesn't play with dice." And now that Luke had started reading so much about the brain, he found things got more confusing. He'd read an article in the *Atlantic* not long ago that posited a theory that belief in God emerged as an accidental by-product of cognitive functioning. Luke admired evolutionary scientists, and he understood how even something as good and noble as altruism probably developed as a by-product of another trait such as empathy, but evolution couldn't answer all the questions. Even some renowned scientists said that one of evolution's weak points was that it couldn't explain how conscious life emerged. He'd found dozens of scientists who admitted that evolution wasn't a certainty, that fossils didn't show gradual changes in life forms and that new species seemed to pop up out of nowhere.

He knew there was some kind of mind-God connection and he also knew it would be his life's work to discover it. There were brain and consciousness researchers who were well along the way. He'd become obsessed with his research to the point of not caring about having a social life. Brain research proved to be far more fascinating than any of the kind of sophomoric recreation in which he and his friends had participated.

Consider the study conducted recently at Johns Hopkins University: researchers gave volunteers a pill containing psilocybin (the active ingredient in hallucinogenic mushrooms). Two thirds of the participants described having a deep mystical experience that left them with a long lasting sense of well-being. The pill was dubbed the "God pill." There were a few volunteers who had "bad trips" and experienced fear and paranoia, but the majority of the participants said they felt connected to the universe, that they had a direct personal experience of the beyond and said that the experience changed their lives. And consider Dr. Raymond Moody, the father of near-death-experience research, who created a pyschomanteum chamber in his gristmill in Alabama, recreating an ancient Greek "Oracle of the Dead" where people go, sit in a dark room, gaze at a mirror, and report experiencing reunions with apparitions of their departed loved-ones. Luke didn't know what to make of this stuff. Some of it seemed legit, but at the same time he knew that the mind could play complex and spooky tricks on itself. A perfect example was a study he came across recently in one of his father's journals. Neurologists showed that stimulating a certain part of the brain with electrodes induced a patient to sense an illusion of a shadowy person prowling behind him and mimicking his movements. Man! Oh yes, there was so much to learn about the brain, consciousness, about the seat of the soul. And some of it was pretty creepy stuff.

There was something to the old adage that ignorance is bliss. Sometimes Luke wished he'd never started delving so deeply into science and parapsychology. He wasn't sure if science and religion could be friends. On one hand natural selection made pretty good sense—not in any intuitive way mind you—but it could be simulated on a computer, and one only had to look at viruses and vaccines to see it at work. On the other hand, doesn't complex and adaptive design need a designer? It was so confusing. It was easier when he was ten, an altar boy, and was told what to believe.

{I wish Luke could just get some sleep. Even when he was little it was hard to turn him off. It may be hard to believe, but we can visit our loved ones in their dreams. Oh, sleep is so much more than you think it is. Cecilia lets me say goodnight to Luke. I look around his room and am shocked at the immensity of the mess! Luke used to be a neat-nick, particular about his surroundings, with everything in its place. Oh, how things change! Luke finally falls asleep on his stomach, all tucked into himself, his right hand shielding his eyes. Cecilia and I walk into his dream. It's noisy. I look around and see that we are at a skate park and Luke is racing around the arena, skateboarding with Danny. He is attempting to "one-up" his brother with death-defying flips and stunts. "At least they're wearing helmets," I say to Cecilia. Just as Luke is about to attempt a Herculean maneuver, he skates off the right side of the ramp and cascades down into a deep blue valley. Lucky for him, I am faster than air—I am there to catch him. "Did you see that, Mom?" the dream-Luke

says to the dream-me. "That was awesome!" the dream-me says to the dream-Luke. "Just awesome!"}

Luke awoke to find himself all tangled up in his navy blue comforter. There were tears in his eyes and residual bits of his dream lingered. Skateboarding. And the faint memory of falling into his mother's arms. He tried to remember more about the dream but then Tess appeared at his door.

"Luke," she whispered, "I had another bad dream."

He took her back to her room and snuggled with her until she fell back asleep. But now he was wide-awake. He wandered downstairs looking for an excuse to be up…food or entertainment. Man, a piece of chocolate cake would be perfect. Problem was no one in the house knew how to make chocolate cake. Tess tried once, the result being little more than brown goo.

In the kitchen, Luke found crumpled dollar bills strewn on the oak table. Danny's probably. It was one of the million things about Danny that bugged Luke: his blatant disregard for money. Danny cared nothing for it. And when he had some, he either spent it quickly, lost it eventually, or gave it away. Once, Luke had seen his brother hand a homeless guy a twenty. And he wasn't all showy about it either; he tried to pass it off on the sly. Luke saw though, and it was one of those moments when he had to stop and look at his brother differently. That was the problem with Danny: just when you were sure he was the biggest asshole alive, he would go and do something decent and throw you off kilter.

The crumpled bills were probably Danny's allowance money since he didn't have a summer job yet. And Luke would almost bet the money on the table that his brother wouldn't land a job this summer. He thought about taking the money, just taking it and throwing it in his dresser drawer. The thing was Danny wouldn't even miss it and Luke would spend the rest of his life feeling guilty about it, so forget it. He left the money where it was and paced around the kitchen.

Why was everything still so hard? Everyone said that time would heal, that after a year things would be a little easier. Well, it had been a year and nothing was easier. Why did he miss her so much? Hell, he was nearly twenty, old enough not to be a mama's boy anyway. But nothing was the same without her.

(LUKE'S FASCINATING BRAIN FACT: The brain is actually an organ of forgetting rather than of remembering. It's like a sieve or a "reducing valve" that stores only the amount of truth that we either need or can endure. Luke was convinced that the process of grief involved an element of sifting. In order to survive, you needed to sort through the entire database of memories you hold of your loved one. Then, you need to put them through a sieve, saving only the ones that keep you healthy—Luke knew that's why memories have more to do with the rememberer than with the truth.)

He sat in the dark. It hurt too much to think about it, and the fact that no one—except he and Danny—knew the entire truth about what happened that awful day. Well, there's no such thing as pure truth but only versions of the truth and he had his version and Danny had his. Sometimes he worried that his mother was angry with him. Sometimes, out of nowhere, he would get an image of her wagging her finger at him or clucking her tongue. "Luke, you're the oldest, you should know better," was something he'd heard all his life. But it didn't really matter. Would the whole truth change anything? Would it bring Annie back? Would it return their lives to normal? No, no, and no.

It was just a matter of semantics when you got right down to it, simply substituting one four letter verb for another. One word, one four-letter word and the truth, the real truth, would be revealed. He and Danny had never discussed it after "*the day.*" Mitch certainly didn't want to talk about it. Only Tess would bring it up. Poor Tess. Luke lay awake many a night wondering if Tess deserved the truth. He had rationalized for almost a year now that it didn't matter. But his heart knew otherwise.

Three months, not even three full months, and he would be relatively removed from it all. He'd talked himself into believing that at school, when his head was filled with undergraduate minutia, he wouldn't have time to think about his mother and worry about Tess and Mitch and okay, Danny. At college, the guilt would melt away because he would be doing what he was supposed to be doing.

But what if he choked? Think of all those international students! Think of UChicago's seventy-eight Nobel Prize winners! What if he'd peaked in high school? And now that he'd be a year older than most freshmen, he felt he was already behind. Well, he'd catch up. He'd "wow" them all. He'd make his dad proud.

So, he'd just get through the next couple of months. He'd work at Barnes and Noble, chauffer Tess around, and help his Dad get the boat in the water. That was the biggest deal for his Dad—to get the new boat in the water, get everyone back on the boat, back on the horse, so to speak.

He headed back to bed, but his room wasn't very inviting. In fact, it was a pigsty. When he turned the light on and was assaulted by piles of clothes, books, DVDs, CDs, shoes, and magazines, well, even he was shocked. He used to be orderly but order had flown out the window. Who cared anymore? The laundry just built up until Mrs. Cally got around to doing it. He picked up a blue denim-covered journal from his nightstand. A gift from his therapist, who thought it would be good for him to put thoughts to paper. Dr. Bonovia encouraged him to write something in it every night. The point was to express his deepest dark emotions but the thing was—what if someone ever found the journal? Then what? It was just asking for trouble as far as he was concerned. Maybe a person's deepest dark emotions should be kept deep down inside. He used the journal mostly to write about science and stuff. He made notes to himself about the brain and little odd bits of interesting (at least to him) information that he'd come across in magazines, books, or in conversation. But then the writing turned, well, poetic. He would die if anyone ever saw his scratchings. He plopped into bed and opened his journal and read his last entry:

I Want Big Al's Noodle

Time and erosion,
Measure the distances of an accelerated universe.
The wonderful thing about Einstein
wasn't his brain but his cosmic smile
and his hair, of course.
Energetic as a cosmic ray
he thought everything was a miracle
and understood
the violence it takes to achieve great grace.
He could see through a patch of fog
the variations in the coupling of nature.
I want to be like Einstein, who said:
"I want to know God's thoughts; the rest are details."
I never want to lose the capacity to startle myself.
I want to think about things
no one has ever thought about.
I want to have wild hair and a thick accent,
I want women to be attracted to my brain power.
I want to be quoted and written about years after I have
gone off to the great wild blue
And I want to leave behind an elegant theory
That will, after much skepticism,
leave people saying, that guy was right,
That crazy son-of-a-bitch was right.

By Lucas Roy Langdon

Crap, Luke thought and scribbled on the poem. A poet he wasn't. Now it was two in the morning and he wasn't even tired, in fact, he was buzzing. Out of nowhere—not again!—his heart started racing and a wave of fear washed over him. His chest tightened and it became hard to breathe. He tried to slow down his air intake, but then his fingers started to tingle and he felt himself flushing from the inside out. He knew what this was—a panic attack. He'd had them before. He wanted to scream and crawl out of his skin. When the nausea hit, he grabbed his wastebasket and sat on the floor with it poised under his chin. Luke, being Luke, had read all about panic attacks and knew that the best thing to do was to use relaxation and reassurance methods. Once the nausea subsided, he lay back on the floor and progressively tensed and relaxed his large muscle groups, one at a time while deep breathing and reassuring himself that the attack would recede in a matter of minutes. He placed his hands on his chest to gage the rapidity of his breathing. His heart was still pounding violently. This time, he might die. Or go crazy. He'd wait it out and see which.

When it ended, Luke lay on the floor, exhausted. The attacks made him feel as though he had just run a marathon. He was sopping wet with sweat. He carefully got to his feet—he'd fallen back down before—and headed for the bathroom to shower.

Afterward, in a clean tee shirt and boxers he felt better. He should be sleepy but he wasn't. He was glad he didn't wake his dad. No one knew about the panic attacks and no one needed to know. Luke was in control. But now what? What to do? What to do? A light bulb went on is his head—the answer was in the basement.

The answer had a cork and a label and came from Germany. His dad would never miss it. Luke found a corkscrew in the kitchen drawer and headed down the basement. He drank right from the bottle because it seemed appropriate for his mood and intention. A few minutes and swigs later, Luke felt better—and worse. Better because he could feel his body give in to the alcohol and relax. Worse, because he'd given in to the alcohol before and it had almost ruined his life. But of course, he could stop any time he wanted to. He just hadn't wanted to in a while.

The wine coated his mouth and throat, and then seemed to relax his vessels and his nerve endings. After a while, it was just Luke and the green glass bottle. Each swig brought him further from guilt and pain and closer to peace and pardon. Then the bottle was empty and he was staggering up the basement stairs. At the top of the stairs, Piper appeared, curious but benign, and startled Luke.

"Pipey!" Luke said. "Come here you little doggie! Come here for a little pet."

Piper accepted a quick massage from Luke. Once Luke was bent down it was hard—correction, impossible—to get back up. He lay down on the kitchen floor's cold ceramic tile. The room began to spin. "Hey Pipey, go get me a pillow and blanket, will you?"

Piper, confused by this sudden and rare bit of attention from Luke, backed up and stared blankly.

"And you're supposed to be man's best friend?" Luke sat up and got to his feet. He trudged his way to the river room and plopped down on the sofa, immediately regretting the "plopping" part. Piper followed and nestled herself on the floor next to him. "I owe you an apology," Luke said to the dog. He closed his eyes, but then opened them again when he realized he'd forgotten to dispose of the wine bottle in the basement. "Awwww, hell," he said out loud, but his body wouldn't move.

{"But Cecilia," I say, shocked at the sight on my son lying drunk on the sofa, "Luke never drank alcohol! Not once in all of high school. I don't understand!" Cecilia just squeezes my hand.}

Chapter Ten

_____

This Watery Place

W E BEGIN LIFE in water—our mother's warm amniotic fluid—and as water—as fetuses we are ninety-nine percent water. The average adult body is seventy percent water and as we age we dehydrate and at the end of our lives we are probably about fifty percent water. The point is, we humans exist for most of our lives as water. Each day we exhale about a liter of water back into the atmosphere, most of which rains or snows back down to our general vicinity in about a week's time. That means there is a bit of all of us in every raindrop, every snowflake, every bit of hoarfrost or dewdrop that is returned from the clouds. I never knew this. I never even thought to wonder about it.

Water holds hidden messages. Water isn't just a substance, after all, it is the most sacred life force of all. In fact, water is a mirror of the soul. This is because water is extremely sensitive to the vibrations of life. Yes, everything in the universe vibrates, even things that seem solid, like a chair or a rock. Water can pick up the unique frequencies that the world constantly emits, and essentially mirrors the outside world.

Without water this pretty planet Earth would never have formed. Water was part of Earth's starter kit. We all—from the beginning of time—have *sought the healing, soothing powers of water for physical and spiritual well-being. Think of holy springs, baptisms, spas, Roman bathhouses, swimming pools, hot tubs, whirlpools, rain showers, jumping in puddles, gazing upon lakes, listening to the ocean or to rain falling on a tin roof.*

Why then did water repel me? There's a name for what I had: hydrophobia (not to be confused with hydrophobophobia, which is the fear of rabies). If you want to get technical, you could say that I also suffered from potamophobia (fear of rivers or running water), ombrophobia (fear of rain or of being rained on), and hygrophobia (fear of liquids, dampness, or moisture).

My parents said it was all because of Amy Giller, the girl who lived next door, the girl my parents hired to baby sit me in a moment of desperation. I don't blame them of course. They had no idea that in her selfish teenage boy-craziness she would force me to stay in the bathtub in the dead of winter for two hours, while she sat on the toilet seat and talked on the phone with her boyfriend, withholding from me both attention and towel. What began as a fear of baths evolved into a fear of water in any form. My mother worked with me, sought counseling for me, and gave me a prayer by St. John of the Cross: "And I saw the river/over which every soul must pass/to reach the kingdom of heaven/and the name of that river was suffering/and I saw a boat which carries souls across the river/and the name of that boat was love."

I learned to live with my phobia, but I never completely conquered it. I adjusted—speedy showers and nippy sponge baths. I owned dozens of umbrellas and carried one with me at the hint of rain. I never owned a swimming suit that got wet, wore them only for sunbathing. I stayed away from wishing wells, water fountains, and I never "got" home aquariums.

People don't understand just how debilitating phobias can be. I once read that Hans Christian Anderson was afraid to go to bed for fear someone would mistake him for dead. He would go so far as to place a note on his bedside table with the words, "I only seem dead." He was also terrified of dogs and fire. My father researched other famous people and their fears and it helped me to see that I was not alone. Sigmund Freud was fearful of travel. Dean Martin was afraid of elevators. Steven Spielberg is afraid of insects. Aretha Franklin and Phil Donahue are aerophobics (afraid of airplanes). Carly Simon suffered from stage fright and couldn't perform live for many years. Brad Pitt suffers from ichthyophobia—fear of sharks. Harry Houdini could cope well in tight places during his acts, but off stage he suffered severe claustrophobia. The French playwright Feydeau had a morbid fear of daylight. King James I feared unsheathed swords. Howard Hughes was one of the most well known phobics of all time. He was microphobic (afraid of germs), agoraphobic (afraid of open spaces and unfamiliar places), and eventually he became panphobic (afraid of everything and everyone).

Like me, CNN's Larry King was afraid of water. As a child he'd almost drowned in the surf off Coney Island. I'd read that sixty years after the incident, at the urging of his wife and kids, he swam in his backyard pool, and I was happy for him. It gave me hope. If Larry King could overcome a sixty-year mortal fear, couldn't I? But then there was Frederick the Great. He was so hydrophobic that he could not even wash himself with water. His servants had to "wash" him with dry towels.

How does the disorder manifest itself? Well, I had frightening movies of water running in my head. I experienced shortness of breath when I got close to water. In the worst cases, I would breathe rapidly, my heart would pound almost out of my chest, I would begin to sweat, and feel nauseated. I sometimes had feelings of dread that I couldn't control. My head would swim, and I would obsess about my fear of water. I would suffer from horrific nightmares where my kids were drowning and I couldn't save them, or that I was a prisoner and my captors were using dunking and waterboarding to torture me. One of my greatest fears was getting trapped in a car and sinking underwater.

Believe it or not, there is a patron saint for running water: St. John Nepomuceno from Bohemia. When I was small and dealing with the hydrophobia, my mother got out her thick Book of Saints and looked up the patron saint of water and there he was. I prayed to him daily.

Growing up I would lie in bed and dream of drowning. And then, as a mother, I would dream of accidentally leaving one of the kids in the bathtub and finding him or her face down, lifeless. I would dream that one of the kids would disobey the house rules and wander down by the river's edge and slip on a rock and slip under the current and slip away from me forever. My nightmares weren't of gruesome monsters chasing me down dark alleys, but of getting soaked in a rain shower. Of standing in a puddle that swells until it becomes a lake and engulfs me.

⚜

While others took water for granted and enjoyed its aesthetics and physics, I found that I could never quite quell the anxiety that proximity to water caused me.

Ironic then to live with people who adored water. I was glad of it, of course. No mother wants her children to inherit her fears. Great swimmers were my children. Danny we had dubbed water boy as a child—he could often be found standing at the kitchen sink filling a water balloon or a squirt gun, playing with a colander or a medicine dropper, filling water bottles, creating his own "tornadoes" as water swirled down the drain. If Danny was water boy then Tess was water girl—garden hoses, sprinklers, and watering cans were her summer toys. Luke was my swimmer, star of his school diving team, and my sailor, the first one to help Mitch with the boat. Water babies, all of them. And I was glad.

And Mitch, well, he revered water. Mitch evolved from fish. I used to check him for fins, for an air hole. (Isn't it interesting how we humans seem to belong to different species: Mitch's ancestors were fish; my brother the pilot came from birds; as for me, I am equine if I am anything.) Mitch found peace in water, be it brook or birdbath or ocean. I have many times observed him admiring the "crown" created by a drop of water splashing into a pool. He loves how water looks when he casts his fishing line and the hook sinks and the bobber bobs. He adores waves and waterfalls and fresh water springs. He loves diamond dew on velvety green leaves and water droplets on spider webs. He is interested in condensation, evaporation, barometric pressure. He loves icicles and igloos. He is fond of rainstorms, snowflakes, watermelon, lava lamps, and water coolers. He is curious about irrigation, ancient Roman aqueducts, water on the moon and Mars and inside of comets. He agrees with recent medical trials showing that adequate water consumption can help to thin the blood and prevent heart disease. He even favors watercolor paintings. Water, water. I was surrounded on all sides by water.

At first, I decided that I wouldn't tell Mitch about my silly disorder. It was so embarrassing! A grown woman, afraid of water. Finally I had to come clean. One night while we sat on his screened porch drinking wine, I told him everything, beginning with Amy Giller and the bathtub. He listened intently and tried to understand, but I'm sure it was like a chocolate-lover trying to comprehend how a person could not like chocolate. How can you not like chocolate? No, he didn't really understand my problem, and, being a man, he thought he could fix it. He would plan excursions on the boat—simple lunches, romantic moonlit dinners, Sunday afternoon rides with neighbors and friends. He thought they helped. I suffered along with a smile, always wearing my life vest. He would splash me sometimes and I would pretend to be mad, but I really was mad. I don't mean to sound melodramatic but no one knew my pain.

I won't kid you, it's hard at first to be separated from your loved ones. We cross over with our feelings and emotions intact, as well as our thinking. But we feel and think with our spirit self and so our emotions are no longer conditioned by our heredity and environment. When we "drop" our earthly bodies we are left with our essence. I know you are wondering how we can feel sorrow in Heaven, and all I can tell you is that sorrow is part of the purification process; it is part of finishing our earthly business. It's tying up the loose ends; it's getting closure. But there's also this—there is a joyful sorrow in Heaven that has no earthly connotation.

Why do we suffer so much on earth? We cry to cleanse our eyes, to prepare them for the sight of God. And our hearts break so that they can be enlarged to contain the Almighty.

I want to tell my kids, and Mitch too, that they already possess Heaven! They need only open their eyes! There are hints everywhere—mostly in human faces, but Heaven's secrets are hidden in water, in light, in sounds and vibrations, in memories and dreams, high in the sky and deep on the ocean's floor. We drive through life asleep at the wheel. Until we crash.

Divine clues abound if we just open our eyes! Remember what St. Mark said: "For whatever is hidden is meant to be disclosed, and whatever is concealed is meant to be brought out into the open."

While on earth, study spirals for they are one of nature's special blueprints. Spirals are everywhere. (Go ahead, Google Fibonacci's sequence.) Some are plain as day and some are less, but if you look, you will find spirals everywhere.

Look at an unfolding leaf, an oceanic snail, the eye of a storm, a human embryo, the patterns of rose petals, the human ear, an empty hair follicle, our fists, hair cowlicks, and even the structure of our own DNA—all spiral-shaped. The fine fibers in our heart muscle construct a spiral. Smoke can spiral. There are spirals in the florets of pineapples and strawberries, daisies, and sunflowers, broccoli and cauliflower. Study the spiraling bracts of a pinecone or the spiral phyllotaxis of the meristem of an artichoke. You can see spirals in the horns of a mountain goat. Bacteria called spirochetes are spiral-shaped. Water circling down a drain is an example of a spiral, as is a whirlpool. Even the flight pattern of a falcon diving for its prey is a spiral motion. There is spiral grain in wood and in marble. (Even the yellow brick road in the classic movie The Wizard of Oz begins as a golden spiral!) Your fingerprint is a unique spiral.

Galaxies form spirals. Stars spew out dust in spiral arcs. There are spiral waves in Saturn's A-Ring and there are strange spirals in the ice caps of Mars. Hot gas spirals into black holes in deep space. The Big Bang is the point of the spiral of the expanding universe.

There are spiral patterns in turbulence and spiral-shaped flames in fire. There are stunt airplane spirals, figure skating spirals. Tornado spirals. A palm fans out in a spiral. The equiangular spiral is the optimal curve for highway turns. Log spirals on Greek columns.

Spirals are used in mechanical engineering (spiral gears, spiral elevators), and in thermodynamics (spiral flow heat transfer) and in physics (low-energy particles seen in bubble chambers produce fascinating spirals). Mutant bacteria can spring into surprising spiral shapes that puzzle microbiologists. On earth moss grows up; but up in space, scientists found that moss grows into mysterious spiral patterns.

In everyday life spirals hold things together and open things up—spiral-bound notebooks and the spiral ribs of a mason jar. Spiral staircases. When my grandmother taught me to crochet hats, we started with a circle that turned into a spiral. Rotating lawn sprinklers shoot out spirals of water. Spirals are in barber poles, on candy canes, and in colorful tie-dyed tee shirts. Spirals can be found at burial sites, in ancient art, on cave walls, and in fact, they have left no culture untouched.

God speaks throughout the universe in vibrations and patterns and sensations and resonance and reverberation. Hush and listen.

Chapter Eleven

It's a Bird, It's a Plane, It's… Stupidman!

{*"I'm worried about Danny," I say to Cecilia. When I crossed over my Danny was floundering. He had just finished his junior year at the same school as his brother and was sick of living in Luke's academic and athletic shadow. Danny didn't have the faintest idea about what he wanted to do in life and his father lost sleep worrying that he would become a professional hippie. Now I watch him as he rides around town with his friend Mathis looking for a summer job. He's driving too fast, but I see that at least he's wearing his seat belt. Look how handsome he looks with his loose brown curls, strong nose, and near-black sparkling eyes. He's tall like his father, but that is the only resemblance. He's my boy—from the shape of his calf to the mediocrity of his report cards. Also like me, he has passions—his filmmaking, his tee shirt business, his music. He never wanted to share much about his love life but I know his heart has been broken at least twice. "Oh my gosh," I say to Cecilia, "is that an earring in Danny's ear? Did that boy get his ear pierced? His father is going to kill him!"*}

*D*ANNY HAD A bumper sticker on his beater that said "0 to 60 in 15 minutes." (He had another one that said, "Unless you're a hemorrhoid, get off my ass," but his mother had made him scrape it off with a razor.) The beater was a tan, old lady Sundance with holes in the floor. Everybody knew when he was coming—especially the neighbors. Mr. Dean, the old guy across the street, once offered Danny five hundred bucks if he would junk it. Danny just laughed. The car suited him. He was attracted to things well worn.

Summer had arrived without a plan. This was not good. Danny had promised his dad he would get a job as soon as school was out. He'd graduated—"matriculated," he liked to say—from Boylan two weeks ago and had been living off his gift money. Time was running out. His dad had threatened to cut off his "allowance" since he hardly did any work around the house anyway.

Now he rode around in the beater with his best friend Mathis killing time before his two o'clock counseling appointment. Mathis had been accepted to every college he applied to and would be attending Northwestern University in Evanston, Illinois, at the end of the summer. Since this was their last summer together as free wheelers, they wanted nothing more than to do absolutely nothing. Of course parents thought differently. Mathis had a job: he was working in the home office of his mother's friend, stuffing envelopes, filing, answering the phone.

"I'm a frickin' secretary," Mathis lamented.

"Well, I'm a frickin' bum," Danny said, taking a corner too quickly. "And I'm almost on empty. Got any cash?"

Mathis patted his pants pockets. "Just some silver, dude."

"Silver works," Danny said and pulled into the Mobil station. He drizzled into his tank exactly one dollar and seventy-two cents worth of regular unleaded. "Where to?" he asked Mathis when he got back into the car. Danny figured Mathis had had his fill of riding shotgun all morning while he ran into businesses and filled out applications.

"My house for some lunch? You've applied everywhere in town. Let's get something to eat and watch "The Big Lebowski.""

"Let's do it," Danny said. "Top five movies of all time," he said as he pulled out onto the street.

"Comedies?" asked Mathis.

"Yes."

"Easy," Mathis said. "One, Monty Python and the Holy Grail; two, Animal House; three, Blazing Saddles; four, Caddyshack; five, Tommy Boy."

"Dude! Here's mine: One, Spaceballs the Movie; two, Wayne's World; three, Jay and Silent Bob Strike Back; four, The Big Lebowski; five, Uncle Buck." Danny flicked on his turn signal to make a left past Village Green Nursery.

"Hey, wait," Mathis said. "Have you applied at the greenhouse?"

"Right. Like I know anything about plants."

"What's to know? You water them."

"I think there's a little more involved."

"It can't be that hard. Turn around. Check it out."

It must have been providence. One of the owners had hurt his back earlier in the week and wanted a "grunt" to lift and carry. While Danny was insulted that the man actually used the demeaning word "grunt," he wasn't one to let pride get in the way of a good thing.

"I've been many things," Danny told the guy, "but I've never been a grunt before. Hmmmmm. Grunt. How much?"

Minimum wage. That was how much. He completed the application and was told to show up on Monday morning at seven a.m.

"You're a genius!" Danny shouted to Mathis as he approached the car. When he realized that Mathis had the car running so he could listen to a CD he changed his tune. "No, you're an a-hole. I'm gonna run out of gas."

"It's my gas."

"I got the job, dude."

"You got the job? Just like that?"

"The old man hurt his back and they need a grunt."

"A grunt. Okay then."

"Dude, I gotta drop you off. I don't have time for lunch or Lebowski. I almost forgot about my appointment at two."

"Drop me then."

Danny and Mathis had been best friends all through high school. They'd met freshman year when they were both getting roughed around for their—well, let's be kind and say "quirkiness." They made an odd pair. Mathis was a light-skinned bi-racial young man with impeccable taste and manners, who dressed sharply and who wanted to follow in his physician father's footsteps. Danny was king of grunge, who had neither the grades nor the desire to pursue medicine. They were thrown together in homeroom and someone commented that other than the shade of their skin, the two boys could be twins. Danny stared at Mathis and conceded there was a resemblance. They became fast friends, discovering they shared a passion for movies and filmmaking, avant-garde art, and song writing.

Just for fun, the day before sophomore year, Danny got a perm and the two boys showed up at school with modified afros. They ended up in the yearbook with their matching fros.

Mathis was the more serious of the two, never letting their shenanigans interfere with his grades. Danny was the opposite of serious. More often than not, they balanced each other out. When they didn't, there was trouble, but not too much. Like the time Mathis on a "Danny dare" pulled the string in the restroom at his dad's clinic that said, "Pull for emergency assistance." Or the time Mathis dared Danny to pretend that he dropped his keys in the toilet at church. With glee Danny had accepted Mathis's dare to shoot a Frisbee through a McDonald's drive-thru window (luckily neither boy could locate a Frisbee). At school, they were notorious for one, wearing the same necktie to school every day their entire senior year (Danny's featured Hawaiian dancers in grass skirts and Mathis's had dozens of yellow smiley faces against a black background); two, singing the Boylan Fight song and/or the National Anthem in squeaky falsettos; and three, "Eddie Haskelling" their way out of demerits. The teachers couldn't help but love these two, but especially Danny, who in spite of the ADHD, in spite of the spontaneous drug holidays from his medications that would test the nerves of all at home and school, in spite of the impulsivity, had that secret something certain people had that resisted reprieve. Call it charisma, call it magnetism, but Danny had it, and "it" got him out of just about any trouble.

By the time Danny pulled into the parking lot of the medical building he was late, not to mention running on fumes. He was only five minutes late, but late just the same. It didn't matter that more often than not he'd have to wait fifteen or twenty minutes for his psychologist Allen. All that mattered was that he, the paying client, was late.

It was all to humor his father anyway. Mitch wanted his kids to be able to "talk" about their mother's death...even if they didn't want to talk about it. So, you make it into a game is what you do. You play with Allen the psychologist's mind. Poor pathetic Allen, who really, truly, honestly believed he could help.

Even though he knew he was wasting precious gas, Danny kept the car running so he could hear the end of the Beatle's "Eleanor Rigby." It was a CD so it didn't really matter—he could hear it anytime, but it was a pet peeve of his to cut off a song before its finish. It was just rude. "*Where do they all belong?*" he sang out loud, slamming the car door shut as the song ended. He was still singing as he crossed the parking lot. It was a nice blue-sky day and unless there was something to be crapped out about, Danny usually defaulted to cheerful. Walking briskly he came upon an elderly man moving at a snail's pace and pulling behind him a canister of oxygen on wheels. Danny passed him by, then turned to say hello, because Daniel Andrew Langdon never could pass a fellow human being without acknowledging him or her in some way. Annie had told him that when he was little, he thought his mom and dad personally knew everyone in the whole wide world. To this day, Danny knew no strangers.

"Good day to you, sir," Danny said, tipping an imaginary hat and then turning back to look at the man. The man didn't say anything, but he abruptly stopped in his tracks, which made Danny think he had frightened the old dude. But then the man sat—nearly fell—onto a concrete bench near the entrance of the clinic. Danny realized he was having trouble breathing—even with that oxygen contraption. "Hey, are you okay, mister?" he asked.

The man's breathing was so labored it scared Danny. He took a few more breaths and then said, "Just…need…to rest…a minute. The wife…is sick…she usually…takes…me."

"Should I get you a wheel chair? Would that help?"

"It would," the man said, his eyes a little glassy.

Danny sprinted up to the clinic entrance and grabbed a wheel chair from the reception area. He wheeled it over to the man, locked the wheels, and helped him into it.

"I can hold…the oxygen on my lap," the man told Danny, smiling weakly. "The name's Alvin," he said as Danny boosted the oxygen tank up onto his lap.

"Like the chipmunk?" Danny asked.

"Chipmunk? No the last name's Conners."

"Well, nice to meet you, Alvin. I'm Danny," he said as he began wheeling the man to the clinic entrance.

"If you don't wanna…end up like me, kid, never take up… smoking."

"Oh, I won't," Danny said, patting the pack of Marlboro Lights in his back pocket. "Hey, Al, can I ask you a question?"

"Shoot."

"When your wife calls you does she say 'Alvin, ALVIN, AL-VINNNN!' like on that Christmas song?"

"I don't follow you."

"You know, the Chipmunks? Alvin? Theodore? Simon?"

"Sorry, don't know 'em."

Danny shook his head and smiled. "Hey Al, can I do a wheelie?"

"If you want me to fall out you can."

"What floor you going to?" Danny asked when they reached the elevators.

"Fifth."

"Fifth it is."

{At this moment, I couldn't be prouder of my son. I want my children to be kind people. I smile at Cecilia. She smiles too. "When he was little," I tell her, "Danny was a 'Mama's boy.'" Even when his brother was off exploring, Danny seemed always to be close by me. Even when he was in high school there were times I sensed he needed some alone time with me. He couldn't actually articulate that need, but a mother's radar picks up these things. So we would sneak out of the house when Tess was in bed, and Mitch and Luke were in Mitch's office reading about nanotechnology or researching colleges. I would let Danny drive and we'd skulk off to McDonalds and pig out on French fries and strawberry shakes. This went on for months, until we ran into a girl Danny knew from school—twice— and Danny, who usually didn't care what anyone thought, cared this time. At least that is what I deduced, since Danny stopped taking me up on my invitations after bumping into that girl. At first I was hurt, but then I realized that the situation presented itself as a good life lesson. "It's because of that girl we saw, isn't it?" I asked one day while we were cleaning up after dinner and he'd declined my invitation once again.

"Mom, no guy wants to be seen out with his mommy. Once, maybe. Twice, forget it."

"I thought you didn't care what people think."

"This is different."

"How?"

"I don't know; it just is."

"Well I do know," I told him. "The truth is you do care what people think of you. But only what people you care about think of you."

He didn't reply but he didn't smart off either. That was the end of our junk food runs. We were probably both healthier for it anyway. But in the end, it wasn't my heart that killed me.}

Once he had deposited Al safely to his internist's office, Danny took the stairs down to the lower level where his psychologist's office was located. His watch said two-fifteen—which was "Danny time" for two o'clock. He stopped at the drinking fountain and splashed some water on his face to simulate sweat. He jogged in place for a minute and then galloped around the corner to meet Francine. Dreaded Francine was a sliver of a woman with long wavy gray hair and a gravely voice. She had a penchant for muted monotones, usually in the brown family. The wheels in Danny's head turned—he needed a good excuse. A really good one.

"Hey, Francine, sorry I'm late. *Dang* if I didn't get stopped by the cops. You won't believe it, but both of my brake lights are out. Both. So they said I couldn't drive. They made me leave my car over by that church, you know, that church with the weird angel on it that looks more like a ghoul. You know the one I mean? The one that's near the cleaners. So I thought I was going to have to walk, but they said they'd give me a ride, so I hopped in the back of the cop car, and we pull up to the stop light and—you won't believe this part—there's my girlfriend in the car next to us. She sees me. Oh, man, you should have seen the look she gave me. So now she thinks that I was like arrested. How've you been?"

"Any changes to your address or your insurance?" Francine asked without emotion.

"As a matter of fact, I have a lot of changes. I should probably fill out a whole new set of forms. You know, those medical history forms where you check off all the little diseases you have. Yeah, recently I've developed—or I guess more accurately 'contracted'—some new diseases. And I'm on some new drugs, too. Blue pills. French blue."

Francine shook her head, grabbed the clipboard and handed it over.

"How important is it to be a hundred percent accurate when I fill out these forms?" Danny asked, trying to get a rise or any old reaction from Francine. Nothing.

He sat on the floor by the window and doodled on the medical history form. He randomly checked off boxes in the diabetes, heart disease, mental illness, and asthma categories. These meetings were such a waste of his time. He used to skip them and hang out at the

North End Coffee Bar for an hour, but Allen called his dad. Narced on him. How do you put your trust in a guy like that? "I was concerned for your safety," was how he had put it, but Danny knew that was psychobabble for "I was concerned for my office fee."

Danny had seen enough movies to know that you could fool some of the people some of the time and mental health professionals (Allen's term, not his) all of the time. It was sad really. But then again, not that sad.

Allen was interested in summer plans. Idleness was not a good thing, he contended. They usually started the sessions with a stare-off. Danny liked to lie flat on the floor when he met with Allen and look at the ceiling, but today for the first five minutes of the session he had reluctantly agreed to sit in the wing chair and talk with Allen face-to-face. "Summer plans?" Allen repeated.

"Actually," Danny told him, "I just got a job a few minutes before I got here."

"Excellent. Where? What?"

"At Village Green Nursery. A grunt."

Allen was also interested—primarily interested—in how things were at home.

"Fine. I'm fine. Luke's fine. Tess is fine. Dad's semi-fine. We're fine."

Basically Allen made sure that Danny stayed on his ADHD medication because he had confessed to skipping it at times. Sometimes he wondered if the medicine made him antsy—it was a stimulant, after all. The ADHD was always there, even with the medicine holding the disorder at bay, always ready to surface. Sometimes he wondered if he had been misdiagnosed. Maybe he had something worse than attention problems and hyperactivity. Maybe he was bi-polar. Or worse—something they didn't even have a name for. Backfire disorder. Mouth muscle dysfunction. Acute Calamity Syndrome.

"Danny, why do you always wear that Superman tee shirt?" Allen asked.

"Whatever's in my shirt drawer."

"I think, in the months we've been together, that I've never seen you in anything else."

"I do wear pants."

"You know what I mean."

{"I do wish he'd take these sessions seriously," I say to Cecilia. "I think he'd get something out of them if he did." He's such a stinker. But he did get a job! I'm so proud of him. This is a big deal and I think it will be good for him.

Here's a great Danny story for you. When he was six years old, he got angry with me because I wouldn't let him sleep over at a friend's house. Well, I had never even met the boy's parents, and I'll be honest, I was a little worried because I'd heard talk up at school about this particular family—marital problems and alcoholism—and while I didn't blame Danny's friend (he was a nice enough little boy), I wasn't at all comfortable with Danny spending the night. He was furious with me. To make matters worse, Luke had been invited to stay at a friend's also, but this little boy was the child of some of our best friends, so it wasn't an issue. Of course, Danny couldn't see the difference and thought I was being unfair. Mitch, I remember, was away at a medical conference, and so Danny had no way of leveraging one of us against the other. He got himself all worked up, punching pillows, pounding on tables, and clobbering his stuffed animals. Fortunately for us his temper tantrums were infrequent, but when he had one the whole world knew it.

He thought he could break me down with his begging and battering, but I wouldn't budge. I continued preparing dinner and did my best to ignore him. After a while he quieted down and I thought the storm was over. But when I called him in for dinner, he didn't come, and when I went searching for him, I couldn't find him anywhere. At first I thought he was taking his revenge in a game of hide and seek. I searched his bedroom and the entire house before I started to panic. Then I searched the yard. How many times had I gone through this scenario in my head: one of my kids at the bottom of the river. I ran down to the edge of the water, getting closer than I cared to. I scanned the area and my heart skipped a beat when I saw Danny's shoes and socks strewn near the rocks. My baby! Oh my God! I didn't know what to do, so I began screaming and running up and down the dock searching the water for any movement. Our neighbor, Judith Spellman, heard me wailing and came running down to the water. All it took was one look at me and the mother in her knew to run and call 911.

By the time the ambulance arrived I was hyperventilating. The paramedics were shooting questions at me, bam, bam, bam, and I was so disoriented and so numb that it took me a moment to realize that Danny was standing next to Judith and staring at the paramedics.

"Danny!" I screamed, and ran to scoop him up into my arms. He wasn't wet at all. Dry as a saltine cracker. "Oh my God, you're all right. Danny!" He let me hug him and even allowed kisses on his cheek.

"What's wrong, Mom? Why are they here?" he asked, pointing to the paramedics.

Well, I felt like an idiot. I felt as if a spotlight were shining down on me, differentiating me from all the "good" mothers in the neighborhood, the ones who didn't lose their children and then presume the worst, thereby wasting the money of decent and hard-working taxpayers.

Thankfully Mitch didn't think I overreacted when he called that night and I relayed the event. "How were you to know? Judith did the right thing in calling. Better safe than sorry. Where was he anyway?"

"That's the strange part. He said he was in his bedroom playing, but I had checked his room. I checked all the rooms. And he would have heard me calling for him."

"Sounds like he was hiding on purpose."

"No, he wouldn't do that. Not Danny. Would he?"

"How do you explain the shoes and socks? Or how did he explain the shoes and socks?"

"You think he planted them? That stinker!"

Mitch laughed.

"Mitch, it's not funny. Think how he connived!"

"Honey, don't make too much of it. He was an angry six-year-old who knew his mother's weak spot."

"I feel violated."

"Welcome to parenthood."

Well, the incident really threw me for a loop. Luke never in his life would have pulled a stunt like that. Danny had a temper and a bit of a mean streak that scared me sometimes. But ninety-nine percent of the time he was pure sweetness. Like, later that night when I tucked him in, he placed his little hands on each of my cheeks and said, "You worry too much, Little Mommy."

Up here, I got to play the scene back in its entirety. I watched from above as my little angel ran outside in tears once he realized that I wasn't going to give in. He swung on the swing set for a couple of minutes, kicked a soccer ball around, and then ran down to the dock. He looked around guiltily before peeling off his shoes and socks and flinging them close to the water. Then he skulked around to the front door and sneaked into his room and hid under the bed. He popped up when he heard the ambulance siren and the look on his face—surprise, horror, shame—was almost comical. He paced around his room a bit and decided to play it innocent and that's when he sauntered down to the backyard and met me at the river's edge, wearing his best sweet little cherub face and nothing on his fat little feet.}

Danny decided he'd had enough of the chair and sprawled out on the floor. Yeah, as if he'd tell Allen the real reason he wore the Superman tee. That when he and Luke were little and played super heroes, Luke always got to be Superman and he always got to be some lesser somebody, some "stupidman" or another.

"So, does that mean anything?" Allen asked. "I mean, are you making some kind of statement by wearing a Superman shirt all the time?"

"My mom gave it to me," Danny said. It wasn't true, but he knew it would make Allen feel all bad and sorry about it.

"Oh, sorry. So it *does* have a special meaning then."

"It's just a shirt." It wasn't just a shirt; it was his favorite tee shirt. The truth was that he'd bought it himself at Media Play freshman year. Sophomore year he bought another one, only long sleeved. What was so bad about Superman, anyway? He was a decent role model.

It pissed Danny off when Allen was right about something. He did speak through his tee shirts and sweat shirts. He actually had quite a collection. He had one that said "Black" on the front and "Sheep" on the back, and another one that said "Mr." on the front and "Disaster" on the back. For his sixteenth birthday Mathis had given him one that had a hangman game on it, with the letters 'F', 'C', and 'K' on it, with a blank line between the 'F' and the 'C' but his mother had confiscated it and cut in up into a dust rag. One of his favorites was a simple black tee with the word "Jump!" on the front and the phrase "Go ahead and jump" on the back. That one pissed Luke off royally.

He owned a variety of tie-dyed shirts and what he and Mathis called "Anagram Tease"—tee shirts they themselves designed, imprinted with anagrams made out of the names of designers they despised. Tommy Hilfiger was: If Met Girl Oh My! Ralph Lauren was: Lunar Lap Her. Abercrombie and Fitch was: Time For A Crabbed Chin. Old Navy was: Van Oldy. He and Mathis loved that none of their friends or family could ever figure them out. Most guessed they were possible names for their garage band. Others just chalked it up to craziness.

It must have been just a coincidence that he always wore the Superman shirt to his sessions with Allen. Or was it? *Dang*! He hated when Allen got him to start questioning himself. He hated being psychoanalyzed. It just made him play harder. Here we go: "Maybe…" he said, letting it hang in the air for effect.

"Yes?"

"Maybe you're on to something. Maybe I wear the tee shirt so often because I feel guilty about my mom. Maybe subconsciously I think that if I were in fact Superman that I could have…well, you know."

"Saved her?"

"Something like that. I don't know. It's probably just because it's what's in my drawer."

"Well, let's see, do you dig for it? Do you say to yourself, 'I want to feel strong and invincible today, I think I'll wear my Superman shirt?' Do you say that?"

"Yeah. Exactly. You're unreal, man. *Dang.* What do you think that means?"

"You tell me."

"I might be wrong, but I think my dad's paying you so you can figure that out."

"No, your dad is paying me so we can figure it out together."

"There's nothing to figure out. I'm fine. I'm a typical specimen of a middle-class American middle child who can't stand his perfect older brother, who is annoyed to no end by his hypochondriac little sister, and who, no matter what, can never live up to his brilliant and successful father's expectations. There. I think I just described about ninety-eight-point-seven percent of all eighteen-year-old WASPS."

"You're not Protestant."

"Okay, WASC then. Whatever. You're missing the point." Danny closed his eyes. These mind games exhausted him. Why wouldn't his father let him quit these useless sessions? It had been a year since his mom had died; wasn't it time everyone moved on? He thought hard, with all three pounds of his brain with its hundred million nerve cells and more connections than there were stars in the universe. He knew his brain was eighty-five percent water, but was it supposed to feel watery? He just didn't know. One thing he knew for sure: he seemed different from just about everyone else in the universe.

"What are you afraid of, Danny?"

Danny turned over to lie on his stomach, burying his head in his folded arms. He'd fielded this question before. Many times. Allen could be a broken record.

"Hey, I'm Superman. I fear nothing."

"Even Superman was afraid of something."

Danny gave it some thought. What did Allen want to hear? The usual probably: fear of death, fear of snakes, of speaking in public, of losing it all in the stock market. Okay, he'd give him something else. "Well, I get freaked out, totally freaked out by toys that can talk. If Tess gets a toy or doll that talks I find a way to accidentally destroy it."

"Toys that talk. What else?"

Dang! He thought 'toys that talk' would garner a little more attention. Fears. Fears. Hmmmm. "I'm afraid of different foods touching on my plate. I can't eat a thing if one kernel of corn snuggles up with my mashed potatoes."

"Be serious about this, please."

"I am. Let's see. I'm afraid of computers. I believe one day they will think on their own and perpetrate brilliantly evil attacks that will make the 9/11 terrorists look like amateurs."

"Hmmmmm."

"I'm afraid of the words 'Some assembly required.'"

Allen smiled. "You stole that one from Dave Barry."

Danny turned over to look at Allen. "I love Dave Barry. He's cool. Hey Al, what's the strangest phobia anyone has ever shared with you?"

Allen uncrossed his legs, which was a signal that he was actually considering the question and that what he said next would not be bullshit. "Oh, goodness, years ago I had a lady who was abnormally afraid of mirrors."

Danny couldn't help laugh. "Was she butt ugly or something?"

"No, no, she was beautiful in fact. That's what makes a phobia a phobia—it's not just a fear, it's an abnormal or exaggerated fear. But I'm not asking you about your phobias, just your everyday, average, run-in-the-mill fears.

"I'm afraid of mispronouncing words in public."

Allen nodded.

"I'm afraid of driving on ice."

"Me too."

"I'm afraid we'll run out of clean water someday, and that we'll run out of places to put nuclear waste, and that we'll never see a Democratic president again."

"Now you're scaring me," Allen said. "Go on."

"I'm afraid of being invisible."

Allen raised his eyebrows.

"I'm afraid of terrorists, being drafted, getting arrested in a case of mistaken identity. I'm afraid of wearing plaids with stripes, of fathering a baby with a woman I don't love, of flunking out of college if I ever get into one—a real one, I mean, not a junior college, or, as I like to call Rock Valley: the University of North Mulford."

Danny looked up to see if he'd earned a smile. Not even a grin. "*Dang*, I'm on a roll here."

"Guess so," Allen said.

"And," Danny said before he realized what he was saying, "I guess I'm afraid of water."

Allen nodded again and Danny decided it was time to change the subject. "Do you believe in cutlery bending?" he asked. (One of his favorite things was to "out-of-the-blue" Allen). He'd overheard Luke talking about cutlery bending with Mitch the other day and he'd wanted to join in on the conversation but it was way too cerebral for him—no pun intended.

"Excuse me?"

"Cutlery bending. You know, bending a metal fork or spoon using just the power of your mind."

"Well, I've never witnessed it myself, but I remember it being a craze in the seventies. The scientific term is 'psychokinesis.' Why, do you want to be a psychometallurgist when you grow up?"

"Allen?" Danny said, from the floor. "How'd you get so smart?" He was being serious, Allen did know a lot about a lot of things—not that it made him a good therapist, but it saved him from being a total loser.

"I pay attention, kid."

"I've heard that silver-plated brass seems to be the best material, although stainless steel is acceptable, but it tends to snap rather than bend," Danny said, mimicking what Luke had said.

"How do you know?"

"I pay attention, too."

Allen smiled.

Danny jumped up from the floor. A smile. Mission accomplished.

At dinner Danny shocked and awed his dad with the timely news of his employment.

"That's great, Danny. Way to go."

"Congratulations, Danny," Tess said.

"You hate plants," was Luke's comment.

"I don't hate plants," Danny shot back.

"Oh, then why was it that whenever Mom wanted help with the yard you told her that you hated plants."

Danny knew what this was. This was Luke acting all jealous whenever Danny did something right. "Because I'm a lazy slob, you idiot."

"Guys, quit it," Mitch said. "Let's be happy for Danny."

"Yeah, you're right," Luke said, "let's be happy that he won't waste his entire summer away like he did last year."

Danny scowled but knew darn well Luke had a point. He was an amateur time-waster. Like, one day last summer when he and Mathis had nothing to do so they sat in the DMV for two hours just staring at the people. Why is that place always so full of characters? Where do normal people go to get their driver's licenses, Danny wanted to know. And he and Mathis did waste a lot of gas driving all around town trying to find the "best" food. For the best lunch, it wasn't unusual for them to drive south across town to 20th Street to get the best sausage sandwich from Anthony at *DiTulio's Italian Market*, and then drive back west to North Main Street to get a *cannoli* from Frank at *Deli Italia*.

They could waste away hours just talking. If they had nothing to do on a Friday night they would sit around the house and "top-five-best" each other for hours…top five best fast food restaurants, top five best movie dogs, top five best Saturday Night Live hosts, top five best spaghetti westerns.

They were quirky all right. They had their own version of Pig Latin called "Lig Latin." You just replaced the first letter of each word in your sentence with the first letter of the first word in the sentence. So "today is my birthday" became "today tis ty tirthday," and "You are so lame," turned into "You yar yo yame." Sophomoric? Yes. Fun? Yes. The best part being, it drove Luke absolutely nuts. Oh, life was good when you could get a rise out of Luke.

"It's your turn to do the dishes," Luke said to Danny, as he brought his plate to the sink.

"No nidding," Danny replied.

Danny knew very well that it was his turn to scrape and rinse the dishes after dinner and load them into the dishwasher, but that didn't stop him from trying to bribe Luke into doing it for him. Luke was fixing himself dessert: a blob of nonfat yogurt in a cup, sprinkled with some Cap'n Crunch cereal, and then squirted with a healthy splash of Hershey's chocolate. Oh my God, the world was coming to an end—Luke, health food nutcase, was eating junk food!

"Please poo pa pishes por pe. Please?" Danny asked, sticking out his lower lip.

"Stop it. Do you know how stupid you sound when you talk like that?"

"Please?"

"No, it's your turn. Just do it."

"Hey, hat hooks hood. Hake he hum, hould ha?"

"Man. No wonder Ashley Pallow dumped you. She probably thought you were mentally impaired." Luke spooned up a heap of yogurt and shoved it into his mouth. Danny snapped him with a wet dishrag and gave his brother a "nothing you say can hurt me" look. But hurt it did. Deeply. He tried covering up. "Top five coolest sounding languages: one, Vulcan; two, Glossolalia—that's speaking in tongues, if you didn't know; three, Yiddish; four, Zulu; five, Vietnamese."

Luke just shook his head and walked outside. Danny, standing there holding the dishtowel, considered drumming up Tess and talking her into doing the dishes, but then he remembered that she was out riding her bike. So he did the dishes. Half-heartedly, which meant he skipped the scraping and rinsing and just stuffed the grimy plates and silverware into the dishwasher. He overfilled the soap compartment with dishwasher powder and pushed all of the buttons.

Exhausted, he headed outside for a rest in his dad's hammock. Sometimes he had to force himself to stay still. Annie had taught him how to downshift from high gear into neutral. When he was little he thought it was a game, until he realized that some kids could regulate themselves naturally. For him, with the ADHD, it was always a chore. How did they know he had ADHD anyway? He'd looked up the symptoms online years ago and almost laughed. *Disorganization.* Check. *Emotional reactivity.* Check. *Under-achievement.* Hey, Cs weren't the end of the world. *Low self esteem.* Now wait just a minute. *Impaired relationships.* Yeah, but only with his brother. Sometimes just thinking about hyperactivity hyped him up.

Mitch and Luke were in the backyard "having a throw" as they liked to call it. When Mitch saw Danny, he called out for him to join in.

"Nah. I'm okay," he said and plopped into the hammock. There was nothing to do. Mathis had to go to a wedding reception with his parents and the other people he hung out with were going to a *Modest Mouse* concert in Milwaukee that had sold out before he could buy tickets, which basically sucked. He didn't read for fun—his attention problems turned reading for pleasure into reading for torture.

He was able to skim through non-fiction books and had over the years purchased several self-help books. The latest one, hidden under his mattress, was called *How to Make People Like You in 90 Seconds or Less*, by Nicholas Boothman. It talked about rapport and congruity and of course communication. He hated that word. It was a girl's word...*I just love people and I'm a wonderful communicator.* Basically, the book preached about smiling a lot, leaning in toward the person, using their name, good eye contact, asking a lot of questions about the person, even mimicking their gestures and tone of voice. Most of these things Danny seemed to do naturally and yet four years of high school and there had been just three girlfriends and they were short-lived at best. It was odd but Danny had found that older people liked him. Little kids didn't, but that was probably because he wasn't crazy about them either. But man, oh man, he seemed to attract the septuagenarians and octogenarians.

Dang, was he bored. What a waste of some solid summer time. He resigned himself to simply communing with nature. He was determined to stay still. He could do it. It wasn't that hard. He tried to tell people all the time that he could slow down if and when he wanted to, he just never really wanted to. It was more fun (and exciting) to be moving. Besides, Annie had told him that people had different learning styles and he was a "kinetic learner" which meant he learned better by hands-on experimenting than by written or oral instructions.

He watched the sky and listened to the sound of catch. He hated baseball but he had to admit, the *thwacking* sound the ball made when it hit the glove was somehow satisfying. Luke, among everything else, had a good arm. And there was the root of the problem—Luke had a good…everything. Danny knew it was impossible to compete with Luke. This he'd learned early on. As long as he could remember he and his brother had fallen into their roles: the smart one and the funny one. Annie would introduce them as her gentleman and her comedian; Mitch would refer to them as the brains and the muse. And although Mitch and Annie made certain that Danny always got an 'A' for effort, he was sharp enough to know that effort counted for nothing in the real world, only results counted, and for results, Luke was your man.

What caused attention problems, anyway? Danny often wondered. How come Luke could get from point A (mow the lawn) to Point B (sweep the sidewalk) with no problems, but if it was Danny's turn, he'd get sidetracked somehow by a neighbor's dog, a great idea for a movie, a new guitar riff, or a pretty girl walking by. And why did he get bored with things so quickly? His father had derided him for being a quitter. His mom tried to soften it by saying he was just a "tryer," but Danny knew that he was both, a tryer and a quitter. The problem was he wasn't great at anything. Luke was great with science and decent with sports; Tess was a great singer and a pretty good gymnast. Danny was a mediocre student, a passable guitar player, a writer of 'B' type screenplays.

His jokes were funny half the time and stupid the other half. He ran below average when it came to dating, and no one had ever loved him enough that she couldn't live without him. Okay, okay, no one had loved him enough to have sex with him either. He had hoped Ashley Pallow would be the one. But Luke went and wrecked that.

The sky was really beautiful. If there was a job as a full-time sky watcher, he'd apply. Not a meteorologist, mind you, but just a person who would watch and report daily on the condition of the sky, simply from an aesthetic point of view. Remember being little and lying in the grass and just contemplating the sky? This was something Annie had taught him to do…to always look up. She said the sky was full of pretty things to look at. *Dang*, if his Dad wasn't out here he'd have himself a ciggy and it would be a perfect evening.

The other morning, he'd awakened early and couldn't get back to sleep. It was nearly daybreak and the birds chirped so boisterously they sounded like old busybodies. He'd gone downstairs to get a drink of something but was beckoned outside by the rising sun—something he hadn't seen in ages. Sitting near the water's edge, he watched the sun's pink head crest and then sneak up on the world. For a solitary moment the lights were mixed—moonlight turning to sunlight. Luke would probably be able to explain the physics of sunlight and moonlight; all Danny knew was that the transition from dark to day was both breathtaking and heartbreaking and he began to cry. It had scared the bejesus out of him because he almost couldn't stop. Where was the justice in life? How come the one time in his life when he was the hero—or the almost hero—no one even noticed or cared? No one ever took him seriously. He was Danny the clown, Danny the cut-up. Well, he knew the truth and it was this: he was the brave one; he was the one that took the chance and jumped.

Now as he lay in the hammock, the early evening sky began to change before his eyes. Thick cotton ball clouds darkened to gray and blocked what was left of the sun. Danny focused on the movement of the clouds and saw that they had become perforated in places. Pale shards of colored light filtered through the gaping holes, and the rays reminded him of spotlights, spotlights from Heaven. As if God were saying, "Look here! Look at how beautiful this is! Don't miss it!" Annie wouldn't have missed it. Danny wondered if she could look down. How beautiful earth must be from a Heavenly vantage point. He thought about the sunset and realized that his sunset was someone else's sunrise. And that the reverse was true as well. It made him think about the question Tess had asked Annie once: "Where does the sun go when it sets?" The question made him realize how egocentric we humans are—we think everything is just for us.

Suddenly, a baseball slammed into his shoulder and he let out a cry: "AHHHHH!" He heard Luke laugh. "You did that on purpose, you ass-hole," Danny screamed at his brother as he sprang from the hammock and took chase. Finally, a good and justifiable reason to beat the crap out of Luke!

"He did not, Danny," Mitch hollered. "I threw the ball."

Danny ignored his father and chased Luke around the yard.

{"Cecilia, would you look at these two! They're nipping at each other all the time. It makes me so sad because when they were little they were inseparable!" Oh, things were so much simpler when they adored each other. As little ones, they played so well together I rarely had to import playmates. I remember the summer when they were five and six and they discovered garter snakes living under rocks in the back yard. They spent hours and hours trying to lure a particular one out from under a rock with magic potions (brewed in my kitchen from ketchup, mustard and vinegar!). When they caught him they named him "Frank the Snake." They would taunt me with him, relishing my predictable squeal. Really, I didn't mind snakes; I was fine with land animals. Throw a fish in my face, though, and I would faint.

They were Boy Scouts together, crying in unison when their cars lost at the annual Pinewood Derby. They were farmhands together at my parents' place, jumping from the rafters into bales of hay, and chasing Sweetie-Bell, my father's pet goat. They were sea captains on their dad's boat. Campers and canoers and fisherman with my brother and their other uncles.

Then they parted ways. Their interests diverged. Their personalities forged. Suddenly Luke was serious, competitive, and driven, leaving his younger brother miles behind in his dust. I can't blame Mitch but surely part of Luke's ambition was because of his father's focus on education, grades, "getting ahead," "getting into a good school," and "making something of yourself." I now know how "earthly" those endeavors are, and while noble, they have nothing at all to do with getting to Heaven. (Competition does not exist in Heaven.) Just as suddenly, Danny turned mellow, carefree, and jocular. (Mitch liked to say slapdash, flippant, and droll.) At the end of the day, we knew the truth: Luke was more like Mitch and Danny was more like me. But before their "separation" they had loads of fun together.}

Danny knew that Luke was a faster runner than he was. His smoking habit didn't help matters, but this time, Danny outsmarted Luke by cornering him on the dock. Luke had nowhere to go but in, but the river was much too cold, not to mention off limits to the Langdon kids. To Danny's surprise, Luke jumped. *Dang*! For a split second Danny thought he was going in too but his body and his will were not in sync and he stopped, stone frozen cold, an inch from the end of the dock.

"Shit! Cold! So cold!" Luke bawled, when he surfaced.

"Oh, sure, now you jump," Danny said.

Mitch ran up, baseball glove still in hand. "Luke, get the hell out of the river. You know it's off limits. "

Tess appeared from nowhere, her female instincts detecting impending danger. "Help him! He's *drownding*!" she screamed.

"He's not drowning," Danny told her, wondering why little kids always added a letter 'd' to the end of the word *drown* when there wasn't one. "But I wouldn't care if he did."

Tess gasped, hand slapping her heart. "How can you say such a thing?"

"Look what he did to me," Danny whined, pulling up the sleeve of his tee shirt to reveal a perfect red circle on his upper arm. "I think I tore my rotator cuff."

Mitch laughed and shook his head, examining the area. "That's not where your rotator cuff is. And *I'm* the one who threw it anyway. And I'm sorry."

Danny watched his brother emerge from the river. "Yeah, well, maybe he didn't throw it but he probably didn't *catch* it on purpose."

"Oh, right," Luke said, checking out his watch, which Danny guessed was not waterproof and would have to be replaced.

Tess said, "Luke, don't you dare walk into the house dripping like that. You're stinking, sopping, soaking wet." Danny couldn't help but think how she looked and sounded at that moment exactly like Annie.

Luke said, "Run get me a towel, will you, Scout?"

Tess smiled sweetly at Luke, who had said the magic word.

Mitch slung his arm around Danny's neck. "Let's get some ice on that arm." Yeah, his upper arm stung all right, but the feel of his Dad's arm around his neck warmed Danny all the way through.

❦

Danny drove to the video store to kill time—the night would be long with nothing to do and no one to "not" do it with. Not to be a baby, but his arm was killing him. He thought about how Annie would have fussed over him, would have put ice cubes in a plastic bag, wrapped the bag in a soft cotton towel, and held it tightly to his arm. She would have offered ibuprofen, and she would have shaken her head at Mitch and Luke as she often did when they roughhoused and one of her boys ended up hurt. Mitch had thrown a bag of frozen corn at Danny and said, "Hold this on your arm for a while. You'll be fine."

He cruised the aisles at BlockBuster. Nothing new: Hollywood crap. He didn't really watch a lot of what Hollywood put out. He picked up some old "friends," a couple Hitchcock classics—*To Catch a Thief* with Cary Grant and Grace Kelly, and *North by Northwest* with Cary Grant and Eva Marie Saint. But as he was looking at the DVD covers, he realized that both leading ladies resembled Ashley Pallow, the girl who had just about obliterated his heart, and he returned the movies to the shelf. No need to rub things in. No need to wallow in Pallow. Oh, that rhymes. Maybe what he needed was a comedy. What he really liked was alternative film: art films, foreign films, and documentaries. His idea of a perfect date—although he could never find a "date" who agreed—was a movie at Storefront Cinema, Rockford's only independent art house, with a bag a popcorn, followed by hours of conversation about the movie. And it would be better if one of them liked the movie and one of them didn't like the movie so the conversation would be animated and interesting. And it would be best if they could talk somewhere outside, if they could sit on a park swing, or sit in the car and look at the river, or sit on a bench on the bike path, or even lie in his dad's hammock in his own backyard.

In the "comedy" aisle (oh, the irony) he nearly collided head-on with Ashley Pallow.

"Danny!" she said, putting her hand to her (cold, cold) heart.

"Oh," was all Danny could get out. Inside he said, "Speak of the she-devil." Out loud he said, "Sorry, didn't see you there."

"How *are* you?"

Hmmm. How am I? Two ways to go here. I could lie my ass off and go with mania. Or I could lie my ass off and go with clinical depression. Or I could tell the truth and say I have absolutely no idea how I am. "I'm alive and well and living in Rockford."

"I got into U of I by the skin of my teeth," she told him. I'm rooming with Brianna Wyner. Remember her?"

"No, no I don't," he lied.

"What about you? Where are you going?"

Hmmm. Where am I going? Probably to hell for lying, but here goes nothing. Hell if he was going to admit to lowly junior college. "Well, I'm still undecided, but I got into Columbia in Chicago and the Manhasset Film School in New Jersey. Both excellent schools, I just can't make up my mind."

"But didn't you have to let them know by May?" Ashley asked, her long blonde hair shimmering even under the unforgiving fluorescent lights.

For a split second he thought about distracting her by pretending that there was a spider crawling in her hair, but the evil urge passed and instead he said, "Of course. I accepted at both places and come the end of August, I'm just gonna show up at one or the other. I'm leaning," he explained, leaning exaggeratingly to the right, "toward Manhasset but only because I like to say 'New Joy-zie.'"

Ashley smiled and shook her head. "Same Danny. You are funny, you know."

Pregnant pause.

"I'm glad I ran into you," she said. "You know I always felt bad about what happened."

"Yeah, well, I apologize on behalf of my brother."

"No, I mean with us. I never meant to hurt you like that. It was wicked."

"Hey, well, it's just part of the journey. I've chalked it up as the first crack in my heart, and you likely have compartmentalized it as your first experience with wickedness. Please don't apologize. I knew who you were when I asked you out."

"What's that supposed to mean?" Ashley demanded.

"Nothing. Just that sometimes film imitates life and sometimes life imitates film." He pointed to the DVD she was holding in her hand: the pop classic *Clueless* starring Alicia Sliverstone.

"Touché," Ashley said, with obvious relief.

He knew that she knew he had let her off easy with a simple "ditzy" description. That wasn't the half of it, but he left it at that.

"Gotta run," he said, reaching a hand behind her to grab the first movie he could. Yikes, it was *Sixteen Candles*. He smiled sheepishly. "My girlfriend just *loves* this movie," he said, rolling his eyes. "Later." He paid the rental fee and made a mad dash to the car. Once inside he realized the same heart that he thought had been obliterated was now beating angrily against his chest. He dropped his head on the steering wheel. What an idiot! All those lies! He bumped his head lightly on the steering wheel and was hit with a frightening revelation. His head popped up. "*Dang*, I've turned into Tess!" he said out loud.

That night Danny watched the movie *Sixteen Candles* with Tess, and he would never ever admit it, but he enjoyed it. A lot. Afterward, he went to his room and wrote a song for Ashley Pallow. She didn't deserve it, but he wrote it anyway. It was a pretty tune and he was proud of it, even if it was a little whiney and melo-dramatic. The guitar sounded nice and he was sure that when Mathis added bass it would sound just right. It went like this:

Late in the day / when the light changes hue / I think about you. / I'm not gonna say / you were the one / 'cuz that'd be dumb / but still / I think about you. / Everything leads to everything else / and the best I can do / is dispense my charm / and do no harm / and try not to think about you.

I'll scream so loud no one will hear it / except my dog / who's too dumb to know it / what's wrong with me? / Anyway / early in the morning / in the mixed lights of June / I watch dawn on the river / and I think about you. I'm not gonna say / I can't live without you / 'cuz that would be lying / and I don't feel like trying / anyway...

The thing was Danny knew he wasn't smart. But he knew something a lot of people didn't know: that you can pretend to be smart. It wasn't that hard, really, to strike an intellectual pose—U.S. presidents did it all the time. The secret is you had to keep them guessing. This could be accomplished easily with a small amount of research. Just find out a little piece of trivia about just about everything—inject it into a conversation—and then pull out quickly. Example: *I have one thing to say about capitalism—it leads to imperialism.* Another tactic was to throw in an obscure or fictional person's name into the conversation. Example: *Does the name Andrew Paul* (always include a middle name) *Frentwick mean anything to you?* (No.) *Then I simply cannot continue this conversation.* And then storm off with an air of arrogance. Worked every time. Or at least he thought so.

Is there anything cooler than a guy with a guitar? If only he could play better, sing better, write better songs. Early on, Danny had figured out that parents were lying when they told their kids they could be anything they wanted to be in life if they put their mind to it. Where do they get off? In reality, there were probably only two or three things a person could do well. Danny just needed to figure out which two or three.

Life is so unfair. His mom used to say no one ever promised that it would be fair, but didn't it seem über unfair? It was like that kid in his high school. Not only was the kid just plain ugly, but he had to wear these magnifying glass eyeglasses, he was skinny as a skeleton, he had one of the worse cases of acne Danny had ever seen, he wasn't smart at all, and during junior year he was in a car accident that killed his little sister. The kid had been on the receiving side of ridicule and the object of many jokes. Danny never made fun of the kid himself, but he had to draw the line at outright defense. The problem with high school, as anyone knew, was that if you stood up for the leper suddenly you had leprosy. What high school kid could risk it?

Danny believed that in Heaven we would be perfect. In Heaven, justice would prevail and your heart would never break and impartiality would be the order of the day. And that poor kid—even his name was awful—Richard Ellert (the kids were so cruel, in the halls they would shout: Dick alert! Dick alert!), even he would be beautiful and happy.

And then there was Petey. Petey was this autistic kid Danny had befriended at summer camp when they were nine. He sort of kept in touch with the kid, not just out of pity, although that was part of it, but also because the kid was actually pretty cool. He looked at the world so differently, and so did Danny. Danny looked at his watch. Ten o'clock on a Saturday night. Pathetic. Wonder what Petey was doing. Give him a call…

Geez, even Petey was out tonight—at a movie with his Dad. Danny had met Petey's parents. They were both doctors and had a look that had set into their faces, into the muscles, a look of longsuffering and heartbreak. Once, Petey's mother had called Danny and thanked him for being so nice to her son and wondered if he would take Petey to the new Star Wars movie. She would pay for everything of course. He did it, he took Petey to ShowPlace 16 to see the movie. Petey spilled his popcorn, then never returned after whispering to Danny that he had to go to the bathroom. Danny found him in the arcade. On their way out, they bumped into some guys from school, who spread it around Monday that Dan Langdon hung out with retards. And even though Danny wanted to think he was bigger than that, he never took Petey anywhere ever again.

No, nothing was fair about this life. Look at what happened to his mom. Of all people, his mom didn't deserve to die. She was careful and health-conscious. She never took crazy risks. She didn't drink excessively, she didn't smoke. She took no medications aside from a pain reliever now and then. She ran and worked out. She bought organic food and prepared healthy meals. She drove the speed limit. She didn't jump out of planes, or bungie jump, or ride motorcycles. She made complete stops at stop signs.

Was this concept of fairness hardwired into the human brain? And if so, why? Wouldn't we be better off if we never expected equity of any kind in any situation? Justice is the Lord's. A religion teacher once told Danny that justice is when you get what you deserve, mercy is when you don't get what you deserve, and grace is when you get what you don't deserve. He wrote it down in his notebook because he had to admit, it made good sense.

Chapter Twelve

A Blessing in 'Da Skies'

*Y*OU MIGHT ASK *what I did with myself all day since I didn't have a job outside the home. (I detested that question, but at the same time realized it was a fair one.) My days were simple and full: car pools, housework, cooking, gardening, laundry, the usual.*

In the winter, I painted and sold furniture. Funky pieces for which I had received a small following among my gardening friends. I always had a chair or a table or a chest of drawers to paint. I employed a technique that was reminiscent of English Hepplewhite but with a modern twist. I donated many pieces to be auctioned off at charity benefits, and it never ceased to amaze me the amount of money people would pay for spiffed-up junk.

In the summer, you'd find me in my garden, my glorious garden! It was filled not only with flowers but with trellises, arbors, pergolas, gazebos, arches, and gates. You would love my flowers! Our front yard gets a lot of sun so it is filled with sun-loving perennials. The back yard is shadier and so it contains mostly woodland plants. My garden was a full time job—even with a sprinkler system and lawn service. It was truly a paradise, a sanctuary. And I had something quite unique—a moon garden. I'd read about moon gardens or night gardens in one of my gardening magazines and I was so intrigued I dug up a spot of ground on the south side of the house off the screened porch and went at it. The idea is to fill the garden with night-blooming flowers and plants with glow-in-the dark silver foliage, like artemsia, lambs ear, silver santolina, dusty miller and silver helichrysum. Moonflower vine is a must. Over the years I added white iris, white roses, phlox, miniature gardenias, white day lily, hosta, and white pansies. For fragrance, you can add daphne, heliotrope, jasmine, osmanthus, heavenly tuberose.

There is nothing as lovely as a moon garden on a summer night. The white flowers look iridescent and there is something holy about it. You know darkness has gotten a bad rap, being associated with evil and impurity, but there's a blessed sacredness about darkness. Cecilia tells me that there is no more perfect backdrop to the brilliant light of God, then perfect darkness. Don't be afraid of the dark.

I also helped with the gardens at church. The lawn and beds at St. Peter Cathedral are simple and elegant and I always enjoyed caring for them.

In the summer, I would give Saturday morning riding lessons out at my parents' farm. Luke was my horseman and so he often helped. I broke a horse here and there for Dad, and in the fall I would drag all the kids out to help bale hay.

That was my life. I tried to live it right. I tried to be a good mother, wife, friend, daughter, sister, and gardener. I tried to leave the world a more beautiful place. I tried to live out my faith. I tried to overcome my fear of water. The best things in my life were my husband, my children, my garden, and my horses. I tried to use my talents. I tried. But there was so much more to do.

Now I'm here in Heaven. Sometimes I think I don't deserve it because my life was too easy. I hadn't thought about Heaven that much while I was alive—we are so grounded to earth. Don't get me wrong, I wanted to end up here. I was Christian—Roman Catholic—and I had been taught that Heaven was the great reward, the pearl, the place to be with God and Jesus and your loved ones who have gone before you. Where there is no suffering or tears for all of eternity. Forever and ever. Amen.

But Heaven always seemed such a mystery. When Jesus' first disciples asked him, "Rabbi, where do you stay?" he answered, "Come and see." He didn't describe in detail his home or his heart, but he invited the men to embark upon a journey of discovery. To come and see. And so it is with Heaven. God didn't describe our future home in great detail, but invites us to "taste and see," to "handle me and see," to "come and see."

And again, I say, I can't reveal anything that could alter your journey, but I can say this: think about Heaven. Don't obsess and walk around with your head in the clouds, ignoring earth and its challenges, but investigate, research, get a conversation going.

Know this: our ignorance about Heaven is a blessing in disguise, or as Tess would say, "a blessing in the skies."

Chapter Thirteen

A Boo Radley Moment

{Cecilia senses that I need to see my baby girl. We find Tess in her room dressing for church. I watch as she pokes around in her closet and tries on different dresses. Tess used to be a dress kind of girl, but not anymore. But her father insisted that she dress nicely for church and brunch so she settles for the least frilly dress she can find. "She misses me so much!" I tell Cecilia. "She's only nine!" She misses me most on weekends and for school field trips. She misses our "girl's nights" where just the two of us would stay home and watch chick flicks, paint each other's toe- and fingernails, eat croissants with homemade raspberry jam for dinner, drink orange juice out of Waterford crystal glasses, and stay up until midnight crocheting scarves for Christmas presents.

Tess, my sweet little chickabiddy! She is so unique and spunky. I know she is obsessed with the story of Scout and Jem and Atticus and Boo, but that's okay. Scout is a good role model. I loved her, too.}

AFTER SCHOOL LET out for the summer Tess became even more obsessed with *To Kill a Mockingbird.* She took to carrying a tattered hardback first edition, in which she had forged Harper Lee's autograph, and to calling her father by his first name, just as Scout had addressed Atticus. She would spontaneously recite an especially clever excerpt when it was apropos to the situation. Overalls became her mainstay. And against her father's protests, she called Mrs. Cally *Calpurnia*. Once, to her face.

Tess's favorite part of the book was when Walter Cunningham joined Scout and Jem for lunch (they called it "dinner") and Walter proceeded to pour syrup all over his vegetables and meat "with a generous hand." Scout explained that he probably would have poured syrup into his glass of milk as well if she hadn't asked him what in the sam hill he was doing. That just cracked Tess up—the 'sam hill' part. She'd read and reread that section of the book. She also loved when Calpurnia summoned Scout to the kitchen to lecture her about her lack of social graces. That Scout was something else. Tess liked her spunk.

Well, there was nothing else to do. She'd refused summer camp. Cried till her eyes were so swollen they were almost sealed shut. And forget about having friends from school over to play. Tess was too embarrassed now that her mom was gone and there was no one to "host" her get-togethers. Annie used to plan fun things for Tess and her friends to do: bake cookies, strip old wallpaper from a bedroom (the girls loved that!), paint a piece of furniture, plant flowers in a window box, create greeting cards, even visit Bumpa and Grans to feed and brush the horses.

Mrs. Cally was nice enough but she had work to do; it was clear to Tess that their housekeeper did not consider "entertaining the children" to be part of her job description. Oh well, in *To Kill a Mockingbird* Scout never had any friends from school over. She just hung around with her brother and Dill.

Now, sitting in the back seat of her dad's old Volvo, Tess pretended she was Scout, her dad was Atticus, Luke was Jem, and Danny was Dill. "Dill" was sitting next to her in the backseat, listening to music on his IPOD. She imagined that they were on a Sunday drive, on their way to a church picnic or a county fair. Calpurnia would have packed an old-fashioned picnic basket filled with fried chicken, potato salad, bread-and-butter pickles and honey almond cookies. There would be a red-and-white checkered tablecloth and napkins, and lemonade squeezed from real lemons. There would be talk of crops, and the weather, and maybe Atticus would meet a nice widow, someone of whom Scout would approve, of course. Tess smiled at the picture. Too bad it wasn't reality.

The day they all dreaded was here. Today was the day it happened: Annie had been gone a whole year. Tess wondered how it could be. The whole family—her real family, not her imagined one—was quiet as they drove to the Catholic cemetery where Annie's ashes were buried. They'd only been there twice before—once when they buried the pretty urn in that weird thing they called a vault and once on Annie's birthday. The second time Daddy cried. The first time, with all the people around, he didn't. Tess remembered her dad saying that Annie never liked cemeteries and had told him in no uncertain terms that when she died she wanted to be cremated. "And don't come visit my grave. I won't be there," she'd said.

Tess always thought her dad would die first. He was so much older than her mother. All her friends had these young fathers who coached their soccer teams and took them camping and snow boarding and gave them piggyback rides. From as far back as Tess could remember, her father was old. Once, when he picked her up from summer day camp, one of the campers asked Tess if Mitch was her grandfather. She'd been so embarrassed she said yes, he was. That night she asked her mother why she had married such an old man. Annie just laughed and said, "You can't control whom you fall in love with, honey." And then Annie pointed out all the youthful things Mitch did: he jogged and water-skied and—well, he jogged and he water-skied. And then she explained to Tess how someone could be young at heart.

The June air was hot and humid as it blew in through the back car window. "This car is as hot as an EasyBake Oven," Tess announced. The air conditioner in her father's old Volvo had broken last year and he had never bothered getting it fixed. This infuriated Tess who had lectured her father that surely it couldn't be good for a man his age to risk heat exhaustion. In spite of the heat Tess rolled the window up when the hot breeze started bending her flowers. This morning she had picked a colorful bouquet to place on her mother's grave. She hated that old grave. It scared her to see her family name engraved on the big smooth headstone. And she never understood why her mom wanted to be burned to ashes.

She still had nightmares about being burned alive. When the nightmares woke her, it was Luke she called for, since she never knew if her father had been called out to the hospital in the night. Luke would come quickly and hold her. He'd get her a drink of water and drag her and four or five of her stuffed animals into his room where he allowed her to climb into bed with him. Often, when she awoke, she'd find Luke asleep on the floor. "Sheila snores," he'd tease. Sheila being Tess's favorite stuffed bear, the one she named after her first grade teacher.

Once when Luke was away for the weekend visiting a friend at college, Tess woke from one of her burning-alive nightmares and called out to her favorite big brother. When he didn't come and she remembered that he was away, she called for Danny. It took him forever to show up, and when he did he was barely awake. Instead of picking Tess up and holding her as Luke had, he simply jumped into her bed and patted her head a little. "Why would Mom want to turn to ashes?" she asked him.

"Because it's better than rotting in the ground and getting eaten up by worms," Danny answered. (In his defense, it should be said that he was still ninety percent asleep when he made this statement.) After this, Tess's nightmares took a new and darker twist and she started sleeping on a foldout cot in Luke's room.

You had to wonder how someone so young could go through so much. At least that's what Miss Miranda, her psychiatrist, said the first time Tess poured out her little heart. Miss Miranda didn't want Tess to call her "doctor," but Tess wasn't comfortable calling her "Miranda"— she was sure Scout wouldn't be so bold—so they compromised and added the "Miss" which made Tess feel southern, like Scout. Miss Miranda was the best listener ever. Tess liked her from the start even though she was not very pretty to look at. She was almost a giant lady, thin as a yardstick, and she wore eyeglasses with turquoise-colored frames, long dangling earrings, and her dark hair shorter than most men. But her voice possessed a soothing quality and she seemed to remember what it was like to be nine.

"Sometimes I'm so sad, you know, about my mom," Tess told Miss Miranda at their last session. "But then other times, like when I'm playing with Julianna, I'm happy, but then I think about my mom and that I should probably be sad, so then I get sad about being happy."

Tess had envisioned the sessions with Miss Miranda differently. She saw herself lying on a couch and balancing a box of tissues on her stomach. Her dad told her she'd seen too many movies. Instead she got to sit in a big swivel chair and swivel to her heart's content, or until she got dizzy, whichever came first.

"The thing is, Miss Miranda, a girl my age shouldn't have to go through everything I've had to go through this year. I mean, my mom and everything, that's the worst thing, but then why does my best friend have to move to Chicago? And I have to take care of my brothers and make their lunches and clean the house and do the laundry and my dad is never home, he's always looking after newborn babies and sick kids, and my teacher this year was a kook. She couldn't spell and couldn't remember anyone's name. And I want a kitten and Dad says no, a dog is enough, and I don't want piano lessons anymore but Dad says it would break my mom's heart if I quit. How much can a kid take? Do you have other kids who have it this tough?"

Miss Miranda explained that just as she couldn't tell anyone what Tess said, she couldn't share any confidential information about her other patients with Tess, but she agreed that Tess had had more than her share for a nine-year-old kid and she hoped that together they could make this a better year. "Ninety-nine percent of happiness is the result of our attitude," Miss Miranda said. "Do you know what that statement means, Tess?"

"I think so. Doesn't it mean that ninety-nine percent of people think they're happy but they're really not?"

Miss Miranda couldn't stifle a smile, which made Tess mad, but then she remembered how she could make her mother smile by saying clever things and so she decided she must have just said something clever and left it at that.

Miss Miranda always made Tess tell her one thing about her mother that she missed and one good thing that was happening in her life. Tess swirled in the chair. "I miss the secret nicknames we had for each other that no one else knew. Wanna know what they were?"

"But then they wouldn't be secret anymore, would they?" Miss Miranda said.

"But it doesn't matter anymore," Tess said, putting her feet to the floor to abort her swirl. "Mom called me her little 'chickabiddy,' which means a little chicken, and I called her 'mommamiddy,' which means nothing, but it made her laugh. You have to know I was like three or four at the time."

"Terms of endearment are important. My mom called me her 'little-diddle.'"

Tess had a hard time picturing Miss Miranda as ever having been a *little* anything, but she said politely, "That's cute."

"Tess, what if your dad called you 'chickabiddy' and you called him 'daddadiddy' or something like that?"

Tess gave Miss Miranda a look.

"Okay, well, tell me something good that happened since we last met."

"Nothing."

"Think."

"Calpurnia let me fold towels with her yesterday."

"That's good?"

"Yes, and she called me 'Scout.'"

"Well, I know *that's* good. Listen, Tess, if you like, we can make secret names for each other and use them only when we meet. Think about it, okay, and we'll talk about it next time. Okay, kiddo, time's up. I bet Luke's waiting for you."

Now, Tess asked Danny if they were getting close to the cemetery but he had his headsets on and so he didn't hear her. She tapped his leg and he reluctantly lifted one of the earphones. "What?" he said, with annoyance in his voice. They were getting close, he told her. "Look for a barn with a caved-in roof, it's right after that." Tess decided it was too much trouble and took Danny at his word. She stared at the back of her dad's head. His hair was graying at the temples but at least he wasn't bald. What if his heart got arrested again? She wondered if a man that old should even *be* driving. His birthday was coming up in September—he would be sixty-four. Sixty-four!

By the time they pulled into Calvary Cemetery Tess's bouquet was wilted and she'd gotten herself all worked up. "I don't want to come," she told her dad when he opened the car door. "Can't I just stay in the car? Please?"

"Are you sure, honey?"

She nodded.

"Are you scared?"

She shook her head. "Just don't want to."

Her dad nodded and brushed some of her hair back.

"Here," she said, thrusting the flowers into his hand. She watched as her dad and brothers walked toward a line of gravestones that bordered the road, baking in the hot sun. Tess looked around. To the left, the graves were in the shade, cool and content under huge leafy trees. Why had her father selected this hot spot for her mother? He knew she liked the sun for gardening and the shade for relaxing. Surely she would bake. What was he thinking?

Tess got back in the car, leaving the door open for air. She could see Danny standing by the grave with his hands in his back pockets, his scruffy hair blowing in the hot breeze. Luke stood beside him with his arms folded, kicking at the grass. Mitch leaned over the grave and gently placed Tess's bouquet near the headstone, and then he knelt on the ground and made the sign of the cross. He nodded to the boys, but neither one bent to his knees. This made Tess teary because her father looked so pathetic. Alone and pathetic. She jumped out of the car and slammed the door closed. As deliberately as Scout, she walked to her mother's grave. No one should have to kneel alone by the grave of someone you loved. She may have been only nine, but this much she knew.

{I wish they wouldn't even go out to the cemetery. I don't think it's good for Tess. She still has nightmares. I know it's because Mitch feels obligated—my mother asks him whenever she sees him if he's been to the cemetery (my parents don't drive anymore.) I don't want death to tarnish Tess's innocence any more than it already has.

"When Tess was little," I tell Cecilia, "she used to get the words to songs mixed up—something we all found absolutely adorable." She thought the words to the national anthem were "Jose, can you see by the donzerly light." "What are spacious guys?" she asked me after we sang "America, the Beautiful" at church. "It's spacious skies, honey, not guys." When Danny turned her on to the Beatles, the first time she heard the song "Lucy in the Sky with Diamonds," she thought the line "the girl with kaleidoscope eyes" was "a girl with colitis goes by." (Only a doctor's child!)

Oh, and here's how Tess recited the "Pledge of Allegiance" as a preschooler: "I led the pigeons to the flag of the United States of America, and to the republic of Richard Sands, one station, under God, indivisible, with liberty and just Tess for all."

Yes, oh, yes, Tess was the little darling of our household. Without prodding or cajoling she would happily recite a poem, sing a tune, tap a dance, provide a riddle, knock a joke, or just sit prettily in a foo-foo dress. Everyone doted on Tessa Camille Langdon. I'll never forget when she was three and all dolled out in her Easter ensemble. I had her look at herself in my full-length mirror, and she said, "Hmmm, I didn't know I was this cute."

Looking back, I guess we exploited her. But it was irresistible! "Tess, say the 'Hail Mary' for Grandma," I'd beg her. "Hail Mary, full of grapes, the Lord is withy, blessed are you, a monk swimming, and blessed is the Fruit-of-thy Loom, Jesus…"}

After the cemetery there was brunch at Cliffbreakers, just the four of them. Danny did most of the talking, going on and on about a new get-rich-quick scheme he and Mathis dreamed up just in case their real summer jobs didn't pan out. (Tess could tell Danny was already bored with his job at the nursery.)

"Here's what we've got in mind," Danny said with his mouth full. "Houses."

"Houses—as in real estate?" Mitch asked.

"No, houses as in miniatures."

"Here we go," Luke said, shaking his head.

"Just listen. You know how a couple of years ago, Sally Dobson went around the entire Churchill's Grove neighborhood and commissioned water-colored sketches of everyone's homes? Well, Mathis and I are going to create perfect miniature facades of homes—out of plywood and stuff—that you can hang on your wall."

"Oh, Danny!" Tess squealed. "They sound so cute! Like doll houses!"

"But just the fronts," Danny said, gesturing with his fork. "People in our neighborhood are in love with their houses."

Tess smiled. Maybe Danny would let her help. Probably not, but at least everyone seemed a little happy. Danny did have a way of injecting cheer into an otherwise somber moment.

Mitch let Tess order three kiddie cocktails. She arrived home on a sugar high only to have her bubble burst when she found Piper lying on the cold ceramic tile in the kitchen, looking sad and lethargic. Mitch had just said, "We'd better get her to the vet," when his pager went off.

"How dare someone need you now! Piper needs you now!" Tess said, after Mitch reported that he had to go to the hospital.

"Tess, it's a very, very sick little two-year-old boy. Luke, will you handle it?"

Of course Luke would handle it. Luke always handled it. There was another man who was old before his time: Luke was only nineteen but he had to act like he was thirty. Poor Luke. It took both Luke and Danny to pick up Piper and haul her to the van. They placed her in the back seat with her head on Tess's lap. Tess noticed a strange goo oozing from Piper's eyes and she got so scared she started to cry. She was sure Piper had eye cancer or macular degeneration, like her grandma. Tess prayed the whole way. Her mother had taught her to talk to God as she would a parent or a best friend. Tess did. "Dear God," she said under her breath, "enough is enough! Give me a break, I'm just a kid! Amen."

God did give Tess a break. Piper just had a virus: conjunctivitis—which was a fancy name for pink eye. On the way home, Tess clutched the bottle of eye drops tightly in her hand. Two drops in both eyes, four times a day. Two drops in both eyes, four times a day. Or was it four drops in both eyes, twice a day. Shoot. Well, Luke would know.

Her best friend was gone. Tess hung upside down from the monkey bars on her swing set and sulked. Mitch sat in a swing and tried to console her.

"It's no use, Dad. Unless you can snap your fingers and get me a new best friend."

"I'm sorry, honey. I'm so sorry."

"What am I going to do without her?"

"Honey, I wish you'd get down from there. You might fall."

Tess ignored him. What a worrywart. "Could I go live with Aunt Maggy for the rest of the summer?"

"Tess! Wouldn't you miss me? And your brothers?"

Tess flipped herself off the monkey bars. "I guess," she said, shaking her hair out of her eyes. Her dad held out his arms to her but she ran off.

"Would pizza soften the blow?" her dad called after her.

Nothing would soften the blow. She fetched her bike from the garage and pedaled as fast as she could down the sidewalk and out into the street. She intended to ride all the way to Aunt Maggy's but soon realized that her front tire was low and hopped off to check it out. It was nearly flat. She sighed and then walked the bike home. How many times had she asked her dad and Luke and Danny to look at the tire, that it seemed low, but as usual, they'd all promised to look at it but never did. Crikey! She could have wiped out and killed herself. After she dumped the bike in the driveway, she peeked around the house to survey the backyard. She didn't want to see her dad. He was nowhere in sight. Luke was on the riding mower and Danny was asleep in the hammock. She moseyed back to her monkey bars. For some reason it felt good to be upside down. Maybe it was because her whole life had been turned upside down and by hanging upside down she could turn the world right side up.

Was it just her, or was the world a crazy place? Even so, she knew she didn't want to die. She thought about death and dying quite a bit. How did you know if you were dying? Or, what would be better, to die quickly from a heart attack or slowly from cancer? And why did we have to die, anyway? Why couldn't eternity just be here on earth? What was so bad about earth that it had to end? It was such a pretty planet, really, unlike Mars that seemed so gray and brown, nothing but craters and volcanoes. Earth had everything we needed. Why did we have to leave?

Then she fell. She hit the ground hard, her right shoulder and upper arm taking the brunt of the fall. Lying still in the grass, she appraised the pain, rubbing her upper arm, her shoulder, her neck. She sat up and opened her eyes, expecting blurred vision and a wave of nausea. Nothing. But then, sometimes these things were delayed. These kind of injuries were nothing to fool around with. She screamed for Luke because Luke was her "Go-To-Guy." A person could depend on Luke.

Luke came running. (Danny, on the hammock, never flinched.) "What's wrong?" Luke said. "What happened?"

"I fell off," Tess told him, rubbing her head, even though her head wasn't what hurt. "I- I- think I have a percussion. Check my eyes and see if they're dialed."

Luke peeked into Tess's eyes. "They're not *dilated* and you don't have a *concussion*. How'd you fall? What were you doing?"

"Nothing."

"Want to get on the mower with me?"

"Dad won't like it," she said, as she got up and started to follow her older brother.

"Dad's not around," Luke said.

"So what else is new," Tess replied.

Tess watched the movie *The Sound of Music* in her dad's office while she sorted socks. That was one thing that never seemed to get done after Annie died. No one—not even Mrs. Cally—wanted to sort socks. What happened was that socks were picked out of baskets of clean laundry and thrown into a plastic garbage can in the basement. The unsaid rule was that everyone fended for him- or herself when it came to socks. Once in a while Tess would grab the can, haul it upstairs, and attempt to find matches while she watched a movie. Danny had gotten to the point where he didn't even try to match anymore and often could be seen walking around wearing two completely different socks. It would probably make her mother sad to hear it, but once when her dad asked her what she missed most about her mother, she had answered, "I miss her matching up my socks."

It was the little things. (It was the big things too but the big things were so obvious.) The little things would stab you when you least expected. Tess missed her mother's movement, her vibrations. Instead of walking, Annie had almost glided. Tess missed observing her mother's little quirks—the cute way she removed her gloves by "biting" the fingers. The way she wigwagged her dinner fork through the air while talking at the kitchen table. The way she knew the fancy name of plants—Baby's Breath was *Gypsophila elegans* and Burning Bush was *Kochia scoparia*—but she didn't know some of the names of things Tess was learning in school—*proboscis* for nose or *Franken food* for genetically modified food.

Tess missed the little quotes her mother used to tuck into her lunchbox or backpack. *"Sweetie, if you want to be loved, then be lovable."* *"The best way to feel like a big girl is to stand up for the little guy."*

Miss Miranda said that Tess was absolutely normal. Miss Miranda said that the grief Tess was experiencing was the perfectly normal grief of a nine-year-old girl who missed her mother. Sometimes Tess wondered: if she had been awake on that dreadful day could she have saved Annie? Unlike her brothers, Tess talked about her loss. Danny and Luke had told her to knock it off but Miss Miranda encouraged her to continue to talk about her mother because it gave a person a sense of "control and mastery," whatever that meant. Miss Miranda was so smart. It seemed she could sometimes read Tess's mind. When school had started and Tess just couldn't handle it, Miss Miranda named her fear: being different because she was the only kid in her class who had lost her mother.

Her dad came in at the part when that old nun sang the climb-all-those-mountains song and since this was her least favorite scene in the movie—it was her opinion that the song dragged on and was unnecessary—she didn't protest when he grabbed the sock garbage can and told her it was time for bed.

In her room she deposited fifteen pairs of sock into her dresser drawer and, because her beloved Miss Miranda had encouraged her to do so, she wrote in her journal before getting into bed. Miss Miranda had presented Tess with the pretty paisley-patterned journal one day and told Tess that journaling was one of the best ways to deal with sad thoughts. "Those sad thoughts are like little fish swimming around in your head. You need to catch them and put them in a net. Your pen is your fishing-pole and this journal is your net."

Tess thought about Julianna. Losing her was like losing her mother all over again. Was this how it was going to be? Was life all about losing people you loved? Tess wrote a friendship poem for Julianna but it wasn't very good. *"Friends are like diamonds, they sparkle forever, friends are like elephants, they forget you never. Friends are like good books with secrets to tell, friends are like …mothers…they leave as well."* She ripped out the page and crumpled it up. It wasn't fair—her mother didn't leave on purpose and Julianna didn't either. But part of her was sad and the other part was mad.

Miss Miranda said write about how you are feeling. Okay. Okay. Maybe she could write a "feelings" poem:

When you have a mother,
Life is all chocolate and cherries
And when you don't
Life is like dark chocolate
It's okay but kind of bitter.
I want to ask my mom about Heaven.
How is it anyway?
And do you like it better than you liked it here?
Is there water? And if there is are you still afraid of it?
I'd like to ask other things too.
You're supposed to be happy in Heaven
But how can you be happy without us?
I'm happy sometimes, but I'm not overjoyed.
I get mad when I can't find two socks that match.
I'm kind of mad a lot.
And Dad forgets me a lot.
And I wonder if it would be easier for him if I were to go live with
Aunt Maggy. Luke and Danny are almost grown and then Dad could just
take care of his patients and come home and relax. He looks pale lately
and I heard him coughing last night. I think he's just too old and too
tired to take care of me. I heard Mrs. Wicker say that I must have been
an "Oooops!" baby and I didn't like the sound of that. I know I should be
taking care of your garden, but I'll be honest, it's a wreck. There are more
weeds than flowers. Bumpa wants me to ride Stella this summer but I'm
too scared. If I fall off and hurt myself, then who, I ask you, who, is going
to take care of this family?

Ooops, back to the poem:

I want to be a morning glory
Because you always said they were a headstrong plant
And that they twine in one direction only.
That's me. And that's why I'll be okay.
   But I do get this pain in the back of my neck and I think I should probably have a cat scan or something, just to be sure. And yesterday I couldn't taste a thing all day and so there must be something wrong with my tastebloods. There's a small bump on the tip of my tongue and it hurts and I can't help but wonder if it's tongue cancer. You would think having a dad who is a pediatrician would come in handy for a kid like me, but if you want to know the truth, it's worse because whenever I complain about my health he just smiles and says, "Well, that's nothing serious." Nothing serious? Nothing serious? Do I have to bleed from my eyes for it to be something serious?

Oh, back to the poem.

Are there flowers in Heaven, Mom?
Are they as pretty as the ones in your garden used to be?
What's the weather like?
I hope it's always like you liked it: sunny and seventy.
   One more thing, can you sit on clouds and swing on stars, like in that song? And one more last thing, is the moon cheese or paper, like in that other song?
   Please write these questions down so when I get there you can answer them.

{"She's a good little writer, isn't she, Cecilia? I'm glad she's seeing Miranda Burns. I think it's helping. But she needs answers, Cecilia. They all need answers."}

118

Enough writing. Tess slipped under the sheet, said her prayers, and then lay awake for hours wondering why God was so angry with her. He must be angry about something for all these bad things to be happening to her. She racked her brain and the only thing she could come up with was the time she was so mean to that Kevin Hennead, that awful finger-sucking boy in her class. She had nothing against the kid if he would just keep his fingers a safe distance from his mouth, but for Kevin, that proved impossible. Once, when they were waiting in the lunch line and Tess told him to get his fingers out of his mouth, he obeyed, but then he wiped his saliva-soaked fingers off on her uniform skirt. She almost threw up. Instead she slugged him. Good and hard on his shoulder. Enough to make him cry.

Reliving the event made her stomach queasy all over again so she switched to reflecting on her family life. She was the model daughter, wasn't she? She was good to animals and God's green earth. And if she was mean to her brothers it was either as an act of self-defense or out of utter frustration. It was mostly Danny because Luke was actually pretty sweet to her. Danny had a warped sense of humor that baffled Tess and his teasing could be mean at times. Danny was the one who would play hide and seek with her and then never come seeking. Once she'd stayed hidden (in an uncomfortable squatting position) in the kitchen pantry for nearly a half hour. Danny was the one who told her she was adopted; that her real mother was an Eskimo and her real father was a Jamaican Rastafarian. Danny deserved any slugs he got and then some. That couldn't be it. Maybe it would come to her in time. She said the *Act of Contrition*: "*My God, I am sorry for my sins with all my heart…*" She rolled over, sleepy at last, and the reason finally came to her. It could be on account of all the lying.

Sitting in church that Sunday, Tess tried to listen to Father Will. He was talking about happiness and what really makes people happy.

It all boiled down to three things, he said: "One, someone to love; two, something to do; and three, something to hope for." That's it? Tess thought. *Baloney!* she almost said out loud.

Danny was fidgety and his squirming made Tess uneasy. She tried to imagine what it must feel like to inhabit her brother's body. It must be thunder and lightning inside there—all electricity. She watched his knees vibrate and his fingers drum a beat on his thighs. She could tell he wasn't listening at all, that he was off in his own weird world. She said a prayer then and there that somewhere out there in the big world there was a girl who would love Danny.

He wasn't totally unlovable. When he wanted to be sweet, he could be very sweet. Take Petey for example, the autistic boy Danny had befriended at summer camp. Danny was actually pretty sweet to Petey. He'd report at dinnertime all the funny and heartbreaking things that Petey would do at camp. Her brother was patient and kind when he spoke to Petey on the phone. It was one of those things that surprised her about Danny.

Tess looked at her brother; he was smiling. He looked beautiful with the colored sunlight that filtered in through the stained glass windows bathing his hair and cheek. What she would give to know what went on in that head of his. Oh, what she would give. She couldn't help herself, she reached over and placed her hand on his knee to steady it. He scowled at her and swiped her hand away. Tess sighed. She should have known better. You can't stop Danny's engine—he simply had to run out of gas.

Before communion Tess said another *Act of Contrition* (the prayer was becoming a daily thing) all the while wondering if she should even be receiving Holy Eucharist. She promised the Lord she would put an end to the fibbing. There, she felt better.

Later that morning Tess wandered through her mother's garden. It was overgrown with monster weeds and this broke her heart. She pulled some plants she was sure were weeds and pinched dead blossoms from flowers (something her mother called "dead-heading"). Piper kept her company, but soon Tess grew bored with the task and lay down in the grass near the fragrant rosebushes. Piper lay next to her. Tess let the dog lick her face. Piper knew all of Tess's secrets. What would Tess do when her beautiful dog died? She was already twelve, which in dog years was sixty-one. (The common belief that one human year is equal to seven dog years turns out not to be very accurate, according to Piper's vet. Dr. Andover explained to Tess that a more accurate formula was to assign 10.5 dog years per human year for the first two years, then four years per human year for each year after. This calculation made Piper nearly as old as Mitch!)

In a while, they were all going to Aunt Maggy's for a memorial dinner, as if they needed a pan of lasagna to remember Annie. But this was a good thing for she loved Aunt Maggy and Uncle Jack and she liked her cousins; they weren't bad for boys. They had a trampoline and they had the most adorable kitten named Jasper. The best thing about Jasper was that he tolerated being wrapped up in a baby blanket and being nearly hugged to death. After Mass, Tess had secretly called her aunt and asked her if she could spend the night. Of course Aunt Maggy said yes, as long as it was okay with her dad. Tess told a teeny-tiny fib and said that she had already asked her dad. When she hung up she tried to find her dad to get permission, but he was nowhere to be found, so she granted herself permission. How she would explain the giant suitcase she'd packed with enough clothes for two weeks, she'd worry about later.

Piper was snoring. Tess wondered if animals went to Heaven. Her teacher told her class that they didn't, but Tess thought they did. What would Heaven be without animals? (Her dad agreed with her and said something about animals having a group soul rather than individual souls…whatever that meant.) It was so hot, she wished it was winter. She flapped her arms and legs making invisible snow angels in the grass. Maybe her mom was an angel. Could people become angels in Heaven? She didn't know. It's the kind of question her mom could have fielded.

{I wish I could tell Tess, no, honey, people don't become angels. People stay people in Heaven. You stay your unique self. I tell Cecilia that I'm worried that Tess thinks she is invisible. I want to clap my hands and scream down to earth: "Pay attention! Tess needs some TLC and quick!" She also needs a good scrubbing. Look at my baby girl! Someone should throw those overalls she insists on wearing into the garbage. Even the people who used to dote on her suddenly seem to have forgotten how vulnerable Tess is. After all, it's been a year and people just assume that the one-year marker means survivors have moved on.

To get attention my little one has turned into a hypochondriac—she'd had that "bent" all along. The other day she asked her dad if he knew of a good "germatologist." "A what, honey?" "You know, a skin doctor. My skin feels funny." "Where?" "My whole skin."

And, yes, she has also turned to lying for attention. "Oh Cecilia, Tess never used to lie. She was the one who was mortifyingly honest!"}

Tess felt a bug crawling up her arm, swatted it, and then mourned the splotch of guts she wiped from her arm onto the grass. She stared at her fingernails, which looked like the opposite of a French manicure—instead of white tips, her fingernails were crowned with black dirt. She thought she knew her mom by heart—her face, her smell, her gestures, her voice—but it was fading. She closed her eyes and pictured her mom in Heaven. Surely she must be gardening or else she was riding horses.

"Tess!"

She jumped when she heard her dad calling her name. Maybe it was guilt. For if her conniving worked, she'd be at Aunt Maggy's for the rest of the month! Aunt Maggy would take Tess shopping at T.J. Maxx and Marshall's, and if she was really lucky, take her to Chicago to the Drake Hotel for afternoon tea (with china cups and a harpist even!) and then on to the American Girl store, like they had done shortly after Annie died.

She ran to the house, with Piper at her heels. *Hmmm, how to explain that suitcase…*

Chapter Fourteen

Heaven-Crammed Earth

'M SITTING ON my first and favorite horse, Carmel, a gorgeous palomino paint. What a sweetie she is! Here in Heaven she has been restored to perfect health and I can ride her to my heart's content. I lost her when I was fourteen (she was fourteen, too!) to a stupid case of tetanus. I was beside myself. Carmel had no equal.

Are you surprised to know that there are animals in Heaven? So was I. I was always told as a child that animals didn't have souls. What nonsense! Animals belong in the "new earth" just as much as trees and plants and flowers and people and angels. Remember Heaven is the new earth and it's not so different that we don't recognize it. The good news is that the whole family of creation is included in God's plan of salvation. Yes, even spiders, bats, and snakes.

Oh, I know you have so many questions about Heaven. I can share a few more things. Music lovers want to know if there is music in Heaven. The answer is of course. But I have to qualify that because there is both silence and sound here. And it's not so much that there is music in Heaven but it's more like Heaven makes music. What do I mean? Just that the entire universe is a musical instrument. Music is simply vibration. And just as on earth—the breath of the wind, the patter of rain, the crashing of waves, the singing of birds, the laughter of children, the voices of humans—music is made naturally here in Heaven.

You may be familiar with the Pythagorean theory about planets producing celestial music. The ancient Greek mathematician believed that planets orbited in perfect harmony and vibrated in musical harmony, according to their different rates of movement thereby producing celestial music. There was also the great astronomer and mystic Johannes Kepler who formulated elegant laws about planetary motion. Kepler also believed the universe made beautiful music, that each planet sang its own unique tune. He calculated each planet's angle to the sun and was able to work out a distinct tune for each. He thought earth's simple song was "mi-fa-mi." Kepler was a brilliant man, but neither he nor Plato nor Pythagoras had it totally right. It's far more fascinating and brilliant. Let me say this—most celestial music comes from the fluttering of angels' wings.

Some people who get a glimpse of Heaven in near death experiences remember most vividly not what they saw but what they heard—the sacred swoosh of angel wings. On earth, you mostly use your sense of hearing to appreciate music, although the musician himself can also enjoy the sense of touch through the instrument. But in Heaven, we experience music with all of our Heavenly senses. You can smell and taste music here. Isn't that cool?

Did you know that you—you as in your heavenly soul melded with your earthly body—make music? Every cell in your body vibrates to your own unique frequency, for we sensual beings are chemical and electromagnetic. The Bible says, "In the beginning, there was the Word," and the deeper meaning is that God is the sacred creative sourcing sound—His "word" vibrates within us; it's what gives rise to our very existence. In other words, our DNA sings!

I am learning so much here. Did you know that the Dutch are the world's tallest people? They have a protein-rich diet and a national health service that takes extra good care of their children. The world's tallest tree is a redwood in California that stands five stories taller than the Statue of Liberty. Humans are not the only animals on earth that copulate face to face. More people are killed annually by donkeys than die in air crashes. Ninety-seven percent of all people, when handed a new pen to try, will write their name. Over eighty percent of professional boxers have suffered brain damage. Did you know that most people are an inch taller at night? That the average person laughs about fifteen times a day and will walk the equivalent of twice around the world in a lifetime? Here's something that might surprise you—the most common last name in the world is Mohammed and the most common first name is Muhammad. Most people have a vocabulary of about 5000 to 6000 words. The average adult has about 3500 square inches of skin. You share your birthday with at least nine million other people around the world. Shirley Temple always had 56 curls in her hair. People who work at night tend to weigh more than people who work during the day. The most common eye color in the world is brown. The chemical and mineral composition of the human body breaks down as follows: 65% oxygen, 18% carbon, 10% hydrogen, 3% nitrogen, 1.5% calcium, 1% phosphorous, 0.35% potassium, 0.25% sulphur, 0.15% sodium, 0.15% chlorine, 0.05% magnesium, 0.0004% iron, 0.00004% iodine, and trace amounts of fluorine, silicon, manganese, zinc, copper, aluminium, and arsenic.

I've learned some very disturbing things too. One of the worst things was that during the Holocaust, the Nazis used human skin as a substitute for leather in the manufacture of lampshades and shoes, among other things. Too horrific to even imagine…

Did you know that if there were no dust in the world there would be less rainfall and fewer beautiful sunsets? That's because rain is formed when water molecules in the air collect around particles of dust, and water vapor and dust particles reflect the rays of the sun and make the sunset (or sunrise) more colorful. Did you know that carbonated drinks bubble more in plastic cups? That ancient Romans used to kiss each other on the eyes when they greeted?

But that's all fluff. The most important thing I've learned so far is this: that God loves each of us as if we were an only child. God loves us for our beauty and not for our morality. Let me say that again: God loves us because we exist, and our being is beautiful just because we exist; morality is something we aspire to and something that pleases God, but it is not what makes God love us. God loves us in spite of our sins and immorality and amorality; and this is why we should love our enemies—not because of some code of righteousness, but because they exist, and if they exist, then God loves them, and if God loves them, then we should also.

Chapter Fifteen

Hop on Papa

{*"Of course no marriage is perfect," I tell Cecilia, "and ours wasn't." I used to tell people I thought I married "Mr. Right" but he turned out to be "Mr.-Always-Thinks-He's-Right." But Mitch and I were well matched and like-minded, and early on we learned each other's hot buttons. I was more social and needed to get out of the house after being home alone all day. Mitch was with people all day and wanted to come home and have some time to himself. We made our marriage work. And it worked.*}

SUMMER WAS PROVING to be wicked in nature. Hot. Mitch used to love the heat, but now the searing, moist air seemed to strangle him when he stepped out from the air-conditioned shelters of his home and office. Maybe he would have to get the air-conditioner in his car fixed after all.

Today was Saturday morning, which meant that before making rounds at the hospital he'd have his Swedish massage. It seemed to be one of the few things he looked forward to anymore. Since Annie died, he felt as if he were living in an alternate dimension, where things that used to give him pleasure—practicing medicine, boating, woodworking, reading—didn't, and things that used to drive him crazy—disorder, tardiness, indecision, idleness—he could slough off without a second thought. He was a different man now, half the man he was when Annie was around to make him want to be a better man. Annie had softened his rough edges, calmed his nerves, challenged his physical stamina, and reminded him daily about living for the moment and being mindful of God's gifts. It was Annie who had taught him how to be a father, for even though his life had been dedicated to the care of children, when Luke was born and he held him in his arms for the first time, he knew immediately that he really didn't have the first clue about fatherhood. He'd had the illusion that parenting would be a simple extension of doctoring, but of course it wasn't.

Annie was his fire and fuel; now he was running on empty.

He drove over to his massage therapist's house. Trina's husband and children were home on Saturdays and this made Mitch feel more comfortable with the set up. He probably would never get over the awkwardness he felt before a massage. Afterward, when he was completely relaxed and redressed he could make small talk with Trina, but before, he could barely make eye contact. He wasn't attracted to Trina—she was elfish with sharp features—but he was attracted to the sensuous art of massage. Trina's skilled hands and her soft voice were what mattered to Mitch. Here were fifty solid minutes of stress-free bliss. He'd come to live for it.

While he undressed in the bathroom, Mitch wondered why it had taken him sixty-some years to discover massage. Massage therapy could have made a huge difference in med school. And before taking his boards. During his residency. Before his wedding. Before and after the births of each of his children...

Trina gave him the option of either being unclothed or keeping on his underwear for his massage. Mitch, being Mitch, kept on his briefs (white, Fruit-Of-The Loom), thank you very much. He lay on the table, draped a soft clean sheet over himself and waited for her soft knock on the door.

Soon he was in another world. The quiet alone was worth the trip. The tinkling music was barely audible and the jasmine-scented aromatherapy was just enough to soothe but not overpower the nostrils. Trina started with a technique called *effleurage*—gliding stokes with the palms, thumbs and fingertips—then used a combination of kneading, friction, vibration, percussion (brisk hacking or tapping), and ended with gentle bending and stretching.

It was amazing how a quiet room, soft music, and the power of human touch could draw toxic stress from the human body. It was a far superior medicine to the variety he practiced. Mitch had learned after a couple of sessions that the trick to clearing his mind during the massage was to concentrate on each part of his body as it was being worked on. He could name the muscles, tendons, ligaments, bones, vertebrae and disks. He could forget about Annie for fifty straight minutes.

Afterward, Mitch thanked Trina for her magic fingers and wrote her out a check.

"Dr. Langdon," she asked, "you live on National Avenue, right?"

"Yes, why?" Mitch said, as he tore out the check from his checkbook and handed it to her.

"Well, one of my clients knows someone who knows the lady who I think is moving next door to you."

"Yes, our neighbors to the west just moved to Chicago. I'd heard the house sold quickly."

Trina nodded. Mitch could tell she wanted to say more but was hesitant. "So, is it a nice family? Kids? What?" he asked.

"Well, if you really want to know… I'm not usually one to gossip, but I guess it's some woman and her teenaged daughter."

"No husband?"

"That's just it, the husband is dead."

"Trina, I'm not interested in dating, if that's where you're going with this."

"No, no, no, that's not why I'm telling you, Dr. Langdon. It's just that, I guess there's a little scandal involved."

"Scandal? First my son Luke tells me they're bohemians and now there's a scandal? What kind of scandal are we talking about here?"

"Like I said, I don't usually gossip, but it has something to do with the husband's death."

"What, did the wife kill him or something?"

"Well, I guess she was tried in court for his murder."

"You're serious. Whoa." Mitch blew air out of his mouth.

"I guess she was acquitted but a lot of people think it was an 'O.J.' thing."

Mitch shook his head. "Wow, I liked it better when I thought they were just bohemians."

"I knew I shouldn't have said anything. I just thought that if I didn't say anything and then you found out that I had heard something you might have asked why I didn't say anything. So there. I said it and that's it. It could be gossip fueled by jealousy. I guess the mother is a gorgeous blonde bombshell."

Mitch felt himself blush. This was the longest conversation he'd ever had with Trina. Usually it was just an exchange about the weather, the children, or weekend plans.

"I think that's why they're moving here, to put the scandal behind them," Trina explained.

"Well, thanks for the warning anyway. See you next week."

On the drive to the hospital, Mitch made a mental note about the new neighbors. What would Annie say? Annie would say don't listen to gossip. Annie would say, "Let's just see for ourselves." Even so, Mitch tucked the juicy tidbit away.

At the hospital, Mitch had to put on a phony veneer of crispness with the floor nurses. Two of them had crushes on him and practically threw themselves at him. Vanessa and Aubrey—a thirty-something divorcee and a twenty-something child. They showed their affection with baked goods and extra good care of his patients. Since his patients (and his stomach) benefited by the crushes, Mitch was willing to put up with them.

{*"The nurses always had crushes on Mitch," I tell Cecilia. "The mothers of his patients often did as well." This was something I had to learn to live with. Mitch was never Mr. Romantic but B.C. (before children) we did have our moments. I remember one winter we lit a fire in the living room fireplace and sat on the floor eating a dinner of cheese, crackers, grapes, and wine. After dinner, Mitch got frisky and starting removing my clothes. It was all so romantic until he removed his own underwear, dangled them on his big toe for a few seconds and then flung them into the fireplace. I laughed so hard it took me a while before I could catch my breath and get back in the mood. Mitch could be very funny and playful when he wanted to be.*

He could also be absentminded and forgetful. And sometimes he just wasn't precise. Ask him to pick up a jar of mayonnaise you needed for a recipe and he'd come back with salad dressing. Ask him to fix a leaky faucet in the kitchen and he'd tighten up the faucet in the bathroom. Ask him to pick up Tess from gymnastics and he would drive to her school and then wonder where in the world she was.

And then there was his work. He was gone a lot. A lot. I had to accept the crazy hours, interrupted dinners, canceled engagements, and middle-of-the-night phone calls, but I never liked it, and I never got used to it.

Like many couples, we often disagreed about money. I was freer with it. Early in our marriage I realized that Mitch might be the type of man who worried more about tomorrow than today. He wasn't a miser but during his bachelor years he'd grown accustomed to socking money away. I did have to nudge him to dig deeper into his pockets, but really, he is a most generous man. We agreed that we wouldn't spoil the kids. Both boys got "beaters" to drive when they turned sixteen. And Tess, she, she, well, I guess by the time Tess came along we did spoil her, but just a little.}

"Good morning, ladies," Mitch greeted. "How's Joshua Terrance doing?" It was one of the saddest cases of his life: a family dog dragged a two-week-old boy from his baby swing and almost mauled him to death. The little guy was hanging on by a thread. Mitch had checked online news archives and found that although rare there had been a few reported cases of family dogs attacking infants in baby swings. An animal behaviorist said that the back-and-forth motion could activate a dog's instinct to chase prey. Mitch had made a note to have his nurse post a warning on his bulletin board urging parents not to leave their pet alone with their baby in a swing.

He went into autopilot. When Mitch was Dr. Langdon, he was focused and intense, and the world beyond the hospital and his patients did not exist. Unlike many of his colleagues Mitch actually got along with the floor nurses. He didn't 'suck up,' but a crusty old professor had once told him that in the doctor/nurse relationship the doctor was ultimately in charge, but that a 'team attitude' went a long way. Many of his colleagues' problems with nurses stemmed from their arrogance, but for just as many it was a simple communications problem. Hey, nobody wanted to be called at three in the morning to be asked if a patient could be given Tylenol for a headache, but in Mitch's opinion and experience, the problem was easily solved simply by giving more specific orders and giving the nursing staff some wiggle room, some choices to get patients what they needed. For example, his professor, an internist, always wrote for Tylenol, a sleeper, an anti-emetic and a stool softener and would write standing orders *not* to be called for fever unless it was above a hundred and two. Mitch adopted this policy early on in his career, which resulted in excellent doc/nurse relationships, fewer stupid middle-of- the-night phone calls, and better patient care.

That's not to say Mitch didn't have to get nasty with nurses at times. He did. Once, when he was fairly new in his practice, an experienced night charge nurse called him at four a.m. to pronounce a five-year-old patient dead. When Mitch arrived at the hospital fifteen minutes later, he found the boy alive and well. The nurse was defensive and Mitch lit into her. Had she been embarrassed and apologetic and explained what had led her to the conclusion, he probably wouldn't have been so upset.

Even with specific orders, he would still get the infamous "patient has a headache" call in the middle of the night. "I ordered Tylenol PRN," he would explain, incredulously. "Yes, but it says PRN pain or fever, not headache. You need to come and write 'headache.'" Most times, it was a new inexperienced nurse who was afraid to make a decision on her own. He could muster up patience with the new ones. But if it was a nurse who should know better, he would bark, "You've got to be kidding! Is not a headache *painful?*"

And of course there was frustration with the nurse who called during the wee hours to "notify" him of every abnormal vital sign. Was she not able to look in the chart and see that this particular patient's blood pressure always ran low and that a reading of 99/50 mmHg in this child wasn't low regardless of what the nursing protocol said?

On the other hand, there were some nurses who were so good, so skilled, so caring that Mitch trusted their every word and action. Karin Fastola was just such a nurse. She never believed she was a "semi-doctor." She believed in nursing and her twenty-five years gave her a cool head when the crap hit the fan. When Karin called at three in the morning, Mitch listened. And the few times that Karin had not followed nursing protocol, her instincts had been dead on.

He left the hospital with a loaf of banana bread and a dinner invitation (which he gracefully declined). Jake Schmelter, a pediatric gastroenterologist with whom Mitch was friendly, stopped him in the parking lot and suggested a golf date. Mitch hadn't shot a ball in over a year. He left it open, saying he'd give Jake a call, but he knew he wouldn't.

❧

He'd left the kids at home sound asleep. When he returned around eleven, they were all in the kitchen eating breakfast with the TV blaring. To a stranger, they may have looked like normal American kids eating breakfast cereal in their cheery, sun-filled kitchen, but closer examination would reveal that they were eating cereal out of stainless steel mixing bowls, and there was nothing normal about that. "All the bowls are in the dishwasher," Tess explained.

Mitch turned off the TV, made himself a cup of instant coffee, and sat down at the table with the kids. He watched as Danny with his bird nest hair slurped the last of the milk from his humongous bowl. Obviously he had spilled chocolate milk on his white "anagram tease" tee shirt that read "I Vox Eels." (Mitch had no idea what this one meant but he guessed it had something to do with sex.) The tension shrouding the table led Mitch to believe the kids had been fighting. Luke was acting all innocent, as if he were just reading the paper but Mitch knew he was reading the paper *and* kicking his brother under the table. Tess was feigning cheerfulness, tapping her fingers on the table, chewing her LIFE cereal, all the while explaining to Piper, who sat dutifully at her feet, why her brothers were dirty, rotten pigs.

"See Piper, Danny has terrible hygiene. He should have been a cave man because he hates baths and loves to grow lots of gross hair all over his body. And he's grown into one of those obnoxious men who think women should do all the housework. It's not that I'm not proud to be a woman, Piper, I am. And you too should be glad you belong to the female of the species. But you might as well know, we girls do most of the work in life. Most of the important work anyway."

The boys ignored her. Mitch waited for an entry. With Tess a lot of it was about timing. But then again, timing often didn't matter at all. Tess was an absolute enigma to him. Just when he thought she wanted to be treated like one of the guys, she'd turn all girly on him. Then when he tried to treat her like a little lady, she'd cry chauvinism. It was exhausting.

"Piper, just know, that because—"

"What's going on here?" Mitch said.

Silence.

"Come on, guys, I know something's up. Luke?"

Danny snapped, "Why ask him? What makes you think his version is always the gospel truth?"

"He's the oldest, Danny, that's all."

"So, that doesn't mean he doesn't lie. Or that he doesn't spin everything to his advantage."

Luke didn't even look up from his shredded wheat.

"Okay, Dan, you tell me then."

Danny looked around the table. Tess gave him squinty eyes. Luke continued spooning cereal. Danny laughed a little. "I guess it will sound really stupid, you know, now, after the fact."

"I'm a pretty good judge of stupid. Give me a try."

"Well—" Tess threw in.

Mitch stopped her with a raised hand. "Danny's telling."

Danny said, "Okay. Well, little miss Girl Scout trespasses into my room this morning at like eight o'clock or something and starts opening and closing my dresser drawers. Opening and *slamming*, I should say."

"I was just—"

"Tess," Mitch said, "let him finish."

"She was just putting clothes away, is what she was doing, and I've told her a million times that I don't want her in my room, even to put my laundry away. Mrs. Cally puts my stuff on the counter in the laundry room and I get it when I need it. End of story."

"Tess, that is what we agreed to. There's no reason to go into Danny's room to put clothes away."

"That's not all, Dad," Danny said. "She switched around my drawers. I keep my socks in the top drawer, my undershirts in the second one down, underwear in the third down, etcetera, and she starts switching everything around."

Mitch looked to Tess for an explanation. "Dad, come on, his drawers are a wreck. They don't make sense. A person's drawers should be arranged in dressing order. Most *normal* people put on their underwear first, then an undershirt, then socks, and then clothes. So the top drawer should be your underwear, the next your undershirts, then your socks, then from there it could be shirts or pants—it doesn't really matter."

"Dad!" Danny said, "Can you believe this?"

Mitch had to stifle a smile. The funny thing was he actually agreed with Tess. They were of like minds when it came to personal organization; they were both lovers of order. Danny was more like his mother—a creative spirit who was comfortable with low levels of disorder. Tess said, "That's how you have your drawers, Dad."

"Yes, I know, but Dan isn't me, and if he wants to have his socks in the bottom drawer and his jeans in the top, that's up to him. Although, our way is more efficient, Dan, you must admit."

"I loath efficiency," Danny answered. "Efficiency is a product of economics which leads to the consumption of wealth which leads to greed and national shallow-ism."

"Tess, leave his clothes alone. Okay?"

"Ohhhhhhhh-kaaaaaaaaaay," Tess said.

"Okay then," Mitch said, getting up to make himself another cup of coffee.

"Hold it just a minute," Luke said. "We're not done here. Talk about spinning, Danny's not telling everything."

"Oh, yeah," Danny said, "she did the same thing to Luke's drawers, but Luke was glad and thanked her because he still needs a mommy to take care of him."

Luke shook his head. "What he left out was that he threw his shoe at Tess and hit Piper instead, who was bleeding from her ear."

"Danny!"

"The dog's fine. I checked her out. Sorreeeeey. You know I'm ornery when I'm sleeping."

"All right!" Mitch said, his voiced raised. "There will be no throwing things. No switching dresser drawers. Do not go into each other's bedrooms and do not touch each other's clothes. Do we all understand?"

"Yes, Daddy."

"Yes."

"Yeah."

Mitch decided he needed something—anything—from the basement. He made his escape. His foot hadn't even reached the first step when he heard Danny say (for shock value, Mitch was sure): "Did you guys know that the cremated remains of the average adult weighs nine pounds?"

"Gross!" screeched Tess.

"Now that was just mean," Luke said.

Mitch stood in front of his tool bench. It calmed him to look at the shiny tools arranged in perfect, logical order. Everything in its place. Everything with a definite purpose in life. A hammer knew its job; a screwdriver, its. They didn't compete. A hammer didn't dream of screwing (that didn't sound quite right…) and a screwdriver didn't wish it could pound. For Pete's sake, Mitch thought, I'm losing it. Wait a minute, what was this? An empty wine bottle? What the hell. *He* certainly hadn't left it there.

Bottle in hand, he shot up the stairs two at a time. The kids had scattered. Tess was at the kitchen sink washing the mixing bowls, and, in the adjacent river room Danny had planted himself on the couch and was watching a stupid cartoon. Luke was nowhere in sight.

"Dan," Mitch said, as he approached, "does this belong to you?"

"What? Huh? No. I hate wine. I don't even like grape juice."

"You're sure?"

"Dad, if I was going to drink wine, it wouldn't be that sissy sweet stuff Mom liked, and if I was going to drink wine in my own house, I would be smart enough to dispose properly of the bottle. I think you are interrogating the wrong son."

"I'm not interrogating, I'm just asking. This is disturbing to me, Dan." He looked around. "Where is your brother, anyway?"

"I don't know. I am not my brother's keeper, but I think I hear the shower running."

Mitch took the stairs (not two at a time this time, but one at a time; his heart rate was already up) and stood outside the master bathroom. When he and Annie had put on the master bedroom and bathroom addition five years ago, they intended it to be their own private sanctuary. There were two other showers in the house, but the master bath was the best room, the most luxurious room in the house, with a huge tub and a separate walk-in shower, and once completed, it was taken over by the entire family.

When Mitch heard the shower turn off, he knew that he had an unfair advantage over Luke, who would emerge exposed, with just a towel wrapped around his waist. That was the idea.

But Luke didn't come out. At least not before Mitch heard an enormous crash downstairs and had to leave his post. He found Tess standing on the kitchen counter and the shattered remains of a pottery bowl on the floor.

"It slipped out of my hand," she said.

"It's okay, honey," Mitch told her. He swept up the shards of clay while Tess sat whimpering on the counter, mourning the loss of one of her mother's favorite bowls.

By the time Mitch made it back upstairs, Luke was dressed and sitting in his room at his computer. Mitch's advantage was lost. As was the bottle: he must have set it down to clean up Tess's mess, and now he was approaching Luke without evidence. Bad move.

He entered without knocking. Luke was startled.

"Hey," he said.

"Hey," Mitch said. This was hard for him. After all, Luke had made it through four years of high school and one year at home without a lick of trouble. He sat down on Luke's bed and got right to it. "I found an empty wine bottle down the basement and I wondered if it was yours."

"Yes," Luke said.

This threw Mitch off. He wasn't even going to deny it?

"Dad, look, it's not a big deal. The other night I went down there for something, saw Mom's wine, and just felt like a swig. I had a swig, didn't like it and poured the rest down the drain. How could Mom drink that stuff? It's nearly like white grape juice," he added, puckering his face.

"Oh, okay. So this isn't a habit or anything?"

"Dad, you know I've never been interested in messing with my brain."

"I know, that's why I was shocked. Of course I thought of Danny first."

"Nope. I can't blame him. This one is mine."

"Okay, well then, I feel much better. You okay? Things going okay with Dr. Bonovia?"

"Dad, I'm fine. Seriously."

"Okay."

"Sorry I gave you a scare."

"That's okay," Mitch said, rising from Luke's bed. But he wasn't so sure. Annie would know what to do. Annie was a human lie detector when it came to the kids. *Annie, is he lying? Annie, what should I do?* Maybe it was time to inventory the wine cellar. And the liquor cabinet as well. Wait, they didn't have a liquor cabinet. Or did they?

Okay, now he was really losing it. He **really** didn't have a clue. This isn't what he bargained for—raising **three** kids and a dog, and caring for a big home and yard without a wi**fe**. He'd envisioned a life of serene bachelorhood, a life devoted to his **patients**. He'd always felt suited to the kind of busy but controlled life **that** would have been his as Dr. Mitchell Langdon, hopeless bachelor, consummate physician. But then Annie came along and changed everything. And then she died and changed everything again. How was he going to do this? He couldn't fail these children, but what if he did? How could he be sure Luke wasn't drinking? He was sure Tess was lying. And Danny, geez, the kid flitted from this to that. Now it was miniature houses, a project Mitch wanted to support but knew damn well would go by the wayside the minute something more interesting came along. Annie would say let him do it, let him express himself. Annie understood art. Mitch understood ability.

He wandered around upstairs rummaging through closets and drawers. Tess found him poking around in the hall linen closet.

"What are you looking for, Dad?" she asked.

"I'm not sure, honey."

Tess rolled her eyes and sauntered off to her room.

━━━━◦⬦◦━━━━

They had a family event that evening—dinner at Annie's folks' farm. It was his father-in-law's birthday. Mitch dreaded going, and not because he had a problem with his in-laws—they were wonderful people—but because Annie had been her dad's favorite and Gerald cried whenever he saw Mitch or the kids. And Annie's mother thought it was healthy for the children to talk about their beloved mother so she inserted Annie's name into every conversation. "Your mother loved this farm." "Carrot cake was Annie's favorite." "Your mom's with us in spirit, you know." They all endured their visits to the farm; they all breathed more easily on the way home.

"Can I ride Stella?" Tess asked Mitch from the back seat of the car on the way over.

"Really, honey?" Mitch asked. Tess had always been frightened of horses and ever since she'd fallen off of Flower, her grandmother's fat and fickle miniature horse, two years ago, she'd refused to ride.

"Uh-huh. Mom would want me to."

"What kind of shoes are you wearing?" Mitch asked, always thinking safety.

"Sneakers."

"Then you may ride Stella."

Dinner was delicious. Annie's mother, Maxine, was a fabulous cook. Country ham, scalloped potatoes, asparagus, and homemade apple and cherry pies. Gerald (the kids called him *Bumpa*) kept his eyes dry through the meal, but when it came time to blow out the candles in his birthday pie, he didn't have the wind and Tess had to do it for him, and then his eyes sprang a leak. He did brighten up though when Tess asked him if she could ride Stella after the pie and presents. Speaking of presents, Mitch had almost forgotten to get one—gifts were Annie's department, of course. What do you buy an eighty-year-old? He ended up taking Maxine's suggestion and bought Gerald the weather radio he wanted, but when Gerald opened it, Mitch felt silly. A weather radio. As if you couldn't just look out the window.

After dinner, they all headed outdoors, which was good, because Mitch needed some air. There'd been tension at the dinner table, but then again maybe it was just Mitch's paranoia. He couldn't really say that he felt judged when he was with his in-laws, but the evening was not without innuendo. Before dinner, Maxine took one look at Tess's fingernails and dragged her to the bathroom to put a scrub brush to them. And later, he spotted his sister-in-law, Maggy, picking a blob of earwax out of Tess's ear and clucking her tongue. At that very moment he wished he had a tee shirt that announced: "I'm trying my best." Maybe Danny could design an anagram tee for him—"Be My Stringy Tim" or "Best Trim Gym Yin" or even "Gib Symmetry Tim." *See, Annie, See?* He was trying to be in touch with his children. He was trying to appreciate Danny's quirkiness.

The worst moment of the evening came when Maggy cornered Mitch in the barn and insisted that Tess needed a bra.

"She's nine for goodness sakes," he said.

"Yes, but she's budding. Plus—"

"Yes?"

"Since Annie's been gone, she's turned into a tomboy, Mitch. She looks like a little urchin."

Mitch looked at his daughter. Maggy's husband, Jack, was helping Tess tighten the cinches on Stella's saddle, explaining to her in a patient voice all the steps required to saddle up the horse properly. She looked like any little girl—like any of his patients. Or did she? He watched as her Uncle Jack helped her with the bridling and finally as he boosted her into the saddle. Perched on the pretty palomino, Tess looked over and waved to Mitch, her face pulled into a nervous smile. Urchin? Tomboy? Well, she was dressed in her usual overalls, but her tee shirt was pink and her sneakers were pink and white. But Mitch knew that under her riding helmet was a tangle of curls and a cherry pie-smudged face. Still, she was a little kid. And little kids should play and have fun outdoors and not worry about getting dirty. He and Annie had liked that Tess wasn't a prima donna.

The 'urchin' comment rubbed him the wrong way, and afterward, Mitch could barely look at his sister-in-law. Oh, she meant well, of course, but Tess was Tess and he wasn't about to force femininity on her before she was ready. Now he just wanted to go home.

After a quick review about neck reigning, Jack led Tess and Stella out of the barn. Mitch followed on foot. Danny and Luke were already up on horses out in the arena, cantering too fast for Mitch's comfort. "No need to show off, guys," he called out, always the overly cautious. It did make Mitch feel good to see the boys with smiles on their faces. Mitch himself didn't ride anymore. These days his back could go out from a mere sneeze and he just couldn't risk an injury. Everything was already going to pot. Imagine what would happen if he was out of commission. No, even though Tess and the boys chided him, he stayed on the sidelines.

Tess did fine. Her nervous smile transformed into a broad, proud one that never left her face as she walked and then trotted Stella around the arena. Each time she passed Mitch, she said, "Dad! Look!" Each time Mitch said, "I see, I see. You're doing great!" On the third time around, he noticed that not only was her face smeared with cherry pie filling, the front of her tee shirt was as well. And her ponytail, hanging out from under her riding helmet, resembled Stella's tail more than Mitch cared to admit. Okay, so maybe he needed to pay a little more attention to his daughter's hygiene. If that was the worst of it, he wasn't doing so badly, was he?

Gerald came up and stood beside Mitch. "She looks good, doesn't she."

Mitch nodded.

"You need anything, Mitch?" Gerald asked awkwardly.

Mitch raised his soda can. "I'm fine, thanks."

"No," Gerald said, "I mean for the kids, or for you. Money? Babysitting? You got everything set for Luke for college? What am

I saying, of course you do. But, can we do anything? We want to do something. Mother and I just don't know what we can do since we can't drive anymore. That's the worst thing, not being able to drive."

"Thanks, Gerald, we're fine. The kids are fine. I'm fine. We're fine."

"You don't look fine. And I can say that because you know I love you like a son. Always have. Well, 'course, first time I laid eyes on you I thought you were too damn old for my daughter. But you won me over."

"What? I look tired?" Mitch opened his eyes wider. "Well, I am tired. But I've been tired since the day I started med school, so that's nothing new."

"No, that's not it. It's that, well, there's no life in your face, Mitch. All the joy's gone out of your face." Gerald teared up, patted Mitch on the back, and walked away. Mitch made his own escape, wandering into the pasture. Dusk was setting in and the sky was almost a teal blue. A couple of horses—Mitch couldn't remember their names—neighed as he approached, jealous that their buddies were getting attention and they weren't. He and Annie had spent a lot of time out here when they were first married. The animals and the land were things they both could enjoy.

Mitch stroked the mane of the old paint he used to ride, *Edwin*, that was his name. Out of nowhere, the tears came. The horses looked at him funny when the tears progressed to sobs. Flower, the fat little miniature horse nuzzled his hip. He hadn't cried in months. He was afraid if he got started he wouldn't be able to stop. (There was a neurological disorder called *pseudobulbar affect* where people suffered from episodes of uncontrollable laughing or crying.) It felt good to cry. Well, not good exactly. No, it did feel good. He wiped his eyes and nose with the end of his Polo shirt. He inhaled deeply and wondered who could take Tess shopping for a bra because it certainly wasn't going to be him.

He sat down in the grass; the rain-thirsty blades pricked his buttocks like needles right through his Dockers. Oh yes, the face was the mirror to the soul and, according to his father-in-law, his face proclaimed his misery to the world. God, he should have gone first. Why had he been granted a second chance but not Annie?

{"Oh, Cecilia," I say, looking down at Mitch sitting in the grass. "His heart is broken! How can I help him?" She pats my shoulder. My poor husband. He's so sweet and sensitive, but so locked up inside. I was the only one who could get him to open up. Did I mention that he made a cup of coffee for me every morning and brought it up to me in bed? He started this when Luke was born and then just never stopped. It was the best, most unhurried, intimate time of our day. Mitch would sit at the edge of the bed and we would talk in hushed voices about the kids and our day. I would sip my coffee and wonder what I ever did to deserve such a beautiful man.}

A cardinal lit on a tree branch directly above Mitch's head; a sharp red contrast against the background of thick green. His brush with death had provided such a contrast.

If his heart was a house, then his cardiac arrest had been an electrical problem, not a plumbing problem. Simply put, Mitch had gone into cardiac arrest because his heart's electrical conduction system had gone out of whack. Instead of contracting, those darned ventricles had started to quiver. If it wasn't for Dean Armour, Sr. and Dean Armour, Jr. all those years ago, there would be no Mitchell Langdon today. Those two brave men had ministered to him and performed CPR until the paramedics could shock his heart with a defibrillator and restore a regular rhythm.

You couldn't even say Mitch was lucky; he was beyond lucky. Most—estimates run between seventy and ninety percent—of ventricular fibrillation victims die before reaching the hospital. Mitch looked into the statistics regarding survival rates from out-of-hospital cardiac arrests. One study showed that only fourteen percents of victims who had received resuscitation by ambulance staff survived as far as admission to the hospital. Of those fourteen percent, almost sixty percent died during admission, usually within twenty-four hours. Of those who survived (seven percent of those who had been resuscitated by ambulance staff) ninety-seven and a half percent suffered a mild to moderate neurological disability and two percent suffered a major neurological disability. That meant Mitch fell into that lucky remaining half a percent of people who walked away with complete recovery.

Annie had called him her "Lazarus." If she only knew how right she had been. But there was something that had always bothered Mitch about those five minutes when he was clinically "dead." Where did he go? And if he really died then why didn't he have one of those "near death experiences" he had read and heard about, where people fly through a tunnel, see a bright light, and hear a deafening noise? All he saw and heard was…nothing. When it happened, he had been driving along, thoughts off somewhere else, when everything went black. No warning, nothing. Just driving and then just black. He had been preparing to turn onto a side street so at least he had slowed down, which turned out to be a good thing: he hit the other driver's car going only about ten miles an hour. Thank God the woman and her three-year-old daughter were not hurt.

But of course Mitch didn't know any of this until later. He wasn't even aware that he had died. He thought he had just blinked. The next thing he knew he woke up in an ambulance surrounded by concerned but amazed faces. He had not only survived, he had come through with no loss of brain function. A simple implantable pacemaker/defibrillator and he was good as new. Or was he? Inside he was alarmed and distressed. Did the fact that he hadn't seen or felt what others at the brink of death had seen and felt mean that he was unworthy?

Four years ago he'd had a patient, a six-year-old girl, who'd suffered a severe asthma attack at home that led to a cardiopulmonary arrest. Her babysitter performed CPR until the ambulance arrived and the paramedic injected her with epinephrine to restore her breathing. Stephanie made a full recovery and later told Mitch about the experience. She remembered waking up and not being able to breathe. The next thing she knew she was floating out of her body and up into the corner of her bedroom. She watched as her babysitter bound into the room and screamed. When the babysitter pulled the covers out of the way, Stephanie could see her own body lying motionless on her bed and turning blue from lack of oxygen. It didn't scare her, but something else upset her: from her ceiling vantage point she could see all the dust that had accumulated in her bedroom light fixture and wondered if the dust had triggered the asthma attack. She also noticed four dead spiders, one big one and three little ones, and a dead wasp in the flat bowl of the light fixture, but didn't think much about it until later. Next there was a loud whooshing sound in her ears and as the paramedics arrived she floated up and out of the room. She said she melted through the roof and found herself swirling in a dark tunnel. She saw a pinpoint of light at the end of the tunnel and was drawn to it. The pinpoint of light increased until it embraced and engulfed her and the light became the landscape—the flowers and trees and then people seemed all to be made of light. And then there was a glowing lady who approached her and bent down to Stephanie and smiled at her. When the "glowing lady" touched her hand Stephanie felt her spirit being sucked back into her body.

Mitch was intrigued by Stephanie's story but wondered if it wasn't the result of a dying brain starved of oxygen. A phone call from Stephanie's mother made him a believer. The little girl's mom was all out of breath as she relayed the story: Stephanie had proof that she had flown out of her body. When she returned home from the hospital she insisted that her father get on a chair and remove the ceiling light fixture in her bedroom. Sure enough there were four dead spiders, one big one and three little ones, and a dead wasp positioned in the ceiling light, just exactly as she described. Stephanie also told her folks that one of the paramedics was a short bald man who had "a funny red mark" on the back of his neck that she could see as he bent over her body. Stephanie had stopped breathing and was unconscious by the time the paramedics had reached her, so there would have been no way to know this. Stephanie's mom confirmed this: the paramedic did have a large red birthmark—a "port-wine stain"—on the back of his neck.

After that, Mitch studied NDEs (near death experiences), getting his hand on all the books he could. He wanted to ask some of his colleagues if they had patients who had experienced NDEs but something held him back: the medical community often dismissed or scoffed at stories of near death experiences. But what he read was fascinating! The stories—especially the children's stories—were so similar in detail. And one thing he knew for sure—children don't lie. Of course they lie about doing their homework and cleaning their room, but they don't lie about life and death.

So then he wondered, why hadn't he had an NDE? He'd read that only a small percentage of persons who are clinically dead have memories of NDEs. One researcher felt that powerful drugs given to patients before or after the NDE could dull the memory of the experience.

Edwin brought Mitch back to reality with a forlorn whinny. The sky grew dark in the east; the air took on a greenish tint reminding Mitch of an oil painting that had hung in his great-grandmother's dining room. How do such thoughts come into one's head? He hadn't remembered that painting in fifty years. He lay back in the stiff dry grass and closed his eyes while his pacemaker paced and his defibrillator ticked, waiting patiently for the day it would have to shock his heart back to life.

⚜

On Monday afternoon, Mitch had an appointment with Dr. Burns, Tess's counselor. Of course he was late. Miranda Burns towered over most people, but with Mitch, she stood neck to neck. Over the years, Mitch had referred many patients to Miranda and the feedback from the parents was always positive, so when it came time for Tess to talk to someone, he thought of Miranda immediately.

Truth be told, she scared him a little. Her stature made her imposing, and although she was only in her forties, she possessed the mannerisms of a grandmother you didn't dare cross, and her handshake was firmer than it should be. Mitch took the seat she offered—the swivel chair Tess so loved—and folded his hands in his lap. Why did he feel as if he had been summoned to the principal's office? As Miranda took her seat behind her desk Mitch observed (and admired) the orderliness of the desk. No pile of pens and pads, compliments of the drug reps, on her desk. No stacks of literature and reprints to get through. His desk *used* to look like this.

"Dr. Langdon—" Miranda began.

"*Mitch*, please." Mitch felt at a disadvantage sitting in the swivel chair.

"Mitch. Well, you know I think Tess is a delightful child and I think she is coming along just fine."

"But…"

"But I'm concerned about the lying. It seems to have increased since our last meeting. What are you seeing?"

Mitch exhaled. "Yes, well, not big rotten lies, but little ones. They are getting more frequent, though. Why do you think she feels the need to lie?"

"Well, children lie for so many reasons: to protect themselves from pain, to save face, to avoid getting caught, to get someone they dislike into trouble, to get something they want but can't otherwise get. They lie so as not to hurt someone's feelings or to get out of doing something they don't want to do. Often children feel powerless and lying gives them control to manipulate their world. Sometimes it's to get attention, and sometimes it's simply because they can't help it, as in pathological lying."

"Tess is not a pathological liar."

"I agree. I think she's lying for attention. She's starving for attention, Mitch. A year has gone by since your wife died and people aren't as attentive as they used to be. People assume that families move on. With Tess it's all about drama. Her world is falling apart. First she lost her mom, now Julianna, and soon Luke. Her lying is a cry for help."

Mitch pinched the bridge of his nose. "What in the world is she telling you?"

"Nothing too terrible," she said, and laughed. "But according to Tess she's running the entire household, cleaning, cooking, gardening, doing all the laundry, ironing, bill-paying, and going unappreciated each and every day."

"Miranda, I assure you—"

"What are her set chores?"

"Almost nothing. She makes her bed when she feels like it. She sorts socks sometimes. She does like to be in the kitchen. I think she pretends to be her mother. She talks to our dog while she sweeps and does dishes. Sometimes she makes soup. That is the extent of her cooking, other than toast."

"I think the best way to handle this is through a backdoor approach. Let's not call her on it. Let's start paying more attention to her and see if it doesn't go away on its own. I think it will. Also, I think she needs some females in her life and I'm sorry but Mrs. Cally, a.k.a. Calpurnia just isn't going to cut it. Is she still spending time with her aunt?"

"Yes, every Friday."

"Good. See if you can expose her to other women—babysitters, camp counselors, church ladies, neighbors. She says she doesn't have playmates over anymore."

Mitch shifted in the chair. "Miranda, I'm trying my best. It's a lot to juggle. I—"

"I can't even imagine," Miranda said, leaning in. "Are you seeing someone?"

Mitch thought she meant romantically and raised an eyebrow.

"I mean professionally, Dr. Langdon."

Mitch shook his head, ready for a lecture. But Miranda sat quietly while he fidgeted.

"We doctors never practice what we preach, do we?" she said. "It could help, Mitch. You yourself said it's a lot to juggle. But listen, Tess wants more details about her mother's death and I think she's ready for them. I think it will help her. Can you talk to her?"

"Unfortunately, she knows everything I know."

"She's not convinced of that. Would you be opposed to bringing the whole family in for a session? I know it would be painful but I think it would help Tess."

"Oh, I don't know. I don't know if I could put them through that. They've been through so much."

"Think about it, okay?"

Mitch stood up to go. He didn't feel like shaking this giant woman's hand, but she offered it and he took it. Suddenly her hand was on his shoulder and she was saying, "I lost my husband two years ago and the most surprising thing about grief to me was that it felt so much like fear."

Mitch had to run to his car before the giant lady saw him cry.

Chapter Sixteen

Lingering

*C*ECILIA SAYS *I must linger in my "Life Review" a bit longer. She guides me to delve deeper to see what it has to teach me. I wish I could accurately describe what a life review is like. Some people who have had near death experiences report that it really is like your life flashing before your eyes, but it's so much more than that. Oh, how can I explain it? You watch scenes of your life, yes, but sometimes you also relive the scenes, so I guess the life review is both self-witnessing and interactive. Sometimes you're the viewer and sometimes you're the player—depending on what lesson you need to learn.*

"What have you learned?" Cecilia asks me, after an especially intense review of a scene from college that I would have rather forgotten. Freshman year, I had forced my roommate, Lila, to attend a frat party with me. She was a shy, bookish girl, and a frat party held no appeal whatsoever. She came reluctantly. We got separated in the swarming crowd and when I couldn't find her I thought maybe she had left, so I went off to another party, leaving her stranded. Later, she was so angry with me she requested and was permitted a dorm room transfer. I had always thought she over-reacted. Until my life review, that is. That's when I saw that two big frat

151

boys at the party had been harassing her and scaring the heck out of her. And then I was her! (Sometimes in the life review, you become the person you hurt—you literally wear their shoes!) Goodness, it was terrifying! The brutes backed me up against a wall and stuck their hands up my skirt. I ended up in tears and had to call the university security to come and give me a ride home, which is what poor Lila had to do.

"Well?" Cecilia asks gently.

"I see now that the Golden Rule isn't just a saying, it's really how things are! Do unto others because you will experience it as done unto you."

I've come to learn that every single thing you do in life—every thought, every feeling, every action—is recorded in eternity. Everything you do in life becomes yours. And we receive back everything we have given out, just exactly as we gave it. The good and the bad. Your whole life is there in your review to evaluate.

"Dear Annie," Cecilia says, "the essential thing to learn is that you are the very person you hurt in life and you are the very person you help."

"Yes," I say.

"You are discovering your authentic self. This is your personal revelation."

It's interesting, but in the life review, you don't feel judged. (Cecilia tells me: "Love heals; judgment kills.") Here, even in your life review you feel only unconditional love. And empathy. Deep empathy. A literal 'walk-in-someone-else's-shoes' empathy. You have almost a telepathic understanding of others' thoughts and feelings; it's as if all earthly filters are removed and you understand completely that we truly are all connected!

"Now," Cecilia says, "let's look at how four simple, kind words that came out of your mouth changed someone's life."

I can't wait!

Some things I'm learning up here about down there: No two people ever see the very same rainbow even if they are standing side by side. This is because rainbows are formed when light enters a water droplet and two people will see a different set of raindrops when looking at a rainbow.

Most people think that what we see is what our eyes see and report back to our brain. But there are many tricks your eyes perform in looking at the world. Your brain adds to the report it gets from your eyes to complete an image. So the brain actually makes things up. Our eyes actually discard a lot of what we see, leaving it to the brain to fill in additional information in its own ways. This process explains optical illusions.

And memories are a peculiar thing. They are so precious but rarely are they one hundred percent accurate because, again, our brains often have to fill in the gaps. When a person stores a memory, she attaches it to an emotion and then files it in a 'concept' area in the brain. It's our emotional memories that mark the mind. Recollections without an emotion attached are unrecognizable—otherwise we would store memories of every time we brushed our teeth or took a drink of water.

Your hopes and memories are a foreshadowing of a Heaven that is time-free. Remember, every thought, action, word, and event exists in Heaven—in active form—where we can see them, review them, and learn from them.

Did you know that memories are not stored in your brain? This is going to sound outlandish, but humor me here for just a moment. Haven't you ever wondered how your brain can process and store every thought and experience you've ever had? There just couldn't be enough room! Some important brain scientists from around the world agree that the human brain would need a processing speed of over 1000 bits per second to store a lifetime of memories. And when you die your brain dies so haven't you ever wondered how you brought your love and memories with you to Heaven? Well, that's because memories are "extra-cerebral," residing outside of the brain. So is consciousness. A Dutch cardiologist named Pim van Lommel has been instrumental in this research. It turns out that our brains are more like antennas than computers (Luke has been reading about this), more like a receiver and transmitter that tunes into specific electromagnetic waves and converts them to our reality. Consciousness and memories are stored in an electromagnetic field that surrounds us all and it's our own unique

DNA that allows us to tap into it. Oh, but I might be giving away too much here. You can research this yourself if you're interested.

I never realized how imprisoned we are on earth by time. We have fears because we have tomorrows and we have regrets because we have yesterdays. But the good news is this: since Heaven includes all todays, tomorrows and yesterdays in its living present, God can redeem mistakes that were made in earthly time. Think about that! That is why God's forgiveness is so awesome! Any sin, mistake, missed opportunity, tragedy, can be reversed in eternity! When God forgives our sins he obliterates them; they cease to be.

Prayer is timeless, too. This is why prayer is so powerful—it can change the past, the present, and the future. We are always praying for something in the future—but don't forget to pray for the past, too. God is not bound by time so He can answer your prayers anywhere and anywhen.

Oh, my dears, it seems that in life we are on an unfamiliar road leading to an unknown destination. But we have traveled the road already—in the other direction. We walked this same path to get to our earthly life, and now we travel it to return home. In your heart of hearts you know that everything visible emanates from the invisible. On earth, our existence can be summarized by two desires: a yearning to explore the world and a longing to go home. Not unlike a child who wants to play and explore out of doors until it gets dark and then wants to go inside where it's safe and warm. We want adventure topped off with a warm bed and a mother singing a lullaby. We want to branch out, but we want to remain rooted. We want to fly but only if there's a safe place to land. Only Heaven can satisfy us for it is truly home, a home to explore for all of eternity.

So, prayer touches eternity. So do dreams, and meditation, and death, and artistic creation. And—you're not going to believe this: jumping. Yes, jumping! Think about it—jumping is levitating. Jumping is actually a very miraculous thing because by sheer will power a person can defy physical gravity and rise into thin air. It's no accident that when we are happy and excited we jump for joy. For fractions of a second we are weightless and free and this is a hint of Heaven. I, for one, never thought about jumping. Go ahead, right now. Stop what you are doing and jump. Come on, you know you want to! Taste a bit of Heaven! Jump!

Chapter Seventeen

Here Come the Hippies

{*When Danny was about six he became preoccupied with death. Mitch's dad and a favorite neighbor had both died in the same week and so death and all its accompaniments besieged us. Of course Danny had questions about Heaven. Not sure where to begin, I turned the question back on him. "What do you think Heaven is?" "It's like a fancy hotel where you can jump on the bed and get a mint on your pillow," he said, with a silly grin. Luke overheard us and said, "You dork, that's not right. Heaven is where your soul starts and ends."*

We really should listen better to the children.

Don't be afraid about crossing over. I say that, but of course you will be afraid, just as a baby cries when crossing over from the warm and cozy world of his mother's womb to the cold and capacious world of physical life. It's frightening. But not wanting to die is like not wanting to be born. What kind of life would it be if we lived our entire existence in our mother's womb? Of course we must be born, and of course we must die. Be not afraid! Everything will come to good!}

*D*ANNY WAS STUCK with his sister for the rest of Saturday afternoon, which basically sucked. When Tess heard the new neighbors were arriving today she set her alarm for six o'clock and had been riding her bike all morning. Luke and Mitch had set aside the morning for cleaning up the boat and getting her "river-worthy." Danny had been appointed to baby-sit Tess, which was not hard work per se, but was definitely hard on the ears. *Dang*, could she chatter. And about absolutely nothing. Danny tried to be patient but the kid kept getting in the way. When Mathis arrived around noon, Danny roasted hotdogs on forks over the kitchen stove and served Tess and Mathis lunch on the screened porch.

Tess had it bad for Mathis. "I just love the color of your skin, Mathis," she said, her mouth full of food.

"Huh?" Mathis asked.

Tess swallowed and repeated her statement.

"Oh. Thanks."

"How'd you get that nice color, anyway?"

"Tess!" Danny said.

"It's cool, man," Mathis told Danny. "My mom is black and my dad is white. Mix the two and you get café mocha."

"Uh-uh," Tess said. "Black and white make gray."

"Eat your hot dog, Tess," Danny said. "And wipe your mouth. You have ketchup all over your face."

"So if I marry a black man my babies will be your color?"

"Maybe."

"Then I'm going to. Mathis, have you ever read the book *To Kill a Mockingbird* by Harper Lee?"

"Tess, can't you just shut up and eat?" Danny said.

"No, I can't. I like to eat while I talk. I am a civilized human being. I can multi-task."

"I read it, Tess. We read it in English sophomore year."

"Do you have a Boo Radley?" Tess asked.

Mathis swallowed his hot dog while considering the question. Danny was interested in how his friend would respond. He knew that

Mathis didn't mind Tess; he'd told Danny that he thought she was a cool little kid. Mathis had only one sibling and he was nine years older. "Do you mean," he asked, "do I know someone spooky?"

"No, not that. We all have that. I mean do you have someone you *thought* was spooky but who actually turned out to be your angel?"

Danny almost choked on his bun. He knew Tess had a high I.Q., even though she often mixed up words, but sometimes she still could surprise him. At nine she was beyond him in many ways. He and Mathis exchanged raised eyebrows.

"Hmmm," Mathis said. "That's a hard one. Maybe I just haven't had my Boo Radley moment yet, but when I do, I will let you know."

"Mathis, do you sing?"

"Enough questions, Squirt," Danny said as he collected the plates.

"That's *Scout* to you," Tess said.

Out in the garage, Danny and Mathis had four new house fronts laid out on card tables. The miniature house front business was actually taking off—almost everyone in the neighborhood had ordered one. There was even a waiting list. "You can glue some peat moss on this one to simulate the bushes near the front porch," Danny instructed Tess, showing her a photo of the real home. Then he turned on the CD player and turned up Pink Floyd's *The Wall* good and loud.

Mathis handed out sticks of gum and the three of them fell into a routine. Danny was glad to see that Tess was concentrating on her work because at least it kept her quiet. Poor kid. He did feel bad for her sometimes; he wasn't heartless after all. Some days she seemed fine and other days, well, other days, he would find her hiding in her closet wearing her mother's clothing, shoes, and jewelry. She started "taking" her mom's things shortly after Annie died and hiding them in the big walk-in closet in her room. Once, in a weak moment, she shared her treasures with Danny and it just about tore his heart out. Tess had squirreled away Annie's make-up bag, her wallet and an old check register, her good jewelry, her foreign coin collection, the big hat box full of cards that the kids and Mitch had given her over the years, her reading glasses, her manicure kit, various high-heeled shoes, and the pale pink bridesmaid dress Annie had worn in her sister's wedding. Tess had even saved scrap paper and notes that contained Annie's handwriting.

"What's all this?" Danny had asked gently.

"Please don't tell Daddy," Tess whispered. "It's just so I won't forget her."

Danny had just nodded and gave her a loose hug. Now Tess was singing along with Pink Floyd's Roger Waters to *Brain Damage*. It was comical to see and hear this tiny little blonde girl singing, "*The lunatic is in the hall.*" Danny watched her as she concentrated on the gluing, her little pink tongue peeking out of the corner of her mouth. *Dang,* she looked like their mom!

Danny got a call on his cell phone from his buddy Petey so at first he didn't notice when the bright orange VW van pulled up next door followed by huge moving van. When he heard a car door slam shut, he peeked through the pine trees that separated the two properties. He covered the mouthpiece of his phone and called to his sister, "Don't look now, but the new neighbors are here."

Tess jumped out of her seat, knocking over the chair but thank goodness not the card table. She exhaled in relief and then took a peek at the vehicles. At the sight of the bright orange van she scrunched up her nose in disgust. "What are they, hippies?" she said out loud. But the people themselves were nowhere in sight.

Danny and Mathis both laughed. "Go find out, why don't you," Danny urged, eager to get rid of her.

"Not right now," Tess said, going back to right her over-turned chair. "Maybe later."

Later came in just five minutes when Tess brushed her hands off on the back of her overalls and said with phony spontaneity, "I think I'll go ride my bike for a while."

"Good idea," said Danny. Now he could re-do the amateur job she'd done with the peat moss while the 'bricks' (made from tiny rectangles of painted balsa wood) dried. They were working on Mr. Abbey's fiftieth anniversary present for Mrs. Abbey. The Abbeys lived three doors down from the Langdons in a huge red brick home designed by Jesse Barloga, a well-known Rockford architect, and Danny thought this was the house front that would make him famous.

While the boys waited for paint and glue to dry, they got their guitars out and jammed in the garage. Their band, *Slime Mold*, together since freshman year, had been forced to take periodic hiatuses when band members got girlfriends. This last hiatus had been an extended one and Danny, the guitarist, was ready to get back to his music. Although now with his job at Village Green and the house-front business, he probably didn't have time either.

You see, he'd found that keeping busy was the secret. That's where he and Luke were different: Luke was too reflective; he went too deep. That kind of thinking would eat you alive. You gotta coast, skim the top, stay cool. Even numb. He and Mathis were rarely without something to do—what with their jobs, their music, their art, and their filmmaking. They were just about finished with their new "mockumentary" (a term coined for the work of genius Christopher Guest and his films: *This Is Spinal Tap and Best In Show*). This one was a satirical commentary on the state of high school in the twenty-first century. He called this film "Split Infinity." It depicted the social, economic, and diversity splits in their high school as well as two of the public high schools in town. The film before that was called "The Parts of a Sentence" and it chronicled the eighty hours of community service two friends of his were ordered to perform after getting caught pouring Joy dishwashing liquid into a downtown water fountain as part of a senior prank. (The ensuing bubbles made the front page of the newspaper, costing the city one thousand dollars to repair the fountain.) Danny filmed the boys as they delivered meals to senior citizens and shut-ins. Mathis interviewed the boys and the meal recipients. They didn't mean for it to turn out hilarious at the expense of the old folks—they loved old folks—but it did.

The secret was not to think about his mother at all. The secret was to self-protect. That was of supreme importance. Luke didn't know how, Tess didn't know how, and certainly Mitch didn't know how. But Danny did. It was a skill anyone could learn. It started with your face: put on the right face on the outside and soon your inner self follows suit. Danny was working up the nerve to ask his dad if he could quit the counseling. It wasn't doing any good. He was on his third professional now and he was no better than when he started. Besides, wasn't the purpose of counseling to help people deal with the truth? Danny had dealt with the truth—by burying it. And if it were up to him it would never be unearthed.

{"I'm thrilled, Cecilia, that Danny has this new interest, these miniature house fronts, but he tires of these kinds of projects quickly. I'm afraid that this will be yet another endeavor he takes on and then abandons, resulting in Mitch's aggravation once again." Mitch doesn't understand Danny. I am the one who understands Danny. What if I'm the only person in the world who understands him? Then what, I wonder.}

"Danny! Danny!" Tess called, all out of breath. She skidded her bike to a burning rubber stop in the driveway.

"What?" Danny said, exasperated in advance.

"Good news!"

"You're going to summer camp for the rest of your natural life?"

"That's mean! No, no, no! The new neighbors have two cats! One's a big fat white one, an angora, called Gloves, and the other one I haven't seen yet but she said it was a little grey kitten named Mittens. A kitten, Danny!"

"That's great, Tess," Mathis said. "But tell us about the people. Any good looking babes?"

"Well, I don't know your type, Mathis, but if it's blonde, skinny, and big boobs, then you're in luck."

"Tess!"

"What? She's really cute! They're both cute!"

Danny and Mathis exchanged loopy grins. "There are *two* of them?" Danny asked.

"Well, one of them's the mom, but she looks really, really young."

"And the other one?"

"The other one is…you're not going to believe this! The other one is Lee. *Lee Harper!*"

Danny looked at Mathis to see if he got it. Mathis did get it because he asked Tess, "You mean *To Kill a Mockingbird* author Harper Lee, only backward?"

"Yes! The book is her mother's favorite, too. And Lee said that when her mom married her dad who had the last name of Harper she told him that if they ever had a girl, she was going to name her Lee. They had two boys first and then Lee came. The brothers are older and live out of town. Just Lee and her mom are moving in and the grandmother is coming later." Tess lowered her voice to a whisper and said, "The dad died. Isn't that sad?"

Danny nodded. "Yeah, sad. Nice detective work, Squirt. Lee told you all this?"

"Of course."

"Lee, who you think is really cute. How old is she, anyway?" Mathis asked.

"Seventeen. She's going to Boylan when school starts."

"Lucky her," Danny said.

"Too bad you won't be able to car pool," Tess said. "Hey, Danny, can I have a lemonade stand?"

"Look around. There's nobody about. You won't have any customers."

"*Duh*. The new neighbors!"

"Better idea: go make a pitcher and bring it over."

"That's a wonderful idea! Sometimes you do come up with wonderful ideas! Could you help me?"

"Sure, get a pitcher, open up the little cup of lemonade mix, pour it in, add water, and stir. There, I helped you."

"Ohhhhhh!" Tess said and dropped her bike to the ground. "Luke would help."

"Yeah? Then go get Luke."

Danny got tired of working on the houses and he and Mathis messed around on their guitars again. Danny had a new song fleshed out. He called it "Dress Warmly." He strummed the melody for Mathis so he could pick up a base line and then he sang in his "folk" voice: *"She told him to dress warmly / the wind was out today / he said okay-fine-sure-all-right / then ran out hatless anyway."*

Mathis was a fast learner. Danny moved on to the chorus: *"Why don't we listen / when we're loved? / We want so to be brave / You never heed my call of love / you always misbehave. / But it's cool; it's okay / I love you any—"*

Suddenly Luke was there. Listening. With a disgusted look on his face. "Where's Tess?" he said.

"She brought lemonade over to the new neighbors."

"Oh, so they're here, huh?"

"Yeah, and too bad. Tess said they are weeeir-errrrd. Two butt-ugly women and a dead husband."

"There goes the neighborhood," Luke said. "Glad I'll be getting out of here soon. Hey, go get Tess. Dad wants us all on the boat for the maiden voyage."

"What?" Danny said, pulling the guitar strap over his head and placing his guitar in the stand. "I don't want anything to do with that boat."

"He's not going to take 'no' for an answer."

"*Dang!*" Danny said, stomping his feet. Stupid boat. Why'd his dad have to go and buy a new boat? Danny wasn't interested in fishing or water-skiing. He wasn't that into water. He'd rather be making his movies or playing his guitar.

"Mathis can come too. Go get Tess."

"You go get her."

Talk about humiliating: Danny sitting on his daddy's boat wearing a banana yellow life vest, his face pinched into a scowl. Only kids under thirteen were required by state law to wear a life jacket, but after last summer, Mitch had made his own law: everyone on *his* boat wore a life vest, even Mitch. *So force me out on your boat against my will and then force me to look like a two-year-old who can't swim. Dang!!*

Mathis, in an identical life vest, seemed to be enjoying himself. Danny wanted to slap that happy look off his best friend's face. Didn't he realize how hard this was for him? He closed his eyes, as water sprayed his face. He felt queasy. What was this? Had he suddenly inherited his mother's fear of water? Was this his punishment? So be it.

He turned around to look at Luke, up on skis. Tess was spotting. How could Luke even *think* about skiing? What a traitor. Luke was smiling and waving to Tess. Why? To demonstrate his awesome talent—he could ski with one hand! Whoopee. Who cared about skiing? Who cared that Danny had tried and tried and tried and never could get up. What was wrong with him? And to add salt to the wound, Mitch had promised Tess that this was the year, this was the year she would water ski!

"How about it, Dan?" Mitch shouted over the motor and the wind. "You want to give it a try?"

"Pass," Danny said.

"Me, Daddy, me!" Tess screamed, jumping up and down. "I'm ready and you promised!"

So there it was. His scrawny little sister could ski. There'd be no living with her now. Danny lowered the visor on his baseball cap and sunk deeper into the leather seat. Mathis was next. Danny wished he could beam himself home. Wouldn't that be cool to be able to vanish into thin air! Wouldn't it come in handy at times like this? So was this how it was going to be forevermore? Would he always come in last? Oh no! Oh, God, no! He was starting to blubber. *Dang!* He spotted his dad's sunglasses. He grabbed them and put them on. There, he was pretty sure no one saw the tears.

{*"Poor Danny! I don't want him to be afraid of the water. I wouldn't wish that fear on anyone," I tell Cecilia. I was always glad my kids were fish. Maybe Mitch should just take Danny out on the boat one day, just the two of them. I used to be the one to push the two of them together. I'd suggest to Mitch to take Danny to a concert or a movie. They did have an annual tradition of going to the Beloit Film Festival and making the Fourth of July fireworks run. They love each other, I know. It's just that they are so different. I was the one that made them try harder.}*

Driving the boat, Luke was in his glory. Danny watched him from behind the sunglasses. Luke's bone structure gave him a look of imperialism, a smug look Danny so many times wanted to wipe off his face. Things would be a lot better when Luke was out of the picture, away at school growing his brain. Without Luke around as a measuring stick, maybe Danny wouldn't always come up short. Maybe he and his Dad could be "buds." Maybe Danny would take an interest in "having a catch" and take a liking to boating. In Luke's absence maybe Tess would begin to dote on him.

Luke was no fun. He was, in fact, anti-fun. One time, Mathis and Danny were in the kitchen enjoying their favorite unhealthy fast-food meal of double cheeseburgers and fries, when Mathis pulled out of his French fry carton the longest fry they had ever seen. It had to be over eight inches long! While Danny went to find a ruler and Mathis went to fetch the Guinness Book of World Records, Luke came into the kitchen and ate the fry. A French fry hadn't touched his lips in years. "It was just sitting there," was his only explanation.

If only his dad knew the real Luke. Mr. Perfect wasn't really so perfect. It was all a ruse, subterfuge. Oh, sure, on the outside Luke looked the part of Wally Cleaver—he had the build and the grades and the polite demeanor. But Danny knew that inside he was a coward. He was a person who didn't think twice about stealing his brother's girlfriend right out from under his nose. He was a person who got that same girl, on her eighteenth birthday, to chug more vodka, rum, and Kahlua than her petite body could handle. By the time Ashley passed out at Michelle Goodman's house, Luke had already booked. Good thing Michelle and another friend were smart enough to throw Ashley's ass in the car and take her to the ER. What a birthday present—getting ditched by your date and having your stomach pumped. And because

Ashley was eighteen, the hospital could not notify her parents unless she gave permission. She did not. The best part is that Ashley came away without any residual damage. The worst part is that Luke got away scot-free.

Did he learn? No. Later that summer, Luke and two of his best friends were drinking in the cemetery. The cops busted them and Luke ran, leaving his two friends with the bottles of Jack Daniels. His friends got arrested for minor drinking and trespassing. Again Luke walked.

These were the events that severed the brotherly bond. His parents couldn't understand what had happened between them. *Dang*, he wanted to narc on Luke so bad. So many times it wasn't even funny. The only reason he kept his mouth shut was he knew how much the revelation would hurt his mother and father. But someday, Luke would drive him to the breaking point.

When the boat ride and his humiliation came to an end, Danny wanted to hide from the world, so he and Mathis retreated to his room to play computer games and chat on-line with friends. Mathis had found out the name of his roommate at Northwestern—a certain Damon Golembiewski—and had tried e-mailing him a couple of times over the last week but hadn't received a response back yet. Danny, jealous of just the *idea* of being replaced, cruelly began referring to the boy as "Gollum," the little slimy creature from "The Hobbit."

"See if Gollum e-mailed you back," he suggested to Mathis. When Mathis signed on and checked his e-mail, lo and behold, there was a response waiting.

"Ask him if he knows what the longest word in the English dictionary is?" Danny said. "Come on, ask him." (The 45-letter word was *pneumonoultramicroscopicsilicovolcanokoniosis*—more commonly known as "Black Lung Disease.") Danny secretly hoped that this Damon kid wasn't a word man, linguist, or polyglot. How could he compete with that? "Come on, I'll look up how to spell it."

Mathis was reluctant. "Not until I know him better. I don't want him to think I'm weird."

But that was just it—Danny and Mathis were weird! Normal people scared them; so why was Mathis all of a sudden so worried about what this stupid Gollum guy would think?

He read the e-mail over Mathis's shoulder. It was just boring introductory information... Gollum was from Indianapolis. He was going to study finance. He was bringing a television; could Mathis bring a microwave? The guy sounded about as interesting as cardboard. And he didn't even spell microwave correctly; he spelled it "micerwave." What a doofus!

It was at that moment Danny decided what he wanted to be. Not a filmmaker but a linguist. Words were really about the only scholarly thing in which he took an interest, and he indeed had a knack for them. When Mathis left the room to take a pee, Danny looked up careers in linguistics on the Internet and found all sorts of interesting options: sociolinguistics, psycholinguistics, diachronic linguistics, or theoretical linguistics. He could even study lexicography and publish dictionaries. There. He felt better. He had a plan.

When Mathis returned Danny said, "Dude, I need a nap."

"Go ahead. Mind if I play World of Warcraft?"

"Be my guest."

Danny plopped on top of his unmade bed. He'd requested that Mrs. Cally not make his bed and so far, she'd abided. It was a thing with Danny, why make a bed when you just wreck it anyway? Who cared? The truth was he was just lazy about some things and this was one of them. The other was hanging up clothes on hangers. Why bother when you could just pile them on a chair? What was the harm? His room was just how he liked it—comfortable chaos.

He closed his eyes and tried to fall asleep while Mathis was gaming, but the sound effects were distracting. Danny drifted into the cushion between sleep and wakefulness. He thought about the humiliation of the day. What was wrong with him anyway—why was it that scrawny Tess could get up on skis and he couldn't? Maybe it was that bad case of Osgood-Schlatter's he'd had during puberty. Maybe it did something to his legs or knees that prevented him from getting up on skis. *Dang!*

Thinking about the boat made him think about the day. *That* day. He didn't allow himself to think about it very often. And he never talked about it with anyone else, not his dad, not his siblings, not even Allen. It was all Luke's fault anyway. That's how he was able to deal with it—not to accept any of the blame. It was Luke's lie, Luke's arrogance, Luke's case of beer. Luke would have to live the rest of his life with the guilt. But Danny had to live the rest of his life with the secret, for neither boy had told anyone about what really happened that day. It was an accident with a tragic result, and in Danny's opinion, the details were incidental. Accidents happen every day. Every minute of every day. Every second of every minute. Every millisecond of every second. Every... Danny slept.

Chapter Eighteen

Storms Like These

{My Luke is an introvert," I tell Cecilia. "And I don't know why it is that introverts get such a bad rap." People seem to distrust people who are reserved and self-contained, and sometimes mistake them for arrogant or haughty. Both Luke and Mitch are introverts, and they are two of the most intelligent, kind, reflective people I have ever known. Luke thinks before he talks, while Danny thinks by talking. It's a little known fact that introverts give energy and extroverts, like Danny and me, suck it all up. Introverts don't babble on endlessly; they are good listeners, skilled observers, and in their own quiet way they discover, invent, and care for things.

Luke needs his alone time. At first I worried about this. I worried that he was anti-social, but my husband's friend, a pediatric psychologist, explained that introverts need down time to re-energize; that introversion is a legitimate personality style and not a failure to be an extrovert. Yes, Luke has a rich inner world and that's part of what makes him so special.}

AFTER THE BOAT ride Luke talked his dad into carryout from Altamore's Ristorante for dinner. Pizza, salad, and cannoli for dessert. Tess wanted to invite the new neighbors, but Luke told her no. She'd brought over the pitcher of lemonade that afternoon—leaving a sticky, drippy trail—and spoke of nothing else all through dinner.

Mitch let them eat picnic style in the river room while they watched *The Best of Chris Farley* DVD. Mathis stayed on for dinner and pumped Tess for information about the new neighbors.

"So what do they do for a living, Tess?"

"Well," she said, wiping her mouth on her sleeve, "the mother has an antique shop and Lee just got a job at a coffee shop. I don't think the grandma does anything but of course I haven't met her yet."

Mitch asked where the shop was.

"I don't know. But I know what it's called. It's called 'Junk for Joy.' Her name is Joya, the mom. Joya Harper. Isn't that a great name for a shop? 'Junk for Joy,'" Tess said, cheerfully. "You know, it's kind of like *Jump for Joy* and her name is Joy. I think it's neat."

"Tell me about this Lee," Luke said. He'd never said a thing to the kids about bumping into Karley Lappos at work and what she'd said about her cousin.

"Well, I call dibs on her. For a babysitter I mean. You and Danny and Mathis will probably all fight over her for a girlfriend."

Yeah, right, Luke thought. With the inside information he had, they could have her. He was staying clear. "I thought she was a dog," Luke said to Tess.

"No, she has a cat. Two cats, actually."

"No, I mean I thought she was ugly as a dog."

"Who said that?" Tess said. "She's really, really, really cute. And so is her mom. They look like sisters."

"You jerk," Luke said to Danny.

Danny gave him a "ha-ha" face.

In the middle of cannoli and Chris Farley's hilarious motivational speaker skit, the doorbell rang—several times—followed by the sound of high-pitched screaming. Mitch told everyone to stay put, but Luke followed him to the front door.

They opened the door to find two women clinging to each other and squealing. Luke knew who they were before they introduced themselves. Mother and daughter blonde bombshells was who they were.

"We're your new neighbors and there's a bat in our house!" screeched the mother.

"We hate bats!" bawled the daughter.

"Can you help us, please?" said the mother, folding her hands in supplicant prayer.

"Of course we can," Mitch said. "Luke, go get a sheet and a broom. Ladies, come in and calm down. It'll be okay. Luke and I will take care of the bat."

Luke headed for the kitchen to fetch the broom as his dad asked the women where exactly they had seen the bat.

Luke was confused. What was Karley Lappos talking about? These two didn't look like bohemians. What they looked like were two hot babes.

Luke heard the daughter say, "Upstairs, in my room. The pink one at the top of the stairs. Hanging upside down from the curtain rod. Eeeeeeeuuuuuu!"

With broom in hand, and forgetting about the sheet, Luke made his way back to the foyer where his dad and the ladies were standing. Now Danny and Mathis and Tess were there, Danny with his tongue all but hanging out of his mouth.

"Ah, damsels in distress. May I be of assistance?"

"You can take these ladies into the river room, '*Dan Juan*,' and get them something to drink while Luke and I catch ourselves a bat. Luke, where's the sheet, buddy? Let's go."

Story of my life, Luke said under his breath as he took the stairs two at a time up to the hall linen closet. How was it that he always ended up with the dirty work while Danny made out like a bandit?

Luke despised bats. The fact that they helped the environment by eating about six hundred mosquitoes an hour didn't matter. Bats were creepy.

Good thing no one had a video camera focused on Mitch and Luke as they tried to catch the bat in Julianna Spellman's old bedroom. The bat was just a baby; nothing to get hyped about. Friends of bats always try to say that bats are more afraid of you than you are of them, but how did they know? Had they interviewed a bat?

They'd done this bat-catching thing once or twice before—for the Spellmans. Lucky for them, the Langdon's home seemed to be bat-free. Mitch had the broom, Luke the sheet. The idea was to lure the creature away from the window with the broom, throw the sheet over it, gather it up in the folds, and release it safely back to nature (so that it could find its way back in at a later date). The problem was they couldn't get organized. Luke was distracted by Lee Harper's hot pink panties and bras that were strewn about the room. And by the large framed color photograph of some guy that looked like an Abercrombie and Fitch model on her dresser.

"Luke, pay attention!" Mitch said.

"I am. I'm just waiting for you."

"The damn thing is hiding behind the curtains," his father told him.

"Rustle 'em a bit."

"I am rustling," Mitch said, but he wasn't getting close enough. "The only thing I hate more than bats are snakes."

"Here, let me," Luke said, feigning courage. He traded weapons with Mitch.

Luke ended up being an excellent rustler, but when the bat came rushing out, circling and squeaking, it spooked him, and he began flailing around with the broom and screaming like a girl. Mitch stood poised ready to fling the sheet over their prey, but the little thing was quick and circled the room in a panicky fight *and* flight mode.

"Luke, lead it to me, over here. Come on! Over here," Mitch yelled.

"I'm trying. I'm trying."

"Come on. Guide it to me, Lukey."

"It's too fast."

"Lucas Roy Langdon, our very manhood is at stake here! We can't go back and tell those good looking ladies that, sorry, we couldn't get their bat."

"It might be a good excuse for them to spend the night at our house. Lee could sleep in my bed, with me."

"Nice try. Come on, when it comes around again, just whoosh it over."

"Okay, okay." But instead of *whooshing*, Luke *whacked*, and the poor little bat flung against the sheet and ricocheted to the floor, dead as a doornail. "Oooops!" Luke said.

"I said *whoosh* not *smash*. Tess will kill you if she finds out you murdered a sweet little mammal."

"Tess will not find out. Tess and the ladies will think we set the little guy free. We are emancipators."

Mitch peered down at the bat. "More like murderers. Damn, Luke. You're in big trouble. You know what this *is*?"

"A dead bat? *Duh!*"

"This isn't just any bat, buddy, it's an Egyptian Fruit Fir Bat."

"Yeah, so?"

"It's protected. It's on the endangered species list. I think it's like a ten thousand dollar fine if you kill one."

"No way."

"You're going to jail."

"If I go, you go, dude."

They stared down at the bat. Then Mitch said, "Psych!"

Luke shook his head. "I should have known better. There's no such bat as an Egyptian Fruit...whatever you called it. You are so lame."

"And you are so picking this thing up and throwing it in the garbage."

"Awww, come on. Not fair. It's disgusting."

"I know, that's why I'm letting you do it." Mitch grabbed some newspaper from a cardboard box that Lee must have been unpacking and handed it to Luke. "Here, wrap her up."

Luke made a face but did as he was told. It grossed him out. He held the thing away from him as he turned to follow his father out of the room. Just on a whim, without really thinking about it, he swiped a pair of Lee Harper's little pink panties with his free hand and stuffed them in the front pocket of his jeans. He didn't know how, but some part of him decided that sooner or later they would come in handy.

Back at the house… Luke heard laughter before he even got through the front door. When he entered the river room Mrs. Harper—or Joya as she insisted on being called—jumped up from the sofa to ask about the bat.

"Oh, it was nothing," Mitch told her, waving his hand. "Just a baby. We took care of it."

"You don't think there are any more, do you?" asked Lee Harper, who was cozied up next to Tess on the sofa.

"Well, I can't promise, but I don't think we've ever found two at a time. Have we, Luke?"

"No, I don't think we ever chased two out."

"You mean this has happened before?" Lee asked, biting her thumbnail.

Luke laughed, inside hoping it *would* happen again. Soon. "Just a couple of times over the years. Not very often really."

"Well," said Joya, "let's just be thankful we have knights in shining armor living right next door."

Luke felt himself turning red. Even more so when he thought about the little pink panties hiding in his pocket.

"I think we ate all your pizza," Joya said to Mitch. "Let me order another one to show our appreciation."

"That won't be necessary," Mitch said. "Let me just throw a frozen one into the oven. Tess, would you do that, please?"

Tess looked around the room. "Don't you just love how *me* really means *Tess*? I can't remember how to make pizza."

What a liar, Luke thought.

"I'll help you, Tess," Lee said, hopping up from the floor.

"So will I," Luke, Danny and Mathis all said in unison.

{*"I don't know about these new neighbors, Cecilia. I know I have to trust, but I just don't see how this all fits together. Of course I'm not being judgmental, but are you sure that these sexy blonde ladies are the liberators of my family? If you say so. I know looks can be deceiving and you can't judge a book by its cover, but Cecilia, can I say something? I'm just going to say it: that woman looks like a hooker!"*}

"It's not delivery, it's DiGiorno," Tess said, quoting the pizza brand's commercial. Luke felt stupid standing there in the kitchen. It didn't take five people to throw a frozen pizza into the oven. He leaned against the refrigerator, arms folded, and watched Danny and Mathis make fools of themselves in front of Lee. Their unfair head start had given them the advantage; they were beyond acquaintances now, interacting as if they had known each other all their lives.

"You guys should come into the coffee bar sometime," Lee said to the group. Lee was long and lean, in cutoff denim shorts, pink tank top and bare feet.

"Lee works at the North End Neighborhood Coffee Bar," Tess informed Luke.

"Ahhh," Luke said, nodding his head.

"She's a barista," Danny said, bumping his eyebrows up and down.

"That's Italian for 'bartender,'" Tess said.

"Yes, I know, Scout, remember where I work?" Luke said.

"Where?" Lee asked.

"At Barnes and Noble. I'm a coffee pusher too."

"Have you ever been to the North End?"

"Actually, no," Luke said, feeling suddenly inept, as if he'd just admitted not voting in the last election.

"No offense to Barnes and Noble and Starbucks, but *our* coffee is better. Not as acidic. You guys need to come in. I can't believe you live on the northwest side and you don't even support your neighborhood vendors."

"I've been there," Danny said, "it's just been a while."

Mathis chirped in. "Me too. I just had lunch there with my Dad last Sunday after church."

Luke glared at Mathis.

"Isn't the food great?" Lee asked. "The ladies that own it, Dana and Luann, are the best. They treat me like a daughter!"

"Luke," Tess said. "Can we go? Tomorrow?"

"I don't work tomorrow, Scout," Lee said, mussing up Tess's hair. "How about Sunday?"

"How about Sunday, Luke?" Tess pleaded, as if he were her father.

"Sure, Scout, we can go after Mass, like Mathis did."

Lee smiled and addressed Luke: "I'll make you the best cup of coffee you will ever have in your life."

"Sure," Luke said, glad the refrigerator was holding him up.

When the pizza was ready they re-gathered in the river room. Outside, the first full-fledged summer thunderstorm was underway. The lightning had a way of coinciding with Danny's clever punch lines and this was really pissing Luke off. God, how did he come up with these things? He was a walking comedy store, with Mathis functioning as his straight man.

Luke got up from his spot on the floor and closed the windows. The rain was dense and slanted and was spraying onto the windowsills. "Thanks, Luke," Mitch said. He and Joya were sitting at the game table drinking cans of Diet Coke.

Assembled on the rug, the kids took turns playing the old *Tetris* game on the even older *Nintendo* unit. (Danny refused to part with it because it was the only game he was good at.) "Luke," Tess called, "it's your turn."

Here we go, thought Luke. He was never going to be able to beat Danny's score. Even Mathis had bested Luke's highest score a while back. Since he hated failure of any kind, he said, "Actually, I better go close the windows upstairs, so skip me."

"Do you need any help?" Lee asked.

"That's okay," Luke said, before he realized what he was saying.

"I'll help you," Danny said, jumping up from the rug.

"That's a first," Tess said.

"You can say that again," Mathis said.

Luke paused to hear if Tess would literally "say that again," but she didn't. He started down the hall and up the stairs with Danny on his tail. At the top of the stairs, Luke turned to Danny and asked what was going on.

"I call dibs on her," Danny announced.

Luke sighed. "You can't call dibs on a person. It's not like she's the front seat of the car or the last piece of pie."

"Listen, if you are any kind of decent human being here's your chance to redeem yourself for last summer."

"Don't worry, I'm not interested. But if I was, you wouldn't stand a chance."

"You're a *biserable mastard.*"

"You're entitled to your opinion."

"It's not opinion, it's fact."

"Go get her, little brother. But first, go shut the windows, since you so gallantly volunteered to help me."

Danny gave his brother a hateful look and recited a line from the movie, *The Princess Bride*: "*Hello. My name is Inigo Montoya. You killed my father. Prepare to die.*"

Luke just smiled and patted the pocket that held Lee's pink panties.

{"What's up with those panties?" I ask Cecilia. "What in the world is he going to do with them? Oh, this can't be good." Cecilia shrugs. "You know," she says, "your boys aren't that different from most brothers that are so close in age. Sibling rivalry is a fact of life." Maybe so, but a mother hates to see it. Is it obvious only to me that these two need a good talking to? If I could, I'd give them both an earful. I'd tell Luke to lighten up and Danny to buckle down. I'd tell Luke to let go and have a little fun; and I'd tell Danny to stretch his brain every so often. I would warn Luke about growing old too fast and I would tell Danny to grow up. I would tell Luke

that junk food in moderation wouldn't kill him and I'd remind Danny that the nutritional value of chips and pop is zippo, and that inside-out sandwiches are just silly. I would tell Luke that he doesn't have to be perfect and I would tell Danny that charm will only get him so far. And then I would tell Luke not to lose his soul to science, and Danny not to lose his soul to a girl. I would tell Luke to quit calling Danny "Ricky Retard-o" and I would tell Danny to quit calling his "bro" "cerebro." I would tell Luke to widen his emotional range and Danny to taper his down. I would tell them to respect and appreciate each other. I would tell them to be nicer to their dad and their sister. And then I'd make them clean out the garage.}

Seeing his dad sitting at the game table talking with Joya Harper (listening to, would be more accurate) made Luke realize how little they had entertained since Annie's death. It used to be the house was filled with family, neighbors, and friends, but for the last year, Annie's sisters had hosted all the holiday and birthday parties. Even Danny's graduation, just a month ago, was held out at Bumpa and Gran's farm. It had been a long time since true guests were in the house.

Luke pretended to fool around with the stereo. He raised and lowered the volume a few times, returning it back to its pre-fiddling level. Who in their right mind had put on John Denver?

"Dad, seriously, John Denver?" Luke said.

"Leave it. It's fine," was the answer.

He lowered the volume and kept it there. He wasn't sure if his dad needed saving, but he suspected it. Joya was L-O-U-D loud, one of those persons whose normal voice was decibels above most people's. Her mouth was her most prominent feature—she had these full, plum lips and big, straight white teeth. A mouth one could refer to as a "kisser" as in "*right in the kisser.*" She was captivating more than she was attractive. She had those haunting-looking green eyes like Sharbat Gula, the "Afghan Girl" that appeared on the cover of the National Geographic Magazine years ago. In the dim light in the river room, Joya's eyes seemed to change from green to grey to hazel to silver like those mood rings of the seventies. Certainly not Mitch's type, and by the look on his father's face, Luke knew Mitch was politely suffering through his neighborly hospitality.

Luke was much more interested in the daughter. She was attractive *and* captivating. Not at all what he'd been expecting. From the moment Karley Lappos threw out the word "bohemian," Luke envisioned a skinny girl with frizzy black hair, a pierced nose, a long flowing gauzy skirt, and ballet slippers. He snuck a look at Lee now—on the floor, playing *Tetris*. Danny and Mathis hovered over her, cheering her on. Lee seemed to be her mother's opposite—soft where Joya was hard, tall and lanky, where Joya was compact and curvy, a natural blonde, where her mother had tons of help. Her eyes were the color of evening skies—as dark as blue eyes come. But her voice, her voice might have been the best part—it was pretty, with a musical timbre. It could give a person the shivers.

(LUKE'S FASCINATING BRAIN FACT: There's a biological explanation for men being sex maniacs—they're genetically wired to be that way. The area of the brain involved with mating behavior, the Preoptic Area of the Hypothalamus, is about 2.2 times larger in men than in women and contains two times more cells!)

What was he thinking? This was no time to be pining for a girl. He was leaving for school in a few short months. There would be thousands of girls at college. Thousands of smart, beautiful women. Besides, Danny and Mathis were already vying for Lee's attention, and one more suitor in the mix would make for a plot of a schmaltzy Hollywood romantic comedy.

So, the thing to do was to ignore her. Not interested. Sending no vibes, no way. He took his plate and his can of Coke and carried them over to the game table. He sat down between his father and Joya and hoped that this simple act said, "I am an adult. I am sitting at the big people's table."

"So you are Luke," Joya said, with a big smile, dangling her strappy sandal from her purple-painted toes.

Luke nodded.

"Thank you so much for getting rid of that damn bat. Oops! 'Scuse the French. They give me the heebie-jeebies. So your dad tells me you're a genius and you're going away to school soon."

Luke concentrated on chewing his pizza. Maybe this wasn't such a good idea. He stared at his father and said, "Only the latter is the truthful part of that statement."

"Oh, you're just being modest, I'm sure."

Luke tried not to look at her, but he just had to: she simply commanded it. She was wearing a low-cut, tight-fitting leopard print sleeveless top and a short denim skirt. Joya caught him staring. Luckily Tess appeared out of nowhere with an apron wrapped around her and holding a pen and small notepad.

"May I take your drink order, Mrs. Harper?" she asked, serious as all get out.

"Why, yes, you cute little kid, you may. I'd kill for a Fuzzy Navel. Do you make those?"

"Do we, Dad?"

"Sorry," Mitch said. "We're all out of Fuzzy Navels."

"Then I'll just have another Diet Coke."

Tess scampered off to fill her guest's order. Joya called after her, "You wouldn't have a little rum to throw in there, would ya'?"

"Mother!" Lee said, looking up from the video game.

Mitch raised his eyebrows. Luke could tell that his father did not approve of Joya Harper. She was way too loose in her appearance, demeanor, and speech.

"Well, that bat did a number on my nerves. Whatever you do, do not tell Gran-Glen about the bat. She'll pee her pants when she comes."

Luke heard Lee explain to Danny and Mathis that "Gran-Glen" is what they called her grandmother, Glenda, who would be moving in with them next week.

"She's convinced I'm moving her to the hicks. Tell me some good things about Rockford that will convince her otherwise."

Mitch said, "Rockford's a great town."

"What are you talking about?" Luke interjected. "It's a rusty old industrial town that's adverse to change."

"Listen Joya," Mitch said, "Rockford has a lot of pluses: we're close to Chicago, close to Milwaukee and Madison. We have an international airport. We're home to Illinois' largest music festival, 'On the Waterfront,' which is held each year on Labor Day weekend. Other claims to fame: we have Jane the Dinosaur, a 66-million-year-old juvenile Tyrannosaurus rex. You know the rock band Cheap Trick, right? They're ours. And the Rockford Peaches of the All American Girls Baseball League which was made into that movie *A League of Their Own* with Geena Davis and Tom Hanks. We have Klehm Arboretum and Botanic Garden, a 155-acre 'living museum' full of unique and unusual plants and trees. Botany experts have said that there is only one other site in the world that compares to Klehm and it's in France. We also have Anderson Gardens, which has been voted the number one Japanese Garden in North America many times."

"Yeah," said Joya, "but are there any good places to party?"

Luke looked at Mitch. They both shrugged. "You're asking the wrong people that question," Mitch told her.

Tess returned with a crystal glass (one of their mother's Waterford crystal glasses) filled with pop and ice. Then she scampered away and returned presently with a huge stainless steel bowl filled with popcorn.

"Popcorn!" Joya cooed. "You are like the neatest little kid around. How'd you get so cool? Look at you! Look at that complexion. Has anyone ever told you that you have perfect skin? I'd pay a million dollars for that skin. Come here. Give me some of that gorgeous skin." Joya pulled Tess up onto her lap and pretended to pinch off bits of Tess's cheeks and add them to her own. Tess giggled and beamed. It occurred to Luke that she hadn't had a female (other than Aunt Maggy and she was family) make a fuss over her in a very long time.

"Tess, you're too heavy," Luke said.

"Are you kidding?" Joya said. "You're looking at a woman who deals in antiques. I pick up old trunks and move chiffarobes."

"Chiffarobes?" Tess squeaked. "Like in *To Kill a Mockingbird*?"

"Yes, kiddo, like in *To Kill a Mockingbird*."

Mitch excused himself when his beeper went off, leaving Luke with Joya and the "kiddo" on her lap. Joya shoved heaping handfuls of popcorn into her mouth. "So, kiddo," she said, "who's your favorite man in the house?"

Luke looked up from his pizza, curious. He watched Tess look over at Mitch who had his cell phone glued to his ear. He was holding up the wall, deep in thought, pinching the bridge of his nose as he listened to somebody's problem. Then she looked over at Danny who was performing his latest stupid human trick for Lee—folding a twenty-dollar bill so that it looked like the World Trade Center and the Pentagon were on fire. (It *was* freaky!) Then she looked at Luke and smiled. "It goes like this," she said to Joya. "In this order: Luke, then Mitchell, and Danny last."

"This guy?" Joya said, nodding at Luke. "This guy's the Tower of Pisa?"

"He's not the tower of pizza," Tess explained. "I just like him the best."

"I think I do, too," Joya Harper said, as she fished a kernel of popcorn out of her cleavage and popped it into her mouth.

<hr />

Wine and the truth are inextricably bound. Someone once said that, Luke just couldn't remember who. But it was true, and also one of the few things he didn't like about drinking his mother's wine. The truth was hard to swallow. Also, he was getting a little sick of white wine. Why didn't his mother like red wine anyway?

Later that night, after all of the excitement wore down and the blonde bombshells went home, Luke realized he had no clean boxers for tomorrow. Now he sat in the basement on top of the dryer, which was filled with every pair of boxers he owned. Mrs. Cally had been sick for a few days and everything in the house was backed up. Danny had resorted to turning his boxers inside out and getting a second wearing out of them but that was just nasty. Luke was particular about his hygiene. In this, he took after his father. It was just easier to be clean and organized. He couldn't really understand why people thought color-coordinating drawers and closets was a symptom of obsessive-compulsive disorder. Wasn't God in the details? Lately, he wasn't sure where God was.

The wine made his mind wander. To that day. He hated his brother for it. It was mostly Danny's fault when you really thought about it. Danny's fault for being such an immature asshole. For being reckless and vindictive. Then why did *he* feel so guilty? And why couldn't he talk about it, not even to Dr. Bonovia whom he could trust and who had to keep everything confidential. With all Luke had shared about Danny, Dr. Bonovia would surely agree that the bulk of the blame lay in Danny's lap. Still, that left some of the blame for him, and even a small slice of blame was too much to bear.

Think of something else. He took a swig of wine and opened up the journal that he had brought downstairs with him. He was studying Savant Syndrome. He opened the notebook and looked at his entries about savants. The word savant comes from French—learned; from Old French—*savoir*, to know; from Latin *sapere*, to be wise. The most well known savant of our time was Kim Peek, the real "Rain Main." And while Kim was fascinating with his encyclopedic memory feats on topics as diverse as the Bible, horseracing, British Monarchs, geography, movies and the space program, Luke found a man named George Widener even more captivating. As a boy, George grew up poor, displaying both signs of giftedness and eccentric behavior. He would get to school early just so he could sit on the floor in a dark, quiet hallway and watch the red 'Exit' sign. He made up counting songs using the 'powers of two.' In 2004 George handily defeated a former NASA scientist in a calendar contest—"What day of the week does June 25th of the year 2,908 fall on?" The most unique thing about George though was his art. He turned his love for calendars, trivia, and magic squares into original artwork. His "Magic Time Squares" were the coolest of all. The guy adapts a regular magic square (a grid of numbers which add up to an identical sum in all directions) into a magic time square where day of the week, month, and year values in each cell add up to identical respective sums in all directions, thus creating a "calendrical portrait" of a person. Luke had looked at some of George Widener's magic time squares on his Web site. There was one for someone named Sarah and one for Queen Victoria, both of which were created with ink pen on stained napkins. They were so cool.

Maybe he would become an expert in Autism, Aspergers, and Savant Syndrome. Autism, in particular, was on the rise and Luke wondered why some people were socially autistic and others seemed only neurologically autistic. And there seemed to be such a fine line between profound giftedness and profound disability.

He could spend hours wondering about and researching the brain. Luke had read about another man, Daniel Tammet, who was referred to as an 'acquired savant,' someone whose exceptional skills appeared following some central nervous system injury or disease. In Daniel's case, it was following a series of childhood seizures that he developed his extraordinary ability with numbers and memory. He can recite, from memory, Pi to 22,514 decimal places; he can calculate 37 raised to the power of 4 in less than one minute; he speaks French, German, Spanish, Lithuanian, Esperanto and Icelandic.

Luke was already thinking about writing his thesis on musical savants. Why were there more males than females? And what about the intriguing triad in some savants of musical genius, blindness, and mental handicap? What was that about? Did savant brains give us a peek into the brain of God? Someone had once called savants "the foolish wise ones," and Luke wondered if they were closer to God than the rest of us. And he would admit this to no one but sometimes he was jealous of his own brother's disability—after all, attention disorders were neurological disorders and he often begrudging came clean (to himself) that Danny's quirky brain was pretty interesting.

(LUKE'S FASCINATING BRAIN FACT: Albert Einstein's brain, for something like thirty years, was kept in jar inside a cardboard box in the somewhat casual custody of a one Thomas Harvey, M.D., of Weston, Missouri, the pathologist at Princeton Hospital in New Jersey who performed the autopsy on Einstein when he died in 1955. This boggled Luke's mind. One would think that the brain of the man who unlocked the atom and came up with special relativity and "E=mc2" would rate fancier digs.)

The dryer shut off abruptly and Luke snapped the journal shut with one hand. It made a nice thwack in the quiet of the basement. He gathered his boxers and since there were no laundry baskets nearby, he stuffed them into a clean pillowcase. He downed the rest of the wine and hid the bottle inside a discarded yellow plastic bag that the salt for the water softener came in and pushed it to the bottom of the waste can. He wouldn't make the same mistake twice. That's where he and Danny were different; Danny made the same mistake multiple times.

Oh sure, those two blonde bombshells were sexy as all get-out, he thought as he trudged up the stairs. And it was true that the young and beautiful Lee Harper had flipped his internal switch to the "on" mode, but Luke had a plan and even his hormones couldn't get in the way.

(LUKE'S FASCINATING BRAIN FACT: Teenage boys usually have three times more sex drive that their female counterparts—a difference that will continue on through life.)

Luke reached into his pocket and pulled out Lee's pink panties. Devious electrical impulses sparked through his brain. This was unlike Luke. Usually it was Danny who went for the jugular.

❦

The next morning, Sunday, Luke slept till ten-thirty. The night before his dad had actually agreed to let them all sleep in and go to the five o'clock evening Mass at St. Peter's. Mitch was making rounds and Tess and Danny were still asleep so Luke had the kitchen all to himself.

He felt like a big breakfast so he gathered up a frying pan and some eggs. Bacon would have been nice but there wasn't any. Crap, there wasn't any milk either. In the middle of scrambling his eggs the phone rang. When he answered, he heard heavy breathing on the other end. "Who is this?" he said.

"Oh, sorry," a woman's voice said. "I'm all out of breath from running up the stairs. To whom am I speaking?"

"To whom am *I* speaking?" Luke asked.

"Oh, sorry, this is Joya, from next door."

Luke knew who it was. "And this is Luke. What can I do for you?"

"Well, first of all, I was wondering what day garbage day is. The realtor never said."

"Tuesday," Luke said. "They usually come around eight a.m."

"Tuesday, okay. Hey, what're you doing right this very minute?"

"Scrambling eggs."

"You wouldn't have just one teensy minute to run over and help me get my attic door open, would ya'? After your eggs, of course. It's one of those pull-down thing-a-ma-jigs and it won't budge. Please? If it takes bribery, I do bribery."

"That won't be necessary," Luke said and laughed. "These eggs kind of suck anyway. I can come over."

Joya opened the front door wearing a tight-fitting denim mini-dress. "You're a prince," she said, as she led him up the stairs. "And I'll make you breakfast if you can get this door open." Luke let her lead the way up the stairs, taking in the view of her from the back—legs and butt and bare feet. He loved women's feet.

It was easy getting the door open and the steps pulled down. They had the same pull-down kind of attic ladder in their house. One swift tug was all it took.

"You're a genius!" Joya said. "I tried and tried. Let's have a look around." She climbed up first and Luke followed her, this time getting a view up her dress. (Leopard print panties!)

Typical attic—all cobwebs and dust. And hotter than hell. Luke could barely breathe. "Listen, handsome," Joya said, "if I make you breakfast would you haul a few boxes up here for me afterward? Please? Please? Please?"

Luke said sure. It felt nice to be needed. Especially for something other than chauffeuring Tess around and paying the bills. Happily, he climbed down the ladder after Joya.

She scrambled eggs and fried bacon and perked coffee while he sat at the counter and answered her questions. Yes, people had told him that he looked like the actor Matt Damon. No, he never considered modeling. No, he didn't go out much; he had to help out with the house and with Tess. Yes, he missed his mother. No, he didn't want to talk about how she died. Fun? What did he do for fun? Well, his life was sort of on hold right now but he was really interested in the brain and so he spent a lot of time on his research.

Joya frowned at him. "On hold? You can't put life on hold. Life keeps going. It'll pass you by if you let it. You gotta live it! Hell, by the time I was nineteen, I had backpacked in Europe, jumped from a plane, got hit by a car and spent a month in the hospital, got pregnant, got married (in that order), and went back to school at night. You gotta grab life by the ass or it'll kick you in the ass, Mr. Handsome."

Luke just chewed his eggs and wished she wouldn't call him that. Anyway, he knew what he was doing.

"I know what you need!" Joya said. "A Bloody Mary! I make killer Bloody Marys." And then she darted around the kitchen, collecting the ingredients, singing lines from Jimmy Buffett's *Margaritaville*—improvising the chorus—*wasting away in Bloody Maryville*. She had a decent voice. Luke watched her as she mixed tomato juice with vodka, then added Worcestershire sauce, hot pepper sauce, and the juice of a lemon. She topped it off with some seasonings, a celery stalk, a dill pickle spear, and three Spanish Queen olives. She handed him the glass and held hers up for a toast.

"To neighbors," she said, and clinked her glass with his. "And damn good-looking ones at that!" She took a broad-shouldered gulp and let out a satisfied sigh.

Luke took a sip of his drink. He wasn't really a fan of tomato juice but he wasn't about to let on.

"You remind me of my son," she told him. "The one I like. You have his eyes—they're like fused glass. He's an engineer out in California. Already has two patents. My other son is an attorney, like his father. He's out in Rhode Island."

Luke nodded.

"I can't tolerate either of my daughter-in-laws. One is a granola— an earth mother, a vegan, a PETA-member—who won't eat anything I cook. The other is a librarian who speaks in complete, perfectly-constructed sentences. Don't *even* get me started."

It looked to Luke like she was already started.

Afterward, Luke helped Joya haul five big boxes up to the attic. The last load was a box of books, heavy as bricks. Joya steadied the pull-down ladder as he climbed up and then down. Finally he pushed the ladder up and closed the door, wiping his dusty hands on the back of his shorts.

"You the man," Joya said and slapped him five.

"Well, I better get home. Thanks for breakfast."

"No, thank you for your muscles."

She walked him to the door and said, "I think I'm going to like living here." Then she winked. *Winked.*

Luke was halfway across her yard when he heard her call his name. She ran toward him. *Now what?*

"Your cell phone," she said, "you left it on the kitchen counter."

"Oh, thanks," Luke said, taking it and dropping it into his pocket.

"Check out the new contact I added for you," Joya said, before she turned around to head back. "My home, my cell, and my store numbers—all listed under 'Joya the Sex Queen!' Call me anytime, Mr. Handsome!" she called. She blew him a kiss and jiggled home.

{"See!" I say to Cecilia. "See what I mean! I just don't—" But Cecilia puts a small hand up to stop me from ranting. She explained to me earlier that until I can trust God completely, I can't move up to the next level of Heaven. It's her job to remind me that it's not about control anymore, it's about trust. Oh, I have much to learn!}

Chapter Nineteen

Into the Bright

HEAVEN IS…HEAVENLY. It's everything wrapped into one thing. It's—oh, it's absolutely unexplainable. And I'm still in the lower vault. I can't even imagine what's ahead. For eye truly has not seen and ear has not heard because the eye's vision is not precise enough to view the beauty of Heaven and the ear's hearing is not acute enough to hear the sounds of Heaven. Be cautious of people who say they know Heaven through near death experiences or mysticism for they may know something of Heaven, but they have only vacationed there. It's like if you vacationed in Hawaii, you would know a bit of Hawaii, but you couldn't possibly know every single thing there was to know because you didn't visit every inch of every island; you didn't live there since the beginning of earth's life. So it is with Heaven. Go, read, explore, research, but always take what others say with a grain of salt for that is the very size of their knowledge of Heaven—a miniscule grain of salt.

We are all searching for the truth in life, but the truth is: you will never find the truth in life on earth. We are meant only to strive for it. We can only understand what we are meant to understand. Think about it, if truth equals that which is, and there is so much going on in the conscious *universe that we as humans don't know, then we will never know the truth until we get to Heaven. Even then, it doesn't all come at once, but is a learning experience. In St. Paul's first letter to the Corinthians he talks about comparing the life we experience on earth to life in Heaven. He says, "For now I see through a glass, darkly: but then face to face: now I know in part; but then I will know even as also I am known."*

Oh, the world would be such a better place if we could understand that none of us—Christian, Muslim, Jew, Baha'i, Hindu, Buddhist, Mormon, Jehovah's Witness, or any other of the followers of the thousands of religions there are—is in possession of the absolute truth. It's so sad that religion has caused the world to be so divisive and destructive. The moment you try to politicize religion you have a problem. Here's what the world has done in trying to define the image of God—we have taken God's omnipotence, omnipresence, and omniscience—and squeezed it all into a bottle to carry around with us as if God were our own personal genie. There are bits of truth in every religion.

I, being a Roman Catholic, believed that my entrance into Heaven was through my faith and trust in Jesus Christ. And for me, that is the truth. Of course other religions have quite different pictures of Heaven and its conditions. The Hindu Moksha or Mukti, the Buddhist Nirvana, and the Zen Satori are afterlives that are indescribable, mystical states of being reached only by the denial of all earthly desires. The Islamic paradise is called Jannah, or the Garden of Eden, and is where one goes at the end of life if one believes in God, the last judgment, and good deeds. Some Native Americans see the afterlife as the "happy hunting grounds," a paradise in which hunting is plentiful and game unlimited, while others believe in reincarnation, returning to earth as ghosts, or going on to another indefinable other world.

The Baha'i faith views Heaven as a symbolic place or a "spiritual condition" where the conscious soul will retain its individuality and memories and will commune with God and other souls. The Latter Day Saints believe that until the Last Judgment, Heaven is divided into two levels. After the judgment, it is divided into four levels, the top three, being referred to as "degrees of glory." In Judaism, Heaven is where God resides and the Hereafter is known as Olam Haba (the "world to come") where the immortal human soul will go after the death of the physical body.

The Kabbalah Jewish mysticism describes seven heavens. The Polynesian tribes divide Heaven into realms—as many as fourteen. One where human souls are created, one where spirits live, and so on.

There are over four thousand religions in the world. More than four thousand different ways people have formed in their genuine and honorable attempts to know God, themselves, and others. Don't worry about the different religions and who is right and who is wrong. God loves variety! Why should that come as a surprise? Think about it. Why would a great God who created and evolved almost a half million species of Beetles (only some 350,000 have been discovered so far in earth time) be happy with only one form of worship? Know this: God delights in the prayer of the Christian, the Muslim, the Jew, the Buddhist, the Hindu, the Native American, and on and on. God has been trying to get through to us for all of time in all different ways.

Life is a maze and a riddle. The Sufi saints instructed people to "Die before you die!" What they meant was to give up all that you think you are. Jesus said it too—"Die to yourself and serve others." Sometimes we see ourselves as a single leaf, forgetting that we are part of a giant tree. Someday our leaf will turn brown and fall to the ground, decomposing into the elements of the earth, blending into the universe. Yes, we are all connected in this beautiful, mysterious dance.

I know you want to know which is the one true faith and I know you want so badly to prove that the one you espouse is the right one. But when others ask you to prove your beliefs, don't go there—earthly answers can never be sufficient to the heavenly questions. You could argue the existence of God with history, desire, conscience, first cause, design, and even with Pascal's Wager, but it's better just to bless the doubter and let your works be the proof of your faith.

I know you've also wondered all your life about who gets into Heaven. I can only say this: the poor in spirit, those who mourn, the meek, those who hunger and thirst for righteousness, the merciful, the pure in heart, the peacemakers, and the persecuted. But if you're asking which people of which religions get to Heaven then the answer (and you're not going to like it) is this: it's none of your business. In Luke 13:22-24, Jesus is asked, "Lord, will those who are saved be few?" And Jesus ignores the question and answers this way: "Strive to enter by the narrow door." You see, not all knowledge is good for us while we are on earth, and details about who and how many inhabit Heaven falls into that category. If we knew we were guaranteed Heaven we would be lazy, arrogant, and uncompassionate. And if we knew we were damned to Hell, we would be lazy, malicious, and selfish. No, find your own way and leave it to God to decide who inherits Heaven.

Be comforted in knowing that God never loosens His grip on us—each one of our names is written on the palm of His hand. There's nothing you can do to undo His love; He loves you just the way you are but urges you to be more.

Life becomes so much more meaningful when you can sense your own spirit. I'm here to tell you that you can do this; not only can you sense your spirit, you can communicate with it. You do this naturally when you talk to yourself and when you dream and imagine. But unfortunately people of modernity spend little time in quiet. We are packed into houses and buildings, into schoolrooms and cubicles, into cars, buses, and planes. We are bombarded with sound and images. But mostly, we are afraid to be alone. It's frightening to come face to face with oneself in all of our weaknesses and failures. But here's the paradox: when you take some time to be alone, you will not be alone because in your own company you will find God.

And here is a great secret: you can get in touch with the Holy Spirit within you through simple breathing. The great yogis knew this. Quiet yourself and breathe.

Heaven is a place, a real place. Beyond the vast blue vault of sky it lies. It's not just a state of mind; it's not an alternate reality or a parallel universe. It's not solid or liquid or gas. And it's definitely not "terra firma." But it is a real place in a different dimension. And it's glorious. In Heaven, all of nature is alive and alert—from a green blade of grass to the pulsating air. The landscape is not a backdrop; it's part of you. You don't tread on the holy ground; your feet just barely touch the floor of Heaven. You move at will. You turn to the right and you are in a magnificent rainstorm in Brazil in the year 708 A.D.; you turn again and you are in Antarctica, in 3049, watching the migration of the penguins; you turn again and you are in the year 65,020,008 B.C. feeding a triceratops. You turn and you are in 32 A.D. listening to the apostles James and John amiably arguing over who Jesus loved best.

Oh, we expend so much energy searching for the meaning of life when it is with us all the time—imbued in every cell of our bodies. It's right in front of you! It's this: existence is the meaning. Pinch yourself. You exist; you were planted on this spinning planet for one reason and one reason only: TO PROVE THE EXISTENCE OF GOD—TO YOURSELF BY YOUR THOUGHTS AND DREAMS AND TO OTHERS BY YOUR WORDS AND ACTIONS. By doing so, you shape your soul for Heaven. And there's a wonderful side effect—you promulgate JOY. Don't you know that you are saved from something for something? We are not man-begotten or cosmos-begotten, but God-begotten. We belong to our God. Nothing else matters.

Chapter Twenty

Donzerly Light

{I realize now I was an overprotective mother. From the start I never knew how I would be able to raise children in a house so close to water. Thank goodness Mitch made a good living and I could stay home with the kids because I never could have trusted anyone else to care for them. As it was I drove them crazy with my rules. Poor Tess was brainwashed so well that she learned to announce her whereabouts throughout the day so I wouldn't have a conniption. "I'm going to use the upstairs bathroom, Mom," she'd call out to me, or, "Mom, I'm going to play with my Barbies on the screened porch." And I never would have been able to raise teenagers without cell phones. "Mom," Danny would say when he called, "We're leaving the dance and we're going to Katie's house and I'm taking Spring Creek to Mulford to Pepper..."

But how do you stop worrying about your kids? Being married to a pediatrician made me even crazier because Mitch would throw around the names of frightening diseases: Meningitis, Reyes Syndrome, Kawasaki Disease, Cystic Fibrosis, Lymes Disease, Stiff Person Syndrome (characterized by stiff and rigid muscles), and even anomalies as odd as Jumping Frenchman of Maine Disorder (a neurological disorder characterized by an unusually extreme startle reaction), and Maple Syrup Urine Disease (a metabolic disorder where urine and sweat have a distinctively sweet odor) and Blue Diaper Syndrome (an inherited metabolic disorder characterized by bluish urine-stained diapers). Oh, I could go on and on because even though a physician is sworn to uphold the privacy of his patients, Mitch would share these heartbreaking cases with me, without revealing the patients' identities. Wrong thing to do, because soon I would be sniffing my kids' urine, licking their foreheads (a symptom of Cystic Fibrosis is salty-tasting skin) and purposely startling them to see if their response was normal.}

*I*T WAS RIDICULOUS when you thought about it, Tess having to run the household, cook the meals, change the linens, and supervise Mrs. Cally. And what thanks did she get for her selfless sacrifice? She got forgotten, that's what she got. Mitch was getting older and more forgetful by the minute. This summer, it was one thing after another. He would forget to pick her up for gymnastics. He would drop her off at a friend's birthday party and then forget to pick her up. He would say he would be up to tuck her into bed, but then he'd never show up. (Sometimes Tess would peek down from the banister and find Mitch asleep in his leather recliner.)

Tess worried that her Dad would have another cardiac arrest. She tried to picture the contraption implanted in his chest that kept his heart beating properly. She imagined it as a TV remote control. What would happen if it went on the fritz? What then? *Crikey*, she didn't want to be an orphan. That would really—of course she wasn't supposed to say this word—suck. But it would. She wouldn't be like Scout anymore, she'd be more like Little Orphan Annie. Tess never cared for that story and that song—*I love ya, tomorrow*—oh my gosh, she hated that song. Why would an orphan love tomorrow? Tess was only half an orphan and what she loved was yesterday. Yesterday when she still had her mother.

Last week she played a trick on herself and pretended, while shopping at Woodfield Mall with Aunt Maggy, that her mother was still alive. Yes, her mother was just back at home while Tess enjoyed a special date with Aunt Maggy. At GapKids, she picked up a flimsy top and when the clerk asked if she wanted to try it on, she said, "Oh, no, thank you, my mom, who is at home right now working in her garden, would think this was inappropriate for a nine-year-old."

Oh, the lies were slipping out left and right. As the summer progressed Tess was getting better and better at dreaming up attention-getting fabrications. It was challenging. It was interesting. It was fun!

But now, Tess has gone and got herself into a pickle. Mrs. Nelson had given her a ride home from Allison Carbeaux's birthday party. Embarrassed that she'd been forgotten again, Tess dreamed up a double doozie: Mitch had recently had a teeny tiny heart attack (I had to call 911) and then when he was in the hospital he was also diagnosed with Alzheimer's. "Our family is really having a bad year." "I'm so sorry, sweetie," Mrs. Nelson said. "Is there anything I can do?" "Oh, no Mrs. Nelson, we'll be fine. I make a really good chicken soup and my dad is a doctor and all so he knows what he needs to do."

In response to Mrs. Nelson's puzzled look Tess manufactured an angelic smile and said, "Thank you ever so very much, Mrs. Nelson, for the ride home. It's always so nice to see you. Michelle is one lucky girl to have a mother as sweet as you."

When Tess got home, Mitch was in the backyard working on the boat with Luke. How could a new boat need so much work—how many times could you polish and wax and spiff and shine? Luke and Mitch loved that stupid boat more than…

The thing that hurt the most was that her dad was clueless. (When she was little she had idolized him to the point of thinking that the 'M.D.' at the end of his name meant 'Magnificent Dad.') She watched him from one of the huge windows that lined the back of the river room. He obviously didn't even realize that he'd forgotten her—again. Well, she would show him. She climbed the steps, stormed off to her room and hid in her closet. But there in the dark, her teeth started to hurt. Then her scalp. Her tongue. Her eyebrows started to itch and tips of her fingers tingled. Swallowing became difficult. Her chin was sore and her cheeks were tender. One of the knuckles on her right hand seemed larger than usual. Could it be a cyst? It certainly could. Here she was with a cyst on her finger. Her whole hand would likely need to be amputated and wouldn't you know she was right-handed. What good was it anyway that her father was a doctor if he missed these obvious illnesses that were staring him right in the face?

{"Now this is breaking my heart!" I tell Cecilia. "My baby is hiding in the closet and no one even cares!" Tess needs me! She needs me. We were attached at the hip, she and I. I used to have to give her five hugs and five kisses every time I left her. Now I think I should have left her instructions. Where would I start? They could fill a book. I guess I would start by telling her that I am pleased that she is such an honest child but that sometimes a person is better off "thinking" those honest thoughts than bringing them out into the light of day. For example, the time she was staring at her kindergarten teacher and the woman asked her if she had a question, and Tess said, "Yes, I was wondering when you started growing that mustache?" Or when she told my mother that the reason she didn't want to spend the night was because the whole house smelled like horses.

I would tell my little girl that when her brothers get on her case to remind them that they started out as females, for it's a biological fact that every fetal brain starts out female. Female is nature's default gender.

I wished I'd remembered to tell her that when she's old enough to wear makeup—maybe a little mascara when she's sixteen—the best eye makeup remover is Johnson & Johnson No More Tears Baby Shampoo. My ophthalmologist recommended it years ago after I got an eye infection, and I never had another infection after that.

Who is going to teach Tess about the precarious balance between ladylike and assertive? Who is going to teach Tess that domestic skills are important for any woman? I want her to be a blend of Suzie Homemaker and someone, someday, people will call "Ma'am." Who but me could teach her how to be both strong and tender?

Well, that's why I'm still here—in this holding place—because I haven't been able to let go yet. I guess I'm one of the stubborn ones. But there's perfect free will in Heaven. I have to be ready to move on. And I will be soon; I just need to know that my family is going to be all right down there.]

Tess decided maybe hiding wasn't the answer. No one seemed to be looking for her anyway. She crawled out of the closet, got to her feet and looked out the window that faced the backyard and the river. Mitch and Luke were still down there in that confounded boat. And there was Piper with them! Her own dog, a traitor! Who cared that Dad had named this boat the 'Tessa?' It was a boat and as they found out the hard way, boats were dangerous things.

Plan B. Cry like a baby. Hmmm. Maximum results guaranteed. It might even get her a kitten. She got up and lay on her bed to strategize but then fell asleep from pure exhaustion. She dreamed of that terrible day. One minute she and her mom and brothers were cruising down the Rock River on the boat (the old boat) and bathing in the sunshine, the next minute, Luke and Danny were screaming and Annie was gone forever. She woke with a gasp, dripping with cold sweat. There was no need for plan B. The tears flowed without pretense.

"Scout, is that you?" Her bedroom door opened and there stood her hero, Luke, so sweet and handsome, so much like Annie in the face and in his build, it made her heart ache. "Scout, what is it? You miss Mom?"

"No, I miss Dad."

Luke sat on the edge of her bed and squeezed her shoulder. "Dad? What?"

"Yes, Dad. I miss my *real* dad. The one who use to pay attention to me. The one who didn't forget me at birthday parties."

"Ooooppps! He did, didn't he? We've been working on the boat."

"I hate that boat."

"Last week you loved it; you got up on the skis and everything."

"I miss my Dad!" she cried, nestling herself in her brother's strong arms.

"I know, I know. But it's been hard on him, too."

"What am I gonna do when you're gone, Luke? Who's gonna take care of me?"

"Oh, Scout, Dad's here and so is Danny. Calpurnia's here during the week (Oh, how Tess loved him for calling Mrs. Cally Calpurnia!) and you've got Aunt Maggy and Grans and Bumpa, and you've got lots of school friends."

"But I don't have Mom and I don't have Julianna!" The tears kept coming. Luke patted her gently on the back. Tess thought that someday Luke would make a wonderful father. "And I want a kitten. Why can't the man get me a kitten? Would it be so hard?" She wiped her nose on her shirt. "Luke?"

"Huh?"

"Do you think we're bad people or something?"

"What would make you say that?"

"Why else would God do this to us?"

"God didn't do it. It just happened. Accidents happen. They just do."

"Tell me what happened. I'm older now. I need to know."

"It was an accident, that's all."

"I fell asleep. Mom had just braided my hair and we put sunscreen on each other's backs. And when I woke up, you and Danny were scream—"

Luke covered his face with his hands. "Tess, I can't, I just can't. I'm sorry. Someday, maybe. Now, listen, Dad's taking us to Giuseppe's for dinner. Do you want to go and wash your face?"

"I don't want to go."

"Well, you can't stay home alone."

"Why not? I'm alone most of the time anyway. I can take care of myself. I got myself home from Allison's birthday party without any assistance from this family, didn't I?"

"How *did* you get home?"

"I hitch-hiked."

"Tess!"

"Psych! Mrs. Nelson."

"Come on, I want a stuffed pizza and Dad won't let me get one by myself."

"Okay, for you I will come. But I'm not talking to the old guy until he buys me a kitten."

❦

Fourth of July was looming and no one had even mentioned what they were going to do this year. Last year, they were all still walking around in a fog—Annie had died just two weeks before and there was absolutely nothing to celebrate. Tess's counselor kept telling her that life had to get back to "near-normal" (it would never be normal again), that she needed to revisit things she had enjoyed, things that had given her comfort. Well, the Fourth of July fit the bill, so she invited herself to make the fireworks run with her dad since Danny, the resident family pyromaniac, had to work at the nursery. They had to drive over the border, to Beloit, Wisconsin, since fireworks were illegal in Illinois. (Mitch always justified his purchases by only buying what he called "stationary" fireworks, ones that stayed in his yard.)

Tess hated having to sit in the backseat. It made her feel like a baby. She did, however, enjoy having this alone time with her dad.

"When I was in college," Mitch told her, on their way up to Beloit, "some of my buddies burned their house down shooting off bottle rockets in the basement."

"Inside?"

"Yes. Pretty stupid, huh?"

"I thought you went to college to get smart. Sounds like all they got was dumber. I hope Luke doesn't try anything like that."

"Nah, Luke's too smart."

Yes, this was nice. Just the two of them, together, talking just to talk. Tess stared at her dad. He seemed more cheerful than usual. He was probably still feeling guilty about forgetting to pick her up the

200

other day from the birthday party. He was even humming a little. It seemed like the perfect time to ask for a kitten.

"Dad?"

"Hmmmm."

"I've been noticing. Piper seems lonely. Don't you think a kitten would be just the thing?"

"We'll see, honey."

At the store, she followed her dad around as he selected various fireworks. She couldn't stop thinking about kittens because of the 'Black Cat' brand of fireworks staring at her from the shelves. And even though the cat was ugly, with its snarling mouth, it made her want a cat even more.

Deciding it might be better not to press her luck about the kitten, on the way home she asked her father instead if they could have a Fourth of July bash like they had had every year since she could remember.

"We'll see."

She sighed. Maybe 'bash' wasn't the best word. "We'll see means 'not very likely.'"

"Well, maybe then."

"Maybe means 'probably not.'"

"Okay, perhaps."

"*Perhaps?* Mitchell, just say 'no' if you mean 'no.'"

"Because I mean 'perhaps.'"

"Define the word, please."

"Perhaps: 'possibly,' 'conceivably,' 'perchance,' 'I don't know.' How would you define it?"

"Here's how *I* define *you* defining it: 'Perhaps means 'no' but I'll break it to her gently by putting off a final answer until later when I can come up with a better excuse like, too bad, I'm on call.'"

Mitch didn't say anything, just kept his eyes on the road.

Tess thought about the Independence Days of her past. They *always* had a party. They had one of the best houses in the whole city of Rockford when it came to the Fourth of July. Situated just so on the Rock River, just at a bend, their backyard provided perfect, front-row seats for the fireworks display. Annie always opened the house up to family, friends, and neighbors for a huge backyard party with the most American of menus: hot dogs, hamburgers, baked beans, potato salad, and ice cream bars for dessert. Simple, but perfect. A kid's dream day, that came to a happy end lying on a blanket on a slim hill in the backyard, hands behind your head, soft summer breeze whispering on your skin, your belly full of ice cream, your best friend Julianna Spellman lying right next to you practicing her "oooohhhhs" and "aaaaahhhhs," and the summer sky all lit up in colorful delight, the sparks reflecting on the calm dark river water before fizzling out. But the best, best, bestest part, was your mom and dad lying on a blanket beside you, holding hands, and making you feel safe and loved.

Tess could go two ways with this. She could play on her dad's guilt—"Mom always had a party, Mom would want us to have a party,"—or she could take a political stance—"A Fourth of July party makes a kid feel like she's part of a good family, a great neighborhood, and an outstanding country. What are you, a Communist?" No, neither one was likely to work. She'd have to go for pity.

"Dad?"

"Yes?"

"I *need* a Fourth of July party."

Mitch turned his head to look at her. "Need? Define need."

"I *need* a Fourth of July party, because I *need* something to do, something to plan, something to look forward to, something that makes me feel needed, something to keep me connected to Mom's traditions. I *need* some women in my life, Dad; you three men are driving me crazy. Even Scout had Calpurnia, Miss Maudie Atkinson, and Miss Stepanie Crawford!"

"Okay, all right, agreed, fair enough. You can have your little party."

"Define 'little.'"

There was so much to do in so little time: invitations, of course, and then renting the tent, tables, and chairs, and calling Logli's to order the beans and the potato salad. Making a grocery list for Luke: hamburger, buns, hot dogs, condiments, pop, beer, wine, and plenty of bottled water. Annie had kept good notes in a little book called "Entertaining Journal and Planner," including vendors, phone numbers, quantities, prices. Tess let her fingers do the walking. Then she let her feet do the walking to deliver invitations to the neighbors, saving the Harpers for last.

"We'd love to come!" Joya said, standing at her front door, after she read the invitation Tess handed her. "Gran-Glen is moving in tonight and by the Fourth I'll need to get the hell out of this house, excuse my French."

"Why do people call swearing *French*?" Tess asked, hoping to be invited in. She'd only been in the house once since Julianna moved out and she was hoping the day would come when she would be as welcome as she once was. (Maybe now wasn't the best time—Joya was still in her nightie.)

"I have no idea, kiddo. But come on in, I want to show you something. Excuse my appearance," she said, pulling her short, short, black lace nightie down over her thighs, "but I would live in night attire if I could."

Tess stepped over the threshold and into another world. Wow! Was it ever different. Mrs. Spellman's decorating was best described as minimalist, with soft earth tones, traditional furniture, and spare decorating. Joya's style was exactly the opposite and just what Tess had imagined: funky, loud, and flashy, but it was simply the coolest decorating Tess had ever seen. Every wall was a different color: the living room walls were four different shades of lavender, the crown moldings were a crisp white, and the ceiling, well the ceiling was a pale yellow.

"The painters just finished yesterday. What do you think? Is it too much? Do you want to throw up?"

"I love it!" Tess said, truthfully. She never could have imagined combining these colors with this furniture: zebra-striped fainting couch, black antique cabinets, glass end tables, and overstuffed chairs covered in pale yellow velvet.

"Now come look at the dining room." The dining room walls glowed in different shades of yellow, and the ceiling was pistachio green. Great big colorful paintings of fruit adorned the walls. Paintings of peaches so delectable, you wanted to pluck one from the wall and bite into it. Grapes with water droplets you'd swear were real. Pears and apples and bananas. Fruit everywhere. Suddenly Tess was hungry.

"You're hungry, kid, aren't you?" Joya said, reading her mind.

Tess smiled and said, "You just read my taste*bloods*!"

"Taste*bloods*. You crack me up. My art always makes people hungry. You want a sandwich? I might have some ham or peanut butter and jelly."

"I love peanut butter and jelly. I could eat it nine times a day. Sometimes I eat it for breakfast, lunch, dinner, afternoon snack, and midnight snack. My grandma makes homemade jam and raspberry is my favorite. But sometimes the little seeds get stuck in your teeth and that is pretty annoying but I love raspberries so I just put up with it."

Joya smiled and said, "Come on in the kitchen. Excuse the mess. I'm trying to get organized before Gran-Glen comes. She wears white gloves."

"All the time?"

"Ha! That's cute. No, it means she's a clean freak."

"Oh."

The kitchen was the best room of all. A chair rail separated the walls with the bottom portion a raspberry color, the top, cantaloupe orange, and the ceiling honeydew, all trimmed in cream. Tess felt like she was inside a bowl of rainbow sherbet. She drank it all in with her eyes. Everything was so light and bright and cheerful—from the colorful pottery to the whimsical curtains. It seemed like such a happy place that it made her sad. Her home, although tastefully decorated with soft, muted colors and botanical prints, had always had a comfortable, welcoming ambience, but without her mother's touch, everything in the Langdon home seemed to droop, sag, fade.

"Is Lee home?" Tess asked, as she climbed onto a stool at the kitchen counter. (Who would have covered stools in leopard skin prints in a room the colors of sherbet? But it worked.)

"Nope, she's working," Joya said, as she moved around the kitchen, gathering what she needed for the sandwich.

"Luke's a barista, too. Did you know that?"

"Yes, I think your father told me."

"How'd you get your name? I've heard of *Joy* but never with an 'a' at the end of it."

"It comes from the Italian word *gioia*, for joy or darling or jewel. My mother knew no one would pronounce it correctly so she spelled it j-o-y-a."

"My real name is Tessa, with an 'a' on the end."

"Cool. We're like twins then. Here, eat your sandwich while I go take a pee."

Tess munched on her sandwich, swirled on the stool and smiled. She had never met anyone quite like Joya before. She was an adult but she kind of acted like a kid. She wasn't like her mother or any of her mother's friends who were more…what was the word…normal? genteel? ladylike? Tess wasn't sure what her mother would have thought of Joya. Oh, she would have been kind to her, of course—that was just Annie's nature—but Tess doubted they ever would have been good friends.

"So who's gonna be at your party, besides you and me?" Joya asked, when she returned, wiping her hands on the back of her nightgown.

"Well, Lee and your mom, of course, my family and all the neighbors on our block except for Mr. and Mrs. Harrister, because Mr. is blind and wears Depends and Mrs. has that disease that sounds like an angora kitten where you can't go out of your house or you'll go nuts."

"Tessa-messa, you're my kinda kid. You tell it like it is and I like that. We're gonna get along just fine." Joya came around and sat on the stool next to Tess. "Couple of things you should know about me, okay? I sleep late. How's the sandwich, okay? Don't you love how

I added a layer of fresh raspberries between the jam and the peanut butter? That's one thing I am, I'm a kick-ass cook, 'scuse my French. Anyway, I sleep really late because I stay up really late. So don't ever call or come over here and ring my doorbell before eleven in the morning. And I got some bad habits I want you to promise not to pick up from me now that we're friends, okay? Promise?"

Tess promised and hoped with all her heart that Joya wasn't a stripper. (She kind of looked like a stripper in her black lace.) Dad would never let her hang out with a stripper. After the other night, he'd commented about Joya's language and the depth of her cleavage, but all Tess knew was that there were few adult females in her life and here was as good of one as any.

"Okay. Here goes," Joya said, tossing her blonde hair back. "I smoke. I drink. I swear. I drive too fast. And I have a temper that will scare the hell out of you. Sometimes, if you're in my yard and I'm not in the mood for five million questions, I'll tell you to get outta my face. It won't mean I don't like you or that I'm mad at you, it just means that I cannot handle any human interaction at that particular moment in time. I love and I mean *love* rock 'n' roll music so I have been know to piss off—'scuse the French—" She put her hand to her head. "Do I need to say that every time I swear, or can you just excuse me now for all the swears I will say from here on out?"

Tess nodded and said, "You're excused," very seriously.

"Good. Thanks. I really appreciate that. Okay, and here's the last thing. The last thing is that I'm a terrible gossip. I love to get the latest shit—excuse my, oh never mind, we've already covered that, haven't we?—on everyone. So dish, girl."

"No thank you, I don't need a dish."

"Not for your sandwich, you ding-bat." Joya got up from the stool and walked over to the refrigerator. "*Dish*. Dish out some gossip about the neighborhood for me. I know you know everything."

Tess swirled in her chair. She was so happy! Finding Joya was like finding a brand new flower species that you never even knew existed.

She was so totally fresh and new and different. Tess fell madly in love. "Where should I start?" she said.

Joya leaned in on the counter and placed a nice, cold can of Mountain Dew (forbidden fruit in the Langdon household due to its high caffeine content) in front of Tess. "Start with Luke, why don'cha?"

So she started with Luke and ended with Mrs. O. who lived on the other side of the Langdons, and lamented about the neighborhood being filled with old fogies. Tess was glad Joya didn't ask directly about her mother. She didn't offer anything. Besides, Dad probably told her the other night. But, Tess was curious about what had happened to Joya's husband.

"Can I ask you to dish something?" Tess ventured. They were friends now, after all.

"Go ahead. Shoot."

"What happened to your husband?"

"Awww, kiddo, he died."

"How?"

"It was an accident, a terrible accident. But you're too young for details."

"How come everyone thinks I'm too young for details? That's what everyone tells me when I ask about my mom. Well, I would like to know!" she wailed, tears starting to well in her eyes.

"Okay, okay," Joya said, gesturing with her hands. "He fell down a flight of stairs and hit his head. He died instantly."

Oh. *Oh.* Tess had been talking about her mother—she wanted the details of her mother's death, not Joya's husband. But this was an interesting revelation: Joya gave in easily to tears. Tess was not manipulative by nature; still, she stored this information for future use. She said, "Oh, that's so sad."

"Yeah, sad."

Tess popped open the tab on the Mountain Dew, and the can let out of swoosh of air that sounded like a sigh. It was befitting of the moment and they both chuckled.

"Hey, Tessa-Messa, you want to ride in my convertible and go pick up Gran-Glen in Evanston with me?"

"Now?"

"Yes, now. Well, after I get dressed. But wouldn't it be a hoot to pick up my mother dressed like this!"

"I'd love to come!"

"Why don't you run home and ask your dad."

"Dad's at the clinic; I'll ask Luke."

"Oh, well, maybe I better come too."

Luke was paying the bills at the kitchen table while watching a baseball game. Bill paying was an adult task and it made Luke seem older than he was. "I don't know," he said, when Tess asked if she could accompany Joya. "Let me check with Dad." As he dialed the phone he said to Joya, "He'll want details like how long you'll be gone and what time you'll be back. He'll want your cell phone number and he'll probably want to be sure that you don't speed or drink and drive or—"

Suddenly Tess remembered that one of Joya's self-proclaimed vices was driving too fast.

"All of the above," Joya said. "I mean none of the above. Here, let me write down my cell phone number and all the rest will be fine. I could drive to Evanston with my eyes closed."

Tess fetched a pen and a pad while Luke rattled off the details over the phone to his dad. Tess and Joya stood listening to Luke's end of the conversation. "Yeah. Yeah. Yes. I guess so. I think so. I hope so. No. No. No. I know. I know. How would I know? Sorry. Yes. Yes. Yes. Okay." He hung up. "You can go," he said.

"Wow, he really gave you a working over. Doesn't he trust me or something?"

"It's not that…"

"Well, if he thinks I need babysitting you could come along too."

"That's okay, as you can see I've got bills to pay."

"It's a convertible," Tess sang, although she really wanted Joya all to herself.

"I thought you drove a Volkswagen van," Luke said.

"I do. But just to haul my antiques. Otherwise I drive—" she said, and then sang "*my little deuce coupe, you don't know what I got.*"

Luke looked at her, cocked an eyebrow.

"The Beach Boys? Remember? The little deuce coupe? Anyway, my little deuce coupe is actually a very awesome but safe 1993 Chrysler LeBaron. It was my late husband's car. It's turquoise blue with black interior. It was his pride and joy."

"See you, Luke," Tess said, happily.

"Go use the bathroom first, Tessa-Messa, 'cuz if you have to pee while we're on the road I'll punch you in the fessa."

"You're hilarious!" Tess said, and obeyed.

"I'm hilarious," Joya repeated to Luke, thumbing her chest.

Tess, wind whipping through her hair, kept checking the odometer. For whatever reason, Joya kept it at a respectable seventy on Interstate 90. Still, with the top down, it felt faster. Tess had never ridden in a convertible before, and she knew she was spoiled forever after.

Joya had pulled her hair into a tight bun, wrapped an animal print scarf around her head, and donned big, dark sunglasses. She looked like a movie star. It was hard to talk with the wind and the CD player blaring the Beach Boys, but just being in the car, away from home, with someone other than her dad or one of her brothers was freeing in a way Tess loved.

"You okay?" Joya asked, over the music and wind.

"Yes, thank you," Tess replied.

Joya turned down the music. "We're almost there, kiddo."

"Why is your mother coming to live with you, anyway?"

"Ever heard of Alzheimer's."

"Yes, my dad has it."

"What?"

"Just kidding."

"Well, Gran-Glen really does have it. She can't live alone anymore—we're afraid she'll burn the house down. Last week she fried eggs in liquid dish soap. And she keeps taking mail out of the neighbor's mailbox, thinking it's hers. She walks around the house in her bra and underwear—not a pretty sight. My brother's wife is a royal pain, a real Buttinski, and she won't take her, and my sister doesn't have room, so guess who gets her?"

It hurt Tess to hear Joya talk about her mother like that when Tess would have given anything to have her mother with her, Alzheimer's or no Alzheimer's. "But you're so lucky to have your mother!"

"Oh, man! I am such an idiot! That was very insensitive of me, wasn't it? Here you're *missing* your mom and I'm *dissing* mine. Hey, that rhymes! Geez, that was insensitive, too. I'm a jerk. Sorry."

"It's okay."

"No, it's not. This last year has probably just sucked for you."

"Oh, you don't know the half of it," Tess said, sitting up straighter. "I have to do everything. My dad is always out doctoring, Luke is schlepping coffee, Danny finally got a job at the nursery, and so I'm left to cook and clean and do the laundry. I pay the bills—"

"Luke was just paying the bills..."

"You're right; he was. I bribed him into doing it for me this month. I paid him fifty bucks," she explained, wondering if her nose was getting longer.

"Uh-huh."

"Anyway, things are pretty tough. My dad has a heart condition, you know."

"No, I was not aware of that. He looks healthy as a horse."

"And has anyone told you about Danny?"

"What about Danny?"

"Danny is crazy. He makes these weird movies. Documentaries and then he makes the whole family sit and watch them and they never make sense. Sometimes he forces me to be in the movies—that part I don't mind so much because I do enjoy a little acting now and then. What was your favorite part in *To Kill a Mockingbird*? The book, not the movie."

"Wow, now there's a segue."

"A what?"

"Nothing. Let's see, my favorite part of *To Kill a Mockingbird*. Oh, I know, I know. Remember when Miss Maudie's house caught fire?"

"Oh, yes!"

"And remember when they went home and Atticus made hot chocolate to warm the kids up and then he noticed that Scout had a blanket wrapped around her shoulders and at first he was angry because he thought she had left the yard but then they realized that it was Boo Radley who had covered her up."

"Yes! Yes!" Tess squealed. "And Atticus says that someday maybe Scout can thank him for covering her up. I love that part too! Joya, I think you just might be my Boo Radley."

"Oh yeah?"

"Yeah."

"That's just about the nicest thing anyone has ever said to me. I think."

"I'm glad to be of service."

Joya pulled up in front of an enormous English Tudor. "Here we are—this is where I grew up. Isn't it awful?"

"It's gorgeous! It's like a castle."

"Complete with dungeon. Hi, Mom!" Joya called out the car window.

Gran-Glen stood on the front stairs, in a pair of peach-colored slacks and a pretty white silk blouse, with a strand of pearls around her neck. She clutched a huge fluorescent lime green leather purse to her chest. On her feet, she wore bright white sneakers, and on her head, a "Go Cubbies!" baseball cap.

"She gets a little discombobulated," Joya explained as they got out of the car.

"Mom, this is my new neighbor and new friend, Tessa-Messa Langdon."

"Tessa who?" Gran-Glen asked, eyeing Tess.

"Be nice to her, Mom, she's only nine."

"I'm nice to everyone."

"Sure you are. Where's Bobby? Is everything packed?" Joya scampered off to talk to her brother, leaving Tess to get to know Gran-Glen.

"Don't get old, young lady, that's all I have to say."

"Yes, Ma'am," Tess said.

"They took away my car last year; now they are taking my house. My son says I'm having memory problems, but I don't remember ever having any problems with my memory. Would you like one last tour of the house?"

"Sure," Tess said and then followed Gran-Glen through the echoing rooms.

"This is the master bedroom where my three children were conceived. My second husband was good in bed. And this is the dining room where my first husband confessed about his affair—I promptly threw him out—and this is the staircase where Joya floated down in her wedding gown, when she married Reid, God rest his soul. And this is..."

Tess felt bad for Gran-Glen. She could see how confused she was. At one point, she showed Tess the laundry room and said it was the kitchen. The kitchen was the master bath and the basement was the dining room. Still, there was a sweetness about Gran-Glen that Tess liked.

"You're a cute little thing," Gran-Glen said to Tess. "Did my daughter tell you that I have scads of money?"

"No, Ma'am, she didn't."

"It's as good a reason as any to be nice to me. I could always add you to the will."

Gran-Glen insisted on the "top up" in the car but said she would take the back seat to perpetuate her reputation as a back seat driver. After one demand to "slow the hell down," she promptly fell asleep.

"She's nice," Tess said to Joya, trying to be polite.

"Nice and loony," Joya said, snapping her gum.

"Joya!"

"What? Oh, sorry. I keep forgetting. Listen, kiddo, if you're so keen on having a mom you can share mine. She forgets a lot but she hasn't forgotten how to mother."

"What's her real name?" Tess wanted to know.

"Glenda."

"Like the good witch?"

"Sans the adjective."

"Pardon?"

"Yes, like the good witch."

"When did she get Alzheimer's, anyway?"

"Oh, it creeps up on you for years and then bam! there it is."

"It's so sad."

"Yeah. But there's a bright side. She likes me better now that she can't remember that she doesn't approve of me."

Tess checked the odometer. Eighty in a sixty-five. But with the top up, it felt the same as seventy with the top down.

"Joya, do you believe in Heaven?"

"Hell yes I believe in Heaven."

"What about Hell?"

"Heavens yes I believe in Hell."

Tess giggled. "You're funny."

"I don't try to be, it's just who I am."

"What do you think Heaven is like?"

"Don't ask me, kiddo, I have no idea. I just think it's a place that's a googolplex times better than earth."

"A googa what?"

"Googolplex. It means ten to the one-thousandth power."

"We haven't done powers in math yet."

"Well, it's a really big number. It comes after a sexdecillion, septendecillion, octodecillion, and let's see, oh yeah, novemdecillion, vigintillion…then there's like a gazillion more and then comes googolplex."

"Wow." Tess hoped that Heaven was a googolplex times better than earth. And that her mom had a googolplex horses to ride—maybe a palamino paint, her favorite horse of all.

"You know what I wish?" Tess said, dreamily. "I wish I could interview everyone in the world and ask them what Heaven is and maybe someone will know."

"Why don't you? Maybe not everyone in the world but everyone you know and even some you don't know. You could even have Danny film your interviews and make it into a documentary. Everybody is curious about the afterlife."

Tess liked the idea. She wondered if Danny would go for it. Maybe if she made it sound like it was *his* idea.

"How would you like to stay for dinner, little girl?"

"I would like to very much. What are we having?"

Suddenly, Gran-Glen woke up and wanted to know what the hell was going on, where the hell they were going, and how the hell far was the nearest bathroom. Joya tried to explain about the house and coming to live with her, but it was as if Gran-Glen were hearing about the plans for the very first time. She became very agitated. "You think I'd come and live with *you*? Why would I want to live with the woman who murdered my favorite son-in-law?"

"Mom!" Joya screamed. She turned to Tess, who had turned white as tissue paper, and said, "Sorry, kiddo, she doesn't know what she's saying. Don't let her scare you."

"It's okay, she doesn't." But actually, she did, quite a bit, in fact.

Chapter Twenty-one

Gentle Thunder

{"Poor Mitch," I say to Cecilia. "He has no one to share his secrets with."
For that's truly one of the best parts of a marriage, the secrets you keep.
For example, Mitch is the only person in the world besides my mother
who knows this story: When I was young—five or six—and my mother
was helping me pick out a bedtime story, I turned from my bookshelf and
noticed a handsome young boy sitting on my bed. For some reason, I
didn't gasp. He didn't scare me. He looked solid enough, but by the way
he glimmered, I knew he wasn't earthly. He resembled my mother, that
much I could tell. And he was smiling. I asked my mother who he was.
"Who?" she said. "That boy, sitting on the bed. Don't you see him? Right
there!" "Where, honey. Who?" Then he was gone. But I could describe
him in perfect detail right down to his blond crew cut, the scar on his
forehead (put their accidentally by my mother with a baseball bat), the red
and black flannel shirt, and the red high top sneakers. My mother almost
fainted. She wobbled a bit and then collapsed onto my bed. She drew me
to her and hugged me. "Annie," she said. "Tell me again what he looked
like." When I repeated the details she started to cry. "That was my brother
Ritchie, honey. Remember I told you about your uncle Ritchie who died

when he was twelve? My brother Ritchie!" Then Mom explained that we had been given a special gift and it was something that probably should stay just between the two of us. Later, I knew she was trying to protect me from ridicule—people are reluctant to believe in miracles even when they slap them in the face. Uncle Ritchie is here, one in a big group of family members who greeted me when I crossed over.

Oh, the glorious things that await the believer! Imagine a place where all the earthly barriers that sin forces people to put up are broken down. Imagine having all the time in the world to deepen precious bonds you had with loved ones, imagine not being distracted by work and health problems, and being able to concentrate on understanding people and experiences and forging friendships with the most fascinating people in the universe. Myself, I can't wait to meet St. Francis of Assisi, Eleanor Roosevelt, Mary Magdalene, Michelangelo, George Harrison, John Denver, John Candy, St. Augustine, Albert Einstein (for Luke, mostly), Steve Irwin (the Crocodile Hunter), Kahlil Gibran, Pope John Paul II, Johnny Carson, Gilda Radner, Lucille Ball.

And this is going to sound absolutely nuts—but women will understand—one of the best things about Heaven is that there's no laundry to do!}

NNIE'S STOCKPILE OF Riesling was diminishing. It may have been pilfered but rather than suspecting Luke Mitch preferred to believe that he himself was drinking more of it. He realized he had acquired a taste for the white wine, a thing he had always teased Annie would never happen. "It's a girl's wine," he'd told her, after reading up on the varietals. Riesling's hallmark, according to *The Wine Spectator* was its beautifully expressive bouquet, suggesting flowers, green apples, and honeysuckle blossoms.

Real men drank red wine—hearty Burgundy, full-bodied Cabernet, versatile Merlot, and good-natured Sangiovese. And red wine was so good for you. According to recent studies, it seemed to be made especially for men. It could reduce the risks of prostate cancer, lung cancer, and non-Hodgkin's Lymphoma. It could ward off heart disease by reducing cholesterol. It could stop herpes and help prevent colds. It was shown to stop brain deterioration and even reverse the aging process. And apparently a good amount of red wine could keep melanoma at bay by preventing sunburns. If only, Mitch thought, we could put it in the drinking water.

Of course the greatest benefit of any wine was its anesthetizing properties. It was the quintessential cure for his ailment: pathological bereavement. Where grief clouded his thoughts, wine simply rocked them and put them to sleep. Miranda Burns had told him she was surprised by how much grief felt like fear, but Mitch was more surprised by the isolation of grief. In spite of the comfort of others, it was something you had to go through alone.

He still wasn't sleeping well. He worried about his critical thinking skills. His executive function didn't seem to be functioning properly. Blame it on the heartache. Enduring Annie's abrupt excision from his life was not unlike an amputation. Annie had been a part of him, just as a limb was a part of him, and without her he was experiencing what amputees lived through: phantom limb pain. After amputation of a limb, a patient can continue to have an awareness of it and to experience sensations from it. Mitch had had a patient born without a limb and phantom limb sensations were also present in that little baby. It seems that perception of our limbs is something that's "hardwired" into our brains and that limb sensations become mapped onto our brain networks as we develop. Annie had been hardwired into Mitch's brain and into his circuitry as well. She was half his heart, half his memory, half his vision. If he couldn't remember the name of a song, Annie could. If he could only remember the month of Tess's birthday, she would supply the day. At family reunions, it was Annie that would have all the cousins' kids' names at the tip of her tongue. It was Annie who remembered everything.

One of the things he missed most about her was their monthly book club. With a membership of just two, one could say it was very intimate. They took turns with the selections, bought two copies of each book (a luxury about which they both always felt a little guilty) and scheduled into their calendars a "book dinner" the second and last Saturday of every month.

This was something people would be surprised to learn about Mitch—that he was such a reader—because he didn't advertise it. People had attitudes about their doctors' free time: they didn't want them to have any. There was this perception about the medical industry. People didn't look at the practice of medicine as just a job; they looked at it as a noble undertaking performed not for the money but for altruistic and benevolent purposes only. Another misconception was that doctors made tons of money. Yes, a busy pediatrician like Mitch did pretty well for himself, but these days a new family practitioner working for a health system didn't make as much as one might think. And they don't get the best tables at restaurants. Nobody really cares that you're a doctor anymore until they're lying on your table. No, doctors shouldn't be reading novels, they should be poring through the medical journals every spare chance they had. And Mitch did do that, more so than many of his colleagues, but reading novels and discussing them with sweet Annie had become one of the great simple pleasures of life.

Since he lost Annie, he was an automaton. He drove to work and when he arrived he had no memory of the drive over. He never turned the radio on anymore, just drove with his eyes and that was all. The parking lot was full and as he slipped his old Volvo into his reserved spot he wished he could enclose himself in a giant soap bubble and just float through the day, doing what he needed to do, but not being bothered by whining and gossip. How nice and juicy that Dr. So-and-So was having an affair with Miss So-and-So, but he really didn't care. And did you hear who got his hand slapped for not attending that mandatory meeting? What meeting was that? And the whole system is going to electronic medical records next year and—surprise—pediatrics is the guinea pig.

This morning, one of the pharmaceutical sales reps brought in breakfast for the office and while Mitch tried to listen to the sales presentation about a newly formulated, great-tasting antibiotic, he really wished he could lay down his head and take a quick nap. Too bad humans weren't more efficient when it came to sleep. Consider the dolphin whose brain appears to sleep one hemisphere at a time. Wouldn't this come in handy at mind-numbing lectures or interminable homilies? Mitch had read that a seventy-five-year-old human sleeps for twenty-five years of his life, and although Mitch understood well enough both the restorative and adaptive reasons for sleep, he used to think it was such a waste of time. He never needed that much—a prerequisite for becoming a physician—but now it seemed he needed more and more just to get through the day.

"Did you know," Mitch said to the drug rep, right in the middle of his product detail, "that bats sleep twenty hours a day? Doesn't that sound wonderful?"

The young rep blinked his eyes and said, "I did not know that. That's fascinating. Twenty hours. Is that a teenage bat? Get it? Teenage?"

"And the albatross can sleep while flying."

"Didn't know that either," the rep said.

"And of course horses can sleep standing up and only need about three hours of sleep a day."

The rep closed his sales binder and shot Mitch a nervous smile.

Mitch returned the smile. He was a nice kid just trying to do his job, sincere as a preacher. It occurred then to Mitch that something might be seriously wrong with him, more serious than sleep deprivation. He was starting to obsess about sleep the way some people obsessed about food or sex or drugs.

The rep seemed to be waiting for an explanation so Mitch made one up. "I originally intended to be a veterinarian."

The rep smiled and sat up straighter. Then, as if someone pushed a button on his back, he started talking nonstop about an array of topics, jumping from subject to subject. Mitch had a hard time keeping up. Just when Mitch was about to blow the kid off, he shared an interesting piece of info. It seemed that a study published in the journal Science suggested that gently bouncing a baby while singing could help the baby develop a sense of rhythm, which is important of course for learning to make and appreciate music. This was just the kind of info Mitch loved to put on his "Parents 101" bulletin board out in his waiting room. He'd ask Liz to "google" it, print out the article, and post it. Mitch thanked the kid, signed for samples of the new antibiotic, and sleepwalked through the rest of the day.

Mitch's secretary Margie promised on the life of her first born (she had no children) to get Mitch out of there in time to take Tess to her gymnastics lesson. He threatened her with a reduced Christmas bonus if she didn't see to it. "It's never that great anyway," Margie teased.

"Did you know," Mitch asked her, "that the mothers of newborn dolphins and killer whales get almost **NO** sleep for several weeks after their calves are born? And that the calves themselves don't sleep at all!"

"Fascinating. I said I'd get you out of here on time."

She kept her promise and Mitch was in his car and home by five-twenty. Tess was watching TV with Piper sprawled out beside her on the couch in the river room.

"Ready, Scout?"

"You're here!" she said and jumped up. "You actually made it. I can't believe it! And you're not on call, right? Wow."

All the fuss made Mitch feel guiltier than ever. Was it really that bad? Was he so undependable?

"And then we're going to Altamore's for dinner, right? Alberto said he would make me pasta with whiskey sauce."

Mitch smiled. It was vodka sauce. "Yes, honey."

He sat on bleachers at the Gymnastics Academy and watched little girls run, swing, and tumble. The other parents—mostly mothers— were twenty and thirty years younger than him. "Which one is your granddaughter?" one woman asked him. He pointed to Tess who was doing her best not to fall off the balance beam. "Oh, she's a cutey," the lady said. "I've seen her in here with her dad." Of course she meant Luke, and Mitch felt another stab of guilt. He had to make some changes to his schedule. This was not fair to his kids.

Afterward, they ate at *Altamore's Ristorante* on North Main Street. Alberto and his wife Annamaria fussed and fawned over them. A wide smile never left Tess's face. She gorged on pasta in vodka sauce, pretending after a few bites to be drunk. Then out of nowhere, she threw a bomb at Mitch: "Dad, what's the difference between a cardiac arrest and a myocardial infraction?"

Mitch smiled. "First of all, Scout, it's myocardial in*farc*tion, not in*frac*tion. Infarct refers to heart tissue that dies because it didn't get blood due to a blockage in one of the arteries of the heart. Myocardial infarction is a fancy name for a heart attack. They're the same thing."

"But you had a cardiac arrest, right."

"Right."

"So, what exactly is that?"

"It's a hiccup in your heart's electrical system. When that happens, your heart beats so chaotically that it can't pump blood properly. But I'm all fixed, remember?" he said, patting his chest. "I have a pacemaker and a defibrillator. I'm like the bionic man."

"The bionic who?"

"Never mind. TV show before your time. Do you want *panna cotta* for dessert?"

"Yes, please."

Mitch looked at his little girl. She was still in her pink leotard because she wanted to show it to Annamaria. Was she always this skinny or was she just getting so tall?

On the way home, in the back seat of the car, Tess burped loudly and asked Mitch what he thought of Joya.

"I think she's a little kooky, honey, but she's probably harmless."

"I think she's cool. It's a nice night, isn't it?"

"It is at that."

"I'm so excited about our Fourth of July party. It's going to be awesome. Hey, Dad, what's the average life expectancy for men these days?"

"Around seventy-five. Why?"

"No reason," she said, but Mitch could see in the rearview mirror her little fingers doing the math. Seventy-five minus sixty-three was twelve years. Twelve plus nine was twenty-one. "Well, maybe we could have a beer together someday."

"I'd like that, honey. I'd like that very much."

Mitch pulled into the driveway, happy to be home. Tess liked to activate the garage door opener—something that reminded Mitch that she was still a little girl—so he pulled the unit down from the visor and handed it to her. Out of the corner of his eye he thought he saw someone run across the backyard. He didn't want to alarm Tess so he said nothing while he pulled into the garage. "Go on in, honey, I'm going to put out the garbage."

"Dad, they come on Tuesday."

"Oh, right. Well, go on in, I just—"

"Mitch! Thank God!" Joya, in a see-through nude-colored short nightie, appeared at the garage door.

"Joya!" Mitch said, unable to hide his surprise. "What is it? Another bat?"

"No!" she squealed. "This time it's a mouse. What kind of critter-infested house did I buy? What should I do? Can you catch it?"

Mitch laughed. "Well, it's a little different than going after a bat. We might have some traps. Come on in." Mitch had forgotten about Tess until he turned to see her bug-out eyes as she stared at Joya.

"Joya, are you naked or something?"

"What?" She looked down at herself. "Oh, wow. I'd forgotten I'd put on my jamies." She wrapped her arms around her chest and smiled.

Sure you did, Mitch thought, as he held the door for her, pretending to avert his eyes. She had perfect breasts, full and round.

While he scouted around the basement for traps, Tess and Joya talked in the kitchen. Mitch heard something about a kitten. When he came back upstairs, Joya pounced on him. "Mitchell Langdon, do you have something against felines?" she asked.

"Not really, but we already have a pet."

"A dog," Tess said. "A dog that would greatly benefit from a buddy to keep her company when I'm not around."

Mitch placed the mousetraps on the counter. "You really think Piper would put up with competition?"

"Dad! What are you talking about? Piper is the sweetest creature in the world! Come on, Dad!"

"Yeah, come on, *Dad*," Joya chided.

"Hey, wait a minute, don't gang up on me."

Joya smiled a wicked smile. "Come on, Tess, let's gang up on him. Let's tickle him until he says yes to a pussycat." And before Mitch could move an inch, Tess and Joya were upon him, fingers digging into his slightly paunchy stomach. The worst thing was, he was ticklish. Extremely ticklish.

"I love you I love you I love you I," Mitch chanted between giggles—their family's version of surrender.

"Really, Mitchell," Joya said, her bountiful breasts spilling out of her nightie as she fluttered her fingers on his neck, "I don't know you all that well, but I love you, too."

Mitch felt himself go red in the face. "Okay, okay, you can have a kitten," he blurted. What else could he do? "We'll get you a kitten."

Tess faked a swoon and fell to the floor. Joya grabbed a magazine and fanned herself. Mitch had to smile. Tess bolted up and said, "Wait a minute. That was too easy! You're not kidding, right? *Dad*. You said it now. It's as good as a promise."

Mitch tucked his shirt back into his slacks. He scratched his head, not quite sure what had just transpired. Was this planned? Did these two jinxes pull one over on him? Mitch cleared his throat. "I found two traps."

"Traps?" Joya said.

"For the mouse."

"Of course! For the mouse. How could I have forgotten? The mouse. What do I do, just put a little piece of cheese on it? Do you think mice like *Port Salut* cheese? It's French."

Mitch gave her a funny look.

"I'm in a gourmet cheese of the month club and June's cheese is *S.A.F.R. Port Salut*, a smooth, delectable cheese made in the province of Brittany."

"I'll just get you a hunk of cheddar," Mitch said, opening the refrigerator.

"Whatever. Hey, listen, can I borrow your little girl tomorrow? I need her assistance in picking up about five hundred marbles and about fifty dollars worth of pennies—what would that be, like five thousand, yeah, five thousand pennies—off the hardwood floor in my bedroom."

Mitch didn't want to ask, but how could he not? "Marbles and pennies?"

"No one to blame but myself. Man, I got a temper. Gran-Glen will drive you to it. Anyway, as a stress release, I like to throw things. Glass was always my favorite—there's something cathartic about the sound of shattering glass—but then once I cut my toe on a shard and had to have a gob of stitches so I had to find alternatives. Pennies work beautifully—any coins, really, but pennies are just the right weight. Marbles are good because they give you that initial satisfaction when they hit the floor, and then you get the bonus—the rolling. Call me crazy, but it beats pharmaceuticals and doctors, no offense intended."

"So you want Tess to crawl around on her hands and knees retrieving your pennies?"

"And marbles," Tess chimed in.

What he wanted to say was *have you lost your marbles?* but Tess gave him a look.

"Tell you what," Joya said, "she can keep all the pennies she picks up, and if she gets all the marbles I'll buy her a cat. I will. I'll take her tomorrow. My treat. I know a guy."

Mitch just stared at this kook in his kitchen. Who was this woman and how had she infiltrated his private sanctuary?

"Dad, I think it's a good offer," Tess said, nodding.

Mitch handed Joya the traps and a hunk of cheddar.

"And I know just what I'll name her," Tess said, as she walked Joya to the door.

"Let me guess," Joya said. "Scout."

"Close. Jean Louise."

"A tabby then?"

"How'd you know?" Tess, said, obviously impressed with this half-naked, barefoot, crazy woman.

"It just fits, kid. But it should be a brown tabby, not an orange tabby. And it absolutely must have an outstanding personality…"

Mitch rubbed the back of his neck. Note to self: maybe this woman *was* a crazy bohemian. He held the door open for Joya, wondering if he shouldn't have grabbed her a robe or something.

"Thanks for the traps, Doc," Joya said.

"Listen," Mitch said, standing at the back door, "Maybe *I* should take Tess to get the cat."

Tess tugged on his shirt. "Come on, Dad, you know you don't have time. Joya can take me. Oh, oh, oh, I'm so excited. I'm getting a kitten!"

Danny came into the kitchen, eyes all bugged out when he saw Joya in her flimsy nightie, standing at the open door, seeped in moonlight. "What's going on?" he asked.

"I'm getting a kitten for picking up marbles," Tess explained. "What do you have to say about that?"

Danny gave Tess his vintage look—arched eyebrow and smirk. "Did you know that you can have the cremated remains of a loved one made into a diamond?" he asked, apropos to nothing.

"Dan!" Mitch said, "Why do you have to be so mean?"

"Oh, I heard about that!" Joya said, inching her way back into the house. "My girlfriend had this humongous rock made out of her big fat old fart of a husband. Good ol' Charlie Rockman. They called him Rocky. Then they turned him into a rock. Isn't that a hoot?" Joya slapped her thigh. Apparently she thought it was a hoot.

Mitch watched Tess's eyes grow big as dinner plates. "Dad, is that true?"

"Well, we are all made of carbon, honey, so yes, I guess it's true. I don't know how appropriate it is, but I guess it's true."

"Biggest ass diamond—'scuse the French—you ever saw. It was blue—this beautiful blue princess cut stone."

"Yuck!" Tess said.

Mitch was sure Tess would have nightmares now, but Joya was oblivious. "Course I didn't dare make my husband into a diamond. What would people have said? They were saying enough as it was."

Mitch stared at Joya. Would she ever shut up? Would she ever leave?

"Okay, well, looks like I've said enough as well. Thanks for the traps and the cheese and I'll see you tomorrow," she said, tapping Tess on the head.

"Uh, Joya, do you want help setting up those traps?" Danny asked.

"Why ain't you sweet," Joya said, with a Southern drawl. "But just so you know, Lee isn't home yet, so if you're offering just to see my beautiful baby, you're out of luck."

"No, no, I just thought you might be grossed out by mouse traps."

"As a matter of fact, I am," she said, holding them far out in front of her.

Mitch couldn't help but feel, as he watched Danny leave with Joya, that he was allowing his son to go off with the wolves.

He felt even worse the next morning, when he watched Tess scamper off next door to pick up pennies and marbles that had been thrown in a fit of rage. What did he really know of the three blondos next door? After they moved in, the night of the bat incident, he'd logged on to the Internet to see if he could find out anything about the alleged scandal. He'd found an article in the Chicago Tribune:

Lake Forest Woman Acquitted of Husband's Murder

A judge acquitted Joya Elizabeth Harper today of murdering her husband, Reid Logan Harper. The 44-year-old woman burst into tears and embraced her teenaged daughter as District Judge Carson Delkin announced his verdict after thirty minutes of deliberation. Mrs. Harper had waived a jury trial.

Reid Harper, a prominent corporate attorney, was pronounced dead on November 22nd, at Lake Forest Hospital, following a fall from a staircase in the couple's home at 2121 Castle Ridge Avenue. Coroner Lawrence Samson had investigated the case and issued a certificate of accidental death, but on November 24th, a woman named Zena Stuckey came forward with information that she was having an affair with Reid Harper and the day of his death was the day he had agreed to inform his wife of their affair and ask for a divorce.

Mrs. Harper admitted to quarreling with her husband, but maintained that he revealed nothing about an affair. She stated the two had a disagreement in the upstairs hall about their daughter. She testified that following the argument, she went to her daughter's bedroom to speak to her, and her husband went downstairs. She said her husband must have mis-stepped on his way down the stairs and fell to his death. Reid Harper suffered a cerebral contusion and died later that night at Lake Forest Hospital.

Judge Delkin said the decision to acquit Mrs. Harper was not difficult because the prosecution was never able to erase doubts raised by the defense. There were no signs of a struggle and the injuries her husband sustained were consistent with those one would get in an accidental fall.

The testimony of the couple's teenaged daughter provided key evidence for the defense. The daughter testified that although she did not witness the accident, she heard her parents arguing, not about another woman, as the prosecutors had stated, but about her. She maintained that she heard her mother knocking loudly on her bedroom door and when she opened it, it was then that she and her mother both heard the loud thumping sounds of her father falling down the marble staircase.

"I'm just so relieved," Harper said. "Now my daughter and I can grieve properly. This has been a nightmare."

In a later interview, Mrs. Harper said that her attorney has filed a suit against Jickers and Sons Construction, the building contractors for Harper's $995,000 home, maintaining that the dimensions of the risers and treads of the staircase in the home varied more than building codes allowed and could have caused her husband to mis-step and fall to his death.

Satisfied that his neighbor had been wrongly accused and rightly acquitted, Mitch had decided he would give Joya the benefit of the doubt. Surely she and her daughter had been through hell and had moved here to start a new life, untarnished by the accident and the case. Still, they were an odd trio over there. He knew one thing: the grandmother's dementia was so severe there was no way she should be without twenty-four hour supervision. Lee seemed like a sweet kid, but Mitch knew you couldn't discount genetics. Madness could be heritable.

Now, he decided to make himself available and visible in case Tess needed him. The yard could use some attention so he recruited Luke (Danny was at work) to help him remove the thick trumpet vines that were creeping up the west side of the house and covering Tess's bedroom window. Mitch loved nothing more than working along side Luke. They made a good team.

Luke was up on the ladder with Mitch below, stuffing the vines into brown paper leaf bags, when they heard a ruckus coming from next door. Mitch heard Tess's giggle followed by Joya's cackle. He looked up at Luke. "Can you see anything from up there?" he called up.

Luke stretched his neck. "What the—?"

"What the *what?*"

"Am I seeing what I'm seeing?"

"What are you seeing?"

"I can't be sure, Dad, but I think Joya just threw a head of lettuce at Gran-Glen."

"What? Let me up there."

Luke climbed down the ladder and Mitch climbed up. Through the large pine trees that separated the two yards, he could see Gran-Glen standing out on the patio. She seemed fine and showed no apparent evidence of being beaned on the head by a crisphead. What's more, she seemed to be snickering. But wait, sure enough, a head of lettuce came flying through a second-floor window, followed shortly after, by what looked like a giant zucchini. Then his daughter's blonde head appeared at the open window. Laughing her head off, she turned and saw her dad. She waved and screamed, "Hi, Dad! We're playing David Letterman!"

Back in the house, Mitch was beside himself. "I don't know, just tell her that she has to come home," he told Luke, as he paced around the kitchen. "Tell her there's something wrong with Piper."

"Dad, I'm not going to lie," Luke said. He climbed up onto the kitchen counter and downed a glass of lemonade.

"Well, tell her we have to run out to the farm. For something or other."

"Dad, *you* go get her."

"I don't want to get stuck in that woman's web," Mitch said. "Do this for me, will you? Go get her and tell her *I'll* take her to get a kitten. We can go right now."

Mitch absentmindedly started opening and closing drawers and cupboards. "We do not have bohemians living next door, Luke, we have fruitcakes." He pulled a drawer out too far and it came off its track. He fiddled with it until he got it back on.

"What are you looking for?" Luke asked.

"Um, uh, uh—"

"Dad, do I have to go over there?"

"No, but I'm begging."

The phone rang just as Luke was hopping off the counter. He answered it, then handed the phone to Mitch.

"It's me, Daddy!" Tess sang. "I'm on Joya's cell phone. We're just pulling out of the driveway, on our way to get my new kitten! We have the top down and I'm so excited!"

"Oh. All right, honey. Uh, Tess, listen honey, Luke was just about to—oh, never mind. Well, actually, honey, Luke wanted to come along, if that's okay."

"No, Dad, it's not okay. This is *my* day. It's all about ME!"

"Oh, well, if you're sure. You're buckled up, right? And you're in the back seat, right?"

"Yes and yes, Dr. Worrywart."

"All right then, I'll be here when you get back, to welcome home our new family member. All right? See you when you get here."

He hung up the phone and looked at Luke. Luke shook his head. "Seriously, Dad. '*Luke wants to come along*'? Seriously."

Mitch ran his hand through his hair. "It's at times like these I wished I knew what your mother would say."

"She'd probably say that you're doing a pretty damn good job."

"I don't know. What would I have done without you? I couldn't have done it without you."

"But you're going to have to, you know."

"Don't remind me," Mitch said, opening the drawer to the built-in desk and sifting through the junk.

"Dad, what *are* you looking for?"

"I have no idea."

The phone rang again and this time Mitch answered it. "Oh, all right," he said, "I'll send him right out." He hung up the phone.

"What?" Luke asked. "*Dad?*"

"It seems that once Blondo found out you wanted to come along she turned the car around. They're in our driveway. Waiting for you."

"Seriously Dad!"

"Seriously, son."

Mitch couldn't bring himself to walk Luke to the car. He'd heard him muttering "you owe me big time" under his breath. When the back door slammed shut, Mitch stood at the counter, listening to the pulsating silence. He poured himself a glass of lemonade and drank it down while his internal cortex and limbic systems fought with one another. What a dirty, rotten thing to do to Luke. But he had to do it, for Tess's sake, for Tess's protection. He grabbed his cell phone and went back outside to finish thinning out the vines. Thank God for Luke, he kept thinking. Thank God for Luke.

{*"Cecilia, how can I help Mitch to understand that God has already given him everything he needs? He'll be fine when Luke goes away to college. I wish I could tell him that he needn't ask for anything ever again because God has planted the seed of every holy possibility deep inside his heart—all of our hearts. The old saying "God helps those who helps themselves" is not just a cliché. Our prayers should be of thanks rather than of supplication, because asking God for something is like asking the waitress for a glass of water when there is one sitting right in front of you. Remember what Jesus said: "I tell you therefore: everything you ask and pray for, believe that you have it already, and it will be yours."*

Know this: God answers prayers that we aren't even smart enough to put into words!}

Mitch spent almost two hours trimming vines from the house. Tired and sweaty, he was just about to call it quits and climb down the ladder when, for a second time that morning, some commotion from next door caught his attention. This time it was a deep, raspy voice and a flash of bright red. He squinted and peered through the trees and saw Gran-Glen dancing in the Harper's backyard. At first he thought she was wearing red, but then realized that she was wearing *nothing* and swirling a piece of red clothing above her head, while belting out that old burlesque striptease melody—*dunt da duh, da dunt da duh…* *Not* a pretty sight! The neighbor in him said, "just let her be" but the physician in him said otherwise. What if she wandered out of the backyard? How could Blondo leave her alone (Lee was at work) knowing her condition was this advanced? Did Blondo even have a clue? What if the poor lady meandered down by the river's edge?

He ran into the house and grabbed a knit throw from the sofa and headed next door. "Glenda," he called out while he was still several yards away, so as not to frighten her. "Glenda."

She wasn't startled when he approached and he quickly realized that she wasn't even aware of her nudity.

"Well, hello there," she said. "Warren, isn't it?"

"Mitch, actually."

"You look more like a Warren; I'm going to call you Warren."

"Fine, fine. Uh, I live next door and I…"

"Well, I know that," she said, waving at the air. "You and Tabitha have lived next door for thirty-two years. How is Tabitha?"

"Fine, fine. Here, Glenda, it's getting chilly, why don't you wrap this shawl around you."

"I'm not cold. I'm—" She looked down at herself. "Oh. I guess I'm naked!" Her hand went demurely to her mouth. She looked at the red sweater in her hand and shrugged. "I must've gotten hot. There's nothing wrong with nudity, you know, it's a very natural thing."

"Yes, but it's also a very illegal thing, Glenda, so why don't we go inside and you can put a dress on and—" His hand automatically went to the small of her back to lead her, but thankfully he caught himself and stopped before touching her.

She just laughed and said, "Now, Warren, you never used to be afraid of touching my naked body. Even after your wife found out about us. Come on," she giggled, "let's go skinny dipping or something."

"Maybe later, Glenda. Your daughter will be home soon and I don't think she'd like it if she caught us, well, you know."

"Oh just say it, you Puritan—fooling around! Lord, we made fooling around into an art form, didn't we?"

"You might say that," Mitch said, cringing inside. "Now let's get you dressed and then we can talk."

"*Talk?* When a man wants to talk you know something's wrong. Darling, are you breaking it off?"

Well, he was this far into it now. "It's not fair to Tabitha. She's been a good wife."

"That's true; she stuck by you even after you two-timed and three-timed her. Oh, but what will I do? I'll miss our escapades."

"So will I, dear. Now let me take you upstairs."

"For one last romp?"

Good lord! What had he got himself into? And how could he get out of it? "Now Glenda, don't tease me. You know I can't anymore. Must you humiliate me?"

"My poor dear stud! I had no idea! What a shame."

Mitch followed her upstairs and down the hall. She started to walk into Lee's bedroom so he took her by the arm and urged her on. She turned and walked into a room which Mitch could only describe as brothel-esque: vermillion-colored walls, strings of glass beads for curtains, bejeweled window shades and lampshades, leopard-skin comforter. It had to be Blondo's room. As he entered, following Glenda, he stepped on something—a marble. Yes, it was Blondo's room.

"This isn't my room!" Glenda exclaimed, turning abruptly.

Finally, she found her room at the end of the hall—a study in pale blue sophistication. It made Mitch wonder what kind of person Glenda had been before she started losing herself to dementia. She certainly carried herself like a grand dame. He was getting used to her nakedness, watching as she walked to her closet and swung open the doors. "What to wear. What to wear. Are we just dining out or will we be dancing as well?"

Mitch sighed. He was tired of this game. "Whatever you want."

She shuffled through her closet and then grabbed something white and lacey and disappeared into the attached bathroom. Mitch sighed and sat on the bed. This was bizarre. This poor woman belonged in a nursing home. He let his tired head drop into his hands as he pondered his next step. He looked up when he heard footsteps approaching, and then at precisely the same moment, Blondo walked into the bedroom as Glenda emerged from the bathroom in a white negligee.

"I can explain," Mitch said sheepishly, rising to his feet.

"Mitchell Langdon," Joya said, "if you were interested in my mother you should have said something. Hey, we can double date. You and Gran-Glen and me and Luke."

Mitch tried to conceal his shock. She was a whack-job, all right. "I was up on the ladder and I found your mother naked in the back yard, doing a striptease."

"Who is this man in my bedroom, Joya?" Glenda said. "I would appreciate if you and your gentlemen friends stayed the hell out of my room."

Mitch just shook his head. "We need to talk," he said to Joya. In the hallway, he stepped on another marble. Not wanting to break his back, he carefully walked down the steps and out the back door. The screen door just barely missed hitting Tess, who was sitting on Joya's back porch cuddling her new kitten.

"Daddy, what are you doing here? Joya was just getting me a rhinestone collar for my kitten and then we were coming home to show her to you." Tess leaned in to give her dad a peek at the little ball of fur wrapped up in a pale blue baby blanket. "Isn't she beautiful?"

"She sure is, honey." Mitch said, sitting down next to his happy little girl. "So, this is Jean Louise."

"Actually, I changed my mind. Her name is Annie."

Mitch gulped. "Annie? Honey, you can't name a kitten after your mother!"

"Why not? People make diamond rings out of their mothers, why can't I name a kitten after mine? Mom loved cats—she couldn't help that she was allergic to them. She'd be honored."

Mitch was quiet for a moment. He rubbed the bridge of his nose. *What would Annie say? What would Annie say? Think. Think.* "I don't know, Tess, don't you think it might make you sad to hear your mom's name all the time? I know it would make *me* sad."

"Well…"

"Well, how about something close. Something that rhymes with Annie. How about Fanny or Franny or Manny or Nanny?"

Tess shook her head. "*Dad.*"

"Okay, what about Annie backwards or Anne backwards—Enna. That's kind of neat. And the meaning of it could be our secret. Just between us."

"Enna. Enna. En-na. I kind of like it, it sounds a little like Emma and that's one of my favorite names."

Joya appeared at the back door with a rhinestone studded kitty collar dangling from her index finger. "I found it, I had to look *everywhere*, but I found it! Let's see how it looks on her." Mitch moved over a bit so Joya could open the screen door without whacking him. She sat down next to Tess and gently took the kitten from her. She laid it in her lap and unwrapped the blanket.

Mitch almost jumped out of his skin. "Yow! Is that a cat or a leopard? I thought you were getting a tabby!"

"They were out of tabbies," Joya informed him. "This young lady is a brown spotted rosetted female Bengal."

"A what?" Mitch actually felt his heart flutter. This thing was wild looking. Gorgeous. Exotic. But wild looking.

"Bengals are a special breed, a hybrid that resulted from crossing the Asian Leopard Cat with a domestic cat."

"I've never seen such a thing. Joya, I'm not sure about this—"

"Dad!" Tess said.

"Where did you get such a cat? Are they legal?"

"Ugh!" Joya said, slapping her chest. "Your words wound me! I told you I knew a guy. A breeder. This little beauty comes with papers." Joya nuzzled the kitten and purred. "Tess could show her someday if she wanted to."

"Joya, this cat must have cost an arm and a leg."

"Just an arm, but I only need one, so don't worry about it. Really."

"I can't let you."

"It was payment for a job well done. Your daughter worked her butt off gathering up all those coins and marbles."

"Are you sure they're good with children, wild blood and all?"

"I anticipated your every question," Joya said. She passed Tess the little bundle of kitten and pulled a folded brochure out of the back pocket of her shorts and handed it to Mitch.

235

Mitch unfolded the pamphlet and read aloud: "*Bengals love children and children love Bengals. Bengals are active, talkative cats and love to play. They are curious, investigative, and intelligent. The Bengal cat is very people oriented, affectionate and loyal. They exhibit dog-like characteristics—they play fetch and can be leash-trained—and they are quick to learn and adapt.*"

"See, Dad, see? Enna is just perfect!"

"En-what?" Joya said. "What did you call her?"

"Enna."

"*Enna*? I thought you were naming her after your mom. Enna sounds, well, it sounds like 'enema.'"

"Gross!" Tess screeched.

Mitch sent Joya a look that could kill, but it went right over her head. "This little girl is an Annie," she said, pinching the kitten gently under the chin. "This face says *Annie*."

"You're right," Tess said, reclaiming her kitten and her first choice name. "Annie it is."

Mitch looked around. Good lord, it had happened again! Outsmarted by these jinxes. Where was Luke anyway, and why hadn't he put a stop to this? "Where's Luke, Tess?"

"He's home," Joya answered.

"Tess, why don't you take your kitten home and introduce her to Piper. I need to talk to Joya for a minute."

"Dad, you better not—"

"Tess, *you* better not, now get home. Now."

Once his daughter was out of earshot, Mitch said, "Joya, about your mother…"

❦

Back at home, Mitch plopped down in his recliner. What the hell was going on? These kids were driving him crazy. Tess! First with the Scout obsession, then with the lying, and now it looked as if she might be cultivating the fine art of manipulation! And the boys, well… He'd read all about teenage boys: they think about sex all the time; they do crazy stunts with their friends, like grinding a skateboard down a flight of stairs; they visit porn web sites and swear it wasn't them; they stomp through the house asserting their dominance, swearing like truck drivers (do most truck drivers swear?); they put their comrades before family members; and worst of all they experience unrequited love, heartbreak, and betrayal for the first time in their lives.

Okay, so Luke got through high school with almost none of the above. And Danny, with almost all of the above. But they'd made it. But what about Tess? She was nine. By the time she was eighteen Mitch would be seventy-two. Seventy-two! He was ashamed to admit it, but he'd let himself think, while lying alone and sleepless in bed, that it might have been better if they had stopped at Danny. Tess had been a gift, but what she required he simply didn't have anymore.

Maybe Miranda Burns was right. Maybe he should break down and talk to a professional. The saying goes that doctors make the very worst patients and Mitch was living proof. The only human soul with whom he could bear his soul was now pure soul. Oh, grieving was such hard work, and such a peculiar and idiosyncratic process that it never followed the same path. He knew that Tess's grieving was different from Danny's, that was different from Luke's.

Why was it that widows seemed to fare better than widowers? They knew how to cash in on the capital they built up over the years through friendships and church and community. But widowers often came up bankrupt in the friendship area. For them, family was their community. Most men are not good at networking. Men would rather not ask for help—it's not manly. Ah yes, grieving for men is a mixed bag of goods: a lonely, all-your-own, quiet endeavor.

Good Lord, he wished he had all the answers.

{Cecilia, I wish I could tell him that one of the most wonderful things about Heaven is that you finally get answers. I'm not saying that you know everything—we don't become mini gods—but you continue learning and

there are some truly satisfying revelations and epiphanies. I just can't tell you how pleasing that is. I mean, I, Anne Louise Hopewell Langdon, of ordinary intelligence and wherewithal, now understand quantum physics. I have seen the sun's heliospheric current sheet and could describe it to you as well as the best physicist (some other time!).

You discover big things and little things. I know why the dinosaurs all died out and what Maureen O'Hara whispered in John Wayne's ear at the end of the movie "The Quiet Man." (This is a secret piece of information that John Wayne and director John Ford took to their graves and Maureen O'Hara refuses to divulge.) I now know why bad things happen to good people and good things happen to bad people. And I understand what seems on earth to be an unjust distribution of pleasure and pain, joy and sorrow, reward and punishment. Anyway, I know things. I know. I know. I know things.

And I'm learning more day by day. And I wish Mitch could know that he's doing a great job. He'll be okay. He doesn't have to have all the answers.}

Mitch heard the side door slam shut which meant Danny was home from work. He looked toward the doorway and watched Danny emerge, a riot of color and energy in the dusky room. He sighed and dumped his tired body in the chair next to Mitch's.

"Hard day?" Mitch asked.

"Oh dear Father, how weary am I! Hunger and thirst twist in my belly. How my tendons and ligaments lament to their overuse. My skin is darkened with filth and alas, my stench is so foul it rivals that of swine. Ah, but dear Father, I toil for good cause, for nothing pleases me more, my Liege, than to please you."

Mitch smiled. "Dan, you crack me up. You really do."

Danny beamed.

"And know my loyal child, thou doest please me greatly. My pride bursteth forth from my very being."

Danny let out a laugh and beamed even brighter.

Chapter Twenty-two

Bless My Soul

CECILIA SAYS I am progressing. "You get an 'A' for effort," she teases. My time of reflection and solitude is over and now it is time to join the community of saints. One blink and I am surrounded by bright souls, waiting to meet me. They gather me into their fold and I feel like a baby just handed over to his mother's loving arms.

Let me say this: if you wonder about the "communion of saints" in Heaven, then study Dictyostelium discoideum (slime mold) while you're on earth. Go ahead, Google it! You'll be amazed. You can find slime mold on every continent on earth. Peer closer at a rotting log or stump, dead leaves or bark. (Wouldn't Luke be awed and dumbstruck that his mom knows about such things! And wouldn't Danny be surprised that the name of his rock band "Slime Mold" is a hint about Heaven?) Well, slime mold, despite its lowly name is one of the most fascinating "critters" in the universe. They are not animals; they are not plants. They are the least understood life form of the five kingdoms of life, the other four being animals, plants, fungi, and bacteria. I know you are wondering what slime molds and saints have in common, and it is this: slime mold oscillates between being a single creature and a swarm.

For all intents and purposes slime mold is an incredibly primitive organism. Slime molds have no centralized brain, yet, in their plasmodium stage they exhibit what looks like intelligence: they can separate into thousands of distinct single-celled units, each moving separately from its other buddies, and then under certain conditions, the myriad cells will coalesce again into a single, larger organism—the "they" becoming an "it."

And so it is in Heaven. We are distinct individual beings and yet we are perfect togetherness. It is difficult to think in earthly terms of collective phenomenon, but it is true, like lowly slime mold that can be chopped up and dropped into a labyrinth, we saints put ourselves together and move unerringly for our prize—God.

It is so interesting to explore what people throughout history have thought about the soul. The Fijians believed the soul was a miniature replica of the body, so small as to be invisible. The Samoans thought that the soul was something "which comes and goes." Some people, such as the ancient Sumatrans and the Dyaks, feared that the soul could escape the body, and during sickness they would bind various parts of the bodies with cords to prevent the soul from slipping away. Plato believed the body and soul were distinct orders of reality, and that the body was the prison of the soul. Aristotle emphasized the closeness of body and soul. The Stoics thought that all existence was material and described the soul as a breath pervading the body, composed of the most refined and ethereal matter.

I knew this one lady who insisted that the soul was a microscopic bubble, delicate as a soap bubble, but strong as a marble, that dwelled in the heart's chamber; literally, in the right atrium. Then there was this scientist who said he proved that the human soul actually lay in the head, by performing a chimpanzee head transplant. Some people think our soul is actually what scientists call "junk DNA."

My dears, the soul is so much more than simply that which animates our bodies. It is more than the ultimate internal principle by which we think, feel, and will. From the beginning of time we have been scrutinizing the mysteries of birth and death. We have considered the lapse of conscious life during sleep. We have mulled over the operations of imagination and memory, which temporarily remove us from our bodily presence. We know *that all these things suggest that something within us exists aside from our visible self. It is internal to our organism, but also largely independent of it. In a sense, our soul leads a life of its own. And even though we can't grasp it or define it, we know our soul exists, just as we know our finger or our toe exists. C. S. Lewis said it best. He said: "You don't have a soul. You are a Soul. You have a body." I also like what Oscar Wilde said: "The soul is born old and grows young. That is the comedy of life." Or how about Meister Eckhart's words: "No one knows what the soul is. But what we do know is the soul is where God works compassion."*

One of my favorite poems about the soul came from Jelalluddin Rumi.

> *Oh soul,*
> *You worry too much.*
> *You have seen your own strength.*
> *You have seen your own beauty.*
> *You have seen your golden wings.*
> *Of anything less*
> *Why do you worry?*
> *You are in truth*
> *The soul, of the soul, of the soul.*

Think about your soul being nourished when you are kind. Destroyed when you are cruel. Nourished when you pray. Destroyed when you stubbornly give in to temptation. Your soul is dynamic, fluid, in the state of flux. Your soul is part of the universe and you may be surprised to know that what connects you to the universe is the right temporal lobe in your brain. (Melvin Morse, a pediatrician/neurologist, calls this area the "God Spot," after he studied patients who had returned from near death and found that this underused part of our brain is what unites us to the universe.)

I will say this: the student who is willing to boldly examine theology, history, philosophy, physics, evolutionary biology, theistic evolution or biologos, world religions, chemistry, quantum physics, water, light, cosmology, mathematics, near death experiences, sacred texts, and prayer and meditation, and then is willing to admit to the world that he still does not have all the answers will be closest to the truth. Humans haven't even begun to learn about the richness of our inner lives and its effects on the world around us. I certainly never focused much on my "inner self," although of course now I wish I had.

I'm meeting the most interesting people here: Ellen Church, who was the very first airline flight attendant; a charming man named Luther Crowell, who invented the paper bag; a Mr. Walter Hunt, the inventor of the safety pin; and Ruth Handler, the inventor of my favorite childhood toy, the Barbie doll. I met spunky Anna Edson Taylor, who was the first person to go over Niagra Falls in a barrel. I met Edwin Cox, the man who invented those steel wool S.O.S. pads—he told me his wife named them S.O.S. for "save our saucepans." I met St. Peter, my favorite apostle, and I can tell you this, he does not guard the Pearly Gates. There are no Pearly Gates. I met Mary Magdalene and I apologized to her for thinking she was a prostitute for most of my life.

I met Mary Anderson, the woman who invented the windshield wiper. I met the Wright brothers, and Charles Dickens, Dr. Martin Luther King, Jr., Mahatma Gandhi, Leonardo da Vinci, and Jacques Cousteau.

I met the inventor of American Sign Language, Thomas Gallaudet; the inventor of crossword puzzles, Arthur Wynne; and the inventor of disposable diapers, Marion Donovan.

And now you'll have to excuse me. Cecilia is calling. There are more people to meet!

Chapter Twenty-three

In the Moon Garden

{"Danny is a shower singer," I tell Cecilia. For as long as I can remember Danny sang in the shower. Big show tunes like "New York, New York" and "My Way," or Beatles favorites like "Maxwell's Silver Hammer" and "Yellow Submarine." He sang off key, at the top of his lungs. It annoyed Mitch and Luke as much as it amused Tess and me. The world would be a better place if more people started off their day singing in the shower.}

THE THING WAS, Danny liked to have a smoke up on top of the roof of the house. Mitch would have a stroke if he knew Danny smoked. Danny never would have been able to pull the wool over Annie—she had a remarkable sense of smell— but Mitch had sinus problems and the family joke was that he could barely smell his own farts. Still, smoking in his room was too risky. In the summer, when Danny couldn't sleep, he simply climbed out his bedroom window and had a smoke with the stars.

Alone time was good but could also be dangerous. Thoughts would creep into your brain that you would rather stay out. It wasn't good to think about his mom and that day. So you fill your brain with dumb stuff. You ask yourself stupid questions that you can't answer without looking them up: If Teflon is nonsticky, how do they get it to stick to the pan? Why do kids scream, "*Olly, Olly, oxen free, last one in is a P-I-G!*" when playing hide and seek? Why do worms crawl out onto the sidewalk after it rains? And speaking of worms, are they really bisexual critters that can self-mate? Why don't people with mono brows pluck them? What do the letters 'OK' stand for? And how much wood would a woodchuck chuck if a woodchuck could chuck wood, anyway? Oh, the things you could think about to keep yourself from thinking about things.

{"Cecilia, my husband needs to open his eyes and clear out his nose—I can't believe that he doesn't know that Luke is drinking and Danny is smoking. They never could have gotten away with these stunts if I were still alive!}

Don't look now, but Danny was getting tired of his job at the nursery. It was hard work being a "grunt," much harder than he had imagined. Muscles he rarely used, muscles he didn't even know he had, now ached on a regular basis. And his allergies had kicked in big time. His dad would kill him if he quit, but he began to fantasize about it daily (and nightly).

The job might not have been so bad if it hadn't been for the crazy drought Rockford was experiencing this summer. Last summer had been one of the coldest, wettest on record, and now this summer seemed to be heading in the other direction, bone dry and hell hot. All he did at the nursery was water, water, water; move heavy plants from one corner of the nursery to another; and heave enormous bags of top soil, manure, and mulch into the cars of little old ladies who didn't know the meaning of the word "tip."

Oh, the money was nice. Especially since the lovely Lee Harper had let him buy her lunch once last week and had also let him take her miniature golfing. Okay, so Tess came along both times, but still…he was keeping his fingers crossed that things would very soon move from nice neighbor to hot lover.

After beating both Lee and Tess at mini-golf and treating them to root beer floats at Dairy Queen, Danny had been encouraged. Lee seemed so comfortable with him. But she seemed just as comfortable with Tess, so maybe it was nothing. Lee loved Tess. Twenty-million-question-Tess.

"Lee, what do you want to be when you grow up," Tess had asked, slurping her root beer.

"I don't know, what do you want to be?"

"I asked you first, but I'll answer first. I want to write the second perfect novel ever written, second to *To Kill a Mockingbird*, have it made into a movie starring Johnny Depp as the dad, and then I want it to be required reading for every high school student in America, and then after the book tour and the movie promos, I'll retire from literature, enroll in veterinary school and then get married, have some kids and a googolplex of animals. Now you."

"Well, I'm not as certain as you are, I just know that I want to help people. So maybe a social worker, or maybe I'll join the Peace Corp or work for Habitat for Humanity or something. My dad used to tell me this little rhyme: '*A friendly look, a kindly smile, one good act, and life's worthwhile.*' I guess that saying has stuck. Danny? What about you?"

"Filmmaking," Tess told her.

Before Danny could explain that he'd changed his mind and was now considering a career in linguistics, Lee was going on about how cool it would be to make movies, so Danny decided that at the moment filmmaking did sound like the cooler career and smiled an 'oh shucks' smile. "I want to make beautiful art films and important documentaries. No Hollywood crap."

And that is how he got himself trapped into helping Tess with her head-in-the-clouds project.

"Speaking of," Tess said, "Joya gave me a great idea the other day: to interview people about Heaven and have Danny film the interviews for a documentary."

Danny glared at Tess. His big mouth almost ruined it for him. "Tess, that's a stu—"

"Great idea!" Lee said.

"A *stupendous* idea is what I was going to say," Danny said, recovering nicely, if he must say so himself.

Tess gave her brother a look of disbelief. "You mean you'd really help me?"

"Of course I will."

"And so will I," Lee said.

"Oh, thank you, thank you, thank you!" Tess said.

Lee smiled—Danny loved how her whole faced smiled, not just her mouth, but her eyes and her eyebrows, her forehead and cheeks, even her nose. "You're welcome, welcome, welcome," she said.

"Well, get your video camera ready Danny, because I would like to start interviewing people at the Fourth of July party. Joya is going to be my first interviewee. Would you be my number two, Lee?"

"Sure, Scout."

So, here on the roof, Danny was thinking about what might be necessary to win over the lovely Lee Harper. Obviously, he'd have to undergo a complete makeover. He'd need to morph into a kinder, gentler Danny. A Danny with a conscience, instead of a Danny with a punch line. And he'd have to back it all up with action. He'd actually have to start thinking of making "goodness" a goal. It was an interesting concept—doing good—yet it seemed to sometimes be self-serving. It wasn't that Danny was such a bad guy, but, he realized, for the last eighteen years he'd been focused on one thing: himself. The words "social action" and "social justice" were not part of his vernacular. Once his father had lectured him about thinking of others and the virtues of altruism. Danny pondered altruism. Where did it come from? He couldn't imagine cavemen donating food or firewood to less fortunate cavemen strangers who lived far away. From a genetic perspective—

the advancement of the species and all of that—it would be like suicide to squander your life's precious resources for no biological benefit. So how did helping strangers ever become vogue? Hmmm.

A little self-evaluation was in order here. Well, he was kind to strangers and helpful to people in general—he held doors open, offered his seat to his elders, would stop to help up a little kid who had fallen. He was a nice guy, wasn't he? But, he guessed he was the kind of guy who was more interested in random acts of kindness than in deliberate altruism. Being kind was more a game to him, a challenge to see if he could get people to smile. Did this make him shallow? He took one last puff on his smoke—literally one last puff—because Lee had said earlier that cigarettes disgusted her. He flicked the butt far out into the lawn and climbed back in through his bedroom window, singing, "*She came in through the bathroom window*," from the Beatles song of the same title.

He'd need a book, some radical change-your-life book. He booted up his computer. Amazon.com was a beautiful thing—the perfect way for a guy with a non-scholarly reputation to get what he wanted without ever setting a foot in a bookstore, especially the one where his brother worked. The last book he ordered on Amazon.com was a book to help make him smarter called "How To Sound Smart," by Norah Vincent and Chad Conway, and maybe Norah and Chad sounded smart when they threw out phrases like "*cogito, ergo sum*" (I think, therefore I am) or called their assistant their "aide-de-camp" or a traitor a "quisling," but the one time Danny tried to use a phrase from the book it bombed. A customer had asked advice on shade perennials and instead of saying "for example" Danny said "*exempli gratia*" (what we are abbreviating when we write "e.g."). The man said, "Those are purple, right? I think my mom always grew exempli gratias." Danny threw the book away and decided to stick with Reader's Digest's "It Pays To Increase Your Word Power."

Anyway.

In his search, he found an interesting book called "This Book Will Change Your Life." One click and it was his. (Luke paid the bills, so Danny assumed that Luke assumed that any charges to Amazon were Mitch's. Everyone knew that Danny hadn't opened a book since graduation.) Satisfied, Danny got back in bed and decided that part of being good was being responsible and that part of being responsible was keeping his job. So he resigned himself as he turned over to sleep on his stomach.

Then he got fired. Well, not fired but "laid off." What with the drought and all, the nursery was not as busy as last summer and the guy who hurt his back was back at work so Danny was superfluous, a word that turned out to be music to his ears. Of course Danny feigned disappointment, and he felt genuinely bad for his manager who looked like he felt genuinely bad. But inside, inside, he was singing! How often does a guy get to quit a job without actually quitting? And after only a few weeks? It was the best of all worlds—his dad couldn't be angry, and now that it was the beginning of July all the summer jobs would be taken by college kids. What good fortune! Now he could concentrate all his efforts on his miniature house front business—several of which lay unfinished in the garage—on the Heaven documentary, and, most importantly, on winning the heart of the lovely and incomparable Lee Harvey Harper. (The "Harvey" part was his joke and thank God she found it funny. Other girls might not have laughed at being associated with Lee Harvey Oswald.)

"*Veni, vidi, vici!*" he sang as he punched out and walked (trying not to skip) to his car. Okay, so maybe he did find something useful from Norah and Chad's smarty-pants book. It captured his feelings perfectly: "*I came, I saw, I conquered!*"

***

The first thing Danny did after getting fired was to call his father and deliver the bad news.

"That's actually good news and bad news, Dan, because I just got a call from Calpur— I mean Mrs. Cally's son, and the poor thing just broke her hip and has to have surgery. I can keep you busy helping out with Tess for the rest of the summer," Mitch told him.

"No problem, Dad. The kid's growing on me."

"Oh, really? Could that have anything to do with her association with a pretty blonde in the neighborhood?"

It was hard to deny it, especially since he had just pulled into the parking lot of the North End Neighborhood Coffee Bar, where Lee worked. "Gotta go, Dad. Sorry about Mrs. Cally-purnia."

The coffee bar was hopping. He liked this place. Even though he didn't drink coffee, he liked the smell of it. Norah Jones was playing on the stereo and most of the tables were filled. His eyes cruised the counter looking for Lee, but she wasn't around. Look casual and cool, he told himself and stuck his hands in the side pockets of his Cargo shorts. In line at the counter, he tried to look nonchalant as he perused the chalkboard menu.

"Hey you," a voice called out somewhere from behind him.

He turned around and found Lee sitting at a table by herself, eating a sandwich. Suddenly, he was shy. "Hey yourself." He started to walk over but then a girl arrived at the counter to take his order. For some crazy reason he ordered lemonade—a sissy drink!—and a cherry scone—a sissy pastry! He paid and walked over to Lee with his wimpy tray of sissy food. "You on break?"

"Yeah. Sit if you want. I've got five more minutes. How come you're not working?"

"I actually got laid off."

"That's not cool."

"Yeah, but the timing is actually cool, because Mrs. Cally—you met her, right?—she broke her hip so now I have to take care of Tess for the rest of the summer."

"Scout's a sweetie."

"Yeah, well. I guess the good thing is that I'll have more time to help her with her documentary. Uh, do you want this scone?"

"No thanks, I just had a sandwich."

"Do you want this lemonade?"

"No thanks, I have coffee."

"Do you want to go listen to this guy I know who's in this new folk-slash-indie band called "The Stoned Throws" play tonight at Minglewood Music Cafe?"

Lee smiled. "Okay, yeah."

"Yeah?"

"Yeah."

"Not bad," Danny said, checking his watch. "I got fired and I got a date—all before noon."

The band sucked. The name of the band fit—all the members seemed stoned. Danny tried to talk over the noise but it was useless so he suggested they go to Zambuca, a new coffee house and piano bar downtown.

Danny wasn't sure if the place would be lively or mellow. He was hoping for mellow. Turned out to be a little of both—the crowd was lively but the music and the ambiance were mellow. The dude at the piano played and sang Stevie Wonder's *Isn't She Lovely?*

"I feel like a traitor," Lee said, as they stepped inside and found a table, "patronizing the competition."

"Aww," Danny said, "the North End isn't even open at night, so technically you're not a traitor."

"Well, let's have some coffee, so I can report back to my bosses."

Sipping coffee and staring into Lee Harper's bottomless blue eyes, Danny almost vibrated. He was smitten. They drank cup after cup—all in the name of professional critique—and soon they both were buzzing. Lee began to chatter and Danny leaned in, elbows on the table, chin propped up with his fists. He could listen all day.

"…Maybe I'll skip college and travel."

"To Europe?"

"Actually I hate to fly. I would take a road trip and visit all of the continental states. In a convertible. And I would visit the tiniest churches in America."

"Seriously?"

"Seriously. My dad and I did road trips. It was our thing. Every year since I was four he took two weeks off in July and we—just he and I—took a road trip while my mom met her college friends in Vegas. We've seen everything! The Big Fork in Springfield, Missouri; the world's oldest working light bulb—it's been working for like a hundred years—in Livermore, California; a forty-eight-foot tall statue of the Blessed Mary in Stony Point, New York; the world's largest praying hands—another statue—in Tulsa, Oklahoma. We've been to the Jackie Gleason mausoleum in Miami. The inscription on the tomb says 'And away we go.' We tried to go to a living ghost town in Arizona, but I chickened out and wouldn't get out of the car."

Danny gave her a look. Lee responded with: "Excuse me, I was like five. He took me to the Titanic Museum in Branson, Missouri, and to this weird museum called *Musee Mecanique* in San Francisco, that had over three hundred coin operated machines. We've seen all the giant Indian statues—of course our own Blackhawk in Oregon, and Hiawatha in Michigan, and Big Brave in Maine. I'm boring you, I'm sure."

Danny shook his head. The last thing she could do was bore him.

"Anyway, our next trip was supposed to be the smallest churches in America. My dad loved churches. The smallest one is in Oneida, New York, so we were going to go there first and then to New Jersey and New Hampshire, West Virginia, Kentucky and end in Georgia. But then he died and so…"

"I'll take you. I love road trips. I've never really taken one, but I love them. Wonder why we never did take any? Probably because being in the car with Tess for hours on end would have driven us off the road."

Lee smiled. "I am drunk on caffeine. Seriously. No more coffee for me," she said, pushing away her mug. "I'll admit it, but never to Dana and LuAnn, but this *is* good coffee. But it's *night* coffee, you know?"

Funny thing was, he did. Danny was surprised to see when he climbed into his car that his hands were a little shaky. He guessed he was a little caffeined-out himself. Pathetic—a guy who couldn't hold his joe. He looked at his watch. Not even eleven o'clock. Lee suggested they go to her house and hang out, maybe watch a movie.

"Now, don't let my grandma scare you," she warned as they turned onto National Avenue. "She might think you're her son or she might think you're an intruder. You just never know."

"I dig old people."

"Do you dig being asked the same question five thousand times?"

"I am related to Tess, remember."

"Yeah, but it's way different."

Danny parked in his driveway and then he and Lee started to cut through his backyard over to her house.

"Wow," Lee said, "look at all the stars."

Danny looked up. The sky was chockfull of twinkles. He sang softly: "*Do-do Do-do Do-do-do which shines around me like a million suns, la la la la la la, across the universe.*"

Lee looked at him and smiled. "That's so pretty."

"John Lennon wasn't all piss and vinegar."

"You have a really good voice."

"You think?"

"Oh, yes."

"I play a little guitar. I can play exactly twenty-three Beatles' songs—most of the slower ones, like "All My Loving" and "Mr. Moonlight.""

"My mom loves the Beatles."

"Your mom has superb taste."

"It's so nice out," Lee said. "Let's sit outside."

"I've got a better idea," Danny said and grabbed Lee's hand. They trotted back to his backyard and Danny pointed to the hammock. "Front row seats to the sky." He hopped on first and offered Lee a hand. She giggled and snuggled in next to him.

"This is nice," she said, gazing up at the sky. Danny agreed, listening to the symphony of crickets and katydids. "I love living on the river," Lee said. "In Lake Forest, we lived in the woods, and I love trees, but I love water more."

Danny savored the moment. Could this really be happening? Lee Harvey Harper actually liked him! She liked his warped sense of humor, she liked his singing voice, she liked his beater car, and his long brown curls, she liked the mole on his chin, and she liked his thick eyelashes. She liked the way he looked at things. "How so?" "Oh, just how you seem to look deeper than most people." And she liked how he didn't even know he was good looking. "That's 'cuz I'm not." "You're such an idiot; you are. But because you don't know it, well, that's part of your charm."

Dang! Suddenly he was insightful and charming! Charming! And now here he was, snuggling with Lee in his dad's hammock.

"Do you think Heaven's up there?" Lee asked, pointing to the velvety sky.

"I don't know. I mean I think about it. A lot. I used to think that maybe Heaven's just a different dimension but now I think it's a real place."

"What made you change your mind?"

"My mom."

"Oh, yeah. Can I ask how she died? Tell me 'no' if you don't want to tell me."

"It's okay. She drowned."

"Oh, Danny, I'm so sorry."

"Yeah, it basically sucks."

"How did it happen? You don't have to tell me if you don't want to."

"I don't, if that's okay."

"Of course, I understand. My dad's death was so stupid. I hate talking about it."

Danny moved sideways a little and slipped his arm under Lee's head. "You don't have to either."

"Maybe sometime."

"Yeah, maybe sometime."

"Oh my God, look at those flowers!" Lee said, popping her head up. "They're actually glowing in the moonlight!"

"My mom's moon garden."

"It's the prettiest thing I've ever seen! She must have been a beautiful person to create something so beautiful."

"She was."

"My mom's crazy."

"Yeah?"

"You think I'm kidding but I'm not. She's certifiable. But she's got a good heart. I've had a bizarre childhood. My dad and grandma were my anchors, and now look, my dad's gone and my grandma's gone crazy."

Danny didn't know what to say, so he kept quiet and just pulled Lee a little closer.

"I miss my dad," Lee whispered.

"I miss my mom," Danny whispered back.

Lee started to cry a little. Knowing there were no words to comfort her, he instead found her sweet, moist lips with his. They tasted of tears and Carmex and were wonderfully delicious.

Quiet for a while, swaying gently in the hammock, they listened to the sweet summer sounds of the night. The moon lit up the river until it shone like mirrored glass. Danny didn't want to blow it, but he leaned in for another kiss. Lee kissed him back.

"So," Lee said, looking into Danny's eyes, "am I going to like Boylan?" While Danny thought about this, she said, "I had better like it. It'll be my third high school."

"Why so many?" Danny asked. He couldn't imagine the pain and suffering involved with decoding the culture and cliques of three different high schools. One had been quite enough. Three schools, *Dang*, just when you figured the ins and outs of one it would be time to move on. Not cool.

"Lake Forest High School freshmen and sophomore year. After my Dad died, Woodlands Academy of Sacre—an all girls high school."

"I always wanted to go to an all-girls high school," Danny confessed.

Lee slapped him lightly on the shoulder.

"Ah, you'll be okay," Danny assured her. Why wouldn't she be? She was gorgeous, sweet, and smart. "One week and you'll be Little Miss Popular. 'Who's the hot new girl?' they'll all be saying."

"Oh, right. I don't make friends easily."

"You made friends with me easily."

"My mom says that after my dad died I got a chip on my shoulder."

Danny placed his hand firmly on Lee's right shoulder and then on her left. "I don't feel any chips. You're chip-less."

She smiled and shrugged. "You're a sweet boy. If you knew what I knew, you'd run."

"Would not."

"Like everyone else ran." She turned her face away. The moonlight lit up her profile, transforming it into a lovely cameo, concentrating major drama into a minute space. Not only did she glow in the moonlight, she smelled good, too. She was his own personal moon garden.

"I'm not running. I'm just lying here. I couldn't run if I wanted to because my foot is like totally asleep." He shook it out a little.

"People tend to keep their distances from scandals."

"Scandal? What are you talking about? The only thing scandalous about you is your smokin' hot body."

Lee smiled. "Oh, hell, I'm just going to tell you. You're going to find out sooner or later anyway. Here it is, our scandal *de jour*: my mom was tried and acquitted of killing my dad. I'm a freak. I'm like O.J.'s kids."

Danny couldn't hide his surprise. Up went his right eyebrow. "Hey, hey, back up, back up."

"Okay. This is what happened: my dad fell down our marble staircase and hit his head and died. The police thought my mom pushed him."

Danny felt the other eyebrow levitate. It wasn't everyday someone threw that kind of news in your lap.

255

"She was tried and proven not guilty, which, I have learned, is way different from being innocent. She went free, my grandmother went crazy, and I went off the deep end—I ran away for three days. You know, to punish her."

"I'm so sorry."

"I know. From the outside I look normal, don't I? So, this is our fresh start. Rockford, Illinois. No offense or anything, but the only reason we came here was because my mom's sister-in-law—my dad's sister—lives here and my mom thought it would be good to be around family, but surprise, suddenly we're not family anymore. They haven't even spoken to us since we moved in."

"Why did the police think she pushed him?"

"All the usual clichéd reasons—he had money, she thought he had an affair. They'd been arguing that night. About me. I wanted to go skiing with my friend's family over Thanksgiving break and my mom wouldn't let me. Why? Because she broke a leg once skiing, like a million years ago, and so I couldn't possibly go skiing because I would break a leg too. I'd overheard them talking. I was in my room eating a peanut butter and jelly sandwich I'd snuck up after refusing to eat dinner, and I hear my dad say 'Let her go, if she breaks a leg she breaks a leg.' The next thing I know my mom's banging on my door and then I hear this terrible thump, thump, thump, and grunts and groans and then my dad was slumped at the bottom of the stairs." She shuddered from the memory.

"You poor thing," Danny said, brushing her hair back with his free hand. He felt sympathy, empathy and desire all at the same time. "But it was an accident, right?"

"Well," said Lee, "that's the big question, isn't it? That's my life-defining question. Memory is not reliable. Unreliable. Did I really hear my mom knock on my door first, or did I hear the thumping down the stairs first? I honestly can't remember—they almost seem as if they happened simultaneously. Am I the daughter of a murderess who got away with it O.J. style? Or, am I the privileged daughter of two very different parents who had different ideas about parenting, people who thought fighting was a sport and children were referees? It's so stupid, but when I'm not mad at my mom I'm convinced she didn't do it; when I'm mad at her, I know she did it. Don't tell Tess, okay? I don't want Tess to know. She loves my mom. Hey. You're looking at me funny." Lee sat up. "Listen Danny, I throw a little melodrama into every story I tell. My mom didn't push my dad. I'm ninety-nine-point-nine percent sure."

Chapter Twenty-four

Cain and Unable

{*"I always wished I could peek inside Luke's brain," I tell Cecilia. I know
there's a great range and a wide variety of emotion inside but Luke never
opened up to us as easily as my other two did. Poor Luke, he's so hard
on himself! He learned early on that self-disclosure opens a person up to
scrutiny and rejection. But as an introvert, he's in good company—Albert
Einstein, Eleanor Roosevelt, George Washington, Shakespeare, Mister
Rogers, Mother Theresa, Thomas Jefferson, Sir Isaac Newton, Abraham
Lincoln, Socrates, Mozart.*

*When Luke was in kindergarten he cut his flashcards into circles. Why?
we asked. "Circles are easier," he said. Years later, when Mitch was doing
some research he came across a study that showed that children learning
with circular flashcards were better able to focus on the content of the cards
because a round shape is least distracting to the brain.*

Luke is so fascinating.}

IT MADE SENSE that someone who wanted to be a doctor
would be interested in the physiology of drowning. After
Annie's death Luke grew obsessed and spent many hours on
the Internet trying to figure out what had happened to his mother.

He discovered that we are designed *not* to drown. Mammals appear to come equipped with something called the *mammalian diving reflex*, which is triggered when we submerge our face in water. The reflex is more pronounced in marine mammals like seals and whales but is found in humans as well. What happens is that the reflex puts the body into an oxygen saving mode so as to maximize the time that can be spent underwater. The effect of the reflex is a decrease in heart rate, restriction of blood flow to the extremities in order to increase blood and oxygen to the vital organs, and a shifting of blood to the thoracic cavity to prevent the collapse of the lungs. Because of this, a submerged person, either conscious or unconscious, can survive longer without oxygen under water than on dry land.

Humans also have a strong breathing reflex that is related to both the amount of oxygen and carbon dioxide in the blood. When a person holds her breath, oxygen in the blood is used by the cells and converted into carbon dioxide. When carbon dioxide levels in the blood increase, so does the breathing reflex. It grows stronger and stronger until it reaches the breath-hold breakpoint, where the person can no longer voluntarily hold her breath.

So you panic and you try to breathe underwater. When water enters your airway you try to cough it up or swallow it, causing the throat to constrict and seal the air tube. Sometimes this prevents water from entering the lungs and water enters the stomach. But after a while, sometime after unconsciousness, water can enter the lungs and cause a wet drowning. If the throat stays sealed until cardiac arrest, it's called dry drowning because water has not entered the lungs.

If one was to study forensic pathology, finding water in a victim's lungs would indicate that the victim was still alive at the point of submersion; if no water is found in the lungs, the victim could have suffered a dry drowning or could have been dead before submersion.

In forensic pathology, one of the most difficult diagnoses to make is that of drowning. It's made based on police investigation, forensic autopsy, microscopic analysis, and biochemical tests. The most certain signs of drowning are froth around the mouth and nostrils, and lung distention. The diagnosis tends to be one of exclusion.

Of course he didn't discuss these findings with anyone. Not his Dad. Not Dr. Bonovia. Definitely not Danny.

"What are you afraid of, Luke?" Dr. Bonovia asked in his soft voice. Sitting in his office, in his massive oak rocking chair, Dr. Bonovia looked like Santa Claus. He looked like Santa, but he sounded like Burl Ives, and could play the guitar like Eric Clapton.

"I'm not afraid of anything," Luke said flatly, looking out the window into a gloriously blue summer sky.

"Oh, come on. We're all afraid of something."

"Yeah, okay. The usual stuff. Fear of failure. Fear of looking stupid. Fear of not being able to perform someday when I'm actually in a relationship. Can your penis fall off from lack of use?"

Dr. Bonovia chuckled.

"I worry about Tess. She's wigging out. Now it's bone cancer. She thinks she has bone cancer. She lies all the time and she's obsessed with this Harper Lee thing. I worry about what will happen to her when I go away to school. And now she's like glomming on to our new neighbors, who are a little odd. I don't know."

"Luke, Tess is going to be fine. Right now, I'm concerned about you. You need to talk to your dad about the bills—does he want to take over the bill-paying or is it something that Danny could do?"

"Are you kidding? Danny can't keep track of five bucks."

"Okay, then. Your dad's going to have to take back the bill paying. Why not get him set up to pay his bills on-line? I do and it's really quick and easy. As for running Tess around, Danny has a car, right?"

"Yeah, but he's so undependable."

"Maybe you underestimate your brother. I've seen it happen where a younger brother will suddenly blossom, come into his own, so to speak. It can't be easy to be your kid brother, Luke. You're a guy who's got a lot going for him. What else are you afraid of?"

"I'm afraid of getting struck by lightning—men are more likely to get struck by lightning than women because they boat and golf and fish more. And speaking of golfing, I'm afraid of getting hit in the head with a golf ball. That happened to one of my dad's friends and now the guy just isn't right."

Dr. Bonovia raised his bushy right eyebrow. "Luke, have you given any thought as to how you are going to deal with the stress of college? You set such high standards for yourself; you're going to need a way to let off steam."

"I'll start running again."

"Good," Dr. Bonovia said. "I want you to be prepared, Luke. Have you thought about how you're going to deal with telling new friends about your mother's death? It will come up, you know."

"I know."

"Every time you meet someone new, someone with whom you become intimate, you're going to have to tell how she died. This is important, because in order to have fulfilling relationships with people—friends, lovers—you are going to have to share this most painful piece of your life. It's something that will shape you forever. It's a part of you that you can't deny."

All this talk of intimacy made Luke uncomfortable. (LUKE'S FASCINATING BRAIN FACT: Studies have shown that men in general tend to be less interested in fostering intimate relationships, both with God and others. Their brains are not designed for intimacy the way women's are.)

Luke attempted to change the subject. "Guess what's in my back pocket?" he said abruptly, knowing that he sounded like a five-year-old, or worse, his brother.

Dr. Bonovia flung his hands in the air. "Luke, I know intimacy scares you, but—"

Luke pulled Lee's pink panties out of his back pocket as if he were pulling a rabbit out of a hat. "You don't need to talk to me about intimacy, Dr. Bonovia, I got intimacy covered." Luke twirled the panties around on his index finger.

"Am I supposed to ask to whom those belong?" Dr. Bonovia asked, eyebrow raised.

"My brother's girlfriend, of course."

"Luke, I don't understand. What are *you* doing with them then?"

Luke continued spinning the panties around his finger. "I'm not quite sure."

"Well answer me this then. Is that a pair of underwear you're twirling or an instrument of revenge?"

Luke stopped the spinning and stuffed the panties back into his pocket. "I'm not quite sure."

Dr. Bonovia shook his head. "Luke, how many times must I tell you? Confession is good for the soul."

Luke was running, in all senses of the word. Yesterday's session with Dr. Bonovia had left him feeling vulnerable. He decided to start his running regimen immediately. Blow off some steam. The bike path, which ran along the Rock River for ten miles, lay on the opposite side of the river from the Langdon's home. When Luke was little, he asked his dad if he could build a bridge from their backyard over, so they didn't have to get to the bike path the long way—up National Avenue to Harlem Boulevard and across the Auburn Street bridge.

Morning had just broken and the new light illuminated the river, making the calm surface look like a shiny glass tabletop. Luke ran unencumbered with weights or IPod. He had thoughts to think.

What a stupid thing he did pulling out those panties yesterday! Stupid! It screamed to Dr. Bonovia: *I'm screwed up! I hate my brother! I blame him for our mother's death!* How obvious. It could only lead to questions and questions only led back to the day. Dr. Bonovia tried to tell him over and over that confession was good for the soul, but whose soul?

Dr. B. had asked what Luke was afraid of. Here's what he was really afraid of: polygraphs; testifying under oath; brain fingerprinting (a method of reading a subject's brain's involuntary electrical activity in response to being shown images relating to a crime and determining if that subject's brain contains records of the most salient details of the crime); and mendacity trials demonstrating that liars exhibit numerous tell-tale physical and verbal clues such as leaning forward, touching their nose, licking their lips, averting their gaze, clearing their throat, handling objects, stuttering, and using expanded contractions (e.g. I *did not*, rather than I *didn't*.)

Annie could always tell when Luke was lying. She said his nostrils swelled. Her success rate was textbook so Luke researched the topic and found that Annie was right: the nose knows. Researchers found that when people lie they often feel guilty about it and this results in a small rise in blood pressure, which in turn boosts blood flow to tissue in the nose that ultimately leads to slight nasal swelling.

Dr. B. wasn't stupid. Luke was sure he was well trained in recognizing lying in patients. Luke knew he knew there was more to the story about his mother's death. But it didn't change anything, so why did it matter. Still, he knew, just as he knew at this moment that he was getting shin splints from not stretching properly before running, he knew in the end someone would pay for his mother's death. For a year, he'd talked himself into believing that that someone would be Danny. *If Danny hadn't—* Well, he couldn't play that game because then Danny could say *he* wouldn't have if Luke hadn't—and this blame game could go on forever.

(LUKE'S FASCINATING BRAIN FACT: At this very moment researchers were looking for ways to medicate away one's conscience. That's right, there are on-going studies looking at drugs that could numb the affects that guilt and remorse have on the brain. When Luke first discovered this research, he was ready to enroll as a guinea pig, but when he thought about the moral consequences of an anti-trauma drug, he had second thoughts. What kind of world would it be if people could immunize themselves against a lifetime of crushing remorse? It scared him.)

As he crossed the bridge and ran passed "Symbol," Rockford's bright red-orange, forty-seven foot tall, thirty ton, Alexander Liberman sculpture, Luke tried to remember all the gems that Dr. B. had shared with him over the past months. "Grief and mourning are not the same experience," he'd told Luke. "Grief is what the mind thinks and feels about death and mourning is verbalizing those thoughts and feelings to others." All Luke knew was that guilt complicated grief and delayed mourning.

Now he was in the zone—he couldn't feel his feet on the ground, he could barely feel his limbs. He was pure energy in motion. He passed two runners that looked like father and son and it triggered a memory of his father's cardiac arrest. The two men that saved Mitch's life— Dean Armour, Sr. and Dean Armour, Jr.—had been running on the bike path and were heading back over the Auburn Street bridge when they came upon the accident. They saved Mitch's life by performing CPR and calling 911. So why did his father live and his mother die? Was it divine providence? God's will? Good luck and bad luck? He couldn't make sense of it.

After his run, Luke drove to Associated Bank. Standing in line, hugging his jumbo size coffee can filled with pocket change, guess who he saw filing into line two customers behind him? Guess. Karley Lappos, that's who. He hadn't seen her since that night at Barnes and Noble. His luck. Normally he used the drive-through service but the tellers wouldn't take coin through the window. He nodded a neutral hello, hoping he could escape without speaking to her. Something about that girl made him nervous. She looked good; he'd give her that. Her skin was bronzed and her light brown hair was pulled up with one of those plastic hair clips with a few wispy curls loose at the top. She was tiny—nothing like her cousin, Lee Harper, who was blonde and tall and as long-legged as a colt.

It took forever to run the coins through the counter and it ended up that Luke and Karley Lappos finished their transactions at the same time. Go figure.

"So you collect pennies?" she said.

Luke couldn't tell by her face if she was making fun of him or making conversation.

(LUKE'S FASCINATING BRAIN FACT: Girls' brains come equipped with larger communication centers and so girls are more adept than boys at reading faces and hearing human vocal tones.)

Luke tried to read Karley Lappos's face but he didn't have a clue as to what was going on inside. "Hey, it adds up," he said, a little defensively.

"I'm sure it does. How's your summer?" she asked, as they walked outside.

"Fine. And yours?"

Hers was dragging on. "I *so* want to get back to school. It's so weird to live back home once you've been away. You'll see. How's my kooky aunt?"

"Pretty good looking is how."

"Yeah, well, looks are deceiving. You mean she hasn't been belly-dancing on the front lawn or gardening in a negligee or running over at all hours of the day to borrow some obscure spice like arrowroot powder for her witch's brew?"

"No," he said. "And Lee is great. We all love Lee."

"Lee?"

"Lee."

"Lee?"

"Lee. Hey, are you sure we're even talking about the same people, Karley? Joya and Lee Harper—two beautiful blonde women."

"Make that three. My cousin's grandma is moving in with them. Or so we heard."

"That's right. My little sister went to Evanston with Joya to get her."

Karley gasped, hand to her chest. "Are you out of your mind? You let your little sister get in a car with my aunt? Is she okay?" Karley acted all concerned.

Luke motioned to Karley to move aside, since they were blocking the bank's entrance. "Look, my sister is fine and Joya and Lee are great neighbors and a lot of fun. We like them."

Karley shook her pretty little head. "Okay, just for the record, this is my second formal warning."

Luke laughed. "Duly noted. See you around."

The next thing you know Karley Lappos is phoning Luke at home and inviting him to go canoeing with a bunch of kids the next day. She wouldn't take no for an answer because she heard from a reliable source that Luke Langdon had forgotten how to have fun. God he wanted to go. "On the Rock?" he asked, stalling for time.

"No, on the Kish. Who in their right mind would canoe the Rock?"

"Obviously you don't remember the Fourth of July, 1997, when the U.S. Canoe Association came to Byron and put the most human-powered crafts in the water at one time on the Rock River and made it into the Guinness Book of World Records."

"Tomorrow at two o'clock. Bring sunblock and something to drink. Do you want me to pick you up or do you want to meet us at Larsen's Landing?"

"You can pick me up. Oh, and could you bring some sunblock for me, and oh yeah, something to drink?"

"Fine."

Luke hung up the phone and realized his heart was racing. What was this? Excitement? Anticipation? Relief? Maybe all of the above.

Luke sauntered through the house looking for Mitch. How weird that he had to run his social life by his dad. When would it end? He wanted to relay the news about the canoe trip (not date) in a casual, off-hand way, but since he hadn't done anything fun in months, he knew his father would see through any attempt at nonchalance. It was Saturday and the house was dead quiet.

He found Mitch in his office, asleep in his chair, reading glasses on and open book in his lap. Not wanting to wake him—Mitch rarely napped—Luke tried to tiptoe out of the room, but the creaky floorboards woke Mitch up. "You looking for me?" he said, rubbing his eyes.

"Nothing urgent," Luke said.

Mitch sat up and closed the book that had put him to sleep. "What's up?"

"You mind if I go canoeing tomorrow with some kids?"

Mitch smiled and held his palm up for a fiver. God, Luke knew his dad would make a big deal about it. He provided a few details and then escaped as soon as he could. On the way up the back stairs, he nearly collided with Danny. "Hey," Luke said, blocking the way, "that's my shirt."

"Yeah, well I needed something nice—I'm taking Lee out to dinner before she goes out of town for a couple days. I'm taking her to Josef's." He raised and lowered his eyebrows a few times as he smoothed down the front of Luke's Abercrombie and Fitch yellow and blue striped shirt.

"Josef's? How can you afford that?"

"I said I'm *taking* Lee to dinner. She's paying. Not that I care, but the Harpers are loaded."

"Remove my shirt."

"You can't be serious."

"I can be."

"You're not going to make a big deal out of this."

"Oh, but I am."

Danny tried to push past Luke, but Luke was all muscles. Luke laughed. "I said remove it. I don't want your stink all over it. It's my best shirt. You know Ashley bought me that shirt, now remove it."

Danny stood his ground and folded his arms tightly around himself. "You remove it," he said.

Good. Fine. Luke was glad for the invitation, was actually looking forward to a fight, especially one he would win. He started to peel

Danny's hands back, but then—just like when they were kids—Danny twirled around once, fell to the floor, and starting kicking. Danny was a wimp in all ways, having no muscles, but the boy was all mule when it came to kicking. Luke took a sharp blow to his lower thigh and realized he had no other option but to dive. And so he dove. Man, it felt good to fight! The boys rolled around on the hardwood floor, tussling about and bumping into walls and furniture. Soon Piper was barking and Tess was standing over them screaming, "Boys! Boys!" and then Mitch was there and Luke heard his father say, "What the hell?"

Luke ignored them all, focusing his attention on the singular objective of getting his shirt back. The truth was he hated the stupid shirt; the shirt didn't really matter at all. But who was wearing it did, so he grabbed the tail of it and pulled just as Danny was rolling over. The sharp hiss of ripping cotton was music to his ears.

The boys fell apart, out of breath. Danny lay sweaty and panting. Luke jumped to his feet, grabbed the shirt and ripped it completely off of his brother. He raised it up in the air in a victory display. Danny sat up and feigned a "what just happened" look.

Luke looked at Mitch and Tess. He slowly lowered his hand. "It was my shirt," he said sheepishly, knowing he sounded like a five-year-old.

Mitch just stared at Luke, which made him feel like a four-year-old. Luke turned to Danny. "Oh, all right," he said, "you can wear the shirt." He flung the ruined shirt in Danny's face and tore up the stairs. He heard Danny whining in the background: "…I just borrowed a shirt…that's all." And his dad grousing: "…like I'm raising Cain and Abel or something…"

{*"Well for Pete's sake," I say to Cecilia, "those two are at it again!" I wish they'd go look at the portrait of the two of them that hangs over the fireplace in the living room. Luke with his arm slung around his younger brother. They look angelic. I always thought my boys would be friends forever. It breaks my heart to think that it may not be so. They used to be such buds. I remember the summer Danny got interested in filmmaking*

268

and made Luke his leading man in all his movies. Luke as the "naked newsman" (naked only from the waist up, I am relieved to say), Luke as the androgynous Health class teacher, Luke as Dale Daleson or Rob Roberson from the fictional Channel 5, W-DUM.

"Now look at them," I say to Cecilia. "It looks as if they could kill each other."}

In the safety of his room, calmed by the electromagnetic lull of his computer screen, Luke continued with his important brain research. He'd been exploring the medical Web sites on strange brain disorders and there seemed to be something for everyone!

One of the oddest was Alice in Wonderland syndrome or micropsia, a neurological condition that affects visual perception. To the sufferer, people and things can appear to be substantially smaller than in reality. There is a disorder called Foreign Accent Syndrome where people who suffered a stroke or other brain trauma suddenly start speaking their native tongue with a different (and convincing) accent—anything from French, Italian, Swedish, or South African. And the weird thing is the person may have never even heard the accent they pick up. It seems what happens is that tiny areas of damage in various parts of the brain cause subtle changes to vocal features, which makes a patient's pronunciation sound similar to a foreign accent.

Another unusual condition that arises from brain trauma is Alien Hand Syndrome. This one is really bizarre. A person loses control of one hand, and although he or she can still experience sensation in the affected hand, it seems to have a mind of its own. The affected hand will gesticulate inappropriately or even unbutton a shirt the owner is trying to button. Yikes!

And then there's Stendhal's Syndrome, a psychosomatic disorder experienced by people who are exposed to large amounts of breathtakingly beautiful artwork, such as can be found in Florence, Italy. The illness causes rapid heartbeat, dizziness, confusion and even hallucinations!

At two a.m. Luke shut down his computer, took a pee, and slipped under the covers of his unmade bed. He thought about his upcoming—more like impending—birthday. In less than forty-eight hours he would turn twenty and he would get a totally new body, for he'd read that each day fifty billion cells in your body are replaced, resulting in a new body each and every year. So there he was, lying there, involuntarily processing his own rebirth. We are such a balance of integration and disintegration. But—and he would bet money on this—his birthday would likely come and go unnoticed. That's what happened last year when it had been overshadowed, and rightly so, by his mother's death. It seemed so petty but he feared that his birthday would always be eclipsed by the anniversary of his mother's death.

{*"Oh, Cecilia, I've thought about that myself—that my death will always taint Luke's birthday." I have to smile when I see Luke's room. Where other boys his age would have bedroom walls adorned with supermodels or rock bands, Luke's are plastered with 20 x 26 laminated anatomical posters—there are four of the brain and two of the heart.*}

The next day Luke woke with a buzz of excitement. He tried to analyze his feelings. Was it Karley that was getting him going or just the idea of socialization? Sometimes he couldn't read his own mind. He prepared brain food for breakfast—whole-wheat toast, a glass of skim milk, and a bowl of blueberries. Starting today anything that went into his mouth was going to be healthy for his brain, enough of the junk food.

(LUKE'S FASCINATING BRAIN FACT: People who have a well-maintained energy supply hang on to their memories longer because the brain draws nearly all its energy from glucose. A dose of glucose-sweetened lemonade can boost the recall of words, faces, events, movements and drawings, the effects lasting long enough that a kid could get through a two-hour exam. Luke made a point of putting sweetened powdered lemonade mix on his list of things to get for college.)

Oh, Luke was full of little scientific pick-me-ups and help-you-outs. Compartmentalized in his brain was an odd and salient array of health trivia: runners should replace their running shoes every five hundred miles; a good cry can boost your immune system, eating a handful of walnuts before bed can help induce sleep, pregnant women should eat broccoli to prevent heart disease in their children later in life. Oh, he knew he was a nerd. There were times that Luke wished he was more like Danny—a singing-in-the-bathroom kind of person, a touchy-feely, slap you on the back kind of guy. Luke shuddered at the thought. What was he thinking? He just must be nervous about his canoeing date.

At ten to two, Luke sat on the front porch and waited for Karley. At ten after two, he got fidgety and started checking his cell phone every twenty seconds to see if he missed a call or a text message. At two fifteen, Karley pulled her black Jeep, music blasting, into the driveway, and Luke breathed a sigh of relief. Karley told him to throw his gym bag in the back and then take the front passenger's seat. A girl with long black hair hopped out of the front seat, said "hi" and climbed into the back with two other girls. If you had told him yesterday that today he would be sitting in a car with four beautiful women he would have told you you were crazy. But here he was. His skin felt prickly. Karley smiled and turned the music up even louder. She backed out of the driveway and sped down the street. The girls in the back squealed.

"Do you know everybody?" Karley shouted over the music.

Luke turned around to get a look at the girls in the back. Vaguely familiar but nothing definite.

"Girls, this is Luke Langdon; Luke, you're looking at the Triple A's—Amanda, Anna, and Amy. I am not kidding."

Luke told the girls it was nice to meet them. The one named Amy said, "Has anyone ever told you that you look exactly like Matt Damon?"

"A few times," Luke said and smiled. Okay, he could relax. He could do this.

They met up with six other kids at Larsen's Landing and since they had an uneven number of people, the Triple A girls agreed to share a canoe, which was allowed if the total weight was less than seven hundred pounds. The other eight kids paired off. Karley slung her arm around Luke's shoulder and said, "You're with me."

The group gathered their gear and hopped on a bus that would transport them to the launch site at Espenscheid Forest Preserve. Sitting next to Karley, staring at her tan legs and arms, Luke's whole being buzzed. Man, he'd spent most of the last year alone.

{She's a pretty little thing," I say to Cecilia. "I just hope she doesn't break his heart. She looks like she's broken a few hearts."}

"I'm glad you decided to come," Karley said, offering a chilled bottle of water from her mini cooler.

"Me too," Luke said, accepting the bottle.

"Hey, I was thinking about this on the way over," she said. "I thought it might be a good idea if we agreed *not* to talk about my relatives today."

"Fine with me."

"Good," Karley said, and held out her hand to shake on it.

Luke shook her hand. He wasn't prepared for what happened next: electricity ran through his hand and up his right arm. Here we go, he thought. Been here, done this. Luke being Luke had studied the science of attraction and here's what he knew. He knew that right about now his brain was being flooded with infatuation drugs, literally exploding with two particular chemicals—*phenylethylamine* (the 'love molecule') and *oxytocin* (the 'cuddling chemical'). In addition to those neurochemicals, his brain was releasing dopamine (to make him glow) and norepinephrine (to stimulate the production of adrenalin). It may not sound very romantic but being in love was not unlike a drug overdose. Luke felt himself rev up like a racecar. Who knew…maybe this day could end with sex in a canoe. He'd like that. He'd like that very much.

(LUKE'S FASCINATING BRAIN FACT: If a woman does not want to have sex with a man she shouldn't be around him when his stress levels are high because a male's love circuits get an extra kick under stressful conditions, for example after an intense physical challenge. Luke wondered if that was why athletes, rock stars, and military men seemed to need so much sex. Maybe this was a chauvinistic excuse. Paddling certainly constituted an intense physical challenge. Yep, sex in a canoe would be nice.)

They pushed off their canoes from the river frontage. It was a good-looking day. The Kishwaukee River was a scenic, quiet river, with minimum motorboat traffic due to its shallow depth. As Luke climbed into the canoe, thoughts of his mother's drowning popped into his brain. He shooed the thoughts away. Not now. Not today.

Relax. Relax. He took his seat and grabbed a paddle.

"This is awesome!" Karley said, lifting her face to the sun and shaking out her hair.

Luke smiled. He hadn't been canoeing in years. That's why last night he'd hopped on the Internet to get some paddling tips. (Pathetic yes, but Luke being Luke, he wasn't going to take any chances.) Keep the paddle as near vertical as possible. Good. Keep your upper hand at eye level. Now dip the paddle blade in the water, push with your upper hand; don't continue the stroke beyond your body because you'll just waste effort. There. Nice and smooth. He got into a groove, switching sides every five or six strokes to keep the canoe going straight and to rest his muscles.

Speaking of muscles, he liked how his looked. He'd rolled up the sleeves of his tee shirt over his shoulders and he watched his biceps flex with each stroke. He hoped someone else might notice, too.

At a turn in the bend, Luke caught sight of a hawk perched high in a tree. "No, I can't see it," Karley said, when he tried to point it out. Further along, he spotted a beaver working on his dam. "Look," he said to Karley, but her cell phone was ringing and she was digging in her purse for it.

"Sorry," she said.

But she didn't seem sorry. She talked to whomever it was for quite a long time, agreeing that someone or other was a "bitch" and a "skank" and that someone else was a "worthless low life." Luke tried to hand her the second paddle but she just waved it away. She sat back, stripped down to her black bikini, and slathered herself with sunscreen, her Bluetooth clutching her ear.

Luke paddled along. It occurred to him suddenly that the only reason he'd been invited was to be Karley's personal gondolier. At least he *liked* paddling. He liked how alive he felt, surrounded by nature, working his muscles. He breathed in the warm air and listened to water and the songbirds. It was a pretty river. He'd looked up some facts about the Kishwaukee River on the Internet too, hoping to impress Karley—that it was one of the most pristine rivers in Illinois, and that its name was the Potowatomi Indian word meaning "river of the Sycamore"—but he now realized Karley was not the kind of girl who would care about such things.

He turned his head when he heard the Triple A Girls giggling in the canoe behind him and before he knew it, they were overtaking his canoe, two of the three paddling their hearts out in an economical and efficient rhythm.

"*Hi, Luke. Bye, Luke,*" one of them sang.

"Karley, get your ass off that phone," another one called out.

Karley threw an empty water bottle at the girl, which missed and bobbed in the water. Luke hated littering and wanted to retrieve it but when he looked at Karley he saw challenge in her eyes and he decided to just let it go. Let it go with the flow. Literally.

Karley finally ended her call and stuffed her phone back into her purse. "Sorry, my roommate from school is having a boyfriend crisis."

"That's okay," Luke said.

"God, look at your muscles!" she declared.

Luke shrugged. He'd wanted her to notice but now that she had he was embarrassed.

"Looks like you don't need *me* to help paddle, which is a good thing because I have no arm muscles whatsoever." She grabbed her bottle of sunscreen and gobbed more on her long, shapely legs.

And there it was: the ulterior motive behind the false compliment. Luke knew "manipulative" when he saw it. He wished he hadn't come.

Silence would have been nice. Just the sounds of the birds and the water and the distant voices of the other kids. But the reality was, Karley never stopped talking. Following her phone call, Luke was forced to hear the entire lurid roommate story. After that she moved on to scandalous narratives about the Triple A Girls, her supposed best friends. Which segued into carping about her mother and her sisters. It seemed as if everyone she knew was a "whore" or a "slut" or a "dirty skank." Unfortunately, by the time Luke's brain had figured this out, it was too late for his body, which was hyped up with love chemicals. Oh well, it was what it was.

When they stopped for lunch, Karley broke her promise. "So you must have found out by now that my aunt murdered her husband," she blurted out just as Luke was biting into a Golden Delicious.

He nearly choked on the apple. "So much for shaking on it," he said, because somehow he was more shocked by this girl's blatant disregard for a 'shake-on-it' agreement than he was by the bomb she just spewed at him.

"Well, I decided that your little sister might be in danger and that I would be remiss if I said nothing."

"Karley, what are you talking about?"

"She pushed him down a flight of stairs. My loony aunt pushed my mom's brother down the stairs and he died! She got off in court, but it's an O.J. thing—we all know she did it. And Lee knows it, too."

"Is this some kind of joke?"

"Oh, I wish."

"Some kind of vendetta, then?"

"What do you mean, *vendetta*?"

For a second, Luke was confused. Did she not know the meaning of the word? Was she an ignoramus? He shook his head. "Are you jealous of Lee or something? Of her looks or of her money? Is that it?"

"Oh-My-God. You are clueless!"

"Is this why you invited me? To get me involved in some family feud? Or just for my paddling muscles."

"You don't know how stupid you are! I'm just trying to help your family."

"Oh, really."

"You know what, Luke, this was a mistake. You're not who I thought you were."

"Well, you're *exactly* who I thought you were!"

"Ha! Why don't you just go?"

"What?"

"You heard me," Karley said. "Just leave. Get off this boat, right now! I don't want to even look at you!"

Luke looked around at the surrounding water. He raised his hands, palms up. "Seriously. You want me to get off of this canoe?"

"Yes!" said Karley, beautiful, superficial Karley.

Good thing the Kish was just about as shallow as she was, otherwise, Luke would not have been able to do what he did—jump out of the canoe and walk to the shore, holding his gym bag high above his head.

"Wait!" Karley called. "Wait! I didn't mean *literally*! Wait! I don't know how to paddle!"

Luke didn't even look back.

Well, he couldn't phone his dad. And he wouldn't call Danny, oh, no. All his friends were on hold. Damn! Damn! Okay, he'd walk home. It would be a soggy, long walk, but so be it. But wait, he was barefoot. He realized he'd left his flip-flops on the canoe.

He hated to do it but there was only one person who could help him. Before he talked himself out of it, he dialed Blondo's cell phone. And that's how he ended up in her turquoise *little deuce coupe* a half hour later. When she pulled up, even though she was dressed like a she-devil in her usual trashy garb, she looked like an angel to Luke. The top was down and the Beach Boys were blaring. She didn't even care that he would get the leather seat wet.

"That little bitch!" Blondo said, when he told her what had happened and with whom. "She's had it out for us from the beginning. My husband's family never wanted us to get married. Said we wouldn't last five minutes. Well, we lasted almost twenty-six years. And if the son-of-bitch hadn't died, we'd still be married."

"Karley says you killed him," Luke said, without thinking. The words just slipped out. He was hot, wet, and exhausted, and now windblown.

"Yeah, her and a zillion other people. They can think whatever they want. Why would I kill my husband for money when my mother is loaded and my brother and I are going to get it all if and when she ever kicks the bucket, which will probably be never since she is the most obstinate person on earth. Some people are just too stubborn to die. And yes, I had suspected that my husband was having an affair, but he swore he hadn't, that this new, young attorney was pursuing him, the little slut, but that he'd put her off. I believed him. I mean, hot sex he didn't need. He was getting that at home."

Luke gulped.

"You know, I couldn't care less what my sister-in-law and little Miss Priss think of me, but I know that it hurts Lee and that really pisses me off."

"So you didn't do it?" Luke asked. He *had* to ask, didn't he?

"That hurts, handsome. Do I look like the kind of woman who could kill her husband?"

"Hell, yes, you do," Luke said.

Blondo grinned. "I do, don't I? Maybe I'll just keep you guessing. Men find me and my lurid past alluring." She turned to him and batted her eyelashes. "Do you find me alluring, handsome boy?"

"I find you *alarming*, Joya."

"That's the thanks I get."

"You know I'm kidding. There's no 'finding' involved. The fact is you are alluring and you know it."

"I do know it!"

They drove through town, passing neighborhoods Luke barely knew existed. A sleazy motel with a message on the marquee read: "*Love Your Neighbor…Here!*" Suddenly a fantasy popped into Luke's head. A fantasy about Blondo and him, making it at that sleazy motel.

"Shame on you, thinking those dirty thoughts," Blondo said suddenly.

Luke did a double take. Was she a mind reader or was she just thinking the same thing? "What?" he said.

"You know what. Thanks, but I'll have to pass because I'm a woman in mourning. But I'll take a rain check. Okay?" She patted his leg.

Man! Luke felt his engine revving up again. He looked at Blondo. Shit, she was at least twenty-five years older than him, still, she was hot. And look at his mom and dad—his dad was almost twenty years older than his mom. And it wasn't like he wanted to marry Blondo…

"You didn't do it," he said.

"You really want to know if I did it? Okay, I'll tell you, IF, you tell me how your mother drowned and why it's such a big frickin' mystery in your family and why your poor pathetic little sister can't get closure, not to mention the attention she needs. I love the kid but she needs to go through a car wash. God! And your dad walks around like a zombie. He doesn't have a clue about what's going on in that house. Danny, well Danny's been busy chasing after my daughter and I have *allowed* him to catch her because I like him. He's a good kid. He's the only one in your family who is living life. You—you hide behind the bills and your brain research, and you're like a hundred years old. And you think that everything will be hunky dory when you go away to school because you'll leave all the *ick* behind. But you won't. You know what you need? You need vodka. What you got can be cured by what I got."

"Joya, just take me home. Please. I appreciate you coming to get me. More than you know."

"Oh, all right. I knew you wouldn't tell me anything. I guess we'll both keep guessing. Just let me stop for vodka."

{"I'll tell you right now, Cecilia, this is not a good idea. I just don't trust this woman's motives. What could she possibly want with my teen-aged son?"}

Once home, Luke made it up his room without being seen. He didn't know, nor did he care, where anybody was. He showered the Kishwaukee River off of himself, threw on some gym shorts and a tee shirt, and ventured downstairs to see if he could drum up something to eat. It was nearly six o'clock and all he'd had since breakfast were a couple of bites of a lame sandwich and a bite of an apple. There was a note on the counter. "Tess and I are at Aunt Maggy's for dinner. See you later. Dad."

Canned soup was all there was to eat. Soup had become the mainstay of the Langdon household. Think of the sodium! No, don't. Cream of Celery. Cream of Chicken. Man, they were down to the cream soups that no one wanted.

His cell phone vibrated. Caller ID prepared him. It was Blondo. "Just so you know, this vodka is superb. Top shelf, this is. It's called the Jewel of Russia Classic. I paid thirty-four ninety-nine for it, now get your ass over here."

"Will you feed me?"

"I will feed you."

Luke pretended it was because he was hungry. But it was really because he was hungry and thirsty and curious and yes, horny. And while he'd interacted with two shallow women in the same day, for some crazy reason that he couldn't wrap his mind around, one repelled him and the other attracted him.

Just as he was locking the dead bolt on the back door, his cell rang again. This time it was his dad.

"Just checking in. How was the canoeing? Or are you still there?"

"Uh, it was fun. *Is* fun. Fun."

"Well, listen, I won't keep you, but Tess and I are at Aunt Maggy's for dinner and she wants to know if you need a microwave for your dorm room. She bought a new one and the old one is perfectly fine."

"Yeah, that'd be good. Tell her thanks. Dad, I gotta go."

Except now, his dad's call had brought him back to reality, and he thought maybe he wouldn't go. Just as he was unlocking the backdoor to go back inside, his cell rang again. Danny. What could he want?

"Dude, it's me," Danny said.

"Idiot, there's this thing called Caller ID."

"Where's Dad? He's not answering his phone."

"How the hell do I know?"

"Can you tell him that I'm spending the night at Mathis's?"

"I'm not your secretary," Luke said.

"I know that. You're my mother."

Luke snapped the phone shut. What an asshole! That was it. Hell, tomorrow was his birthday. He would toast himself with a shot of vodka or two. He'd never had vodka. He relocked the door and headed next door. Man, he really was starving.

Gran-Glen opened the door. "Let me guess, you're selling magazines."

"No, Ma'am, I'm here to see Joya."

She stepped back to let him in. More like sashayed. She wore a floor-length silver gown, the kind girls wore to their senior prom, and plenty of diamonds. "Oh, I remember you," she said. "You're that racecar driver. Nice to see you're still alive."

How does one respond to that? Luke said, "Thanks. It's good to *be* alive."

"I have no idea where my granddaughter is," she informed him, adjusting her fallen spaghetti strap.

"Well that's okay because I'm here to see your *daughter* not your granddaughter."

Gran-Glen squinted her eyes at Luke. "You're younger than I remembered. Do you know how old my daughter is?"

Luke laughed. "Oh, I'd guess mid-forties."

"Age is irrelevant, thank you very much," Joya said as she came into the foyer. "I'm just a smidgen over forty, right Mom?"

"Don't ask me, I can't even remember how old *I* am. I used to know my age. I think my birthday is in September. *Try to remember the kind of September*," she sang, and danced away.

Joya raised her eyebrows and led Luke into the living room. "Welcome to the loony bin. This is why I drink heavily."

"Poor thing."

"Oh, no. Save your pity for me. *I'm* the poor thing. She's never been happier in her life."

"Still."

"Yeah, still. So, come in. I cooked for you. Nothing fancy. Something to soak up the vodka."

While Luke followed her he checked out her butt. "Is your entire wardrobe animal prints?" he asked her, for once again, she was wearing a zebra-print halter top with a short, tight black skirt.

"Almost. I think I was some kind of wildcat in a past life. I mean all you have to do is look at my eyes." She turned suddenly, and stuck her face in front of Luke's to show him her eyes.

"Ahhh, yes, very feline-looking."

Joya clawed the air in front of Luke and growled. Then she turned and walked into the kitchen.

Whatever she was cooking smelled wonderful. "Sit at the kitchen table while I finish things up," she commanded. He obeyed. But what was this? The table was set for three. Who else was she expecting? Gran-Glen? Not Lee, because she was in Lake Forest, spending the weekend with a friend.

"I took you for a meat and potatoes man, what with all your muscles." (She pronounced it 'musk-uls.')

"I'll eat just about anything except beets and lima beans."

"Well, shit! We're having pot roast, potatoes, beets and lima beans!"

"Oh, well—"

"I'm just shitting you; I hate beets and lima beans, too. We're having the roast, potatoes, carrots and salad. Would you mind lighting the candles on the table? There's the lighter."

"Sure." Would it be rude to ask who the third person was? Maybe tonight wasn't what he thought it was. But, Joya had been coming on to him from day one, hadn't she? Was he so out of practice he was misreading things?

"Mom needed something to do while I was cooking so I asked her to set the table," Joya said, as she removed a roasting pan from the oven. "She set herself a place, but don't worry, she never eats at the table anymore. I have to serve her breakfast, lunch, and dinner in bed. She thinks I'm her maidservant. What am I talking about? I am her maidservant. But you know, after my husband died and before she thought I murdered him, my mother took good care of me. So. Hey, what are you waiting for? Grab that bottle of vodka and start pouring."

Luke walked over to the counter where the bottle, two glasses, and an ice bucket were sitting. *You weren't wrong*, he said to himself, *it is just the two of us.* But then a flash of sanity whizzed through his brain telling him he was stupid and crazy and he might be on the path to making one of the biggest mistakes of his life. *Okay, okay,* he said to himself, to quiet the voice, it'll be just a neighborly dinner and nothing more. There, he'd come to his senses.

But then Joya came up behind him to retrieve her drink and she smelled so good and her bare legs were so tan and shapely and those crazy green eyes! What was it about green eyes that made them so sensual, so carnal? Whew!

"I hope you're hungry, Luke Skywalker, 'cause when I cook and people don't eat, I get so ornery."

"Oh, don't worry, I'll eat."

"How do you like that *wodka*?"

He liked the "wodka" very much. He liked the dinner very much, too. He hadn't had that kind of roast—the kind that is nice and stringy and oh so tender—since his mom had died. (Man, if he could count the times he'd ended a sentence or a thought with the phrase "since Mom died.")

Once they finished eating, Joya excused herself to fix a plate for Gran-Glen. She arranged the plate of food and settings on a fancy silver-handled tray and headed for the back stairs. "Be right back, handsome," she said and winked.

But she was actually gone for a while. Long enough for Luke to finish off a few more glasses of vodka. He'd decided he liked the taste of vodka; it was smooth and prickly all at the same time. By the time Joya returned he was nursing his sixth glass.

"Sorry I took so long," Joya said. "My mother is in one of her moods. Shall we retreat to the living room?"

Luke meant to say "*sure!*" but it came out "*slur!*" Joya looked at him funny. When he stood up and walked toward her, he almost toppled over. Joya moved to steady him, but Luke was so wobbly he pulled her off balance and they both fell to the floor. Joya lay there laughing, with Luke on top of her. *What the hell*, he thought, and leaned in to kiss her.

"Hey!" she shouted, rolling away. "No kitchen floor action for you, my friend."

The next thing Luke knew he was being dragged across the hardwood floor. When he opened his eyes he saw Joya pulling one of his legs and Glenda pulling the other.

Between her grunts, Glenda said, "What, did you kill this one, too?"

He woke up on the sofa in Joya's family room. He tried to swallow but his tongue seemed to have grown in size and was glued to the roof of his mouth. Somebody was sitting on his foot. Glenda. She sat there, staring off into space. On his foot. Man, he had to pee!

"Uh, Glenda?"

"Don't even talk to me, Warren! If this drinking doesn't stop I *will* divorce you."

"I'm sorry," Luke muttered.

"You better be."

"Mom," Joya said. Luke blinked. Had Joya been lying on the love seat the whole time? "Telephone's for you."

"I didn't hear it ring."

"Warren, you heard it ring, didn't you?"

"Uh, yes," Luke said. Was he dreaming? Things were fuzzy.

Off Glenda went. Joya slid into her spot on the couch, right on his foot. "Listen, kid, what do you remember?"

Now he was *kid*? What happened to Mr. Handsome?

"Uh—"

"Yeah, that's what I thought. Don't worry. I covered for you."

Luke tried to sit up. Bad idea. "Covered?"

"I called Danny and told him that if he loved my daughter he would tell your father that you spent the night at the house of one of the guys on the canoe trip."

"What?"

"Look at you. I didn't have a lot of options. I couldn't *carry* you home. So, sleep it off and sneak home later. I take full responsibility for this. But let's just keep it between us, huh? I don't think your dad would ever talk to me again and the truth is, you guys need me!"

She leaned in. Those green eyes were like missiles coming at him. She lifted his eyelids with her ice-cold fingers and peered into his eyes. "Ahhh, you'll live," she said and then kissed him. On the lips. "Now, I'm going up to bed to get some real sleep."

Luke got up to pee and then made himself a cup of instant coffee. Kitchen clock said eleven-fourteen but he didn't believe it so he pulled his cell phone out of his pocket to confirm it. Yes, eleven-fourteen. He checked for missed calls. None. He drank his coffee, splashed some water on his face, and skulked home.

Chapter Twenty-five

I'll Take That to Go

{"Tess seems so grown-up!" I tell Cecilia. "Suddenly she has cheekbones!"
Why just yesterday I was taking her to the American Girl store in Chicago
and staging fashion shows with her Barbies. It couldn't have been so long
ago that she announced to me that she would like to go to China on our
next vacation. "China. That's an interesting choice. Why China?" I asked.
"Because they have the biggest toy store in the world." "They do?" I asked.
"Mom, everything is made in China!"}

TESS WAS SO in love with the three new ladies in her life
that she just tucked away that bit of scary information she'd
heard from Gran-Glen in the car all those weeks ago. Oh,
what was it, something preposterous, something about Joya killing
her husband. Well, Tess wasn't born yesterday, if someone killed her
husband someone would be in jail. *Duh!*

And when Joya bought the kitten for her, the deal was sealed—Tess
would love her forever, even if her dad and Luke thought she was a
kook. The kitty had made Tess so, so happy. Piper had taken to her
immediately, even though the kitten had been somewhat aloof. But

Piper had won her over. And when Danny saw the kitten and told Tess the name 'Annie' was too plain for something so exotic and suggested 'Cleopatra,' Tess found herself actually agreeing. She renamed the kitten 'Cleopatra' even though she had been 'Annie' for an entire day. Cleopatra soon became Cleo and even her dad seemed to be happy with the name, although he also seemed to be a little afraid of the kitten. To be honest, when Tess first saw the kitten, she was a little afraid herself. But how could she say anything to Joya, who was being so sweet and generous? Annie used to tell Tess not to look a gift horse in the eye, or was it the mouth. Anyway. The kitten made her happy.

Every waking minute was spent either in the company of Joya, Lee, and Gran-Glen, or devising a plan to get into their company. As far as Tess was concerned, Joya was absolutely mesmerizing, Lee was big-sister sweet, and Gran-Glen was, well, entertaining. Tess had overheard her dad telling Luke and Danny that he caught Gran-Glen doing a striptease in the backyard the day Tess got Cleo. She would never tell, but just yesterday, she saw Gran-Glen sunbathing in the nude, and last week she had wandered off and was found lying on the front lawn of the alderman's house. She had her clothes on that time, thank goodness.

It occurred to Tess that maybe her mother had sent Joya and Lee and Gran-Glen her way—angels to the rescue! People who made time for her, doted on her every word, and seemed to enjoy her company and didn't get annoyed by her questions: Why is it *freeze* and *froze*, but not *squeeze* and *squoze*? And if you call a word that modifies a verb an *adverb*, shouldn't the word that modifies a noun be an *adnoun* rather than adjective? And why do both of our eyes blink at once?—we could see the world *all* the time if we blinked one eye at a time.

At her last session with Miss Miranda, Tess had announced that she was in love. Miss Miranda asked who the lucky boy was. "Not *that* kind of love," Tess explained. "I'm in love with my new neighbors."

Miss Miranda explained that the term 'in love' usually referred to romantic love.

"Well, anyway, I love them. The mom's got spunk and the grandmother is funny because she has Alzheimer's, and—"

"Tess, Alzheimer's is a sad and serious disease. There's nothing funny about it."

"You're telling me," Tess said, before continuing with her story. "And the daughter is so sweet. Danny likes her. I think Luke does too, but he would never admit it because all he has on the brain is well, the brain, and he doesn't want anything to get in the way of college. Not even blonde bombshells."

"Blonde bombshells? Next door?"

"That's what my dad calls them. What's a bombshell, anyway?

"It's what one calls a very attractive, sexy, desirable woman. Like Marilyn Monroe."

"Who?"

"Never mind. So tell me more about the neighbors."

"Well, the mom is Joya Harper and she is a rich widow who has flaming taste."

"Do you mean *flamboyant?*"

"Does flamboyant mean glitzy and colorful?"

"Yes."

"Then I mean flamboyant. She likes animal prints, short skirts, and cleavage. And she gets a kick out of me. She even bought me a leopard—a real one, for a pet. And she's the best decorator I have ever seen. She owns this antique shop called 'Junk for Joy.'"

"Wait, back up. A leopard?"

"That's what I said, a leopard named Cleopatra. And the daughter is Lee. She's not so flamboyant, but she does have big boobs. She is so sweet and nice and she talks to me like a friend and not just a kid. And the grandma, well, I know her disease isn't funny, but some of the stuff she does is very funny—like running around naked and doing stripteases in the backyard. And she gives me money. Once, a fifty-dollar bill."

"Does you father know about all this?"

"Who cares?"

"Tess?"

"He's barely around, so why should he care?"

"He's been working a lot?"

"All the time. Sometimes I'm home by myself at night and I hear noises and get scared."

"Where are your brothers?"

"Danny is busy chasing after Lee, the girl next door with the big boobs, and Luke is studying pickled brains at the School of Medicine. Yesterday I tried to make a meatloaf and I started a fire in the kitchen, and when I was doing laundry the washing machine overflowed and the suds filled the room and came up to my knees, no my neck, just like on TV."

"Now, Tess, I think you're exagger—"

"I'm not! And I know I told you that I love my new neighbors but I'm also a little afraid of Joya."

"Tess, did she do something inappropriate? If she did you really have to tell me so I can help you."

"Would you call *murder* inappropriate?"

Miss Miranda gasped and Tess congratulated herself inwardly on her dramatics.

"All right Miss Landgon, this is serious. No exaggerations, please tell me what you are talking about."

Tess told Miss Miranda about her car ride with Joya and Gran-Glen and what Gran-Glen had said about her favorite son-in-law.

"But, Tess, do you think it was this Gran-Glen's Alzheimer's talking or do you think she was serious?"

Tess swiveled in her chair. *Blooming heck!* What had she done! No, no, no, no! Now Miss Miranda would call her dad and have a meeting and this whole thing would blow up and she would be banned from seeing her three ladies. She slowed down her spinning. Oh, *crikey*, what had she done?

{*"Oh, Cecilia, what's happening to my baby? She used to be honest to a fault. Honest to where I had to give her permission to hold back on the truth sometimes." I had to explain, like all mothers, that little white lies were permissible sometimes to save hurting someone's feelings. Tess was*

288

notorious for her veracity. "Tess, do you like the custard?" my mother might ask her. "No Grans, it tastes like Elmer's glue." "Tess, say thank you for the birthday gift." "Thank you for the game but I already have it." "Good morning, sweetie!" "Mom, your breath smells like throw-up!"}

On the morning of her favorite brother's twentieth birthday, Tess baked. At least she called it baking. The chocolate cake she was just now removing from the oven was born of a box. As were the blueberry muffins that were cooling on a rack—the ones she had hoped would serve as entrée into the Harper's house later that morning. With her dad and Luke at work and Danny sleeping happily until his full bladder woke him, the house was closing in on her. It used to be bustling. Now sometimes the loudest sound in the house was the refrigerator's icemaker or Piper's toenails clicking against the wood floors.

While Luke's chocolate cake cooled Tess ventured next door to the Harper's to share the muffins. Lee invited her in and made a fuss over the muffins saying they were just the thing to get her lazy bones mother out of bed. They went into the kitchen and Lee poured Tess a glass of orange juice and put on a pot of coffee. While they waited for it to brew, Tess sat swirling on a kitchen stool, basking in Lee's sweet presence. She'd never had a big sister, and until she met Lee, she never knew what she'd been missing.

"I can't believe your mom sleeps this late," Tess told Lee. The kitchen clock said eleven-thirty. Her own mother, being a gardener, considered it a waste if she didn't make good use of every ray of sunshine in a day.

"She loves sleep," Lee explained. "And the more she sleeps the better off the rest of us are. Believe me."

"Could you paint my nails like yours? I just love that shade of blue."

So while they waited for the coffee to brew and Joya to awaken, Lee painted Tess's fingernails and toenails sky blue.

Almost on cue, the coffee finished dripping in the pot and Joya trudged into the room. Wowza! What a mess! Tess couldn't believe it was Joya—her hair stuck out as if she'd just been electrocuted and she had black mascara smudges underneath her eyes. "What are you looking at, kid?" Joya asked. "This is just the *before*. You've already seen the *after* and it's spectacular."

"She means she cleans up good," Lee explained, pouring the coffee and handing a cup to her mother.

"My *favorite* cup! I'll put you back in the will. Why do I smell nail polish?"

"Sorry," Tess said, holding up her little blue fingers.

"Good thing you don't have to worry about my will, kid. Did you bring these muffins?" she asked, sliding onto the stool next to Tess.

"Yes, I made them myself from scrap."

"From *scratch*. You are hilarious! Come here and give me a hug."

Tess obeyed. Joya smelled like cigarettes and alcohol and sleep. She could hardly keep her eyes open. "You want to do some sweeping at the shop today?"

Tess nodded.

"I need to go check up on that nutcase I got running the place. Now there's a piece of work. She questions my accessorizing. I mean, come on, one of my millions of talents is accessorizing, isn't it Lee-Lee?"

"Right."

"She's just a window dresser, where I, on the other hand, am a Visual Merchandiser. I have degrees in graphic and interior design for cripes sake and I got this low-rent trying to tell me where to put vases and throw pillows. I might fire her today."

"Mom, don't do it."

"She *annoys* me."

"So? You're hardly there. And I like my job at the coffee bar. I'm not quitting to work for you. I'm not."

"How's the cat, kid? You like?"

Tess propelled herself into a big, dramatic twirl on the stool. When she completed the three-sixty and returned to face her benefactor, she smiled and said, "I love!"

Tess had never been so excited about the opportunity to sweep a floor. While Joya and Lee accessorized (which Tess discovered meant moving a pillow here, a vase there, dragging a chiffarobe to a corner and then filling it with pink, amber, and green Depression glass) she carefully maneuvered the broom around the wood floors. She'd been to Joya's shop a few times before but this was the first time she'd been "hired" for a job. She would rather have been accessorizing, but if sweeping was her assignment she would do it well.

The shop was sweet; her mother would have loved it. 'Eclectic,' Annie would have called it, one of her favorite words. It wasn't a big shop, but every corner, nook, and cranny was packed with little finds—from vintage jewelry to English antiques. It was an inviting place with so many wonderful things to look at—a woman's wonderland—the kind of place a man wouldn't be caught dead in. That was the idea, Joya had told her. She almost named the shop "The Sissy Shop," but Lee had talked her out of it.

Tess curbed her urge to pick things up, afraid that if she dropped and broke something she may not be invited back. She couldn't risk it. So she devoured everything with her eyes and swept and greeted customers with a pleasant smile. She followed Lee around as much as she could because she knew that Danny would be picking Lee up soon. He hogged her!

Well, sweeping wasn't so bad. She was really getting into the groove of it until she came face to broom with her school friend Michelle Nelson and her mother. Tess remembered the doozie of a lie she had told Mrs. Nelson when she had given her a ride home from Allison Carbeaux's birthday party: that Mitch had had a heart attack and Alzheimer's. Where did she come up with this stuff? Yikes!

"Tessa Langdon," said Mrs. Nelson, "what in the world are you doing here?"

"Just helping my neighbor. She's over there," Tess said, pointing to Joya, even though she knew that pointing was impolite.

"How's your dad, honey? Did he like that lasagna I sent over? Luke called to thank me. He is the sweetest young man. You're going to miss him, aren't you? We all feel so bad about your dad."

Tess gulped. *All?* Had she told others? The entire church? The entire neighborhood? Did everyone in town think that her dad had Alzheimer's? Oh, this was not good. "Actually, Mrs. Nelson, my dad is doing great now. He's actually cured. He went to this special Alzheimer's clinic and they gave him this new medicine that killed the Alzheimer's bug and so there is nothing to worry about. He's fine now! All he has to do is keep taking the medicine and do like two or three crossword puzzles a day and he'll be fine. Okay. I better get sweeping!" Tess sang out goodbye and danced away with her broom. She hid behind a chiffarobe and took a couple of deep breaths. What was wrong with her? It seemed like every time she opened her mouth, lies flew out.

On the way home from *Junk for Joy*, Joya told Tess to open the glove compartment. Inside Tess found a scarf and a pair of sunglasses. "Just a little something for helping out today," Joya told her. "You gotta look good in my ride."

"Wowza! Thanks, Joya!" Tess put on the sunglasses and tied the scarf around her head. Now, if only she had high-heeled sandals…

"Is your brother home?" Joya asked.

"Which one?"

"Which one. *Which one*, she asks. The one I have a crush on, that's which one."

"Oh, I don't know. Probably. He hardly goes anywhere, remember?"

"He hasn't mentioned that he's mad at me or anything, has he?"

"No. Why would he be mad at you? The only person Luke ever gets mad at is Danny."

"No reason. He just seems kind of quiet lately."

Tess removed her sunglasses and looked at Joya, but Joya's sunglasses concealed her facial expression. Tess felt a lie coming on. "Maybe he's quiet because of what happened."

"What happened?"

Tess paused—not for effect but because she didn't know what happened. She was making it up as she went along.

"Well, my dad found out what he did."

"What did he do, kid?"

"You're not going to believe this: he forgot me last week at Woodfield Mall in Schaumberg. He brought me to the Rain Forest Café for a special treat, but his stupid girlfriend, Alexandria, just had to come along."

"Girlfriend?"

"Ugghh! I can't stand her. She's so 'like' and 'actually' and 'seriously' and 'you know.' So anyway, he was paying so much attention to her that he forgot all about me and got halfway back to Rockford before he realized that he'd left me behind. I was crying and then this strange man with red sores all over his face started following me in and out of stores so I finally ditched him in the *Build a Bear* store but then the store lady thought I was shoplifting…come on! I'm way too old for stuffed bears. Finally, the police and the detectives and I think the National Guard showed up and…"

"Tessa-messa!"

"What?"

By now they were pulling into Joya's driveway. "Have you ever heard of Radar?"

"Yes."

"Radar detects radio waves. Have you ever heard of *Gay-dar*?"

Tess scrunched up her face. "No."

"That's when you can detect if someone is gay. You know what 'gay' is, don't you?"

"Yes."

"Okay, do you know what *Lie-dar* is?"

"Maybe?"

"*Lie-dar* is an internal detection device that only mothers have that enables us to have eyes in the back of our heads, to perform remote viewing when our children are miles away from us, and to know when someone is feeding us a crock of shit. Kid, my *Lie-dar* is buzzing. Now listen, I know you lost your mom and that sucks big time, but you have GOT to cut out all this LYING, right now, or one, NO ONE is going to like you; two, NO ONE is going to trust you; and three, you are going to RUIN your entire life. *Capisci?*"

Shocked and shaken, Tess didn't answer but jumped out of the car, and without looking back, ran home. She heard Joya calling her name. She could call for all of eternity for all Tess cared. *Crikey*, she had done it again! Someone had better tape her mouth shut before she lied to every person on earth.

Once inside, she grabbed Cleo and with Piper at her heels, climbed the stairs to her room. The tears spilled, hot and ample, onto her pillow. Cleo snubbed her and squirmed out of her arms. Piper, though, dear sweet Piper, comforted her by jumping up onto the bed and settling herself next to Tess. Oh how she missed her mother! This world was too big and complicated for her to navigate without her.

She cried for a long time, waiting for someone to find her. She cried really loud. She opened her bedroom door and cried even louder. She tried a hoarse, nearly hysterical cry. Nothing. No one. She screamed a fake, shrill horror movie scream. A blood-curdling, oh-my-god-someone-is-trying-to-kill-me kind of scream. Nothing. No one.

It was almost funny. Yes, it was funny. "No one loves me, Piper," she said, "except you. And you have bad breath."

Just before dinner, Luke roused Tess and piggybacked her down to the kitchen, slid her into her seat at the table in front of a plate of chicken quesadillas, and patted her on her head. She was uncharacteristically quiet. Didn't even fold her hands for prayer.

"Tired, honey?" her dad asked from across the table. He seemed acres rather than just a few feet away.

"I'm fine."

"So tomorrow's the big Fourth of July bash. Are you ready?" Danny asked her.

"Yeah."

"Yeah is for yaks," Mitch said.

"Yes, yes, yes. Everything is all set."

Mitch set down his quesadilla and looked at Luke, who shrugged, then at Danny, who also shrugged. "What's this?" Mitch said. "You begged for a Fourth of July party and now you seem unenthused? What gives?"

"Nothing. I just have a ripping migraine and I may have Uvulitis."

"Now that's just gross!" Danny said with a mouthful. "Can't you please park your female problems somewhere else before coming to the dinner table?"

"Dan, *Uvulitis* happens to be an inflammation of the uvula, the small tongue-shaped piece of tissue that hangs from the top back of the mouth. You're probably confusing it with *Vulvitis.*"

"Sick," Danny spat. "Now I can't eat." He threw his quesadilla onto his plate. The phone rang and Danny jumped up to get it.

"Smurf, it's for you," he called, holding the phone impatiently, even though it was a cordless and he could have easily carried it over to Tess.

"Dan, we're eating," Mitch said, exasperated.

"We're eating," Dan said flatly into the phone and hung up.

"How rude!" Tess said. "Who was it, anyway?"

"Blondo. And she'll be right over."

Mitch shook his head. "Doesn't she know we're eating? And you really shouldn't call her that."

"You heard me tell her we were eating. And *you* call her that."

Luke stood up and said abruptly, "I need to be excused please."

"What's with him?" Mitch asked Danny as Luke dashed up the back stairs.

"My diagnosis would be a clear case of *Shame-itis.*"

Mitch raised his eyebrows.

"It's a neurological condition resulting from being overridden with guilt and shame and self-contempt. "*Shame* plus *itis,*" Danny explained as they heard Joya step through the back door, yoo-hooing.

Mitch gave Danny one of his looks. "Your clever sarcasm is not helping things."

Joya pounced into the room. Dressed in yet another animal print pencil skirt and tight fitting brown tank top and stiletto heels, she was nothing if not cat-like. "Sorry to interrupt your dinner, but I'm leaving for a hot date and I needed to give this to Tess. Here, hon. Sorry I yelled at you."

Tess accepted the jade green plastic bag Joya handed her.

"Hurry up and open it. As I said; I have a hot, hot date."

Tess peered inside the bag and then pulled out a little knit something or other. She held it up.

"It's a cat hoodie!" Danny said, sitting back down at the table.

"Isn't it adorable?" Joya announced. "It's for winter, of course."

Tess didn't want to forgive Joya so quickly. Her words had stung, but this little kitty sweatshirt was so cute, what was a girl to do? "It's so, so, so, sweet!" she sang. "Thank you, Joya!" She came around to give her a hug.

"You're welcome! Hey," Joya said, sitting herself down in Luke's empty place, "mind if I have just a nibble of this?" She didn't wait for an answer but grabbed Luke's half-eaten quesadilla. "I didn't eat all day so I could fit into this skirt and now I'm feeling a little woozy. My stomach's filled with butterflies. The last time I was on a date was—oh never mind. Anyway it's been forever. I don't know why I even said yes. Where's Luke?"

"Upstairs," Tess said.

"Did he like the birthday cake you made him?"

"Birthday!" Mitch bellowed. "We forgot Luke's birthday."

"I didn't forget," Tess said. "I made him a cake this morning. And I made him a present, too. I crocheted him a scarf for college."

"Go get him, sweetie, and we'll have cake," Mitch said. "Can you stay, Joya?"

"Love too, but I got this stinkin' hot date, remember?"

"Who's the lucky guy?" Mitch asked.

"I'm too embarrassed to say. He's a lot younger than me. I almost feel as if I'm robbing the cradle." She flicked her hair out of her face with her free hand.

296

Tess looked at Joya sideways. Wait just a cotton-picking minute. Joya couldn't be talking about Luke could she? She sure had an awful crush on him, but Tess always took it for just that—a crush. The thought of Joya actually dating Luke was disgusting.

"Joya," Mitch said, "this thing between you and my daughter. Is it something I need to know about?"

Tess's eyes darted between her dad and Joya.

"No, it's nothing serious," Joya said. "Nothing to worry about. I just get short-tempered sometimes and I lost my cool with her." She winked at Tess and Tess winked back.

"Tess," Mitch said, "I expect you to show Joya respect. She's not your playmate, you know; she's an adult and you need to treat her as one."

"Yeah, Tess," Danny said.

"I know, Dad. And who asked you, Danny? Geez. Joya, who is your hot date with? Tell me and I'll be your best friend forever!"

"Tess, I just said you can't treat Joya as a playmate—"

"Oh, it's okay. You don't know him, kid. He's my attorney from Lake Forest and he only likes me for my money. But he's take-your-breath-away-gorgeous and he likes to dance, so there you go."

"Oh, that's a relief," Tess said before she realized she'd said it.

"What's a relief? That he likes to dance? You're a real nutcase, kid, you know? Okay, well I gotta go." She came around the table and planted a kiss on Tess's cheek leaving a perfect ruby red imprint. Then she planted one on Mitch's, too. She tried to get Danny but he was too quick for her.

"Lee told you about us going to a movie and then to Mathis's, right?" Danny asked her.

"Yes, and I told that girl to be home by midnight and to keep her legs crossed." She slapped Danny's cheek gently and sang, "Bye, kids! Don't wait up!" on her way out the door.

"That woman is crazy!" Mitch said.

"I heard that!" Joya called back.

Luke claimed he had an upset stomach and didn't want to come down for cake. Tess wouldn't take no for an answer. Danny had left for the movie with Lee and Mitch was making an emergency run to Best Buy to pick up a gift card for Luke, so Tess made use of the time by taping up streamers in the kitchen and setting the table with Curious George party plates, leftover from who knows when. She put nine candles (all they had) on his lopsided cake and placed the cake in the middle of the table. Then she rung up Luke on his cell phone, a desperate measure since she knew it annoyed him.

"I still have a stomach ache, Tess. Thanks anyway."

"But Luke, I made the cake just for you. From scrap."

"Maybe later, okay?"

When Mitch returned with the gift card, Tess went upstairs and knocked on Luke's door. He didn't answer, so she turned the knob and peeked in. He was asleep on top of his bed.

Some birthday! she said to herself.

At nine o'clock that night, Mitch told her to forget about it. They could have cake tomorrow, for breakfast even. But Tess couldn't let it go. She removed the candles from the cake, sliced a whomping piece, slid it onto a plate and carried it up to Luke, along with his gift-wrapped scarf. She set the plate on the floor and knocked on his door. No answer again, only this time his door was locked. She called his name and then sat down outside his door and waited. He'd have to come out sometime. At least to pee. She waited for a full hour. By the time Mitch came looking for her she had eaten most of Luke's cake and her face was streaked with chocolate-stained tears.

"Birthdays used to be happy occasions around here," she told her dad, as he scooped her up and carried her off to bed. She decided there was one redeeming thing about the whole day and it was this: the old guy still had enough strength to pick her up and carry her to bed!

Chapter Twenty-six

Lightning, Camera, Action!

{*"Danny almost didn't finish the third grade," I tell Cecilia. "Was he a poor student?" she asks. "No, no, it wasn't that. He came home from school one day with one of my bras in a plastic bag. I had run out of fabric softener dryer sheets and the sweatshirt he was wearing had a bad case of static cling—my bright pink bra was stuck up one of his sleeves and it fell out at recess! He threatened never to return to school ever again. I thought he'd never forgive me!"*}

*D*ANNY YELLED, "CUT!"
Two hours before the Fourth of July party, Danny found himself in the Harper's lavender living room filming the first installment of Tess's documentary. The room made Danny feel jumpy and nervous. He remembered reading somewhere about prison wardens painting jail cells pale pink to both calm and intimidate prisoners. That's how this room made him feel: pacified yet threatened.

There was something sacrilegious about Joya being interviewed about Heaven while she sat on her zebra-patterned sofa, or settee, or whatever it was, in her hot pink satin nightgown, with matching robe and open-toed slippers with fur around the edges. It just didn't seem right. Lee, who was standing near the picture window chewing on her thumbnail, had warned Danny that this would happen, that her mom would Hollywood it up.

"Joya," Danny said, "uh, you're sure you don't want to get dressed, because I'm kind of having a hard time with the light and that fluorescent color you're wearing and the purple walls."

"The walls are not purple, kid, they're a lovely lavender."

The hint sailed right over her head.

"I have three other sets just like this. One in red, one in black, and one in jade green. The green really sets off my eyes."

"Mother!" Lee whined and rolled her eyes.

"Well, it does."

"Never mind," Danny said. "We'll make this work."

"Make me look young," Joya commanded.

"*Mom*," Lee said.

Tess sat fidgeting next to Joya on the sofa, or settee, or whatever it was, with a prop notebook and pen in hand. She wore an uncharacteristically feminine sundress and sandals for the interview, and Danny detected a hint of lipstick and blush.

Danny said, "Ready...action!"

"So, Mrs. Harper," Tess began.

"Oh, please. Call me Joya—it means jewel in *Italiano*."

"Certainly. Thank you, *Joya*. My question for you is this: What is Heaven?"

"Oh my," Joya said, touching her heart and calling even more attention to her cascading cleavage in the process. "Heaven is whatever you want it to be."

"Can you elaborate, please?"

"Yes, of course. Well, if you love chocolate, then Heaven will be wallpapered and carpeted in chocolate. If you can't get enough of downhill skiing, you will probably spend eternity downhill skiing. If kittens were your passion, you'll have hundreds. If you—"

"Thank you. I think we get the picture. Do you think we'll wear clothes in Heaven?"

"No way, Jose, we'll all be buck naked. Clothing will be so 'earth' darling."

"Who goes to Heaven?"

"Not my job to say, but if you think everyone will look like you and me, I think you'll be surprised."

"What color is Heaven?"

"Well it's not white, I'll tell you that. I don't understand why people and Hollywood portray Heaven as white—white clouds, white clothes, white everything. If anything, Heaven is as colorful as Peter Max pop art. Do you know Peter Max? You're probably too young, but he was the father of this fantastically cool psychedelic art."

"One last question. Are you afraid of dying, Mrs. Harper—I mean Joya?"

"Why, yes, yes I am. I have to be truthful."

"And why is that, would you say?"

"Honey, you're looking at a girl who has lived big. I need about seventy more years to clean up my act, and I'll get thirty or forty more if I'm lucky."

Outside it was the perfect day for a Fourth of July party. The weather cooperated with sunshine and temperature in the low nineties. Not a rain cloud in sight. Tess proclaimed it a "blue star day."

Pontoons, motorboats, and jet skis took over the river; walkers and bicyclists invaded the bike path on the other side of the river. People water-skied and tubed, and the Forest City Queen, the city's riverboat, ferried people up and down the Rock, the sun-tanned tour guide providing historical information about the river's history. All of it added to the excited buzz of the day.

The party proved to be a good thing for their family. It seemed to Danny that they all were happy to bring back a much-loved tradition. Everyone pitched in: Mitch and Uncle Jack were in charge of grilling the hot dogs and hamburgers. Donning stupid aprons (Mitch's said "*What*

301

part of 'it's not done yet' don't you understand?" and Uncle Paul's said, *"I'd tell you the recipe but then I'd have to kill you"*), they brandished their grilling utensils like swords. Danny was glad to see his dad smiling.

Aunt Maggy was in charge of the side dishes. Annie's brother, who the kids simply called "Unk," was in charge of the drinks. Luke was the ice-cream man, a job he'd held since he was six. And Danny, well Tess knew better than to assign him anything other than documentary-maker. And document he did.

He followed Tess around the backyard as she worked the crowd. She asked her father's partner, Dr. Penter, a Lutheran, what Heaven was. "Tess, honey, I think Heaven will be like pre-school."

"Pre-school?"

"Yes, and here's why. Remember when Jesus said that we must become like little children before we can enter the kingdom of Heaven. Remember that?" Tess nodded. "Well, he didn't mean act childish, but child-*like*. And children possess two great things: simple faith and endless curiosity. Hence, Heaven will be our preschool."

Tess smiled and gave Dr. Penter a hug. Then she said to the camera, "Let's see if we can interview a non-Christian. Our neighbors, the Weinsteins, are Jewish. Let's see what they think about Heaven." Tess smiled at the camera and motioned with her hand to come along. Danny followed her as she zigzagged through mingling guests. When she stopped in front of Mr. Weinstein, Danny was surprised to see that Tess was almost as tall as the old man—he must have shrunk over the years.

"What was that, Miss Langdon?" Mr. Weinstein said, cupping his good ear. "What's that about Heaven?"

"What do you think Heaven is, Mr. Weinstein? *Jewish* Heaven."

Danny cringed behind the camera at Tess's political incorrectness, but Mr. Weinstein grinned widely. He'd loved Tess best of all, since she was one of the few little girls in a neighborhood of rowdy boys.

"Well, my dear, Heaven is where good people go to experience the greatest pleasure possible—the feeling of closeness to God. It's not equal for everyone, though. I like to think of Heaven as going to the symphony or the opera. Some people get front row seats, some are way back in the balcony. You earn better seats by your good deeds. It's a good thing for you to think about, Heaven. A good thing. I'm happy to see it. You're a good girl. You too, Dan. Hello. Hello." Mr. Weinstein waved and smiled, waved and smiled. Danny kept the camera on him, zooming in for a close-up of that pencil-eraser-sized mole on Mr. Weinstein's left cheek.

"Now I'd like to find out what Indian people think of Heaven," Tess said to the camera. "And by Indian, I am being politically right because I am talking about Indians from India and not Native Americans from America. Although I wish I knew one so that I could interview a tribal person. Did you know there is a Canadian tribe called the Bella Coola? Isn't that the coolest name—Bella Coola? Okay, over here is Dr. Singh, a friend of my father's. Dr. Singh is not a pediatrician like my dad and Dr. Penter, but a gas-tro-en-ter-ol-o-gist, which is a doctor of your stomach, your intestines, and your butt, too. Hi, Dr. Singh!"

"Well, hello, young lady. And how are you? And hello Daniel a.k.a. Mr. Spielberg."

"Dr. Singh, I'm interviewing people about Heaven. Can I ask you a couple of questions?"

"Of course, my dear."

"What religion are you and do you believe in Heaven?"

"I am a Hindu, Tess. My religion is Hinduism. It is difficult to assign a dogmatic orthodoxy to Hinduism, because there are many sects. But almost all of us believe in a three-in-one god known as "Brahman," which is composed of Brahma—the creator, Vishnu—the Preserver, and Shiva—the Destroyer. We believe in Karma, the law that says good begets good, and bad begets bad. Every action, thought, or decision a person makes has good or bad consequences that will return to each person in his or her present life, or in one yet to come. And finally, we believe in *Samsara* or Reincarnation. This is a journey on the "circle of life," where each person goes through a series of physical births, deaths, and rebirths. With good karma, a person can be reborn into a higher caste, or even to godhood. Bad karma can relegate one to a lower caste, or even to life as an animal in their next life. Our goal is *Nirvana*—our 'Heaven'—which is the final release of the soul."

"Wow!" Tess said. "That is very interesting. Were you an animal before you were a man?"

"Mrs. Singh insists I was a baboon in a prior life," he said, with a mischievous grin.

{*"It's good that Tess is thinking and wondering about Heaven," I say to Cecilia. Usually, no one talks about Heaven until someone dies, then we say, "Well, he's in a better place," or when we pray the "Our Father" we acknowledge that God is in Heaven (although when Tess was little she thought the phrase went: 'Our Father who* aren't *in Heaven' and she asked me why God wasn't in Heaven. She also thought the phrase 'hallowed be thy name' was 'how do you say your name').*

I remember once at an intimate family gathering, my sister asked my husband what he thought Heaven was. My ears perked up. Mitch was a very spiritual person, but also very private. He surprised me with his answer, honest as it was: "I have no idea."

"Oh, come on," she said. "You must have given it some thought."

"Well, sure, but there's not much to go on. The Bible says: 'Eye has not seen, ear has not heard, what God has ready for those who love him.' I've always taken that to mean that there's no way we can know."

My sister persisted. She'd recently lost her best friend to cancer and Heaven was on her mind. "What do you think *it will be like? I won't hold you to it or anything."*

"Well," Mitch said, "It can't be a 'nothing to do' kind of place because it seems God created everything to move. The material universe is in constant motion. From the tiniest electron to the biggest planet, everything is moving. As we speak, suns and moons and stars are speeding through the universe. Humans, animals and plants are moving about, growing, evolving. Water is flowing, trees are swaying, the wind is blowing. Everything is moving because life is vibration. Life is energy. So Heaven has to be a very active place—one of pure and holy energy—and not an idle, stagnant place where we would just loll about with nothing to do, sitting on clouds twanging on

harps. I think Heaven will be a vibrant, busy place; where we will continue to learn and grow. Why would God put us in Heaven with revitalized powers of body, mind and spirit, and then leave us with nothing to do?"

"But what do you think there is to do?" my sister asked. "Do we eat, do we pee, or do we fly around? Will we care about how we look? What about sex? Can we see earth and what's happening with our loved ones that we left behind, because if so, how could we ever be happy, watching all the sadness on earth?"

Mitch shrugged.

Mitch was right to shrug. Hints of Heaven are all we are meant to have while we're on Earth. Anything more would distract us from our incarnation. Heaven is so much better than our small minds could ever concoct! Here all of our senses overlap and interact in a way that they never could on earth. (The exception would be the person with synesthesia—an extrasensory condition where senses merge and overlap. Sounds can be visual, letters of the alphabet can appear colored, music can be tasty, a blue sky can smell like blueberries.) I had always thought there were five senses—the sixth, being ESP or extra-sensory perception, about which I was curious but dubious. But on earth humans are blessed with more than just five senses. There are the standard exteroception senses of sight, taste, smell, touch, hearing and balance, but there's also the sense of humor, common sense, sense of reasoning, sense of dread, sense of time, sense of place. There's thermoception (perception of heat), and nociception (the perception of pain), and proprioception (which is our unconscious awareness of where the various regions of the body are located at any one time).

In Heaven, there are even more senses. There's the sense of infinity, there's the sense of pure consciousness, there's the sense of perfect unity, there's the sense of home. It's hard to explain, but you can smell colors, you can taste music, you can hear a gorgeous vision. And to see the Almighty face-to-face, well, I can't wait.

Angelus Silesius, a seventeenth-century philosopher, mystic, and poet wrote this about coming face to face with God:

In Spirit senses are
One and the same. 'Tis true,
Who seeth God he tastes,
Feels, smells and hears Him too.

I'm not ready yet—as I said I'm still in the lower vault of Heaven, but, the way I understand it is that when we see God we will see, taste, feel, smell, hear, and experience Him with all of our senses. I'm told, the Beatific Vision, well, it will complete our being.}

"Let's see, who next?" Tess said, looking around. "Let's get a female point of view."

Danny trailed Tess around the yard as she interviewed (interrogated) their guests on their views of Heaven. Mrs. Archer, their old piano teacher described Heaven this way: "Heaven is the long-awaited return to the pre-fallen state of humanity. The true Garden of Eden, where humanity is reunited with God in a natural and perfect state of existence for all time."

"Do you think it will be fun?" Tess asked.

"Fun?"

"Yes, fun."

"I think it will be pleasurable, young lady, but fun—I just don't think 'fun' is the right word."

"Of course it will be fun," Aunt Maggy, who was passing by with a big bowl of potato salad, interjected. "I think God would want us to be playful and cheerful. It will be fun and amusing and entertaining and enjoyable."

Mrs. Archer looked hurt and stiffened up like a cramped muscle. Danny panned in on a mole she had on her chin. (Did all their guests have moles and he just never noticed before?) The mole on Mrs. Archer's chin had a hair growing out of it. What were moles anyway, Danny wondered, knowing that Luke would know if he asked him because Luke knew everything.

"Let's see who else we can interview," Tess said, smiling into the camera. *"Let's see who else has a mole,"* Danny muttered under his breath.

This was getting tiring. The camera was one of those older, heavier models, and Danny's arms were starting to ache.

Tess approached another colleague of their father's. Dr. Ahmed was a Muslim and his version of Heaven did in fact sound fun. "Dear one, Heaven is luxurious—reclining in silk cushions in comfortable homes, attended to by young servants. All the delights are present— lovemaking, wine, good food. Heaven is all of the positives without any of the negatives."

Tess asked Dr. Ahmed if knew anything about the religion of Native Americans. "All I know, dear one," he said, wiping perspiration from his forehead with a handkerchief, "is that the Native American religion is a land-based spirituality. They believe the Great Spirit is imbued in the buffalo as much as in the man. I'm not sure they have one precise belief about life after death. Some believe in reincarnation while others believe humans return as ghosts. Some believe people go to another world after they die. Hmmm, now you have me curious myself."

"Cut!" Danny said. Tess shot around and gave him a look.

"What? We're not finished, Daniel."

"Yeah, well someone needs to take a pee."

"Who?"

"Your cameraman, who do you think?"

"Come right back."

"Here, you hold the camera."

"Come right back!"

He really did have to pee, even though he didn't realize it until he started walking to the house. Mathis showed up right as Danny opened the screen door, so he waited on the steps for his friend.

"Johnny Mathis," Danny greeted.

"Tater," Mathis greeted back.

"I'm so glad you're here. You gotta help me film some of these people for Tess. I promised her and it's just getting old, dude."

"I can do a little digital."

"You the man."

But after his pee, he and Mathis grabbed a can of pop and decided the air-conditioned kitchen was the place to be. So they hopped up on the counters and drank and burped and tried to figure out the anagrams in each other's homemade shirts. Danny's said "jolt your huff" and Mathis's said "day inc need peed." Neither one could decode each other's shirts so they fessed up: "Jolt your huff" was "Fourth of July" and "Day Inc need peed" was "Independence Day."

"Dude, we themed ourselves!" Danny said. "That's never happened before."

Mathis gave Danny a disgusted look. Danny felt like they were girlfriends wearing matched sweater sets. "Don't worry, no one is ever smart enough to figure out our anagrams," Mathis told him.

"*There* you are," Tess said, appearing out of nowhere. "You were supposed to come right back."

"I was thirsty."

"*I like your haircut, Mathis,*" Tess said, in sing-song.

"*I didn't get my haircut,*" he sang back.

"*Looks like it,*" she chanted.

"*Okay then,*" he sang back.

"*Get the hell outta here,*" Danny sang.

"Hey, wait a minute," Tess said in her normal bossy voice. "Wait just a minute."

"What skunk, I mean Scout?" Danny said.

"I think I know what your shirts say. I couldn't figure yours out at first, Danny, but now that Mathis is here, I think I know it. Yes, I know them both."

"That's highly unlikely, Smurf, I mean Scout," Danny said.

Mathis said he'd have to agree.

"Oh yeah? You wanna bet something?"

"Like what?"

"Never mind. I thought I knew it but now I'm not a hundred percent."

"Thought so, squirrel, I mean Scout," Danny said.

"Well, I think I was close anyway. I thought yours said 'Happy Fourth of July' and Mathis's said 'Happy Independence Day.'"

Mathis said, "Tess! Take out the word 'happy' and you would be—"

"Close, but no cigar," Danny said. No nine-year-old was going to accuse them of theme-ing.

"Come on, Danny, time's a wasting."

"Okay, trout, I mean Scout."

Outside they found Lee talking to Luke the Ice-Cream Man. She was a sight to see with her hair pulled up in a clip and her tanned legs looking longer than ever. Mathis said, "WAHAM," code for 'what-a-hot-awesome-mama.' A spark of jealous electricity ignited inside Danny, but it was set off by Luke, not Mathis, and Danny shot his brother a look. But the spark fizzled out when Lee saw him and said, "There you are, Danny!" She trotted over. Tess hugged her and updated her on her interviews. Danny drank her in while she chatted and attempted to eat an ice cream bar. It was melting faster than she could lick it and finally a gooey chuck fell onto her bare foot.

"Let's get the hose," Danny said. He turned to Mathis and held out the video camera. "Dude, would you? For me?"

Mathis acquiesced but not without griping. "You owe me," he said, as Tess took hold of his free hand and led him away.

Danny led Lee to the side of the house where he snuck a kiss and made her giggle. He sprayed her foot with the hose, wishing he could lick the ice cream off instead. Suddenly she grabbed the hose and shot Danny smack in the face. He let go a scream that sent Mathis running to see what was wrong. "Get her, get her," Danny called to his friend. What ensued was the best water fight ever.

The kids were in heaven, filling water balloons then lobbing them at each other. The older kids made ice water bombs (Styrofoam cups filled with ice and water) and hurled them at their targets. Danny spotted Joya chasing Luke with her can of beer, Luke running as if being pursued by a boogey man. Even the older people were having fun, some joining in simply by dipping their fingers into their beverage and flicking the cool liquid on the person next to them. Tess, happily saturated, forgot about the documentary for a while as she chased her cousins around the yard. Danny cornered Lee, tackled her to the ground and poured ice water down the back of her tank top.

Helping Lee to her feet, Danny said, "Let's get Mathis. He's too dry." He grabbed her hand and led her through the side garage door and sneaked through to the kitchen. They peeked out the kitchen window over the sink and saw Mathis talking to a neighbor girl. "Perfect," Danny said. He slowly and quietly raised the kitchen window and then quickly grabbed the faucet sprayer and shot Mathis with a flash of cold water so quickly he couldn't have known what had hit him.

"Son-of-a—!" Mathis screamed, turning to find Danny and Lee's smiling faces in the window. Danny grabbed Lee's hand and they hid in the laundry room and smooched until they thought the coast was clear. Man, Danny had fallen for this girl! He could have stayed in there all day just kissing her juicy lips! Finally they emerged from their hiding place and went outside to look for Mathis. The screen door had barely banged behind them when they heard Joya's shrill scream. Outside, there was Gran-Glen—who had told Danny and Lee earlier that she wasn't up for the party—standing near the dessert table for all the world to see, dressed in a pair of red, high-heeled pumps, a white bra, and a pair of purple bikini panties, carrying a bottle of something—vodka maybe. Danny couldn't help it and burst out laughing. Lee covered her face in horror, but when she realized that Danny was laughing, she cried, "You jerk!" and took off running.

Danny ran after her. Her long legs and his former cigarette habit made it a long chase. Finally, after three blocks, Lee stopped and fell onto the grass, crying.

Danny fell to the ground next to her. "I am so sorry. I didn't mean to laugh, it was just so..."

"*Funny*. It was funny, I know. It's just, you don't know what it's like. My family is crazy!"

"Oh come on, they're not crazy, they're just a little eccentric."

"That's just a ten-dollar word for crazy. You've heard the saying—the only difference between crazy and eccentric is money. That describes my family perfectly."

"They're just a little unconventional, that's all."

"They're weirdoes! Oddballs. Screwballs."

"Yeah, but at least they're interesting. I can't stand predictable conformists. They're unadventurous and common."

"People don't appreciate ordinary and common. There's something special about being nothing special."

"I disagree."

"But you laughed, Danny."

"It was a gut reaction. I'm so sorry. I didn't mean to hurt you. Dementia is not funny, but the fact is that people with dementia sometimes do funny things."

Lee looked at Danny and smiled. "You're right. You're very wise."

"Wise? That's the first time I've been called wise without the word 'guy' following it."

"How can I face everyone now? I mean, my goodness, the sight of her."

"You know, actually, she didn't look half bad. Great legs and—"

Lee slugged him. "What I want to know is how she got a hold of my underwear!"

{"Okay, now this girl I like!" I say to Cecilia. "She's perfect for Danny." I always told Danny there was a girl out there who would appreciate his uniqueness, and here she is! She's a bit wounded herself and her scars are the genesis of her compassion.}

Danny got up and gave Lee a hand up. She smiled at him, but her smile was a temporary work of art—like a snow flake. She grew reflective, so Danny took her hand and they walked back slowly to the house where they found a semi-irritated Mathis and a fully-annoyed Tess waiting for them. Danny laid on the charm and smoothed everything out. Lee went home to check on her mom and her grandmother.

"Come on, Danny," Tess whined. "We still have more people to interview. With Mathis's help, they interviewed a dozen more (by now, sodden and heat-exhausted) guests.

At dusk, as promised, Lee returned for the fireworks. She and Danny and Mathis lay on a blanket near the other kids and watched the sky explode in color. Later that night, lying in bed, Danny thought about the day. He was so buzzed he couldn't sleep. Lee. Lee. Lee! She thought he was wise! How crazy was that? Ooops. Poor choice of words. How cool was that? All he could think about was that he didn't want to blow it with her. He had to be smart. He tried to understand her. He tried to think about how it would feel to be part of a family that wasn't like his—safe, conventional, respectable even. It was ironic really, because his parents' traditional standards were something he always defied. And here was Lee who longed for the very object of his rebellion. Had he taken respectability for granted? How could this work? A girl who longed to be ordinary and a guy who wished to be extraordinary? A thought popped into his head, a thought so wise and sage that certainly it couldn't have come from his small mind: *why not just be authentic?* it said. Hmmm. It was something his mother would have said, he thought, as he drifted off to sleep.

<hr />

He'd spent every day since the Fourth of July with Lee. Usually they swam at Mathis's or at the neighbor's on the other side of the Harper's. Lee had grown blonder and bronzer as the summer progressed and Danny had grown besotted and lovesick. He was never happier.

"I'll be at Mathis's with Lee," he called out to his dad, after they'd returned from Mass and he'd quickly changed into his suit.

"Do you have sunscreen?" Mitch called back. Danny pretended he didn't hear. Geez. Of course he didn't. He'd run out just yesterday.

And of course he got sunburned. He and Lee and about a dozen other kids stayed in the pool most of the afternoon, getting out only to partake of the tacos that Mathis's mom had prepared.

On the way home Danny and Lee stopped at Walgreen's to get aloe vera gel for Danny's sunburn. He knew his dad was going to flip out—Mitch had recently had a non-melanoma skin cancer nodule removed from his neck and had been harping on the kids to protect their skin.

Perched on a stool in Lee's kitchen, Danny accepted a glass of iced tea from Joya and waited for Lee to change out of her swimsuit. Joya seemed extra jumpy today as she flitted around the kitchen. She filled a thermal cup with ice and Coke and a healthy shot of rum, took a huge gulp, and closed her eyes and sighed. Danny tried to make small talk. "Did you know that if you multiply one hundred eleven million, one hundred eleven thousand, one hundred eleven by itself you get the number 12345678987654321, which is a palindromic number?"

"Tell me some more stinkin' useless information," Joya said, lighting up a Marlboro Light.

Danny spun on his stool. He didn't know Joya well enough to determine if this was sarcasm or interest. He went with interest and continued. "Let's see. Um, did you know that if all the people in China, the entire population, were to walk past your house in single file, you would not live long enough to see the last person in line?" Joya blew her cigarette smoke over her right shoulder, out of Danny's direction. "Keep going."

Danny rubbed his blistered shoulder. "Uh, in any given hour, there are, on average, sixty-one thousand people flying in planes over these United States."

"Well, aren't we just full of interesting shit? You're hurting, aren't you? Here," she said, "placing her cigarette in an ash tray, "throw me that tube of lotion and I'll lather you up."

Danny actually had asked Lee to lather him up—he'd planned it for foreplay—but he didn't want to piss off Blondo here so he tossed her the tube.

She caught it and came around the counter, stood behind Danny and commanded him to remove his shirt. He obeyed. "What other good stuff you got for me? I like how you think, kid," she said, as she squirted lotion into her hand.

"Lightning strikes about six thousand times per minute on this here earth," he said, as she rubbed the lotion on his back.

"And it's going to strike right now if you don't get your damn hands off my boyfriend." It was Lee! Danny turned around to see her angry blue eyes concentrated on her mother like a laser beam.

"Chill, girl. The poor boy was in pain."

"Mother!"

"Okay, here, you do it. I was just trying to help. Danny was cheering me up with worthless trivia that was helping me to forget about my problems, the primary one being what the HELL AM I GOING TO DO WITH YOUR LOONY GRANDMOTHER?"

{"Okay, Cecilia, I'm sure you will agree, this woman is off her rocker. I don't understand how she is the person who is supposed to help my family get back on their feet. I've had reservations all along." Cecilia just smiles.}

"Mom, please!"

"Danny, hurry," Joya said, returning to the other side of the counter. "Tell me something else. Come on, something no decent person in the twenty-first century should live without knowing."

The pressure was on. He needed something good. He watched as Lee screwed the cap back on the tube of aloe vera. She looked so sad. As if the tube were adulterated now, contaminated; tainted by her own mother. Wow, Danny thought, this was one strange mother-daughter relationship. "Okay, okay. Uh, did you know that rats can have sex twenty times a day? Yeah, and that one pair of rats, because they can multiply so quickly, can have more than fifteen thousand descendants in a year?"

Joya downed her rum and Coke and slapped the counter. Hard. "Okay, now you just wrecked my entire day. I hate rats! I frickin' hate rats. Just go, you guys. Just go and rub each other with that goo. Go at it."

"Sometimes I hate you!" Lee screamed and grabbed Danny by the arm.

Up in her room, Lee sulked in a club chair while Danny fondled all her stuff that lay about. "Who is this guy?" Danny asked, picking up from her dresser an eight by ten framed photograph of some kid who looked like a model.

"That's my brother."

"Oh, yeah, I forgot you had a brother."

"*Two* brothers. And that one has forgotten he has a sister."

Danny set the frame back on her dresser.

"He's eight years older and was lucky enough to escape before everything went to hell. He lives in Santa Barbara. He says I should come out there for college. I might. My other brother's in Rhode Island. My mom called his wife a "floozy" once, so we don't see them very much."

Danny pretended to be interested in other things on her dresser—jewelry, cologne, magazines—but he was really stalling. "Hey, listen, I'm sorry about that. What happened downstairs."

"It's not your fault. I probably overreacted but she's been drinking all day and she gets so stupid around men. Not that she would do anything other than flirt with you but I've had guy friends who ended up being more interested in my mother than in me."

"Well, you don't have to worry about that," Danny assured her. He walked over to the chair she was sitting in and fell into her lap.

She giggled. "You're squishing me."

"That's the idea."

Danny kissed her and then scooped her up and sat back down with her in his lap and kissed her some more. *Dang*, he was on fire, burning alive—and it wasn't due to his sunburn. But alas, neither the kissing nor the lotioning proved in the end to be foreplay. Beautiful Lee had other things on her mind. Philanthropy for one thing. She lay her head on Danny's shoulder and asked him if he was rich.

"You mean my family? My dad?"

"Yeah. He's a doctor and all."

"Yeah, but I never thought of us as rich. We have a nice house, decent cars, a boat, private schools. We're not hurting, that's for sure, but we're not loaded if that's what you mean."

"My mom is loaded."

"Good for her."

"Filthy, stinkin' rich. My dad was a self-made man. He came from nothing and made a fortune. My mom came from money and will inherit a fortune. Plus she sued the company that installed the stairs that my dad fell down and got even more money. It's obnoxious the amount of money she has."

Danny nodded. Money was obnoxious, a bothersome necessity, but obnoxious.

"And she doesn't need to work. Her junk shop is just for something to do. A tax write off."

"At least she's not a poor, starving widow."

"Yeah, but think of all the destitute people who have nothing. My mom didn't lift one finger to merit this kind of wealth. It fell into her lap and she doesn't know how to manage it. She feels so guilty about my dad that she gives me a one-hundred-dollar-a-week allowance, which I don't need or want because I have a job and she pays for my car and gas and insurance and clothes and everything else. *'You need any money, kid? You need any money?'* That's all she ever says to me."

Danny readjusted Lee on his lap. "Think of all the people who would trade places with you."

"Oh, I know. Poor little rich girl. I'm not trying to say I want to be poor. I'm not that stupid. But then Gran-Glen feels sorry for me too—when she remembers who I am—and she slips me twenties and fifties and once even a hundred dollar bill. 'Buy yourself a cone,' she'll say. I just feel so guilty about all this money."

"Well, give it away then," Danny said.

"I do, I give to Catholic Charities and to the Red Cross and to Habitat for Humanity. But I hate mailing checks out and how do you know they're really using it for what you intend—" She was interrupted by her cell phone. "What?" she said in a put-off voice, after looking at the caller ID. She rolled her eyes and lipped the words *my mom.* "Why? Mom!" She handed the phone to Danny and stood up. "It's supposed to be important."

Danny took the phone tentatively while Lee paced. "Hello?"

"Listen kid, I forgot to have the talk with you," Joya said, her words a little slurry. "And by the *talk* I mean my killer talk about my daughter still being a virgin and that she promised on her dead father's grave to remain a virgin until she's twenty-one. And just so you know, her father and I have arranged a marriage for her to some European royalty and if you defile her they will probably hunt you down and castrate you, so there you go, you've been warned."

Danny felt like saying, "More like threatened," but instead he said, "Yes, Ma'am," and handed the phone back to Lee. She flipped it closed and said, "I don't even want to know what she said, but one, it's probably a lie and two, don't let her scare you."

"She doesn't scare me," Danny said. But she did, a lot actually. Well, Joya had succeeded in leaching all the desire out of him and he sat back in the chair, shaking his head. What a piece of work!

Lee flung herself onto her bed and Danny thought she was going to have a good cry, but instead she hung her head and arms over the side and pulled something out from underneath. A shoe box.

"Danny?"

"Yeah?"

"You need any money, since you lost your job?"

Danny smiled. She was so sweet. "You forgot. I am a high-paid nanny now."

"Oh yeah. But look at this," she said, removing the lid from the box and revealing a bunch of bills.

"Wowza!" Danny said.

"This is all from my mom and Gran-Glen. I don't need it. I don't want it. Help me think of something good to do with it."

Danny raised his right eyebrow. "Give me a minute," he said.

"Go ahead, think. I have to run to the bathroom and then let's get out of here. Let's go do something."

"I have to 'nanny' Tess in a little while."

"Can I be your co-nanny?"

"You can be my 'co' anything you want."

<hr />

Tess scarfed down three pieces of stuffed pizza at Altamore's. Danny watched as she wiped at the sides of her mouth with her napkin and then realized that she wasn't wearing her overalls, but instead was dressed in a frilly white top and a short jean skirt. Her hair had been brushed and was held away from her face by a black and white polka dot headband. For once she actually looked like a normal nine-year-old girl. But that was as far as the improvements went—she still talked non-stop and interrogated Lee about her entire life. Still, Danny could put up with anything—sunburn, Joya, Tess, a disfiguring disease—if it meant being with Lee.

When they were finished eating, Tess ran off to play with Marco, the owner's youngest son, and Danny had Lee all to himself. He stared at her from across the table.

"Quit staring at me!" Lee said, wiping her mouth with her napkin.

"I'm not staring, I'm 'gazing.' There is a difference."

Lee smiled, leaned into him, and whispered, "Tell me something about you that no one else in the universe knows." Danny gave it some thought. This was his entrée to confess to one person in the world what really happened with his mom. He swallowed. No. He couldn't do it. "There was this one thing," he said "but Mathis knows about it 'cuz he was with me, but we're the only two that know."

"What?"

"Junior year, Mathis and I were sick of being losers and so we got into his Dad's liquor cabinet. All he had was some lame French raspberry liqueur. Well, we finished it off and we drove—I was driving—to this senior party and we were wasted, believe me, and we're on Spring Creek, which is like a 45 mph speed limit, and out of nowhere this cop pulls us over. And I'm trying to act all in control and everything—you sober up real fast—and I roll down my window and I go, "Gee occifer, was I speeding?" and he says, 'No son, you were going six miles per hour.'"

"Oh my God!" Lee squealed, covering her mouth to stifle her giggles. "Did he bust you?"

"No, believe it or not, I talked my way out of it. Said I had a charley horse in my calf. I acted like I was all in pain and everything and I got out of the car and started rubbing behind my knee and panting. Ends up the cop used to get leg cramps all the time. 'Hurts like a kick from a palomino, don't it?' he said. Then he checked my license and registration and wrote down the name of some kind of supplement that would help and sent us on our way."

"Oh my God!"

"I know. It was the first and last time I ever got drunk. I make a sloppy drunk. Besides, Mathis and I both thought it was a sign. Now you."

"Oh, well, I don't have anything as good as that."

"Come on, you started it."

"Yes, I did, didn't I? Okay, no one on the planet knows this, but exactly one week after my dad died I found a book under my pillow. Not a printed book but a journal, a leather bound journal with a built-in lock."

"Cool."

"Except there was no key."

"Can't you just bust it open?"

"I could but…"

"But what?"

"It might wreck it. See, I talked myself into believing it's from my dad—somehow—I don't know. I can't bring myself to open it and find out that it's empty or worse, that it's from my mother." She leaned in and whispered, "I've had nightmares that it contains my mother's confession. Aren't I a dreadful person? Do you hate me?"

Danny leaned in closer and took her hand. "Of course not. But doesn't it drive you crazy? I'd have to open it."

"I'm too chicken. But it haunts me, it does."

"Someday you'll open it. The time will be right and you'll open it."

"How will I know?"

"You just will."

⁂

Before they'd left for dinner, Mitch had pulled Danny aside and asked if he and Lee would mind taking Tess shopping after they ate. "No problem. What does she need?" he'd asked, as Mitch pulled money from his wallet.

"A new bike helmet and a bra."

"As in a *brassiere*? A Flopper Stopper? A Boob Tube? Breast Cozies? Hooter Hoods? Knocker Knickers? Chest Compressors? Mountain Cappers? Bounce Busters? An Over-the-Shoulder-Boulder-Holder? Come on, Dad! She doesn't need a bra. She's flat as a bookmark. Flat as a phonograph record. Flat as a—"

"All right, Dan, I get the picture, but apparently her overalls have been concealing her budding womanhood. According to your Aunt Maggy anyway."

"She's got vanilla wafers for boobs."

"Yes, well, see if Lee might help us out with this, would you?"

Lee had let Contessa—her new nickname for Tess—in on her quest to find a home for her unwanted gift money, so on their way to Target Tess threw out suggestions. "Why not donate it to the Doris Day Animal League or PETA?" Tess the animal-lover proposed.

Lee nodded and said she would consider it. Tess was quiet for a while in the back seat and Danny could tell that she was racking her brains to come up with the most perfect, most deserving charity. "Have you ever heard about The Smile Train?" she asked.

Danny and Lee shook their heads. "Dad told me about it. It's for babies born in cleff palaces."

"What are cleff palaces?" Lee asked.

"She means *cleft palates*," Danny explained. "Babies born *with* cleft palates."

Lee smiled. "I'll keep it in mind, Miss Contessa."

Lee was glad to help Tess out at the store, so while they shopped for a bra and a bicycle helmet, Danny roamed the electronics department. When they reunited, Danny said, "Let me see your new bra, Squirt."

"No way," she said, pulling the bag closer to her.

Danny snatched it anyway and felt the bicycle helmet through the plastic. "Wow! What do you wear, a size double D?"

"Danny! Give me that!"

"Danny, stop teasing her," Lee said.

On the way home, they decided they would stop at the video store to rent a movie, but instead Danny pulled into the parking lot of the Goodwill store.

"What are we doing here?" Tess asked.

"I thought you might need another bra."

"Very funny," Tess said.

"Just follow me," Danny said to the girls. "I might have a solution to Lee's money problems."

Inside, Danny weaved in and out of the aisles, picking up items that sparked his fancy. Then he whispered in Lee's ear and was pleased to see a smile materialize. Then Lee whispered in Tess's ear and by the time they left the store, they'd stuffed pockets and purses and shoes and cookie jars and rain coats and mittens and books and record albums with one dollar-, five dollar-, and ten dollar-bills. They stealthily slipped bills into anything and everything—all without being seen by the employees.

When they emerged from the store they whooped and cheered. What a heady experience! "That was so cool!" Lee exclaimed.

"What did we just do?" Tess asked. "I mean I know what we did but what do you *call* what we just did?"

Danny hopped into the driver's seat. "Well, it's like the opposite of shoplifting. It's like shop-*gifting*. Yeah, shopgifting."

"It's ingenious is what it is," Lee said, beaming. "Thank you, Danny. Tomorrow, let's do the Salvation Army."

"Can I come too?" Tess asked.

"I think you'll have to," Lee said, "you're our partner in crime now."

"You mean the opposite of crime," Tess said, happily.

Lee smiled. "It's like sneaky charity."

"It's Sharity!" Danny said. They drove home singing John Mellencamp's *I Need a Lover Who Won't Drive Me Crazy* at the top of their lungs.

{"Don't I have great kids, Cecilia? I only wish Mitch knew about this. He just doesn't understand Danny the way I do." It's funny, Mitch and I spent so much time worrying about Danny and now it's Luke who needs worrying about.}

Danny drove home feeling pretty good about himself. And not just because he'd pleased Lee. He thought about the dude that would come into the Goodwill shop today looking for a pair of shorts, finding a nice pair, bringing them home and discovering a ten-spot in the pocket. Or the young mother who might need a bathrobe and selected the soft powder blue one with a fiver in the pocket. Or the kid that gets that Dr. Seuss book and when he turns to page thirty-five finds a crisp new dollar bill. Yes, it made Danny feel really good.

The good feeling popped when Danny pulled the car in the driveway and almost hit Blondo. Visibly shaken, she banged on the hood of the car, yelling something about Gran-Glen. "She was in the kitchen and then I thought—anyway, I can't find Gran-Glen! I can't find her anywhere!" she cried, pulling on her hair.

Lee settled her mother down enough to get the particulars out of her. Joya explained that she left Gran-Glen in the kitchen sipping a Virgin Mary while she "took a quick pee" and when she came back she was gone. Luke came out of the house to check on the commotion.

"Get Dad," Danny said. "Gran-Glen is missing."

Luke shook his head. "He's not inside. I think he's down fixing the dock."

Joya gasped and took off running through the backyard, toward the dock, with Lee and the rest of them trailing close behind.

Chapter Twenty-seven

Give Me a Kiss, I Gotta Go

I LOOK DOWN *from Heaven and see my husband flirting with another woman. No, I'm not jealous; Mitch is just being the sweet person he is.*

Somehow Glenda Arlington, from next door, has found her way into my husband's boat.

Cecilia allows me to watch in real time (earth time) because she says there is an important lesson here. She tells me that once Glenda was beautiful and smart and rich, but now she has lost her mind. Glenda thinks my husband is her lover. Mitch is talking to her and playing along to be kind. Just because a person's heart is broken doesn't mean it doesn't work.

Although she's in her seventies, Glenda moves as if she were a sultry younger woman, with graceful hand movements and regal carriage. She wears a filmy gauze caftan, her platinum blonde hair pulled back in a tight ponytail, and holds in her hand what looks like a Bloody Mary (there's a celery stick protruding from the top of the glass, anyway). Cecilia allows me to look but not to listen. Looking is enough.

Mitch is not in the boat. He's squatting on the dock next to the boat and looks to be attempting to coax Glenda out. She'll have nothing of it.

She keeps waving him in to join her, holding up her drink in a celebratory manner. Then she stands, sets her drink down, and proceeds to remove her covering. Oh my dear, she's wearing a black bikini! All bones and wrinkles in a black bikini.

My poor husband does a double take. He looks around for help but no one is around. Again, he holds out his hand to her. I read his lips: "Come on," he says. Glenda shakes her head. Suddenly she starts crying. Then she grabs her Bloody Mary glass and flings it into the river. Wailing, she holds her head in her hands and then falls to the floor of the boat. Mitch jumps into the boat to help her. I look at Cecilia, who just holds my hand tightly. My husband helps Glenda up to a sitting position on the boat's floor. She seems to be okay physically, but she's crying harder now; she can't seem to catch her breath. She's hyperventilating. Mitch is patting her back, trying to settle her down. He's used to placating youngsters at his office with sugarless gum and stickers. This is harder. Glenda looks up lovingly at my husband and takes his face in her hands. It looks as if she'll kiss him, but she doesn't, she lets go of his face and buries her own in the hollow of his shoulder. A particular bewildered look (one I know so well) spreads over my husband's face—he never did do well in the presence of a crying woman. I love him so much at this moment. He sits there holding Glenda, patting her on the back. The bewildered look on his face slowly transforms into one of steadfastness. He lets her empty herself.

Next I see Joya and Lee and Luke and Danny and my baby Tess running toward the dock and everyone seems to be talking at once. And Joya is gesticulating wildly and jumping up and down which doesn't seem to help matters any. Cecilia squeezes my hand again. Mitch gets to his feet and nods to Luke to come aboard to help; my gallant son complies. My two men help Glenda to her feet and then we all watch in disbelief as she unexpectedly frees herself from their grasp and falls or jumps or flings herself into the river.

Even from here, the rest seems like it plays out in slow motion. Mitch's face contorting into shock and horror. Mitch diving into the water, followed by Luke. Danny running to the end of the pier, holding Joya back. Lee with her hand covering her mouth. Tess, looking bewildered. Cecilia holds my hand even tighter. She knows what I'm thinking. Why? Why hadn't Luke jumped in after me?

❦

Be it gentle or brutal, there is terrible beauty in death. It's time to tell you about the day. I've kept you wondering long enough. It's not fair.

Mitch promised and then broke his promise. It was almost the end of June and we hadn't yet been out on the new boat. All that wet cold spring, Tess was driving us crazy with her excitement and anticipation. She had it in her head that this was the year she would get up on skis. She had tried so hard the year before. This year, due to record rainfall, we'd had a no wake order, and so the new boat sat in its slip for weeks. Mitch and the boys tinkered with it, sat in it, and slept on it. It killed them that they couldn't cruise on it. Finally, the order was lifted and Mitch told Tess we could take the boat out on Sunday, weather permitting.

The weather did permit. Finally, we had a sunny, calm day, with temperatures in the eighties. A perfect boating kind of day. After church, we began preparing for the maiden voyage. The week before, Tess and Mitch had stenciled the name of the boat on its side: "My Girls" for Tess and me.

Mitch had promised, but then he got a call from one of his partners who was having chest pains and needed Mitch to take his call. No sooner had Mitch hung up the phone with Dr. Penter then the hospital called. Emergency. Sorry Tess, no boat ride. And he was out the door. Mitch was the kind of doctor who would still make house calls if he could get away with it, and while that kind of dedication made for a wonderful physician, it made for an undependable daddy.

Tess was inconsolable. A real drama queen. "But he promised. He promised. He crossed his heart!" There was nothing I could say that could calm her down, until I blurted out, "Okay, okay, I'll take you out. Your brothers and I can do it, right guys?"

326

Luke and Danny stared at me, their mother gone loony. But I had had it up to there myself with Mitch's ungodly schedule. I was serious. "Come on, guys, we can handle it, right?"

"Mom," Luke said, "I don't know." Luke had decided long ago that I would never get over my fear of water, no matter how many times Mitch got me into a boat.

"What? You're an expert," I said to Luke. "The new boat isn't that much different from the old one, is it?"

"We can do it, Mom," Danny said. "I know how to drive it. Let's go."

So we went. I finished packing up the picnic basket and Luke filled an ice chest with cans of pop. Tess grabbed Piper's leash because we didn't want her jumping into the river—once in we could barely get her out. I sent Danny to fetch the bug spray and the sunscreen and we were ready to go.

The sun was like a yellow diamond in a sky just dusted with powdery clouds. I breathed in some deep breaths of fresh warm air—my flowers were so fragrant that week—as we walked down to the dock. Tess pulled Piper along on the leash, lecturing her about staying in the boat. "There'll be plenty of time for swimming later on," she promised.

I know nothing about boats, but I know that Mitch had had his eye on this one for years. It was the only extravagance of his life—he drove an old model Volvo. This boat—a Sea Ray 270 Select Ex—was something else. All I know was that it cost too much and here we were looking at college soon for the older two. But I couldn't deny my husband, who worked so hard and never asked for anything, this one thing. It was beautiful, big enough that I didn't get splashed much, and it did have a tiny bathroom on it. The kids were in love with it, too.

When I approached the boat, I was hit by the familiar feeling of anxiety. Water. Ugh. And I wondered for the millionth time why I couldn't overcome my irrational fear of the most blessed and basic element of life. I said a prayer to St. John Nepomuceno and climbed aboard.

"First things first," I said. "Danny, will you get the life jackets out? And help Tess into hers, okay?" I always wore a life vest myself—I didn't care who laughed at me. Tess (because she was under thirteen and required to) and I were the only ones in the family who actually wore our life vests.

327

The sun was bright and I wished I had remembered my sunglasses or at least a visor. In the old boat, I could have dug around in the storage compartments and found a pair of glasses or a variety of hats. But this boat was pristine. For now, anyway.

Luke took the wheel and tried to start her up. And tried. And tried. "You flooded it," Danny said. "Here, let me try," he said and attempted to slide in front of Luke.

"Mom," Luke whined. "You said I could drive."

"Who died and made you captain?" Danny demanded, trying to shoulder Luke out of the way.

"Mom!" Luke shouted.

"Danny, let him do it. He's right. I did make him captain this time. You can be captain next time."

Luke gave Danny a smug look and Danny retreated but not before slugging Luke good and hard on his upper arm. A full-fledged fight ensued, with my two darlings batting at each other like cats.

"Enough!" I shouted. "You guys want to go or not?"

"You guys better not wreck this for me!" Tess bellowed, her face scrunched into her bossiest scowl.

"All right, all right," Danny said, laughing and getting in one last slug. Sad but true, my youngest son loved a good fight. "But if he can't get the thing started in two more tries, can I have a go at it?"

"I'll get it going," Luke said. "It always takes Dad a few tries too, if you recall."

I was glad when the engine rolled over on the next try. You would like to think that your own kids understood your phobia and would do whatever it took to make the boat ride easy on me, but teenage kids don't think that way. In this, my boys were completely normal. Tess, on the other hand, was always worried about me. Being a fish herself she could think of nothing sadder than a person who was afraid of the water. She wanted me to love it as much as she did. She wanted us to be "synchronized swimmers." She wanted me to slip down water slides with her. She wanted me to swim with the dolphins with her. She wanted me to dive for quarters in our neighbors' pool. She wanted us to kiss underwater—something she did with her daddy. She was convinced that one day I would come around. That I would "grow out of it." She even tried psychology. Sometimes when Mitch and I were watching TV in the river room, Tess would bring in a small plastic bowl of lukewarm water and have me soak a hand or a foot in it—just to help me "get used to it." But my boys, well, they just called me a "wuss."

When we pulled away from the pier, Tess lifted her small arms to the sky and shouted, "Wheeeeeeeee!" The few powdery clouds that moments ago had dotted the sky had dissipated and the sky was now cloudless and bright. I wished again for my sunglasses as the sun on the water was almost blinding. Oh well, I could squint.

We were off! I swallowed a couple of times and decided I was going to try to enjoy myself. It was a gorgeous day, the wind was in my hair and on my skin, and my children were robust and healthy and relatively happy. I was blessed. Truly blessed.

Luke wasn't a daredevil. He was good at the wheel. I liked the look on his face—proud and confident—and decided maybe it was okay that Mitch had to work after all. This was good for Luke. I was going to miss him so much when he left for school at the end of the summer. I was so proud of him. How many kids get through four years of high school without giving their parents a lick of trouble? No girl problems, no grade problems, no curfew problems, or discipline problems. Not a single demerit, not so much as a parking ticket. Just a good kid, all the way around. Little did I know. Little did I know.

We cruised up the river, heading north, honking at the houses of friends along the way. Surprisingly, there weren't that many boats on the river that day. Some people we knew from church were sardined onto a pontoon boat, one of their children hanging precariously over a railing. I wanted to shout out a warning but I held my tongue and simply waved. I tried to relax and enjoy the ride. I really tried.

There's an island we like not far up the river and so when we came upon it, I yelled over the wind and gestured for Luke to pull over. Danny put out the anchor and we jumped out onto the small wooded area, but the mosquitoes attacked immediately so we reboarded and instead docked *near Martin Park to eat our lunch. As I laid out the food, Danny teased me, calling me June Cleaver "on account of" (as the Beaver would say) the perfectly nutritious and delicious little lunch I had thrown together: turkey and havarti cheese sandwiches with the crusts cut off, apple slices soaked in lemon juice, carrot sticks, string cheese, and homemade chocolate chip cookies. "What a lovely lunch, Mrs. Cleaver. Wally and I really enjoy your cooking," Danny said.*

"Why thank you, Eddie," I said, playing along.

"Mrs. Cleaver?" Danny asked, his mouth full of turkey sandwich.

"Yes, Eddie?"

"Would it be okay with you and Mr. Cleaver, if, after lunch, Wally and I threw the Beaver overboard?"

"Eddie!" I said, feigning shock. Even Luke smiled. We all enjoyed Dan's impressions. He did a great Eddie Haskel, a perfect Darin Stevens from Bewitched, and a mean George W. Bush.

"This is nice, isn't it Mom?" Tess asked.

"This is nice," I agreed. "Nicer than nice."

"And you're not afraid?" she asked.

"Just a wee bit."

"Good," she said, and smiled big, stuffing an apple slice into her mouth. The wind blew a loose strand of hair into her mouth that got mixed in with chewed apple, so when we finished eating and Luke and Danny worked on their tans, I sat Tess in my lap and braided her hair. "It won't stay," she pouted. Then Tess and I took off our life vests and lathered sun block onto each other's bodies. We joined the boys, lying on the seats in the sun and listening to Danny's Pink Floyd CD. It was so relaxing. Soon, I was asleep.

I woke up to fighting. Danny and Luke were at it again. What they were fighting about, I didn't know. Until I got here. In Heaven, I have been able to travel back in time to that scene. Remember how I told you that in Heaven you get answers? That you get to finish the puzzle of your life? That you get to solve some of the mysteries, fill in some of the blanks, find the missing links? To this end, we Heavenly saints are given the greatest gift: the gift of perfect memory, unadulterated by our earthly selfish ego.

The second order of business when you die—after your "welcome home" celebration—is to process your own life, death, and transition. It is very surreal to die and inhabit only your spiritual body. I'll be honest, it takes a bit of getting used to; we are grounded for such a long time after all.

It's your guardian angel's job (your spiritual guide) to help you through. Who better than your angel—who walked with you every step of your earthly life—to help you transition? Cecilia showed me that fateful day.

I saw Tess and myself asleep on the boat. My vanity left on earth, I was able to see myself objectively and not obsess about how I looked lying there in my swimsuit, or rather, how my thighs looked. Anyway, it was eerie to see myself in 'real' time but there I was. I saw Luke and Danny sitting on the starboard deck fooling around with the CD player. I heard them arguing. Danny had set a song—I think it was Pink Floyd's "Money"—on repeat just to annoy Luke, and Luke, thoroughly annoyed, was trying to get his brother to change the song. Just dumb brotherly sparring. Typical as dinnertime in our household.

"Why do you love to annoy me?" Luke asked.

"Because boo bet be."

"I do not."

"Yes, you yu."

"Well, sop it."

"Sop it?" Danny repeated, laughing. "Okay, I'll sop it."

"I said 'stop it' you idiot."

"You may have meant to say 'stop' but it came out 'sop.'"

"Danny!"

"All right. I'll 'sop' it." He pressed the button to turn off the repeat function. Then he threw his empty pop can at his brother.

Luke dodged it. "You're an asshole," he said, using a calm voice to prove that he wasn't annoyed, only disgusted.

"Mom's wrong, you know," Danny said, as he picked up the can from the floor of the boat. "You're the Eddie Haskell, not me."

"Shut up."

"Don't you mean 'sut up'?"

"Danny!" Luke shouted, loud enough to wake me up, but I slept on.

331

"*You are pretty perfect,*" *Danny continued.*

"*I'm not perfect, Danny. Nobody's perfect.*"

"*If nobody's perfect than everybody's imperfect.*"

"*Yes, that's right.*"

"*No, it's wrong. You are perfect.*"

"*How am I perfect?*"

"*Your looks, your grades, your attention span, your thought processes. All perfect. Boring, but perfect.*"

"*Come on, Dan. Let it go.*"

"*Oh, so now you're agreeing. You are perfect.*"

"*You twist everything.*"

"*You twist everything. Dad thinks you're perfect. Mom thinks you're perfect. But I know otherwise.*"

"*You're contradicting yourself. You've just spent ten minutes on the perfect me, now, suddenly, I'm not perfect. You don't make sense.*"

"*I make perfect sense. I know things.*"

"*What things?*"

"*Various things.*"

"*What things?*"

"*I know about Ashley Pallow. I know about the hospital and pumping her stomach and everything.*"

Luke said nothing, but his eyes registered surprise.

"*I guess she almost died, huh? But did you learn? I don't think so. Because then there was that other time, at the cemetery, when Drake and O'Conner got caught, but you ran away. You and Logan got away. You guys left Drake and O'Conner there with the bottles of Jack Daniels and let them take the rap. And then you guys dropped them like they were losers. You told Mom and Dad you weren't hanging out with them anymore because they were getting into drugs and alcohol. What a crock! You're such a phony.*"

"*We all ran. They just didn't run fast enough. They would have done the same if the tables were turned.*"

"*That's how you justify it?*" *Danny asked. He didn't wait for an answer.* "*How do you justify Ashley? She loved you, you asshole.*"

"*That I regret.*"

"*You do not!*"

"*Where do you get off telling me what I don't regret?*"

"*Because I know what you have hidden under the blankets and the life vests in the storage compartment.*"

I watched Luke's eyes grow big and guilty. In a split second both boys sprang up and raced to the storage compartment at the back of the boat. Danny got there first, opened it, and heaved out a medium-sized corrugated box—I could see through it so I knew inside was a case of Heineken. Luke tried to grab it but Danny swerved quickly and the box flew out of his grip and went overboard. The kerplunk must have set off my "mother" alarm. I watched myself awake to blinding brightness and to Luke screaming "Danny! Danny!" When my eyes adjusted, I saw Luke, leaning over the boat, with a look of horror on his face. Danny was nowhere in sight. How could I have known that Luke had pushed him down and that Danny was laughing to himself as he lay on the floor of the boat? I did what any mother would do: I pushed Luke out of the way and I jumped into the river to rescue my son. It didn't matter that I couldn't swim. It didn't matter that I had taken off my life vest. It didn't matter that the water was still shockingly cold due to the terrible spring we'd had. Nothing mattered but Danny.

The scene ended. I didn't need to see my own death.

Glenda didn't die. The old wiry thing could swim like a spiny dogfish. Mitch was able to hook his finger on the strap of her bikini and tow her in. Joya called 911 and now Glenda is resting comfortably at Rockford Memorial Hospital. I trust my husband will help Joya find a suitable place for the poor woman. I look at Cecilia and she reads my thoughts: why me and not her? Why her and not me? Cecilia smiles her "I know" smile. I have much to learn.

Chapter Twenty-eight

Go Jump in a Lake

{"Look at those worry lines around Mitch's eyes!" I say to Cecilia. He's aged so! He used to come home so happy sharing all the cute little things his patients said and did. Like the time he had to examine a little boy who had recently been potty trained and was so proud of himself he wore five pairs of big boy underwear, one right over the other. Or the time he was checking a little girl's coordination and asked her if she could please stand on one foot and she walked over and stood on Mitch's foot. Mitch would have our kids in stitches (while I feigned shock) at the dinner table telling us all the different names his young male patients had for their penises—joystick, corncob, twig 'n' berries, tallywacker, Magic Stick, bacon and eggs, ding-a-ling, little buddy, Gilligan, calizone, Mr. Winkie. Once a little guy came in and told Mitch that his 'kickstand' was broken! Oh, how I wish Mitch could smile again!}

MITCH WAS HIDING. A dark cloud had descended upon him when he awoke this morning and had followed him around on his hospital rounds, during clinic hours, and it even had the gall to follow him home. Would there be no end to this?

He'd gone underground—to the basement—where it was cool and quiet. As long as he was hiding he might as well get some work done.

It was August now, summer was winding down. Tess was talking about school supplies; Luke had begun to pack up some boxes for college. (Danny had only one thing on his mind—Lee.) Just thinking about Luke leaving was enough to moisten Mitch's eyes. With Luke gone, the family dynamics would change yet again.

Maybe hiding in the basement wasn't such a hot idea after all. His family had accumulated an embarrassing amount of junk over the years and standing in the midst of his own past, the walls began to close in on him. He'd had a nightmare last night that he couldn't seem to shake. He'd dreamed he was a walking corpse. (There's a real disorder called Cotards, or Walking Corpse Syndrome, where patients think they have died and exist as walking corpses.) The dream scared him because he felt like a walking corpse. The incident with Glenda had taken a lot out of him. He'd decided to get rid of the boat. To hell with getting back on the horse. Tess was traumatized or retraumatized and her therapist recommended keeping Tess off the boat and away from the water for the rest of the summer. Mitch had a mind to sell the house too, to get away from the water completely. Buy a farm maybe. Land, anyway. He needed high ground.

There was no doubt about it, they were hanging on by a thread. Theirs was not the happy home it once was. Yesterday, driving home from the hospital, after the ordeal with Glenda, Luke and Danny were at each other's throats again, arguing about utter trivia. Mitch had just turned onto Rockton Avenue when Danny, in the back seat, told Luke to go take a jump in a lake. Suddenly, Luke dove into the back seat and tackled Danny. When they got home Mitch sent them all to their rooms.

"So now we're two-year-olds," Tess had said.

And today the whole house seemed to be enveloped in a fog of melancholy. When he returned home from work, the kids were back in their separate rooms, Luke lying on his bed reading a book, Danny belly up to his computer, and Tess, reorganizing her closet. "I'm growing, Mitchell. I need a new wardrobe."

New wardrobe! This basement was filled with boxes of clothes. To whom did all these clothes belong? Organization hadn't been one of Annie's strong points. None of the boxes was even marked. Should he just haul them off to Goodwill? Was he supposed to save them for…his grandchildren? Who knew? Worn out from just opening and closing boxes, Mitch decided to give up and come out of hiding.

At dinner—if you could call toast and eggs dinner—everyone was despondent, shoveling up their eggs and then hauling the load to their mouths. Danny cut the meal short with this gem: "There's this guy in Bangkok—an art student—who makes these gruesome edible human heads and hands and other body parts out of bread and sells them at his family's bakery. He uses red food coloring for blood and they look completely real with veins and everything."

"Sick" screeched Tess.

"Thanks for that image," Luke said, putting down his fork.

After dinner, Mitch made Danny hit the grocery store—it was his turn and he liked to shop at night when the stores were less crowded. Mitch had prepared a long list and instructed Danny not to deviate from it. Tess helped Mitch clean up the dishes while Luke sat at the kitchen table and folded a load of laundry. CNN blared on TV: the war, the elections, a senator scandal.

"Dude," Luke said to his dad, holding up a dress shirt, "you need some new shirts. Two of these are missing buttons."

"Do you sew?" Mitch asked, coming over to take a look at his sorry shirts. Even his receptionist, Margie, had recently commented on the state of his shirts. "Is your iron broken?" she'd asked.

"I draw the line at sewing," Luke said.

"I can sew," Tess said. "Let me get Mom's sewing basket." She scampered off but was sidetracked by a knock at the back door. Mitch sighed. He was in no mood for company and prayed it wasn't Blondo.

It was Lee. "Hey Scout," Mitch heard her say. "I'm looking for Danny and my mom is looking for you. She wants you to bring Cleo over to play with Mittens and Gloves."

Mitch heard his daughter gasp and then ask, "Lee, can you sew?" And then, "Mitchell, can I go next door for a while? Cleo, here Cleo! Where are you?"

Lee came into the kitchen, all golden and lovely.

"Danny's grocery shopping," Luke said, without even saying hello.

"And hello to you, too. Hi, Dr. Langdon."

"Hi, Lee. Say, I wonder, honey, are you any good at sewing on buttons?"

"I can sew. I had to take sewing at my last school—it was an all-girls' school."

"Would you mind sewing on a couple of buttons for me?"

Lee said sure and Mitch took the back stairs up to the linen closet to fetch Annie's sewing basket.

When he returned to the kitchen he found Luke and Lee playing Scrabble at the table. Was time playing tricks on him? How long had it taken him to find the sewing basket? Of course, it wasn't where he thought it was, in the hall linen closet. It was in Annie's walk-in closet in their bedroom and once he was in the closet, besieged by Annie's things (he had yet to remove a single item) he had found it hard to leave. He'd pulled her clothes to his face and inhaled deeply. Her scent was still there, a year later. Oh, Annie! And before he knew it he had found himself shuffling through the built-in drawers, peeking inside shoeboxes, unzipping garment bags. He'd even spilled the contents of several purses, finding pennies and half sticks of Double Mint gum. There was a hatbox filled with greetings cards he and the children had given her. So many birthdays and Mother's Days, Valentines and anniversaries…

Now he was too embarrassed to interrupt Luke and Lee's game of Scrabble for a couple of lousy buttons. For once, Luke actually seemed to be enjoying himself, especially when he spelled out the word 'squeeze' for seventy-five points with the triple letter score.

"Seriously!" Lee squealed. "Now I'll never catch up. I can sew that button on, Dr. Langdon," she said when she saw Mitch standing in the doorway.

"No, honey, you play. I can do it." He plodded off to the river room carrying the silly sewing basket. But he couldn't do it. He was out of practice with a needle since these days most of the wounds he saw in his office were minor enough for steri-strips rather than sutures. He'd licked the end and trimmed the end of the thread with scissors over and over but that damn thread would not pass through the eye of the needle. Aggravated, he dropped the needle and thread back into the sewing basket. The collars on the shirts were showing wear anyway. Why bother with buttons?

"Dr. Langdon," Lee called from the kitchen, "*Zymurgy* is not a word, is it?"

Happy to leave the sewing behind, Mitch joined the kids in the kitchen and took a look at the word Lee pointed to on the game board.

"He's making it up," Lee said, "I know he is."

"Hmmmm. Z-Y-M-U-R-G-Y. I've never heard of it myself, but that doesn't—"

"See Luke, and he's a doctor. He should know."

"It's got nothing to do with medicine," Luke explained. "Zymurgy is the study of brewing beer."

"I suggest a dictionary," Mitch said. "There's one in my office."

Mitch grabbed the basket of laundry Luke had folded and headed upstairs to put the clothes away. On his way up, he shook his head and bemoaned Luke's way with women. He would never get a girl if he competed so fiercely. Mitch had learned the hard way that nothing good could come from a man trying to make his woman feel inferior. A thought pierced his mind. A time when he'd corrected Annie's grammar: "Honey, it's *he and I*, not *me and him*." She'd cried for days. "You're ashamed of me. I'm not as smart as you. I'm not as educated…"

He placed Tess's clean underwear in her drawer and remembered that she was next door. He decided she might need rescuing from the blonde monster and headed back downstairs.

Luke and Lee stood waiting at the bottom of the stairs. "The dictionary's not in your office," Luke said.

"He's stalling because he made the word up," Lee said.

"Check in my room, on my nightstand. I'm going to your house, Lee, to check on Tess. She's probably driving your mother to distraction."

<hr />

Hot as she was, Blondo liked to keep her house cool. It was freezing in there. Mitch couldn't imagine the Com Ed bill. Standing in the kitchen talking to Joya, he couldn't help but notice that she wasn't wearing a bra—her nipples were standing at attention. Lord, she was a sexy thing. Funny how a man's body could be attracted to a woman but his mind could be turned off by that very same woman. Funny how she had him thinking this way.

Blondo handed Mitch a highball glass filled with some clear liquid even though he'd politely declined a drink. "It's vodka," she said. "The Jewel of Russia. You look like you need it."

He almost lied and said he was on call. But he wasn't on call and maybe he did need it. The first sip went down easy enough and while Tess was running around the house trying to find Cleo, Mitch found himself accepting a second glass.

They moved to the living room because Joya said no one ever sat in the living room. Joya, on her zebra print fainting couch, with her long legs pulled up under her; Mitch, across from her on a sissy pale yellow velvet club chair. He couldn't help staring at her. She got an 'A' for legs and an 'A+' for cleavage. He was still a man; he still had equipment. "How was your date with the lawyer?" Mitch heard himself say.

"Oh, please don't call him a *lawyer*. It's *attorney*. And fine, thank you. He's eye candy and, well, never mind. Can I be frank?"

"Are you ever anything but?"

"Touché. Are you aware that your daughter is a big fat liar?"

This took Mitch by surprise. He was ready for some juicy tidbit about the attorney. "What are you talking about? Tess is petite and skinny." Normally, Mitch would have been offended by this kind of talk. Normally, he would have civilly asked Blondo to mind her own beeswax. But the vodka had softened him—he was tenderized meat.

"You know what I mean. She lies like a rug. It's all for attention, you know."

"Yes, I know. And we're working on it. Her therapist and I."

"Actually, it's more than just attention. You know why people lie, don't you? They lie to change reality. Tess's reality sucks."

"Well, I wouldn't—"

"Well, I would! That's what our little tiff was about the other day. I caught her lying and I called her on the carpet. She needs a good kick in the pants sometimes. Figuratively speaking, of course."

Mitch sank deeper into the velvet chair. Up until now, he'd let no one but his children's therapists discuss their well-being. He looked around. This living room kind of intimidated him. What was it?

"And the boys."

"What about the boys? They're fine."

"Fine? Open your eyes, Doc. Those two would kill each other if left alone. Oh, Danny's a sweetheart and gosh almighty if Luke was ten years older or I was ten years younger—"

"Joya, please."

"Sorry. Anyway. They are both bubbling with something. Rage, I'd guess. Or guilt, they could be seething with guilt. I think those two are hiding something. And you better watch that Luke. He's a budding alco—"

"Okay, Joya, now you're out of line," Mitch said, as he sat up straighter. "I appreciate the hkindness you've shown Tess and I'm glad that Lee and Danny are friends, but the boys are fine. Tess is fine.

TESS!" he called. "Honey, find your cat and let's go." He smiled at Joya. "We're all fine."

"Fine."

"Fine. Okay then, thanks for the drink." Mitch rose to his feet and was surprised to find his legs a wee bit wobbly.

"Drink*s*," Joya said, emphasizing the plural.

Mitch meant to say, "What's that supposed to mean," but it came out, "Wha's sas supposs su me?"

"What?" Joya said, covering her mouth and snickering. "Did you say *so sue me?*"

Mitch started to laugh and flopped back down into the chair. "I don't think so," he said between chortles. "But I can't be sure!" The laughter bubbled and effervesced from a dormant place deep inside him that he had forgotten existed. It wasn't until that moment did he realize that lately he'd been about as carbonated as a glass of flat Seven-Up.

How does one sense trouble? Can you smell it? Even in this imbibed state, even though he was busy chortling, Mitch knew something was wrong a millisecond before Lee came crashing through the front door. "Come quick! It's Danny and Luke!"

Mitch sprang from the chair and followed Lee out the door. When Joya started to follow, he turned around and barked, "No, you stay with Tess."

Lee was crying as she ran. "Oh my gah, oh my gah, oh my gah," she repeated over and over. Mitch felt the alcohol in his stomach slosh around as he ran behind her. A million thoughts bombarded his brain. He stumbled on a fallen tree branch, but didn't fall. *Sober up, man*! he told himself. *Brace* yourself.

In the driveway, the van sat parked, with the side sliding door open, revealing bags of groceries lying in waiting. As he climbed the back steps, he missed one and nearly fell a second time. Finally inside, it was dead quiet.

"They're upstairs, Dr. Langdon," Lee told him, grabbing his arm and pushing him ahead of her. "Hurry!"

"Boys!" Mitch called as he ascended the stairs. "What the hell is going on? Luke? Dan?"

In the hall he heard mumbling and whimpering coming from his bedroom. At first, Mitch didn't see them but when he came around to the other side of his bed he found both boys on the floor, battered and breathless. And bloody, too. "What the!" he said as he fell to his knees. "Lee, get me some wet towels from the bathroom. Please." She did as she was told. Mitch hovered first over Luke and then Danny, turning them gently, inspecting their wounds, wishing with all his heart that an intruder had broken in and had done this to them. Surely they didn't do this to each other, for even though neither boy seemed seriously injured, they both looked like victims of a barroom brawl. Could Danny's nose be broken? Would the gouges in Luke's cheek scar? Danny's eye would surely turn black. Suddenly a swell of emotion overcame Mitch and he began to cry. "Who did this?" He pounded his fist against his open hand. "Who did this? Why?"

Lee returned with wet towels and came around to minister to Danny's bloody nose while Mitch swabbed the bloody abrasions on Luke's face. Danny sobbed softly, breaking his father's heart. Luke, too, cried hot silent tears as he lay there, sweaty and spent. Luke didn't cry easily.

The phone rang and Mitch asked Lee to get it, saying it was probably her worried mother. He was right. Lee spoke in whispers: "*It's okay, Mom. They got into a fight. Keep Tess there. I'll call you later.*"

Mitch took a deep breath and got a hold of himself. "Okay, let's deal with the physical first and the emotional second." He asked the boys what hurt the most as he touched and pushed on their limbs and fingers for signs of broken bones: swelling, numbness, tingling, or blue tinge to the skin.

The boys lay there almost lifeless. Now that Mitch knew they would survive, they looked more pooped than anything. Upon Mitch's request, Lee fetched bandages and antibiotic ointment from the medicine cabinet in the bathroom. The phone rang again and Lee intercepted it while Mitch got both boys to sit up and lean against the wall. "Any dizziness?" Mitch asked. "Any nausea?"

"Tess is worried," Lee murmured. "Mom said she wants to come home."

"Ask her to wait fifteen minutes," Mitch said. Lee nodded and spoke softly into the phone. To his sons he said, "Who wants to start?" Luke looked down at his hands. The knuckles on his right hand, his punching hand, were cut and swollen. Mitch said, "Lee, maybe you could run down and throw some ice into a couple of plastic bags and also grab a couple of bottles of water from the fridge. Thank you, honey." Danny sat with his head leaning back on the wall, eyes closed. His southpaw was fine—Danny was more of a kicker than a hitter.

The three of them sat in silence. When Lee came back with the ice bags and water, she sat on the floor next to Danny. "I guess Lee is going to have to tell me what happened then. Lee?"

Lee looked to Danny for help, but his eyes remained closed. "Well," she said, tentatively, "it's all because of me, I'm afraid. It's a big misunderstanding. I was up here with Luke—we came to look for the dictionary." She turned to Danny to explain that she had been playing a game of Scrabble with Luke while she waited for him to get home from the grocery store. "I guess when Danny got home he heard us laughing up here and then he found us sitting on the bed and he got the wrong idea." She turned to Danny again. "Danny, you got the wrong idea. We were just looking up a word in the dictionary. Honest." Danny would not open his eyes.

"So then what?" Mitch asked.

Danny suddenly came alive. "So then I ask what the hell is going on here and Luke says, 'what does it look like, I'm having my way with your woman.' And I say like hell you are and I jump him."

"I was kidding, you asshole!" Luke said.

"Yeah, right," Danny said. "So we're wrestling around and then suddenly a pair of pink panties falls out of Luke's back pocket."

"*My* panties," Lee says, patting the front pocket of her jeans where they seemed now to be safely stored. "And I swear to God I don't know how Luke got a hold of *my* panties. Honestly, neither one of these boys has had access to any of my undergarments. This is SO embarrassing, you guys."

"He had her *panties*, Dad. What am I supposed to think?"

"Luke, where'd you get the panties?"

"It doesn't matter."

"Yes it does!" Lee shouted.

"Yes it does," Mitch repeated.

"Dude, I swiped 'em that day that we got the bat."

"Luke! How could you?" Lee said, covering her mouth.

Danny sat up straighter. Eyes wide open now, he sent daggers Luke's way.

"Luke, I'm surprised," Mitch said, and stood to his feet. (Something told him he needed some height advantage here.)

"You think he's so perfect, Dad," Danny said. "You're finally seeing his true colors. And if you're wondering who has been depleting Mom's wine, here's your guy."

Luke didn't deny it.

"Luke, this is shocking," Mitch said. "I don't know what to say. But I think you owe both Dan and Lee an apology. I'm extremely upset right now. Extremely. And I'm disappointed in you, Luke. You lied about the drinking and you really hurt your brother."

"Wait a minute," Luke said, struggling to get to his feet. "I take full responsibility for the drinking but look at my face! He started this. I was just sitting on the bed and he comes in here, jumps me, knocks my head into the headboard, pushes me to the floor, kicks me in the nuts, and it's all my fault? Dad! I hurt *him*?"

"Your dirty trick with the panties is what hurt him, Luke."

Danny snickered and rose slowly to his feet. "See, he still can't even admit he's wrong. Can you, Mr. Perfect."

"Dad, he *jumped* me!" Luke said.

"That's what it comes down to, doesn't it?" Danny said to Luke, sneering. "*Jumping*. You can't live with yourself because *I* was the one who jumped and you didn't. I am the jumper. I am the one who jumps."

Mitch demanded to know what the hell Danny was talking about.

"He's talking about mom, Dad," Luke explained. "He's talking about mom, okay? He jumped in to save her and I didn't. I- I- guess I just froze. And he won't let me forget it. So he jumped; in the end it didn't make a difference, did it?"

Mitch was taken aback. He'd never heard the boys talk so cavalierly about the accident. "Luke," Mitch said, "you don't have to feel guilty about not jumping. It was too dangerous to jump. Danny shouldn't have jumped—he could have drowned too. No, I don't want you to feel guilty about not jumping."

"Yeah, well, maybe he should feel guilty about *mom* jumping. How about that?" Danny said.

"Don't go there," Luke warned, pointing his finger at Danny.

"What do you mean mom *jumping*?" Mitch said. "Mom *fell*. Mom fell, right? What do you mean mom jumping? What do you mean? Luke, what's he talking about?"

"Maybe I better go," Lee said and slipped out of the room.

"Luke, tell me. Tell me now!" Mitch's face and neck were turning red. He grabbed Luke by the shoulders and shook him. "Tell me!"

"Dad, oh God. Oh God! She *did* jump. She did. It was all a crazy mistake!"

Mitch released his grip on Luke and sat on the bed. He felt himself perspiring, wiped his brow, and swallowed an urge to vomit. If he let himself, he could collapse, crumble, cave in. But from deep inside him a rage ignited and instead of folding up he launched himself up from the bed, pointed his finger at Luke and screeched in a throaty voice that wasn't his: "Tell me what happened to my wife or so help me God, I'll finish what you both started here!"

"Okay, okay," Luke said. "You see, I'd hidden a case of beer on the boat and Danny found it and he threw it in the river and mom had been sleeping and I yelled "Danny" and she must have thought Danny had fallen in because he was hiding on the floor and so she jumped in after him. It all happened so fast!"

Mitch covered his head with his arms. He pulled on his hair. His heart was playing heavy metal music in his chest and his ears were ringing. This time he collapsed on the bed and curled into a fetal position. He couldn't wrap his mind around this. Annie hated water! Annie couldn't swim! Annie couldn't have jumped! But to save her own child, yes, she could have; she *would* have. And suddenly it all became clear. He sat up. And then in a voice he didn't recognize, he shrieked: "YOU MEAN TO TELL ME THAT YOUR MOTHER DIED TRYING TO SAVE A CASE OF GOD DAMN BEER? IS THAT WHAT YOU BOYS ARE TRYING TO TELL ME?"

"Dad," Danny said, "she thought it was *me*! She was trying to save *me*!"

"Get the hell out of my sight, both of you. You deceived me and you dishonored your mother. All this time. All this time! You're murderers and I will never forgive you! Get out of here. Both of you!" He fell to the floor.

As the boys limped out of the room, Tess and Joya bounded in. When Tess saw her dad on the floor crying hysterically, she said, "Mitchell, what have they done to you?" Joya, who was used to moving large chifforobes, lifted Mitch up under his arms and helped him get into bed. Tess climbed up and bore in next to him, stroking his old gray hair. "Oh, Mitchell," she cried.

Chapter Twenty-nine

Between Animals and Angels

{"So, Cecilia, the truth is finally revealed. Mitch finally knows." He needed to know. And the boys needed to release it. The truth is a relief; a burden lifted! Just as a skin wound needs air and light to heal, so it is with emotional wounds; they need to be exposed, brought to light, uncovered and bared. Only then can life produce a scab and begin to heal. A well-formed scab protects a wound from additional injury and infection. Exposing a wound is necessary. Hidden wounds only fester.}

SO THIS IS how a boxer must feel, Danny thought. He sat slumped in the passenger seat of Lee's car. They were making a get-away. He would have driven himself but the stupid van full of groceries was blocking his car.

"I'm taking you to the hospital," Lee said.

"No, you're not."

"Danny, you look terrible."

"I'm fine. And I've been examined by a doctor, remember? I'm just sore."

"Is your nose still bleeding? Can you even breathe out of it?"

Danny pulled away the towel and the ice bag. It hurt like hell but he dramatically inhaled to prove that he could in fact breathe.

"I need to stop for gas," Lee told him, "and I'll get you some ibuprofen."

"And some Coke, please?"

While Lee gassed up the car and bought provisions, Danny closed his eyes and tried to imagine what was happening back home. While he and Lee made their escape through the back door, he had seen Luke in the downstairs bathroom retching. Well, Joya would take charge. She would let Tess cuddle with Mitch. She would lay Luke on the couch and she would haul in all the groceries and put them away. She would make a pot of coffee and stay up all night, smoking cigarettes on the screened porch, waiting to be needed, waiting for her daughter and Danny to return from wherever the hell they had gone. Danny barely knew Joya—but he had the feeling that she was the kind of person who would come through in times like this. In times of crisis.

And certainly this constituted a crisis. It was a catastrophe of mammoth proportions. *Dang*! He would never forget the look on his Dad's face. He and Luke might as well have hurled a grenade at him. Danny gasped and opened his eyes just as Lee was getting back into the car.

"What's wrong?" she asked, handing him a small bag.

"What if my Dad's heart can't take this?"

Lee didn't say anything. What could she say? She started up the car and drove off. Danny shut his eyes again, but tears seeped through. The car came to a stop and when he opened his eyes he was looking at the emergency room entrance at Rockford Memorial Hospital. Lee reached over him, opened his door, and said, "I'll meet you inside."

Danny was touched. "Lee, honey, listen." He closed the door. "I'm really okay and if I go in there, I'd be hurting my Dad even more. This is where he works. I guarantee this would get all over the hospital— Dr. Langdon's kid came in all beat up—and the rumors would fly. I can't go in. I'm fine."

"Fine," Lee said, and stepped on the gas. "Where are we going then?"

"I don't know, but I can't go back home. He—he told me to get out."

"He was upset."

"Lee, he called us *murderers*!"

"People have been calling my mom a murderer for a long time now. You know you're not a murderer."

"But what if I am?"

"I heard Luke explain what happened. It was an accident. It doesn't matter if she fell or jumped; it was an accident."

"But we were so stupid, messing around like that. Who in a billions years would have thought something like that would happen?"

"That's why they call them 'freak' accidents. Who would have thought my dad would fall down a flight of stairs?"

Danny slumped back down in the seat. Once again, he and Luke were in character. Danny on the run; Luke sticking around to face the music. Luke wouldn't leave. Luke was the prodigal son's perfect brother. Well, *he* was leaving. And he wasn't going back. He had some cash and a credit card. As a matter of fact, he still had the debit card his dad had given him to pay for the groceries.

"Lee, here's what I'd like you to do for me. Drive to East State Street and drop me off at one of the motels. You go home. I don't want to get you in any trouble."

"I'm not leaving you, Danny."

"Listen to me, you're not even eighteen. I could be charged with kidnapping or something."

"That's just stupid. Besides, I *am* eighteen. I lie about my age because I was held back in first grade and it was humiliating."

Danny smiled. "Lee, it killed me to think of you with Luke."

"How could you even think such a thing?"

"Because there's a history here. He stole a girl from me once before."

"But I'm not her. I can't be 'stolen.'"

"I'm so sorry. I went crazy."

"I know."

Lee pulled up at the Red Roof Inn on East State Street and insisted on going in to get a room. "One look at you and they're sure to call an ambulance or the police." She was in and out in seconds flat. No luck—the check-in age was twenty-one or older.

"*Dang!*" Danny said. "I guess we need to go sleazy. Something with hourly rates."

"Danny!"

"Not for— You know what I mean. Go west on State. There's got to be something."

But it seemed as if all motels and hotels had a check-in age of twenty-one. Lee drove further and further west until they found themselves at the outskirts of town.

"Danny, what should we do?" Lee asked.

"I seem to remember something around here. Keep going a little further."

Sure enough, they passed something called the "Stop and Stay Inn." Lee did a U-turn at the next intersection and they pulled into the parking lot. It was not pleasant to look at—a dung-colored squat one story, long as it was cheap. And cheap it was: twenty-nine bucks a night.

"Seriously, Danny."

"Seriously. And I can check myself in. I'm sure this is the kind of place where they accept cash with no questions asked."

And sure enough, they did. Danny walked out with a key to Room 118. (That was the room number of the dean's office at his high school. Pure irony, since he'd been a guest in that room many a time during his high school career.) Well, the room was as bad as he had expected. It smelled of a million different odors—perspiration, sex, cigarette smoke, even dog. Lee started to gag. She pulled a bottle of cologne out of her purse and sprayed the stale air until the room smelled like perspiration, sex, cigarette smoke, dog, *and* flowers.

"Seriously Danny."

There was a bed, a television, a sink, a toilet, a stained bathtub. Torn industrial carpeting, dirt on the walls. Clean towels, though. And look! A Gideon Bible in the nightstand drawer.

"I have a blanket in the trunk of my car," Lee said and went to get it. They laid it across the seedy brown bedspread. Lee made Danny lie down and cuddled in next to him. "Danny, let's go home. I'm sure my mom will let you stay at our house."

"Lee, I want *you* to go home, but I can't. But it's okay. This had to happen. It's been brewing for a year."

Lee kissed his forehead. "Your dad will forgive you. And think about Tess."

"No, he won't. And I can't think about Tess right now."

"I'm not leaving you here."

"Then stay with me." Danny pulled her closer and kissed her.

"They'll be worried. It will only make things worse. What if they call the police?"

She had a point. But he didn't care. To appease her, he told her they would just rest a while and then go back. Later, he would take his own car and drive to Wisconsin. He'd always wanted to live in Madison. He'd find cheap housing, work for a year, establish residency, and then apply to the university. He wondered if they had a good Linguistics program. He fell asleep wondering. In his dreams, Annie came to him and rocked him in her rocking chair. "You boys shouldn't fight," she reprimanded. "You boys love each other."

When the ibuprofen wore off the pain woke him. He was even sorer now, stiff and aching. Daylight shown through the dusty threadbare drapes and the first thing Danny saw was Lee's sweet sleeping face. Now he'd really done it! On top of everything else, he *was* a kidnapper. "Lee, wake up. Honey, wake up!" He shook her arm gently.

She stirred and then shot up. "What?" She looked around. "Oh no! Oh no! We are toast! We are— Where's my cell phone?" She found her purse, fished out the phone and reported twenty-two calls from her mother. "We're dead, Danny. This is bad!"

"Call her now and tell her you're okay and you're on your way home. Don't tell her where we are. Please."

"Okay, but let's go now. I'll call her in the car."

Since they had pre-paid for the room, they could leave right away. In the car, Danny checked his cell phone while Lee and Joya took turns screaming at each other on Lee's phone. Not one missed call. Not even a lousy text message.

Chapter Thirty

Burn Baby Burn

*L*UKE HEARD A blast but thought he was dreaming. Maybe it was thunder. But when he got out of bed to use the john he saw plumes of thick black smoke wafting up from somewhere out in the backyard. Fire! "Fire!" he yelled. He ran—oh, how it hurt—into his dad's room, but found only Tess, tangled up in the sheets, snoring. He took the stairs as fast as he could. A lump formed in his throat. The house was dead quiet. Where was everybody? His first thought was to call 911 but then he heard the sirens approaching.

Forgetting the pain, he ran outside and toward the dock where Mitch and Joya stood watching bright hot flames of fire and thick black angry clouds of smoke devour Mitch's beautiful boat. The firefighters were right behind Luke, yelling for him to stay back, dragging their hoses behind them. The men pushed Mitch and Joya back out of the way and then the hoses exploded powerful jets of water onto the burning boat. Luke sat on the ground near an oak tree and watched the inferno in horror. Even from this distance the fire was hell-hot. He felt a hand on the back of his shoulder. He turned and saw Joya.

"It was my fault, Luke," she said over the tremendous roar of the fire and the deafening spray of the hoses. "My cigarette must have started the fire. I'm so sorry."

Mitch walked over and stood next to Joya. The incredible blaze was reflected in his eyes. And it made Luke understand that his father had been to hell and back. If that's how he wanted it to be, Luke could go along with it. But Mitch wasn't fooling him: he smelled the gasoline on his father's hand when Mitch squatted to the ground and placed it on his other shoulder.

Soon an onslaught of curious neighbors invaded the backyard. The police showed up, too. Luke stayed sitting on the ground amid the smoldering charred debris, watching the commotion with an odd sense of detachment.

(LUKE'S FASCINATING BRAIN FACT: The reason the human brain is wrinkled and looks like buckled carpet is that as the primate brain evolved, the neocortex grew at such a rapid pace that it folded in on itself to make room for the new neurons. It is said that we have one hundred billion neurons, and still, look how stupid we humans are. What in that wrinkled mass of grey matter brings people out of the comfort of their air-conditioned homes on a scorching August morning to watch a boat burn? This was something Luke would like to know.)

By the time Danny and Lee arrived home the fire was out and what was left of the boat was sadly sinking. Luke watched Joya pull her daughter roughly to her, hugging her too hard, then slapping her butt. She hugged Danny, too, then pointed a finger in his face as she gave him a good piece of her mind. She pointed to Mitch who was talking to the police now and to the pier, obviously explaining about the boat.

Was it a crime to burn your own boat? Even if you had no intention of trying to get insurance money for it? Luke was sure there were ordinances against it. Pollution and safety and all. But he understood why his dad did it. He would have done it himself. He watched his dad as he talked calmly to the police. Mitch motioned for Luke to come over.

"Luke, this is Officer Carson. He's filling out the police report."

"Wow, I'd hate to see the other guy," Officer Carson said to Luke.

"Yes, well," Mitch said, "this is what happens when a beautiful woman comes between two brothers."

"I see," said the officer, raising an eyebrow. He looked at his clipboard. "Wait a minute. Mitch Langdon? As in *Doctor* Mitchell Langdon?"

"Yes."

"Hey! You're my kids' pediatrician! You probably don't remember me because my wife always takes our kids to the doctor, but you saved my daughter's life. Sammy Gray Carson's her name. About six years ago. She had a heart murmur and our last pediatrician missed it!" He looked at Luke. "Your dad is an amazing man, you know that don't you?"

"Yeah," Luke said, "I know that."

He also knew how lucky his dad was to get this particular officer to write up the report. Officer "Grateful" wrote up the report word-for-word from Joya's testimony. Blondo smoked a cigarette while she answered all the questions and Luke overheard Officer Carson say, "Ma'am, maybe in light of the situation, you should put that thing out." Joya smiled and flicked the cigarette into the grass. Officer Carson smashed the butt with the heel of his boot.

Tess had slept through the entire thing and boy, was she mad. "I always miss the important things," she bellyached when Luke went up to get her out of bed and tell her what happened. "I hated that old boat anyway. Good riddance."

Luke, not ready to face Danny, scooped Tess up, had her throw on some clothes, and took her for a ride in the car. But not in the van, in Joya's convertible, top down and Beach Boys blasting. "This is the life!" Tess said, her loose hair whipping in the breeze. "Howd'ya manage to get the car?"

"Blondo and I are friends, Scout."

"Friend-friends, right? Not lover-friends."

"What are you talking about? Just friend-friends."

"Can I have ice-cream for breakfast? I never even had breakfast."

Luke drove through the drive-up at McDonald's on Auburn and got Tess a hot fudge sundae. "Where are we going, anyway?" Tess asked, digging in with her spoon.

"Listen, Scout, I got to talk to you about what happened yesterday. I thought we'd go out to the cemetery where it's quiet and we can bring some flowers for Mom, too."

They stopped at a nursery and bought a nice pot of pink geraniums. "She always liked this shade of pink," Tess told her brother.

Sitting in the sun at Annie's grave, Luke explained everything to Tess. He told her how he and Danny were screwing around that day, about the case of beer going overboard, and Annie waking up and thinking it was Danny. About he and Danny feeling so guilty that some sick unspoken bond had formed between them, never to talk about it. Never to tell that Annie had jumped, not fallen.

Tess's eyes filled with tears. "Oh," she said. "*Oh.*"

Luke also told her what happened with Lee and Danny. He came clean about swiping the pink panties. "I don't know why Danny and I bring out the worst in each other, Tess, we just do. I guess part of it is simple genetics. Did you know that siblings are pre-programmed to compete for their parents' attention and resources? That's a fact of survival."

Tess nodded her head.

"So then when Danny and I were fighting, the truth came out."

"Poor Dad!"

"I know. Poor Dad."

"How could Mom think a case of beer was Danny? She wasn't stupid you know."

"She was asleep. The sun was blindingly bright. She acted on pure instinct, Tess. It's called muscle memory. She probably didn't even remember that she couldn't swim!"

"Wow! Think of the love, Luke!"

"I know, Scout. I know."

"You know what? I think I want to be called 'Tess' again. Mom picked my name because she loved it. Call me Tess. It means someone who harvests. Does that mean a farmer? Am I a farmer? Do I look like a farmer?"

"Not anymore, but you used to when you wore those overalls. Tess, listen. There's more. I've made a decision. I'm not going away to school."

"You're not?"

"No. I've let Dad down. I'm going to stick around another year and try to make things right with him. And with Danny, too. The thing with the panties was my fault. I guess I was jealous of him and Lee."

"Lucas Roy Langdon, I'll hear of no such thing."

Luke blinked. She sounded just like Annie.

"You *are* going to school. I will be fine. I can take care of Dad and Danny. I've got fortification now."

"Now there's a two-dollar word. What fortifications?"

"Joya and Lee. That's what fortification. Mom sent them, you know."

"What? How do you know?"

"Joya told me. And you know what Luke? She may be crazy, but she's got a big heart. And she sure kicked this family into gear!"

Luke had to laugh. Maybe Tess was right.

When Luke and Tess drove the convertible back to Joya's house, she wasn't home. "She's at your house, Lee told them. "Kick her out if you want," she said, laughing and taking the keys from Luke. "Tess, come and look at my new Boylan uniform. Seriously, it's the worst thing I've ever seen!"

(LUKE'S FASCINATING BRAIN FACT: Many scientists believe humans actually have three brains or central operating systems. There's the familiar one in the head and two more in the heart and in the gut. The brain inside the skull gives rise to thoughts, but we feel emotions with our hearts and stomachs, hence "gut feelings," and "listen to your gut," and "he doesn't have the guts," and "heartsickness," and "I love you with all my heart," and "I know in my heart it's true," and "follow your heart.")

As Luke walked across the yard he thought about the heart. Maybe he'd been wrong all this time. He'd thought by studying the brain he could figure out what made people tick, what made *him* tick. But maybe he only had part of the story—a third to be exact. Maybe you needed to look at how the head brain, heart brain and gut brain worked together. Or maybe Tess was right, maybe all that mattered in the end was a big heart.

{Luke is right—humans do have three brains, but the heart is the control tower. Ancient poets and philosophers have known this for ages. Your beautiful heart beats—a hundred thousand times a day—on its own without any connection to the head brain. As a matter of fact, it's the heart that forms first in the fetus, then the brain. The brain and the heart participate throughout your life in a two-way dialogue, communicating through nerve impulses, hormones, neurotransmitters, pressure waves, and electromagnetic fields. The head brain is an organ of forgetting; it's the heart brain that remembers.

Trust your heart. The love in your heart binds you to the eternal source of love—God. The brain gets in the way, locking onto a piece of the truth and then defending it till death. The heart knows that the truth doesn't come in words. For the truth is love. "God is love and he who abides in love abides in God and God in him."}

That night his dad knocked on his door and told Luke that before school started he wanted him to set something up with UChicago's Student Counseling and Resource Service.

"Actually, Dad, I wanted to talk to you about school. I've decided to take another year off. I need to fix things around here first."

Mitch looked at him sternly. "You ARE going to school, son. You just need to get some help. Call Dr. Bonovia tomorrow and get him to help you get things set up. I'm worried about this drinking, Luke, and we're not going to let this turn into a problem. Are we clear?"

"Yes, sir," Luke said, ashamed and embarrassed that it had come to this, but relieved that he was still going to school.

Chapter Thirty-one

Standing Rapt in Awe

I AM COMMUNING *with the saints, enjoying spirit-to-spirit fellowship. It's odd and wonderful, but when you meet someone here you meet their "total" being, somehow you comprehend their entire life just by standing in their light and feeling their vibration.*

"What have you learned about people?" Cecilia asks me. I am taken aback; it is I who has been asking all the questions. What have I learned about people? "That they are who they are for a reason. That they fit perfectly into the puzzle of life. That even someone we perceive as evil is imbued with holiness, a holiness they have denied. That our earthly incarnation spans the exact number of years needed to prepare our souls for Heaven." Cecilia nods. "I've learned that there is nothing more important in life than loving God with all your heart, your soul, your mind, and body, and loving your neighbor as yourself. That we shouldn't judge hearts, only behaviors. And that judging the authenticity of another's faith is presumptuous, and not to do it."

Cecilia nods. "What else?"

"That God is a progressively self-revealing, self-disclosing God. That the Creator reveals Him/Herself to the inner nature of man and to the outer

nature of the universe. That we should treat others as we would like to be treated. And that people are always more important than things. Don't worry; be happy! Say please and thank you. That's all I know.

Cecilia says, "It is enough."

Then she shares with me something wonderful—that all great religions have a version of the Golden Rule. She insists I listen as she rattles off a few examples:

- *Ancient Egyptian: "Do for one who may do for you, that you may cause him thus to do."*
- *Baha'i Faith: "Lay not on any soul a load that you would not wish to be laid upon you, and desire not for anyone the things you would not desire for yourself."*
- *Confucianism: "Surely it is the maxim of loving-kindness: Do not do to others what you would not have them do to you."*
- *Native American Spirituality: "Humankind has not woven the web of life. We are but one thread within it. Whatever we do to the web, we do to ourselves."*
- *Shintoism: "The heart of the person before you is a mirror. See there your own form."*
- *Sufism: "The basis of Sufism is consideration of the hearts and feelings of others. If you haven't the will to gladden someone's heart, than at least beware lest you hurt someone's heart, for on our path, no sin exists but this."*
- *Taoism: "Regard your neighbor's gain as your gain and regard your neighbor's loss as your own loss."*

"You see," Cecilia says, "despite the great number of religions, almost everyone believes in the same core things: the existence of a soul, an afterlife, miracles, and a divine creator of the universe. That is the core truth—the rest will be revealed when the time is right."

"But how much longer must I wait?" I ask, knowing that I sound like a child.

"Not much longer. Your soul is your story," Cecilia tells me. "The book according to you. It's your true home. You take your home with you, for you and God are the only true witnesses to the events of your life. Only you and God know the true, authentic you. Only you and God know if you truly lived the Golden Rule or just talked the talk."

Chapter Thirty-two

Muddy Miracles

ON FRIDAY MITCH did something he *never* did. He called in sick. Then on Saturday, he did something else he had never done: he forgot about his eight o'clock massage. It just completely slipped his mind.

With his partner seeing his two hospital patients, Mitch was free to sleep in, and sleep he did. After the boys' fight and the boat burning, Mitch was spent. For two days he shut himself up in his room. When he wasn't sleeping, he was reflecting. There was a lot to process.

Oh, the secrets people keep. He'd been hard on the boys, he knew. But how stupid and selfish could they be! He was sick of this rivalry and its biblical proportions. They should both be punished. But how do you punish your children for causing their mother's death? Maybe burdening themselves with this terrible secret was punishment enough.

Poor Annie! What a stupid way to die! It was like a sick joke. It was something you could never explain to people… "Oh, my wife? The silly little thing drowned last summer saving a case of beer she thought was our son, bless her heart."

Well, people died for stupid reasons all the time. Skiers crashed into trees. Divers got eaten by sharks. One of his patients—a twelve-year-old—died when he was crushed by a vending machine he was fighting with for a can of pop. People died bungee jumping, racing cars, and jumping from planes. People died from eating tainted food. They died from sticking a knife in the toaster. They died from cleaning their gun or playing with fire. They died running from bulls. They died setting off malfunctioning firecrackers. Mitch had read once that Attila the Hun had died from a nosebleed on his wedding night. (Apparently he was too drunk to notice that his nose was bleeding and he drowned in a snoutful of his own blood.) Oh yes, there were plenty of dumb ways to die.

Maybe it wasn't important how a person died. Maybe it was as moot a point as how a person was born—vaginal delivery or Cesarean section. Maybe birth and death are just delivery systems.

How could he wrap his mind around this? There was a knock on his door. "Not now," he called out.

"But it's me, Joya."

Like that was going to make a difference!

"I made you a sandwich. You gotta eat. It's chicken salad and my chicken salad kicks ass!"

Well, he was hungry. He got up and unlocked the door. Who cared that he was in an undershirt and boxers. Maybe he'd eat Joya's sandwich and then jump her bones. Maybe sex with Blondo was just what the doctor ordered.

She entered carrying a sterling silver tray (Annie's favorite, a wedding gift from her sister) loaded with good stuff: a huge sandwich on multi-grain bread, a bowl of fresh fruit, a pitcher of iced tea, and three homemade-looking chocolate chip cookies.

"Wow!" Mitch said. Feeling like a kid, he obeyed Joya and climbed back into bed.

She placed the tray on his lap. "You gotta eat."

"So you said."

She sat down on the edge of the bed. "So eat. And I'll update you on your children."

She looked different. What was it? Oh, she wasn't dressed like a whore, that was it. She was wearing a loose-fitting white tee shirt, navy blue running pants, and sneakers. Her hair was pulled back in a ponytail and her face was makeup-free. She looked more beautiful than she ever had!

"What are you staring at? This is just the *before*. You've already seen the *after* and it's spectacular."

Embarrassed, Mitch said, "I wasn't staring. And if you want to know the truth, I like the *before* better."

"You're kidding, right?"

"I'm not kidding."

"Well, you're too damn old for me. Besides, I could never love a man who got it on with my mother."

"How is she?"

"Blissfully crazy is how she is. That nursing home—Anam—is actually working out. She even has a man-friend. But listen, since you haven't been out of this room in two days, someone had to run things for you and you're looking at her."

"Really?"

"I've been cooking and cleaning and organizing. I rearranged all the furniture. I threw out a bunch of files in your office."

"Joya!"

"God, I'm just kidding. I made pancakes, a pizza, some chicken salad, ran a lousy load of laundry, and played like a zillion games of 'Uno' with Tess."

"Oh, well, thank you."

"So, what's the next step?"

"Hell if I know. Have my sons arrested?"

"Mitch! Listen. Don't you know what this is, you moron?"

Moron? That was a new one! Mitch couldn't for the life of him remember anyone ever calling him a moron!

Joya was standing now. And pacing. Gesticulating wildly. "This is your defining moment! The decisions you make now will shape the direction and focus of the rest of your life and your kids' lives. How you handle this will have far-reaching consequences! Will you spend the rest of your life a bitter, humorless man? Will Luke and Danny go through the rest of their lives thinking they're murderers? Will Tess become a pathological liar that people will shun? Tune in tomorrow for—"

"Okay. Okay."

{And finally, here is my epiphany! "I get it, Cecilia! Joya really is my family's Boo Radley. She might scare the heck out of you, she might yell and scream and kick you in the butt, but she has a heart of solid gold. I'll be forever indebted to her for getting the heart of my family beating again! I get it! God bless her! All of her, even her sizeable cleavage!"

One thing I wish I knew while I was on earth: that people usually try their best. For the most part, they utilize all their inner and outer equipment the best way they know how. If we could only understand that, we would not miss opportunities for love.}

Joya continued lecturing. "Let me tell you about *my* defining moment. You know why we moved here, don't you?"

Mitch nodded. "I *Googled* you and found the article in the Trib," Mitch admitted.

"So you *know* what my defining moment was: I could hide and live my life in shame and give people reason to believe that I really did fricking kill my own husband, or I could try for a fresh start for myself and my daughter. *That* was my defining moment. And believe it or not it was my mother who kicked me in the ass. Before she was loony she was pretty wise. When I was wallowing in grief she told me something so powerful, it hit me right between the eyes. She said, 'The death of one parent could be the resurrection of the other.' God, it's so true. When my husband was alive, somehow he became the *main* parent and I was ancillary. Mister you got 'ancillary' written all over your face. You the man, now, Mitch. You gotta do what I did. And

I'm here to tell you, I know I got a long way to go with myself but I think I did good by my daughter. She's happy. She's in love. She's actually excited about school!"

Mitch nodded. "You did do good by your daughter."

"How's the chicken salad? Kick-ass, isn't it?" she said, as she kicked a leg high up into the air. "It's time to get your balls back, bud. Get your boys and hug them good and hard. They're good kids. Tess is easy—just pay attention to her. As for your wife, been there, done that. That doesn't get much easier. You can't put her death behind you, but you can put the *accident* behind you."

Mitch exhaled deeply. "Thank you," he said, simply.

"You're welcome. Let's be friends, okay? You don't have to be afraid of me."

Mitch threw a pillow at her. "I'm not afraid of you."

Joya laughed. "You're not afraid of *Joya*, but you're scared out of your flippin' mind of *Blondo*!"

She left him to his thoughts. God, how he loved his kids. Poor Luke and Danny. What a burden they'd been carrying! How could he have called them murderers? He knew now that the hurtful words he'd hurled at them had their genesis in pain. It all made sense to him now. The truth was Annie didn't fall; she jumped! She jumped into that river to save her child. It didn't matter that her child was really a case of beer. *She* didn't know that. And the neat thing was, this fact transformed Annie from a phobic clumsy woman into a martyr! Yes, his sweet Annie was a martyr.

He slept more and then surfaced at dinnertime. Joya was still there, in the river room, sitting at the game table, playing her zillion and one-th game of 'Uno' with Tess. Danny and Lee were lying on the sofa together watching a skateboarding competition; Mathis was sitting at their feet. Luke was asleep on the floor.

"He is risen!" Joya announced when Mitch appeared in the doorway.

"Daddy!" Tess said. "You're in your underwear!"

"Tess, let's finish this game tomorrow," Joya said, getting up from the table. "Lee-Lee, come on, we need to get home. Johnny Mathis, I think

I hear your mother calling you." She gave Luke a little kick with her bare foot and then pulled her daughter off of the sofa and onto the floor.

"Seriously, Mom!" Lee said, but she followed Joya to the back door, massaging her tailbone. "Call me later," she called back to Danny.

Mitch plopped on the sofa, sitting on Danny's legs. "Hey!" Danny cried, retracting them to make room.

"Tess, come here, honey. Sit on my lap," Mitch instructed. "Luke, wake up. Come on."

Luke popped up. "Okay, but I'm not sitting on your lap."

"Very funny. Just scoot over here. Okay." Mitch cleared his throat. He'd never called a family meeting before. That was Annie's department. He looked at the faces of these three beautiful children—Tess and Danny on either side of him and Luke sitting on the floor right beneath him—and was filled with emotion. He and Annie had raised some pretty great kids. He saw their futures in their faces: Luke was a world-renowned neurologist, Danny was an independent filmmaker, and Tess was an author/veterinarian. So what that he got their dreams wrong. So what if he'd missed the revisions and now Luke wanted to be a cardiologist, Danny a linguist, and Tess, the first woman president of the United States (she was a good liar after all!). It didn't matter. He loved them. And he had the rest of his life to help lead them into the future. "Well, so, I've been thinking," he told them. "This is our defining moment!"

Luke and Danny looked at each other.

"Our *what?*" Tess said.

"Oh, goodness," Mitch said, already tearing up. He pinched at his tear ducts with his thumb and forefinger. "Where do I start? First, I'm sorry. I'm sorry that I yelled at you guys. I'm sorry that I've been living in a fog for the last year. I'm sorry that I'm not as strong a person as your mother was."

"Dad, you're strong," Tess said and hooked her arm around Mitch's neck.

"I made a colossal mistake. The experts say that everybody grieves differently and I guess I took that to mean that it's a solo endeavor. I now know that a family can grieve differently but still grieve together. You guys, it's time to—"

"Please don't say," Luke interrupted, "it's time to *move on*. I hate when people say that."

"No, no. I hate that too. It's time to *continue on*. Moving on makes it seem as if we're putting Mom behind us; continuing on means that we continue on with our lives with Mom with us in spirit. Does that make sense?"

Luke and Danny nodded. Tess said, "I think so."

"I love you guys so much. I feel bad that you had to live with this secret for so long. You boys should have come to me. Why didn't you?"

Danny looked up. He was crying. "I was so afraid!"

"And I was so ashamed!" Luke said, his eyes welling up as well.

"You should have told the truth," Tess scolded.

"And you should practice what you preach, Pinocchio!" Danny returned.

"All right," Mitch said. "Tess, your brothers have suffered enough. Guilt is a terrible thing to bear. And I never should have called you guys *murderers*. You're not murderers, you're just kids. Some really great kids."

"Group hug!" Tess said, tugging on Luke's arm. Luke rose and plopped on top of Tess who squealed. Mitch pulled them in close where they stayed for a good while. Tears flowed freely from the three Langdon men until Tess made them all laugh by saying, "I said group *hug*, not group *cry*!"

{"They'll be all right, won't they? My family?" I ask Cecilia.

"Yes," she says, gently. "They belong to God. They will be all right. They'll miss your physical presence but in their hearts they'll know your spirit touches them daily. It's time for you to let go," she tells me, and I feel it, too. "You have reached the point where a longing for your family has been supplanted with a longing for God."}

369

Chapter Thirty-three

My Little Chickabiddy

ESS SPENT MOST days in her room now, waiting for school to begin. Miss Miranda wanted Tess to take it easy before school started. "Take time for yourself," she told Tess. "Let your dad and brothers take care of you for a change."

Tess could get used to the pampering. Suddenly all the men in the house were attentive, maybe too attentive. A girl needed room to breathe, after all. She enjoyed the attention and tried to take it easy, but Tess just didn't have a gene for 'take-it-easy.'

A week before school she laid out all of her school supplies on her bed and neatly printed her name on each item with permanent marker. Then she packed everything up in the adorable pink "Hello Kitty" backpack Aunt Maggy bought her. (Good thing she was over her Scout infatuation, because the backpack would have been way to foofy for Scout.) She tried on her St. Peter's uniform to make sure it fit, and 'broke in' her new school shoes. She tried to read *To Kill a Mockingbird* one more time before her time for pleasure reading would be severely limited by homework, but the words were so familiar, she found herself distracted by the littlest thing. Maybe it was time to expand her reading. Don't misunderstand, she still loved Scout and Jem and Dill and Atticus. And Boo, too. But she needed some new friends.

She was working on the lying. She was determined to lick this problem once and for all before school started. She lay on her bed with the personal DVD player Danny had lent her (he didn't know he had lent it to her, but that wasn't important) and watched Disney's Pinocchio. She had faked a case of diverticulitis that morning because she didn't want to go to church. Ahh, but Mitchell had seen through her scheme and now she realized just how pathetic it was: lying to stay in bed so that she could immerse herself in a childhood fantasy in an attempt to break this dreadful lying habit. *Crikey*, she was flying in a fast jet to Stupidland.

So after Mass, and despite the fact that it was a beautiful August day and she should be outside riding her bike or hitting tennis balls on Joya's court, just to prove that she indeed had diverticulitis, she came upstairs, put on her nightie and took to her bed. Bored after only three minutes she had sneaked into Danny's room and swiped the DVD player.

Pinocchio was a joke. When she was younger she thought he was adorable. Now he seemed a dolt. She wasn't like him, was she? She forced herself to watch that old nose grow.

Why didn't stupid Pinocchio have a mother? Or Bambi for that matter? Tess lay back on her pillow and thought about all the animated kids' movies she'd seen where the main character was motherless: *Cinderella, Snow White, Land Before Time, Lion King, Hunchback of Notre Dame, Pocahontas, Tarzan, Aladdin, The Little Mermaid, Peter Pan, The Jungle Book, Lilo and Stitch, Finding Nemo, Beauty and the Beast*. Why? Was there something special about losing your mother? She couldn't imagine what.

Why did everyone have to die? Why did God work things out that way? Tess thought that certainly there could be a better way to set up and manage the world.

Just as she was about to start the movie for the second time she heard a soft knock on the door. She was hoping for Luke, but he was out to lunch. He was leaving for school tomorrow and Joya and Lee and Danny had treated him to a farewell "afternoon on the town" in Chicago. Joya even called it a double date and Luke let her get away with it! Tess was glad that Luke finally got to be a kid again and go to school. She was sad for herself though. She didn't want to think about it.

The door opened and her dad peeked in. He walked over and sat on the edge of her bed. Tess could tell that he was holding something behind his back. Maybe it was an injection for the diverticulitis. She would gladly endure it. But it wasn't medicine. It was the DVD of *To Kill a Mockingbird!*

"I know your mom and I had agreed to wait until you were twelve before you watched this but I think you're ready now."

"Really?"

"Yes. Would you like to watch it together? I'm not busy right now."

"You're not on call?"

"Negative."

"Wait. Don't you mean *positive*, you are *not* on call? *Negative* you are not on call means that you *are* on call."

"Try it again."

"You're not on call?"

"Positive-negative."

"Dad!"

"Honey, I'm not on call. Let's watch the movie."

"Can we watch it in your room, on your bed? Like Mom and I used to?"

"Sure. How's the diverticulitis by the way?"

"Better," she said. "I think it was actually just a mild case of 'sick-as-hell-anemia.'" She followed her dad into the master bedroom, Piper right behind her. Tess climbed into the mess of covers—the sheets were wrinkled and smelled like her dad's aftershave. It was the best bed in the house! Piper cuddled in beside her and Mitch slipped the DVD into the player. He plopped down next to Tess and said, "Pay special attention to Dill."

"I know. He's really Truman Capote. Mom told me."

"No, I mean pay special attention to the *character* of Dill," Mitch said. He situated his pillows and was sound asleep before Dill even showed up in Miss Rachel Haverford's collard patch. Had it been any other movie Tess might have cared. But this movie, this story, well, to be honest, she preferred to watch it alone.

She watched Dill in his blue linen shorts that buttoned to his shirt. He was exactly how she had pictured him! She watched as he returned to Macomb from Meridian, telling tall stories that he had eaten dinner in the train's diner; had seen two twins hitched together get off the train; and that he had seen his father, who was taller than Atticus, had a black pointed beard, and was the president of the L & N Railroad. He said he even helped his father engineer for a while, but Jem didn't believe him. Tess watched later as Dill was caught in his own lie when he said his dad didn't have a beard and Scout reminded him that he said before that he did have one, and Dill said if it was all the same to her he had shaved it off last summer. Oh, and his father had sent him a letter and two dollars. And his mother had entered his picture in a Beautiful Child contest and he had won five dollars and went to the picture show twenty times on the prize money. Among other things, he said he'd been up in a mail plane seventeen times, he'd seen an elephant, had traveled to Nova Scotia, and his granddaddy had been a brigadier general and had left him his sword. Then there was Dill's fantastic story about how he ran away from home because his new father had bound him in chains and left him to die in the basement. He claimed to have kept himself alive by eating raw field peas. He finally escaped by pulling the chains from the walls, and wandered two miles out of Meridian, still in wrist manacles, and then traveled with an animal show where he was hired to wash the camel. Eventually, he walked to Macomb. Jem made him come clean—he'd really taken thirteen dollars from his mother's purse, caught the train, and then walked the rest of the way.

Tess scratched her head—Dill came clean for Jem because he knew he wouldn't tolerate the fibs. And then he came clean for Scout when he explained that the reason he had run away was that "they just wasn't interested in me."

"Oh," Tess said out loud. Loud enough to stir her father.

"Huh? What, honey?"

"Mitchell, I just realized something. I'm not Scout. I'm not even Pinocchio. *Blimey heck*, I'm Dill!"

"You paid attention!" Mitch said, propping himself up on his elbows. "And now it's my turn to pay attention. I'm so sorry, honey. I've been living in a bubble. It's not been fair to you and I'm going to do better. So, that being said, telling stories and fibs and lies just isn't going to be necessary anymore. Okay?"

"Okay."

"Now come here and give your old man a back rub, will you?" Mitch turned onto his stomach.

"Dad, can I ask you a question that will probably make you sad?" she said as she climbed onto her dad's backside.

He said of course, she could ask him anything, but Tess saw him scrunch his eyes closed.

"Are my brothers really murderers?"

"Honey! We talked about that."

"But you called them murderers."

"I know. I regret that. And I apologized to them—you heard me. But I was angry. They hadn't told the whole truth, honey, for an entire year. And that secret was eating away at both of them, even though they weren't even aware of it."

"They were jerks to mess around like that on the boat."

"Yes, they were. But I guess that kind of same-sex sibling rivalry is something that neither you nor I will understand completely because you only have brothers and I only had sisters. It can be tough for some kids. You should hear some of the stories mothers tell me about sibling rivalry."

"Is Luke going to be okay?"

"Luke is going to be more than okay. Luke is going to be great."

"Danny's in love, don't you think?"

"I do think. Lee is good for him. And I'm so glad he registered at Rock Valley College. That's a huge relief."

"He's happier, isn't he, Daddy?"

Mitch nodded.

"We all are. Why do you think?"

"You tell me."

"Well, because now we know the truth and the truth will set us free?"

"I couldn't have said it better myself. I think we know now that Mom doesn't want us to go on being so sad. She wants us to live fully. She wants our highest good. Now what about my backrub?"

"But I still miss her and I miss Julianna, too. And I've got one more really important thing I have to tell you since the truth will set me free."

Tess slid off of her dad's back. Mitch sat up and turned over.

"First promise that you will still let me be friends with Joya and Lee. Promise, Dad, you gotta promise."

Mitch crossed two fingers and promised.

"Okay, here goes: I think Blondo murdered her husband."

Mitch fell back onto the pillows and laughed louder and longer than Tess had heard him laugh in a long, long time.

{*"Does this mean the lying will stop, Cecilia?" I ask, hopefully.*

"Annie," Cecilia says, "Tess is human and all humans lie. But yes, Tess's need to lie will be markedly reduced!"

"That's a relief," I say.}

Chapter Thirty-four

Life is Not a Circus; it's Circular

*D*ANNY AND LEE rode in the back; Luke drove. Blondo rode shotgun in her movie star sunglasses and with her leopard print scarf around her head. (Earlier Danny told her she looked like Grace Kelly and he got a big fat kiss in return.)

After parking Joya's convertible safely in a public garage, they took a cab to Navy Pier, had lunch, shopped, and rode the Ferris Wheel. They took an Odyssey boat cruise, and stopped by Fox and Oble, Chicago's premier food market, before heading for home.

For days now, Danny and Luke had been keeping a safe distance from each other. They spoke when they needed to, but neither had talked about what had happened between them. Their physical wounds had healed. Danny knew the ones inside would take longer.

His dad tried to ground him for running off with Lee that night, but as usual, he was able to wiggle out of the punishment. "Dad, what would you do if someone called you a murderer? I was beside myself!" It wasn't a lie.

Inside Fox and Oble, while Joya was sampling cheeses and Lee was checking out the enormous barrels of olives, Luke put his arm around Danny's neck. "Dude, are we okay?"

Danny knew that this was as close to an apology that he would ever get from Luke. "Dude, we're solid," he said. And then, right there, at the delicatessen counter, with the pastrami and the sausages and the corned beef watching, Luke pulled Danny in for a bear hug. People were staring, but Danny didn't even care. Let 'em stare!

On the way home, Danny didn't even complain about the Beach Boys. In fact, he sang along, not realizing until that moment that the lyrics were implanted in his subconscious.

Just after the Elgin tollbooth, Lee leaned over and kissed Danny on the cheek. "What was that for?" he asked.

She shrugged and smiled. "Meet me in your mother's moon garden tonight after it gets dark," she whispered. "And bring a flashlight."

Dang! Was this it? Was this the night he'd been waiting for all his life? Could this mean what he hoped it meant? Lee must have read his mind, or maybe his shitty grin gave it away. "It's not for sex, Danny."

Well, a guy could hope, couldn't he?

Right before they got home, something weird happened. They had stopped at the traffic light at Alpine and Spring Creek and a black Jeep full of girls pulled up to the left of them. The girl in the passenger seat squealed, "Look, it's Luke Langdon." The driver chicken-necked her head to see for herself. Danny didn't know who the girl was, but Luke nodded to her, put his arm around Joya, and revved his engine.

"Who was that?" Danny asked as they sped away.

"My cousin, Karley," Lee answered. "The one who won't talk to us. I wonder how Luke knows her."

"Heck if I know. Am I my brother's keeper?"

"You're a keeper, anyway."

It was getting dark sooner now, so at about eight-thirty Danny headed outside to wait for Lee. His mother's garden was a battle zone—flowers and weeds fighting for territory. Mitch promised Tess he would hire a gardener next year to help out.

What was this about? he wondered as he walked on the stepping-stones through the garden. The moon was almost full and he made a mental note to be sure to ask Lee if she knew that the moon had once been a part of the Earth, a part that had broken off. He had just found that out the other day. How was it he didn't know that? It seemed like he should have known that.

Lee arrived carrying a canvas bag and a blanket. She fanned out the blanket along side the moon garden and motioned for Danny to sit with her on the ground. From the bag, she pulled a flashlight and a can of mosquito repellant.

"You'll get eaten alive," she said, insisting that he let her spray him down.

"Is this foreplay?" he asked, hopefully.

"Danny, this is serious."

"What is serious?"

"Seriously."

"I'm being serious."

"Okay, look." She pulled a leather-bound book out of the bag. "This is it. The book I found under my pillow after my Dad died."

"Ahhh. The book."

"And this is going to sound really, really weird, but last night, in bed, I felt something pricking my leg. I tore my entire bed apart and found this!" She held up a small key.

"A key?"

"*The* key. It fits at least. I couldn't bring myself to turn it. Not alone. Now, here's what makes this story even weirder. I found the book under my pillow when we still lived in Lake Forest. Now, all these months later I find the key in my bed here in Rockford. How weird is that?"

"Pretty weird, dude."

"Seriously."

"Do you have the same bed? Same mattress?"

"Yeah."

"Then maybe it was there all along."

She hugged the book to her chest. "Danny, I'm scared. What if this really is my mother's confession? Or what if it reveals something that will make me despise my dad? I don't want to hate my own father. I loved him so much!"

"Okay, okay. I'm here for you. What do you want me to do?"

"Can you just hold me for a while?"

"Of course." He pulled her close.

"When I'm ready, will you open it up and read it? If you think it's something awful, I want you to burn it." She fished inside her bag again. "I brought matches, too."

They sat quietly for a while in the moonlight. Then Lee said, "Okay, Danny, go ahead and open it, please." She handed him the journal and the key.

Danny hesitated.

"Danny, please!"

He looked at the book in his hands. What if Joya was a murderer? What would that mean? Would Lee turn her into the police? Would they need to run away again? He turned the key and the lock sprung open. He looked at Lee. She handed him the flashlight. He opened the book and shined the light on the first page and read the words to himself:

July 23rd—Here in Arizona with Lee. She was so excited to see the ghost town but now she won't get out of the car. She's as fickle as her mother! I don't know who is enjoying this road trip more, her or me. She's keeping me on my toes, telling me when I'm speeding and when the gas tank is low. She won't admit when she needs a bathroom stop but instead asks me if I need to go! Vintage Lee!

August 28th—Lee is starting first grade! She looks so cute in her plaid uniform dress. Last night when I tucked her in she got all teary eyed. I asked her if she was nervous and she nodded and said, "I'm not very good at math!" I told her that was why she was going to school—to learn math and other things. That seemed to help. What a stitch!

Danny skipped ahead some pages:

May 2nd—My Lee is a woman! Joya told me that she started her period today, on her seventh grade field trip of all places. The poor kid! How can my baby girl be a woman! It scares me to death. Soon she'll outgrow our summer road trips. That'll be a sad day for her old man.

September 13th—Joya went to see the doctor and he put her on Prozac. I hope it settles her down. She's been so touchy—one minute she's singing "Good Day Sunshine" and the next minute she's a cloudburst. I've cancelled my business trip to L.A. to be with her. I wish I knew how to help.

Good quote I found the other day: "When we come to grips with the world around us, the world beyond us, and the world within us, we sense a revived faith, no longer quarantined by the questions of life."–Joseph M. Stowell

December 20th—I'm so excited! Both of the boys will be home for Christmas with their wives. I just hope Joya is nice to Eve. Last year was a catastrophe. Joya seems more even-tempered now that she's on medication but she's still a handful! God help me, I love her!

Another quote I like: "You don't really understand human nature unless you know why a child on a merry-go-round will wave at his parents every time around—and why his parents will always wave back.—William Tammeus

March 19th—I love that Lee is such a compassionate person. She has a heart for the underdog. I know she sometimes feels guilty about being privileged. Last week she used her allowance money and bought ten pairs of gloves and made me drive downtown so she could set them on a park bench where we sometimes see homeless people. It warmed my heart.

"Lee," Danny said, looking up from the book, "Lee, honey, it is your Dad's. It's notes from your road trips, first day of school, some quotes, and some private stuff, too. It's good! It's a piece of your dad!"

Lee covered her mouth with her hand to stifle her cry. Danny scooted over and handed her the book. He shone the light on the journal, happy to illuminate such a special treasure for such a beautiful girl. He watched as she read to herself, smiling and crying at various passages. She randomly and hungrily turned pages and then read some excerpts out loud. "Listen to this one," Lee said.

December 25th—Joya forgot she had hidden all of Lee's Christmas presents in the neighbor's attic. This morning there was nothing under the tree for Lee. Tons of stuff for her brothers. I had to quick call Marilyn next door and ask her to leave the bag near the side door. Then I led a tearful Lee to the door and said, "Look, your bag of presents must have fallen off of Santa's sleigh!" She was so angry with Rudolph—she felt he should have paid better attention!

Lee smiled. "Oh, Danny," she said, hugging his neck. "It's not my mother's confession! Thank God!"

Danny was relieved for her. What would it be like to even suspect one's own mother of such a thing? It was foreign to him. He was thankful his mother was who she was.

Lee pulled Danny into a bear hug, then they lay on the blanket in his mother's moon garden, under a lovely and lustrous moon that used to be a piece of this earth. Peace and closure are awesome things, Danny thought. But love is the awesomest.

{"Wow!" I say to Cecilia. "Yes, wow," Cecilia says.}

Chapter Thirty-five

How Heaven Goes

*C*AN I SAY *a few things before I move on? Don't stop searching!
We all seek our origins whether through scientific investigation,
metaphysical speculation, or religious belief. That's okay. That's
good. Jesus wasn't kidding when he said seek and you shall find, knock
and the door will be opened. But remember: no searcher will ever get it
one hundred percent right. It's an impossibility for the human mind. In
our searches, we are gathering tiny pieces of the infinite cosmic puzzle.
Science and religion lead us to successive approximations of the truth. Keep
searching! God loves a searcher! (You'll be happy to know that science
and religion are not only connected but one needs the other. Science can
help remove error and superstition from religion; and religion can remove
idolatry and untruths from science. The two provide a sort of checks and
balance system.)*

*Some people say that we come from dust of ancient stars. Some say that
we originated from a virus, specifically, something called the Mimivirus.
Others say that life began in hot water. Some say asteroids delivered the
sugar-like substance that seeded life on earth. There's the Big Bang theory
and the Cosmic Inflation theory. There are so many hypotheses about the*

origins of life that one can become so confused. There's Panspermia (that the seeds of life are ubiquitous in the universe and they delivered life to earth); there's Geogenesis (that life originated on earth) and Exogenesis (that life originated elsewhere in the universe and was transferred to earth). There's the Rare Earth hypothesis that asserts that because life on earth required an extremely unlikely combination of geological and astrophysical circumstances, life similar to ours is probably rare in the universe. There's Young Earth Creationism and Intelligent Design. There's Theistic Evolution or BioLogos.

All that really matters about our origins is that we were made in the image and likeness of God, as was the entire universe. How we got here doesn't matter as much as where we are going and how we are getting there. Yes, we are just passing through, but just because our earthly incarnation is temporary doesn't mean it's not important. It is. We view the universe through our mind's lens, which is shaped by time, space, biology, genetics, hormones, and neurochemicals. How could we ever figure out life's origins from our earthly vantage point? People really should stop fighting about the origins of life and start living it. All you really need to know is that you came from God, you belong to God, and one day you will return to God.

We humans make things so much harder than they need to be. If you wake up and approach the day believing that every being and every thing is imbued with God's grace, you will live right. There is more beauty and grace and mercy in this world that we can bear; we have been given precious things and we must honor them.

Here, we are not bogged down with petty desires and selfishness. On earth we spend so much time just resisting temptation—food that is bad for us, sexual encounters that harm us, easy money that we think will make us happy, and power that corrupts us—that we miss so much beauty. In Heaven we don't have to fight these selfish impulses so we seek heavenly graces.

We learn, create, experience, remember with perfect memory, we predict, we see, we know. We are "energy" perfected, and perfect energy is always in a state of motion. And so are we. Helping, growing, basking in the presence of our Creator. There is something unique that each one of us *brings to Heaven. Think about it! You possess some something that only you can bring to Heaven, some way that only you can worship God.*

Even the best minds on earth are undersized. You can't even imagine what Albert Einstein, Isaac Newton, and Galileo Galilei are cooking up here in Heaven. What a threesome! And can you imagine Jackson Pollack, Claude Monet, and Michelangelo collaborating on a grand painting! And I hear that Leonardo di Vinci, Henry Ford, Enrico Fermi are meshing their brilliant minds on a grand enterprise. Nothing on earth can exist, be discovered, invented, or created until it exists, is discovered, invented, or created in Heaven. We pull knowledge from Heaven through our imagination, muse, and sleep. Be assured that all of Heaven is working to better the earth, for earth and Heaven are not separate entities, but just different levels of the same house. Take comfort that Louis Pasteur, Hippocrates, and Angela Maria Robatello (you won't know that name yet but someday it will be a household name) are working for the advancement of medical science.

In Heaven, there are great problems to solve and heightened mental faculties with which to tackle them. Our immortal mind will never fail to delight in the wonders of the creative power we share with our God and the endless proof of his redeeming love. Here, we are not like little children sitting in desks, weary of learning, but rather we approach our infinite existence with amazement and with certainty that we can carry out grand enterprises and that our loftiest aspirations and ambitions will be realized. Heaven promises newness and freshness; the concept of boredom does not exist, for all the treasures of the universe are opened up to the communion of saints.

Oh, all you dear people down there who are hurting so, missing the loved ones who have gone before you, don't you know that they are nearer to you in death than they ever could be in life? And take comfort in the fact that their love for you never ceases, but in fact increases in power and clarity in Heaven. Be assured your loved ones still cherish you and care for you. Rejoice that they can see you from Heaven. I know it's hard to wrap your mind around it: How can they be happy in Heaven then, if they can look down and see all the pain? It seems like a contradiction. I can say four things: 1) We do feel pain and sorrow in the first stages of Heaven; 2) In Heaven we love with a more pure and perfect love, a love that is more active than passive, a love that doesn't worry about being hurt; 3) There is, in Heaven, such a thing as joyful suffering; and 4) Heaven is timeless, so what we see from our vantage point isn't just the one dimension of earth. In Heaven, time is time eternity. But eternity doesn't just mean a timeline that has no end; that is still a linear way of thinking. Eternity is a circle. Oh, I know it's confusing!

How about this? The time in Heaven is NOW. In Heaven, past, present and future mesh into one. It's as if you can predict the past and remember the future. And here's something that will certainly blow you away... Wait, let me make sure I can share this... Yes, yes I can. Prayer touches eternity and has the power to change the past! You heard me correctly! This is one of the biggest "WOWS!" of eternity! Let me give you an example— Oh, okay, I guess I can't get that specific, but just know that your prayers are not bound by time because God is not bound by time. God works forward, backward, sideways, circular, perpendicular, micro, macro, up, down, in, out, over, under, and through.

How can I explain that you already possess Heaven? In your heart you know this. Just as a baby in his mother's womb is already in the world (but unaware of it because he isn't developed enough to know it) so we are already in Heaven (but we aren't developed enough to know it).

There is so much more I wish I could tell you, but as I said, saying too much would be like giving away the ending to a good book. We each have our journey on earth. Just remember that no one dies finished—we are all under construction, so to speak. Each of us will die incomplete in our relationship with ourselves, our neighbors, our God. And that's how it is meant to be. That's why Heaven isn't boring, because we spend eternity learning, exploring, and understanding ourselves, all other humans, and God.

And it's the understanding that makes Heaven Heaven. That's how you can deal with all the pain of earth—because it's all put into context and perspective. Heaven is one big light bulb moment.

Chapter Thirty-six

Beautiful, Beautiful Annie

SHE HAD JUMPED in blindly, frantically. *Danny! Danny! Where are you?* That's how mothers are when instinct takes over, thinking only of their children. The reptilian part of the brain kicks in, the part that controls a mother's instinct to protect her young, without thought of her own safety.

The coldness of the water hit her like a punch in the stomach and even then she didn't question what she had done. The water knocked all the breath out of her and she felt air bubbles escape from her mouth—an odd sensation that made her think of cartoon characters talking underwater. Pinocchio or Sponge Bob Square Pants. When the dirty river water swirled into her mouth she started choking. She clamped her mouth shut, but was unable to swallow the water that was already inside, and she began to thrash wildly.

It never occurred to her the river water would be so murky that she wouldn't be able to see six inches in front of her. What was up? What was down? She turned and caught a glimpse of light—the sun glinting off the top of the water. But how could she go up without Danny?

Where was her baby? Her hands were her eyes now as she "felt" the water for him.

Maybe he had already surfaced. She tried to swim to the light, but her chest began to ache fiercely, the cold river water burning her esophagus and lungs. Her chest began to contract, desperate for air. She felt dizzy. And then suddenly, she felt paralyzed. She began to sink and a strange calmness came over her. She closed her eyes. *I am going to die*, she thought. But then the violent pain in her lungs intensified and she fought against the deceptive calm. Her mouth involuntarily opened and more water rushed in. Her lungs were burning and freezing at the same time. *No*, she thought, *this can't be happening*! Where was everybody? Surely, Luke would jump in after her. She couldn't know that it was Danny who had jumped in after her, that she had jumped in to save a case of beer, and that Luke, the champion swimmer, had frozen when she jumped, his legs cement, his feet glued to the deck. She couldn't know that Danny was already in the water, just a few yards away from her, feeling for her with frantic hands. The indifferent current carried her, curling around her like the wind around a leaf.

She opened her eyes, searching, for now she had lost the light and all she could see was murky water and bubbles—the last of her breath escaping her. Then, there in the distance, she saw the light on the water. But now she was dizzy and weak and her limbs stopped moving. She gave in to the power of the water and watched as the light faded further and further away.

She blacked out.

Up above her, Danny swam desperately in circles. The water was so cold and opaque; he seemed to be moving in slow motion and looking through a brown fog. *Where was she?* He could see nothing but muddy water as he turned his head in every direction. His toes were starting to go numb. He needed air. He swam upward, toward the light. Like a fish he surfaced and gulped hungrily for air. He heard Tess wailing and Luke hollering from the boat, but he dived back down. There was no time to stop.

On the boat, Luke had called 911 on his cell phone and now stood helplessly holding the rope that was attached to the rescue tube he had thrown out. Tess was running around the perimeter of the boat, shielding her eyes with her hand, looking for any movement or sign of her mother. "Help us! Someone please help us!" she wailed into the wind.

In Rockford, the Winnebago County has jurisdiction over the river and so a fire truck and a patrol boat were dispatched to the scene. The firefighters were the first to arrive, lights flashing, sirens screeching. Then the sheriff's boat. A man in a diving suit shouted to Luke, "Which way?"

Luke pointed to the general direction. "My brother's down there too," he called.

"What the hell," the man said, and dove in.

Seconds later, Danny surfaced. One of the sheriffs ordered the additional divers, who had just arrived on a second boat, to "get the kid out of the water." Two men pulled Danny, pale and exhausted, into their boat.

Then Mitch was there, running through someone's backyard. Dodging trees and hurdling shrubbery. He sprinted over someone's dock and jumped into the river, swimming swiftly to the boat.

After some time, the operation was downgraded from a search and rescue to a search and recovery. Annie was gone.

The moment she came up for air she knew she was somewhere else for she found everything anew. There was no river, no sky, no boat with her children in it, just a dense darkness, then a loud rushing sound in her head. Like a train or a tornado! It seemed she was in a deep dark valley surrounded by a thick and impenetrable blackness. But she wasn't afraid! Psalm Twenty-three came to her: "*Yea, though I walk the valley of the shadow of death, I fear no evil, for thou art with me.*" She thought: *this must be the dark valley!* And then she was moving! Propelling at a fierce speed through what seemed now to be a dark and moist tunnel or passageway. It was frightening *and* fun—not unlike a roller coaster!

And then, all at once, she was swimming. Annie Hopewell Langdon swimming! You really do swim to Heaven! she realized. Thoughts came to her as if someone was speaking the words directly to her: '*Water returns to water. Sacred liquids are the passageways to birth and to death: just as we swim out of our mother's womb, we swim through a golden river to Heaven. You are baptized into Heaven. You swim to clean and refresh yourself, to cleanse away your earthly dust. You swim to help you forget the loamy earth, sand and soil, your feet and legs, even gravity and the burden of standing up. You swim to find your ancient fins, for we all begin in water. And you swim to prepare for Heavenly movement, which is more like swimming than flying, for here, only the angels have wings.*

Annie swam and swam and she never seemed to tire. Her surroundings grew lighter and she marveled at the scenery as it came into view. Everything was different, from the quality of the air to the intensity of the light, yet somehow she recognized this place. Had she been here before? Of course. She realized her spirit had started here before she jumped into her mother's belly, and visited here every night in her dreams.

At the end of the tunnel shone a glimmer of light, tiny as a firefly. It grew larger or came closer, Annie couldn't tell which. And then she felt the light's warmth. And suddenly she was nearly blinded by a river of white light. She felt herself become wrapped in its golden embrace, feeling complete peace and love and understanding beyond anything she'd ever experienced on earth. She looked around and could see nothing but light, a quivering, pulsating, brilliant light. And then a little girl, a beautiful glowing little girl, stepped out from the light, shining with a most unearthly brilliance, and took Annie by the hand. "I'm Cecilia," she said, although not really in words. Annie knew her—she'd been with Annie all her life, her guardian angel, her spiritual guide. It was her light that identified her.

"You mean I died?" Annie asked. "I really died?"

Cecilia nodded. "You are water returning to water," she whispered. "Let's look at how you flowed."

And then suddenly Annie was watching—but more than watching!...living!—her entire life. It was as if she was living each and every moment all over again in chronological order but in a flash of a moment! What she was seeing, if you could call it "seeing," were images that were vibrant, colorful, three-dimensional, and moving. It was the home-movie of her life playing back for her to review! But the odd thing was, she was in the movie *and* watching the movie! She could feel and smell and taste and see and hear, but not only her own perceptions, but those of the other people in the life review as well!

Annie watched in astonishment. She realized that what mattered in life were all the little things—the small acts of love and kindness as well as the moments of impatience and insensitivity. In the end, these things are the measure of you, the everyday, ordinary opportunities for love. For in your life review you become the very people you hurt and you become the very people you helped. Every selfish sin, every act of anger, every vain thought is there along side of every kindness and gentleness and act of unselfish love. She truly walked in others' shoes. And she now knew, really knew with all of her being what Jesus meant when he said, "Love your neighbor as yourself." You find out in the end that the Golden Rule is how it all really works! Every thought and action and unit of energy is recorded for all time in the matrix of the universe to be reviewed, reflected upon, and learned from. In her life review Annie found that SHE was the very person she was urged to love.

Cecilia whispered gently: "Everything, every single thing you do becomes yours."

And then Annie thought a zillion thoughts in what seemed to be a second. We affect the universe! Little ol' Annie had had an effect on plants, animals, people, soil, clouds, even the air. Then Annie felt lighter than air. The life review in this strange panoramic form was healing. She felt transparent, she felt genuine—all that was not her authentic self was wiped away.

Cecilia smiled. "All that's left now is YOU—your personality, your knowledge, and your love."

Annie felt a warmth exuding from her being. She looked down and saw that now she glowed, too! And she understood that her spiritual body, composed of the universe's sacred elements glowed with the same intense radiance of the stars. She felt somehow that the grandeur of the whole cosmos gleamed in her and she laughed out loud. Filled with joy, she remembered a Scripture verse from Ephesians: *Once you were darkness, but now you are light in the Lord!*" It all made sense now. The greatest pleasure of life was the joy one derived from making a difference in the world, of creating goodness with your life. Of shining! "*This little light of mine…!*"

Cecilia took Annie by the hand and led her toward an even brighter light. It seemed to Annie that here everything, even the smallest creature (for yes, there were insects and animals—horses!—and birds and flowers) shared in the magnificent brilliance. Annie pulled back. "But my family!" she said, thinking of Mitch and the kids.

"Don't worry," Cecilia said. "They're right here." She pointed to the right or the left—in Heaven, there is no left, right, north, south, up, or down. Everywhere is right here. Annie's eyes looked to where Cecilia pointed and she was able to get a heavenly view in earthly time of Mitch and the kids having dinner at the kitchen table. Mathis was there, too. Piper sat at Tess's feet. They were eating soup and laughing at a story Danny was telling about the time Mathis was working at Logli's Supermarket and he slammed the back hatch door of some lady's SUV on his tie. The lady took off. Thank goodness the tie was a clip-on! Imagine the look on the lady's face when she got home and found the tie in the door! Everyone was laughing. For some reason, Mitch in particular, found the story hilarious and wiped tears of laughter from his eyes. Annie soaked in the scene. She looked at the faces of her beloved: Mitch, Luke, Danny, and Tess. She smiled and squeezed Cecilia's hand.

Cecilia told her that she could love them more from Heaven than she ever could on earth. On earth you could only be close to someone who was physically near you, and even then your mind may be someplace else, but in Heaven our risen body transcends earth's space-time boundaries and takes us wherever our mind wants to go so love becomes limitless!

"They can only cease grieving when you can begin rejoicing," Cecilia said. "It will take a little while, but you and they will get there."

Cecilia told Annie it was time for her welcoming party! And instantaneously they were surrounded by hundreds of beings of light. Annie recognized her friends and relatives by their light, which varied in color, intensity, and vibration. Her loved ones formed a mantle around her. There were angels, too, the swoosh of their wings producing the most sublime music!

"This is the true meaning of a family reunion!" Cecilia explained. "Even for those who stayed far away from family reunions on earth because they were too painful, that's not the case here. Since there is only love and no judgment, everyone can run into the embrace of their loved ones without reserve. If you were a black sheep, you are now pearly white; if you were a failure, you are now a success; if you were mediocre, you are now excellent; if you were selfish, you are now, not selfless, but pure self. For now you are everything you once were, everything you are now, and everything you will come to be—simultaneously."

And then a beautiful woman approached, resplendent and dazzling. She opened out her arms to Annie, smiling luminously. Annie knew who she was. "Mother," she said, bowing. "Blessed Mother." And Mary embraced her.

Later when she was ready, she would meet God, the source of eternal love. Her loved ones tried to prepare her. "God won't look like a person," her Uncle Ritchie explained. Cecilia added, "Annie, being in the image and likeness of God is beyond the physical nature of the earthly world. It is our spirits that were created in God's image and likeness."

Uncle Ritchie said, "God is so good and big and we have all—people of all religions—tried to put God into a box that we can understand in the context of our own evolution, intellect, and culture. But God is so much more! God is not even a HE!"

Cecilia explained that there is but one God manifested in three persons. "To help humans embrace the concept of the trinity God created many triads. The three states of matter (solid, liquid and gas); white light (which is the manifestation of three colors red, green and blue light in one); the dimensions of time (past, present and future); the dimensions of space (height, width and depth); the three physical forces (gravitational, electromagnetic and nuclear); the three facets of an atom (electron, proton and neutron); the nature of man (mind, body and spirit); the three domains of life on earth (land, air and sea). The three-in-one nature of God allows our Creator to reveal a whole but different aspect of Himself-Herself to us. God, the parent (some would say father), the transcendent, infinite, and beyond our understanding. Jesus, the son, God expressed in human form so that we can both know God and know who we can aspire to be in our most divine form. And the Holy Spirit, the voice within, who lives in the heart and soul and counsels those who listen to His-Her quiet voice."

Annie hung on Cecilia's every word. It all made perfect sense.

Cecilia said, "The Beatific Vision is this wonderful union, Annie, a *reunion* really, with the Triune God. You will see God with an intuitive vision. The union is an indwelling, a consummation of the divine in the sanctified spirit. You shall be brought to fruition and you shall share in God's own happiness!"

Uncle Ritchie hugged her...or danced with her. It was hard to tell. Everything was so light and fluid. They were dancing, yes! And as Annie danced her mind's eye caught sight of a door. The most beautiful thing, massive in size, intricate in carving, cut from the precious wood of the montadu tree. The door was the color of sky and imbedded with precious gemstones that glimmered and gleamed with the most brilliant and heralding light of all. She couldn't wait to go through that door and bask in the presence of that holy light! She realized that all of her life the Holy Spirit had been luring her to this unquenchable light!

And her soul sang, vibrating with light and melody.

A Real Life NDE

In researching *Annie's Heaven* I read numerous books about near death experiences or NDEs as they are called. Here's an account of an NDE from my dear friend Giacomina Francik. In November 1996, Giacomina's father, Frank St. Angel, had a near death experience when an abdominal aneurysm burst. He survived and wrote this note, which was later found by his family. I remember Giacomina telling me that she wished he would have completed the last sentence, but maybe he didn't need to! Thank you, Giacomina, for sharing this inspiring note!

(What I felt deep inside my being was a great, loving presence, a surge of warmth and peace so powerful and bright even though I was standing in the shadows. I knew with absolute certainty...)

In Appreciation

Thank you to the authors and publishers of the following books. These masterpieces influenced my thoughts as I crafted this story.

The Bible

To Kill a Mockingbird
　　Harper Lee

Everything You Ever Wanted To Know About Heaven
But Never Dreamed Of Asking
　　Peter Kreeft

Hello From Heaven
　　Bill and Judy Guggenheim

90 Minutes in Heaven
　　Don Piper

Closer to the Light
Learning from the Near-Death Experiences of Children
　　Melvin Morse, M.D., with Paul Perry

Where God Lives
　　Melvin Morse, M.D., with Paul Perry

Mere Christianity
    C. S. Lewis

What God Wants
A Compelling Answer to Humanity's Biggest Question
    Neale Donald Walsch

Why Do Catholics Do That?
A Guide to the Teachings and Practices of the Catholic Church
    Kevin Orlin Johnson, Ph.D.

What Jesus Meant
    Garry Wills

Why I Am A Catholic
    Garry Wills

Lessons from the Light
What We Can Learn From the Near-Death Experience
    Kenneth Ring, Ph.D. and Evelyn Elsaesser Valarino

Life After Death: the Burden of Proof
    Deepak Chopra

Eternity: Reclaiming A Passion For What Endures
    Joseph M. Stowell

You Are the Answer: An Extraordinary Guide to Entering the Sacred
Dance with Life and Fulfilling Your Soul Purpose
    Michael Tamura

Thomas Aquinas
Preacher and Friend
    Mary Ann Fatula

The Applause of Heaven
    Max Lucado

Talking to Heaven
    James Van Praagh

Grace For The Moment
    Max Lucado

The Intention Experiment
Using Your Thoughts to Change Your Life and the World
    Lynne McTaggart

Going Home
    Thich Nhat Hanh

The Seat of the Soul
    Gary Zukav

The Only Dance There Is
    Ram Dass

Life After Life
    Raymond A. Moody, Jr., M.D.

Reunions
Visionary Encounters With Departed Loved Ones
    Raymond A. Moody, Jr., M.D.

The Case for Christ
A Journalist's Personal Investigation of the Evidence for Jesus
    Lee Strobel

The Poem of the Man-God
Maria Valtorta

The Probability of God
A Simple Calculation that Proves the Ultimate Truth
Stephen D. Unwin, Ph.D.

The Language of God: A Scientist Presents Evidence for Belief
Francis S. Collins

The Universe in a Single Atom:
The Convergence of Science and Spirituality
Dalai Lama

The Varieties of Scientific Experience:
A Personal View of the Search for God
Carl Sagan, edited by Ann Druyan

The Hidden Messages in Water
Masaru Emoto

Great Waters: An Atlantic Passage
Deborah Cramer

The Snowflake: Winter's Secret Beauty
Kenneth Libbrecht and Patricia Ramussen

The Little Book of Phobias
Complied by Joe Kohut

DNA: Pirates of the Sacred Spiral
Dr. Leonard G. Horowitz

Eureka! 81 Key Ideas Explained
Michael Macrone

The Little Book of Science
John Gribbin

Time: A Traveler's Guide
Clifford A. Pickover

The Fabric of the Cosmos
Brian Greene

Shadows of Forgotten Ancestors
Carl Sagan and Ann Druyan

Why We Believe What We Believe
Andrew Newberg, M.D., and Mark Robert Waldman

The Better Brain Book
David Perlmutter, M.D. and Carol Colman

The Female Brain
Louann Brizendine, M.D.

Mind Wide Open
Steven Johnson

Emergence
The Connected Lives of Ants, Brains, Cities, and Software
Steven Johnson

The Book of Useless Information
Noel Botham and The Useless Information Society

Stuff You Should Have Learned at School
    Michael Powell

So Now You Know…
A Compendium of Completely Useless Information
    Harry Bright and Harlan Briscoe

Brain Power: Practical Ways to Boost Your Memory, Creativity, and Thinking Capacity
    Laureli Blyth

Mind Games
    Michael Powell

Liberating Greatness
    Hal Williamson and Sharon Eakes

Divine Proportion
Phi in Art, Nature, and Science
    Priya Hemenway

Sacred Architecture: Symbolic Forma and Ornament Traditions of East and West Models of the Cosmos
    Caroline Humphrey and Piers Vitebsky

Eveything I Need to Know I Learned from Other Women
    B.J. Gallagher

Rockford
    Jon W. Lundin

Printed in the United States
127975LV00005B/73-273/P